Second Edition

Mental Health Social Work Practice in Canada

Cheryl Regehr | Graham Glancy

Oxford University Press is a department of the University of Oxford.
It furthers the University's objective of excellence in research, scholarship,
and education by publishing worldwide. Oxford is a registered trade mark of
Oxford University Press in the UK and in certain other countries.

Published in Canada by
Oxford University Press
8 Sampson Mews, Suite 204, Don Mills, Ontario M3C 0H5 Canada

www.oupcanada.com

First Edition published in 2009

Library and Archives Canada Cataloguing in Publication

Regehr, Cheryl, author
Mental health social work practice in Canada / Cheryl Regehr and Graham Glancy. — Second edition.

Revision of: Mental health social work practice in Canada / Cheryl Regehr and Graham Glancy.—
Don Mills, Ont. : Oxford University Press, c2010. Includes bibliographical references and index.

ISBN 978-0-19-900119-4 (pbk.)

1. Psychiatric social work—Canada—Textbooks. 2. Mental illness—Diagnosis—Canada—Case studies.
3. Mental illness—Treatment—Canada—Case studies. 4. Mental health policy—Canada.
5. Mental health laws—Canada. I. Glancy, Graham, author II. Title.

HV690.C2R43 2014 362.2'04250971 C2013-908203-4

Cover image: Paper Boat Creative/Digital Vision/Getty Images

Oxford University Press is committed to our environment.
This book is printed on Forest Stewardship Council® certified paper and comes from responsible sources.

Printed and bound in Canada

3 4 — 16 15

Contents

Preface *viii*

1 **The Context of Mental Health Social Work Practice in Canada 1**

Learning Objectives 1
The Role of Social Work in Mental Health 3
Social Work and the Interprofessional Team 4
An Ethical Framework for Social Work in Mental Health 7
A Recovery Model for Mental Health and Social Work Values 8
Psychiatric Medications and Social Work Practice 10
Evidence-Based Social Work: An Ethical Responsibility? 12
Multiple Levels of Influence: A Social Work Perspective in Mental Health Practice 17
Summary 19
Discussion Questions 20
Suggested Readings and Websites 20

2 **A Policy Framework for Mental Health Practice in Canada 21**

Learning Objectives 21
Background 21
Health Policy in Canada 25
Mental Health Policy in Canada: History and Reform 31
Summary 39
Discussion Questions 39
Suggested Readings and Websites 39

3 **Mental Health Law in Canada 41**

Learning Objectives 41
Case Example 41
Mental Health Law 42
Consent to Psychiatric Treatment 55
Elements of Consent to Treatment 56
Advanced Directives 60
Substitute Decision-Makers 61
Community Treatment Orders 62
Protection of Financial Security 65
The Duty to Warn and Protect 66

Mental Health Records 68
Possible Social Work Interventions in the Case Example 71
Summary 72
Discussion Questions 72
Suggested Readings and Websites 72

4 Social Work Assessment in Mental Health 74

Learning Objectives 74
Assessment within a Cultural Context 77
Assessment and Gender 82
Social Work Assessment 83
Mental Status Examinations 87
The *Diagnostic and Statistical Manual* 92
Summary 95
Discussion Questions 96
Suggested Readings and Websites 96

5 Suicide and Self-Harm 97

Learning Objectives 97
Case Example 1 97
Case Example 2 98
Case Example 3 98
Case Example 4 99
Suicide 99
Incidence and Prevalence 100
Factors Contributing to Suicide 103
Self-Harm Behaviour 105
Assessment of Suicide Risk 105
Ethical and Legal Duties in Working with Suicidal Clients 111
The Impact of Suicide on Family and Friends 113
Interventions 113
Crisis Intervention with Acute Suicide Risk 114
Possible Social Work Interventions in the Case Examples 119
Summary 121
Discussion Questions 122
Suggested Readings and Websites 122

6 Trauma and Traumatic Grief 124

Learning Objectives 124
Case Example 1 124
Case Example 2 125
The Nature and Prevalence of Trauma Reactions 126

Types of Trauma Response 131
Intersections between Grief and Trauma 135
Interventions 140
Possible Social Work Interventions in the Case Examples 145
Summary 146
Discussion Questions 147
Suggested Readings and Websites 147

7 Schizophrenia and Related Psychotic Illnesses 148

Learning Objectives 148
Case Example 148
The Nature of Schizophrenia 149
Incidence and Prevalence of Schizophrenia 150
Factors Contributing to the Development of Schizophrenia 151
Course of Illness 155
Symptoms and Challenges 156
Other Related Psychotic Disorders 160
The Recovery Model and Schizophrenia 161
Psychosocial Interventions That Promote Recovery 162
Pharmacological Interventions as Part of Recovery 166
Possible Social Work Interventions in the Case Example 171
Summary 172
Discussion Questions 173
Suggested Readings and Websites 173

8 Depression and Mania 174

Learning Objectives 174
Case Example 1 174
Case Example 2 174
Case Example 3 175
The Nature of Depression and Mania 175
Incidence and Prevalence 176
Factors Contributing to Disturbances in Mood 177
Course and Symptoms of Depression and Mania 182
The Recovery Model and Mood Disturbances 185
Psychosocial Interventions That Promote Recovery 187
Pharmacological and Medical Interventions as Part of Recovery in Depression 190
Psychopharmacological Treatment of Mania and Bipolar Disorder 197
Possible Social Work Interventions in the Case Examples 198
Summary 199
Discussion Questions 199
Suggested Readings and Websites 200

9 Anxiety 201

Learning Objectives 201
Case Example 1 201
Case Example 2 202
The Nature of Anxiety 202
Incidence and Prevalence 203
Causes of Anxiety 204
Symptoms and Types of Anxiety Disorders 207
The Recovery Model and Anxiety 212
Psychosocial Interventions That Promote Recovery from Anxiety 213
Pharmacological Interventions That Promote Recovery from Anxiety 215
Possible Social Work Interventions in the Case Examples 216
Summary 217
Discussion Questions 218
Suggested Readings and Websites 218

10 Neurocognitive Disorders 219

Learning Objectives 219
Case Example 1 219
Case Example 2 220
The Nature of Neurocognitive Disorders 220
Incidence and Prevalence 222
Factors Contributing to Delirium 223
Factors Contributing to Traumatic Brain Injury 225
Factors Contributing to Progressive Neurocognitive Disorders 225
The Course of Progressive Neurocognitive Disorders 226
Special Issues for Family Members Caring for Relatives with Neurocognitive Disorders 231
Abuse of Older People with Neurocognitive Disorders 232
Recovery-Oriented Approaches to the Treatment of Delirium 234
Recovery-Oriented Psychosocial Interventions for Traumatic Brain Injury 235
Recovery-Oriented Interventions for Progressive Neurocognitive Disorders 236
Possible Social Work Interventions in the Case Examples 239
Summary 240
Discussion Questions 240
Suggested Readings and Websites 241

11 Substance-Related Disorders 242

Learning Objectives 242
Case Example 1 242
Case Example 2 243
Case Example 3 243
The Nature of Substance-Related Disorders 243
Incidence and Prevalence 245
Factors Contributing to Substance Use Disorders 245
The Association between Substance Use Disorders and Other Mental Health Problems 247
Drugs of Abuse 249
Screening for Substance Use 254
Canada's Anti-Drug Strategy 253
Harm-Reduction Interventions to Assist with Recovery 255
Other Recovery-Oriented Psychosocial Interventions 258
Pharmacological and Medical Approaches to Support Recovery from Substance Use Disorders 261
Possible Social Work Interventions in the Case Examples 264
Summary 265
Discussion Questions 266
Suggested Readings and Websites 266

12 Personality Disturbance 267

Learning Objectives 267
Case Example 1 267
Case Example 2 268
The Nature of Personality Disturbance 268
Incidence and Prevalence 269
Factors Contributing to Personality Disturbance 270
Types of Personality Disturbance 274
Recovery-Oriented Psychosocial Approaches to Intervention 280
Pharmacological Interventions 285
Possible Social Work Interventions in the Case Examples 286
Summary 287
Discussion Questions 287
Suggested Readings and Websites 287

Glossary 288
References 294
Index 332

Preface

- Sarah, age 26, was sexually abused as a child between the ages of 10 and 15 by her stepfather. At age 15 Sarah disclosed the abuse to her mother, who called her a whore and threw her out of the house. As an adult, Sarah struggles with alcohol use and is frequently in and out of relationships with men, all of which at first seem perfect but then end in a **crisis**. Sarah has periods of intense despair where the memories of her abuse and her mother's rejection overwhelm her. Sarah cuts herself at times of extreme distress and has made several attempts on her life.
- Tom is a 19-year-old male admitted to the local general hospital psychiatric unit. He is the third child born to middle-class, first-generation immigrant parents. Recently, his parents became concerned because he was burning pieces of paper in his room, which he said would keep the aliens away. He barricaded the door of his room; it took a local police officer to persuade him to go to the hospital, where he was admitted for assessment on an involuntary basis. On admission his speech was difficult to understand because of the severity of his thought disorder. He reported that aliens had been taking thoughts out of his head and had been constantly occupying his room, whispering. Tom was diagnosed as suffering from schizophrenia.
- Stefan is a 38-year-old married accountant. His father had episodes of severe depression and, although Stefan is not sure of the details, he believes that his grandfather committed suicide. Stefan always feels a little down every winter. He feels that it has been a little bit worse every year. This year his depression is so severe that he could not go to work and reports that he wakes up every morning at 4 a.m. and can not get back to sleep. He has no appetite, feels nauseated all the time, and has lost 10 pounds. He complains of feeling worthless and feels guilty about letting his father down and being a failure in life.
- Bill and Jean worked together for 28 years in a family-owned business. They were known as the perfect couple. As Bill approached his seventies he had increasing difficulty remembering names and phone numbers; gradually this forgetfulness extended to his long-term memory. Bill began to have difficulty finding words that he would previously have used in everyday conversations, and eventually he forgot how to use familiar objects such as the kettle. At times he would become confused, especially in the evening, becoming agitated and fearful. Their son and

their family practitioner suggested that Bill should consider a long-term care facility, but Jean felt it her duty to look after him, for better or for worse. On one evening Bill thought he heard a stranger come into the house and when Jean tried to calm him, Bill became increasingly upset and pushed Jean out of the way, hitting her with his cane.

Approximately 20 per cent of Canadians will experience a mental illness at some point in their lives. Thus, mental illness and mental health problems affect the lives of almost all individuals, families, and communities throughout Canada. Social workers are ideally suited to assist individuals and their families adapt to and overcome challenges associated with mental illness because of our focus on multiple levels of influence and multiple targets of intervention. Social workers are concerned with and trained to work with individuals and their families, drawing on client strengths to attain optimal functioning. Social workers assist individuals who are experiencing mental health problems to evaluate the challenges they face and the opportunities available to them and to facilitate the processes of making choices. Social workers support affected family members, assist families to deal with issues associated with mental health conditions, and help them to develop creative ways to manage change.

Social workers add to the understanding of other members of the interprofessional team by focusing on the social and community contexts as contributing factors to the experience of mental illness. This includes the family and social environment in which the client lives; opportunities and challenges that exist within the community; systemic forms of oppression that influence the individual, including factors affected by race, gender, sexual orientation, ability, and social class; and social policies that influence choices. Social workers are able to advocate for changes in the environment through mobilizing and accessing community resources or working to change policies and practices that undermine mental health.

Historically, the dominant model of mental health focused on a deficit-based approach that had clear assumptions about normality and pathology. Overall, treatment programs and policies were designed around the assumption of chronicity, that is, people having a persistent and long-lasting condition, and mental health facilities were thought to be required to provide long-term care. However, practitioners and policy-makers have now progressed in putting consumer choice and recovery at the forefront of mental health policy. This has contributed to a recovery model for mental health practice and an inherent belief that individuals can and do recover from severe mental illness. Social workers have integral roles to play in this recovery process.

This book is intended to provide a guide that will allow social workers to understand the nature of mental health issues, become aware of the Canadian legal and policy framework in which mental health treatment is provided, and learn about evidence-based social work practices that will best assist individuals and families struggling with mental health challenges.

Reviewers

We wish to thank the following reviewers, whose thoughtful comments and suggestions have helped to shape this text:

Karen Schwartz, Carleton University
Gail Baikie, Dalhousie University
Rick Enns, University of Calgary
Rick Sin, McMaster University
Patrick Konkin, Vancouver Island University
Nan Lowe, Algonquin College
Tammy Stubley, University of Northern British Columbia

Research Assistants

Thank you to Kate M.R. Hardy for her invaluable assistance in gathering research updates for the second edition of this book.
Thank you to Annabel Pitts for compiling the terms in the glossary.

Funding Assistance

The research contained in this book was generously supported by:

The Sandra Rotman Chair in Social Work Practice.

Note:
Some sections of this book that discuss legal issues related to mental health are reprinted from Regehr, C. and Kanani, K. (2010) *Essential Law for Social Work Practice in Canada*. Toronto: Oxford University Press.

Dedication

This book is dedicated to Kaitlyn and Dylan.

1 The Context of Mental Health Social Work Practice in Canada

Learning Objectives:

- To outline the nature of mental health and mental illness in Canada.
- To outline the role of social work in mental health.
- To describe the role of social work on the interdisciplinary team.
- To discuss ethical guidelines for social work practice in mental health.
- To outline the recovery model for mental health practice.
- To consider the application of evidence-based practice to mental health social work.

The Canadian Association of Social Workers (CASW, 2001) suggests that mental health encompasses: psychological and social harmony and integration; quality of life and general well-being; self-actualization and growth; effective personal adaptation; and the mutual influences of the individual, the group, and the environment (see Box 1.1). Similarly, the **World Health Organization** (WHO) definition of mental health focuses on the ability of individuals to realize their potential, cope with stresses, and contribute meaningfully to society (WHO, 2007). Social work skills and knowledge are ideally suited to the practice of mental health because of our focus on multiple levels of influence and multiple targets of intervention. Social workers are concerned with and trained to work with individuals and their families, drawing on client strengths to attain optimal functioning. In addition, social workers focus on social dimensions of well-being and consider opportunities and barriers in the environment. Social workers are able to advocate for changes in the environment through mobilizing and accessing community resources and by working to change policies and practices that undermine mental health.

Mental illness is an issue that touches all segments of Canadian society and all people within our country. The following statistics illustrate the impact of mental illness in Canada:

Box 1.1 Definitions of Mental Health 

"Mental Health is the capacity of the individual, the group and the environment to interact with one another in ways that promote subjective well-being, the optimal development and use of mental abilities (cognitive, affective and relational), the achievement of individual and collective goals consistent with justice and the attainment and preservation of conditions of fundamental equality."

(Canadian Association of Social Workers, 2013)

"Mental health is a state of well-being in which the individual realizes his or her own potential, can cope with the normal stresses of life, can work productively and fruitfully, and is able to make a contribution to her or his own community."

(World Health Organization, 2007)

- Approximately 20 per cent of Canadians will experience a mental illness at some point in their lives (Health Canada, 2002).
- According to the Institute of Health Economics (2010), $14.3 billion in public expenditures went towards mental health services and supports in Canada in 2007–8, representing 7.2 per cent of all government expenditures.
- In 2003 the economic burden of mental illness in Canada, including direct medical costs, work absence, and loss of productivity, totalled $51 billion (Lim et al., 2008); the World Health Organization predicts that depression will be the leading cause of workplace disability by 2020.
- Only one-third of those who need mental health services in Canada actually receive them (Statistics Canada, 2003).
- Suicide is the second leading cause of death among 15–34-year-olds in Canada; accidental death is the first (Navaneelan, 2012). The suicide rate among people suffering from schizophrenia is 12 times that of people in the general population (Cohen et al., 2010).
- Delirium occurs in up to 50 per cent of elderly people in acute-care health settings (Canadian Alliance on Mental Illness and Mental Health, 2006).

Despite these facts, only in the last few years has Canada begun to formulate a National Mental Health Strategy (Mental Health Commission of Canada, 2009, 2012). We are far behind other Western nations in our focus on mental health services and on mental health promotion. On the other hand, much has been done with regard to our understanding of mental illness. Biological research is furthering our understanding of some factors in the **etiology**, or origin, of specific mental illnesses, which is not only contributing to more effective medical interventions, but has also moved us away from blaming individuals with mental illness and their families for their own misfortune. The WHO and governments, such as the government of Canada, have come to recognize the **social determinants of health** and mental health that provide a basis for advocating for basic human rights such as adequate housing, food, income, education, and employment. Research is moving forward in determining effective psychosocial treatments for assisting clients with mental health problems and their families to regain control and enhance their own lives. Clearly, there are important roles for social workers in the area of mental health to identify problems, assist clients, advance knowledge, and create systemic change.

The Role of Social Work in Mental Health

In 1952, Mort Teicher, the first chief social worker at the Toronto Psychiatric Hospital (now the Centre for Addiction and Mental Health), wrote an article for *Canadian Welfare* entitled "The Role of a Psychiatric Social Worker" (Teicher, 1952a). At that time he indicated the job of a social worker falls into two broad categories:

1. Intake: The social worker helps the patient and his/her relatives express feelings about the hospital and clinic services (they may have to work through feelings of anger, shame, and panic before they can really use treatment). The social worker then assesses the family's attitude towards the patient and the extent to which both patient and family are able and willing to participate in treatment.
2. Continued service: The social worker helps the patient to move into and use the psychiatric hospital or clinic and helps him find his way in the community after discharge (as cited in Skelton, 1996: 240).

Mora Skelton, who was the first social worker hired at Toronto Psychiatric Hospital (TPH) in 1947, indicates that at that time social workers were hired to work on discharge planning and rehabilitation in order to reduce **recidivism** (or **relapse**) and **readmission**. As a member of the multidisciplinary team, the social worker focused on the world in which the client lived, the world in which he or she had become mentally ill and to which he or she would return upon discharge. This analysis included the attitudes of relatives, job pressures (or the pressures of no job), finances, and housing (Skelton, 1996). Social workers at that time also played an important role with respect to patient advocacy and social justice. For instance, Teicher (1952b) wrote an article entitled "Let's Abolish the Social Service Exchange" that shifted social policy throughout North America with respect to patient confidentiality. "Social service exchange" was the name of a central database where agencies and hospitals, without the client's consent, would share information regarding named patients or clients who had accessed services. Therefore, any former client of the psychiatric hospital obtaining services in the community would have a notation that she or he had been treated by TPH. Teicher, concerned about the stigma that this created for the client, was outraged; after many attempts at publication, his article was finally published in *Social Work Journal*. Despite the firestorm of letters and objections that followed, policy and practices were changed.

Skelton's description of social work in mental health in the 1940s and 1950s shows it as remarkably similar to today's role. The Canadian Association of Social Workers (2013) identifies three broad areas of social work practice in mental health:

1. *Prevention:* reducing the incidence of mental illness and dysfunction through modifying stressful environments and strengthening individual, family, and community coping.
2. *Treatment:* reducing the impact of mental illness through early assessment, intervention, and treatment.
3. *Rehabilitation:* reducing the lingering effects of mental illness through the provision of retraining and rehabilitation.

In 2006 a survey was conducted in association with the Ontario Association of Social Workers in which 339 social workers in mental health described their duties (O'Brien and Calderwood, 2010). Six major responsibilities, in order of prevalence, emerged: (1) assessment and referral (88 per cent of respondents engaged in this activity); (2) supportive counselling (84 per cent); (3) crisis intervention (71 per cent); (4) psychotherapy (56 per cent); (5) advocacy (55 per cent); and (6) case management (52 per cent). Activities related to education, discharge planning, addictions counselling, outreach, administration, research, and teaching of activities of daily living were each identified by 18 to 46 per cent of respondents. On the basis of this survey, the OASW developed the list of professional services offered by social workers in the mental health field (see Box 1.2).

Social work practice in mental health is highly diverse and offers many career opportunities. Of particular note, 83 per cent of social workers responding to this survey reported that they believed they were having a significant impact on the delivery of mental health services.

Social Work and the Interprofessional Team

The **interprofessional** team is "a fully integrated practice by a team of professionals from a diverse background of disciplines. Each member of the team

Box 1.2 Specific Aspects of Social Work Practice in Mental Health

- **Psychosocial assessment:** Perform a comprehensive assessment of individuals, families, groups, and communities based on identified needs, strengths, and coping; assess formal and informal support networks; recommend an action plan.
- **Counselling and psychotherapy:** Apply a therapeutic approach based on bio-psycho-social-spiritual and environmental factors.
- **Individual and family psycho-education:** Provide education and promote awareness of mental health and mental illness issues and services.
- **Case management and discharge planning:** Co-ordinate interdisciplinary services for a specific client, family, or group; advocate for equitable access to services; assist individuals and families to prepare for transitions; engage in relapse prevention.
- **Supervision:** Provide clinical supervision to students, volunteers, and employees.
- **Consultation:** Provide a social work perspective with interprofessional teams; provide consultation to colleagues.
- **Community capacity-building:** Participate on boards/committees and develop partnerships with the community; identify gaps in services and advocate for resources.
- **Program management/administration:** Ensure accountability and monitor clinical and systemic outcomes; oversee programs; contribute to organizational development.
- **Teaching:** Provide or facilitate workshops, courses, and presentations.
- **Program, policy, and resource development:** Analyze and establish standards of practice; participate in or lead quality improvement initiatives.
- **Research:** Contribute to the development of best practices through discipline-specific or interdisciplinary research.
- **Social action:** Advocate for improvements to systems, policies, funding structures, and services; support self-help and self-advocacy associated with mental health and mental illness.

Source: OASW (2006).

has an integrated knowledge of the other team members' roles, and all work from an equally valued team mandate. . . . When two or more professions purposely interact in order to learn with, from and about each other . . . to improve effectiveness and the quality of care" (Gilbert, 2008). Interprofessional teams are found at the policy and program-planning level of practice where other members of the team are economists, political scientists, and management professionals. Teams are found at the community level and at the direct practice level where other members are from other health disciplines, such as medicine, nursing, occupational therapy, and psychology.

The role of social work within the context of the interdisciplinary mental health team is well recognized. According to statistics provided by the National Association of Social Workers (NASW) in the United States, social workers provide 60 per cent of mental health services in that country, whereas psychiatrists provide 10 per cent, psychologists provide 23 per cent, and psychiatric nurses provide 5 per cent (NASW, 2009). An analysis of the Canadian Community Mental Health Survey by Towns and Schwartz (2012) revealed that 16.1 per cent of respondents sought mental health services from their general practitioner, 9.0 per cent from psychiatrists, and 8.3 per cent saw a social worker for the purposes of mental health treatment. When phrased slightly differently, however, 12 per cent of respondents indicated that they spoke to a social worker about their mental health concerns. In direct service mental health practice, there is some overlap with other professionals, for instance, in the areas of assessment and some individual interventions. However, social work provides specific expertise in building partnerships among individuals, families, and professionals; collaborating with communities to build supportive environments; advococating for services and resources; challenging and changing social policies to address poverty, employment, housing, and social justice; and supporting the development of preventative programs (CASW, 2001).

The US Department of Labor defines the role of social work in the context of mental health as assessing and treating individuals with mental illness or substance abuse problems. Such services include individual and group therapy, outreach, crisis intervention, social rehabilitation, and teaching skills for everyday living. Social workers also help plan for supportive services to ease clients' return to the community. It further notes that social workers in health care help doctors and other health-care professionals understand the effects that diseases and illnesses have on patients' mental and emotional health (US Department of Labor, 2012). Evidence indicates that other members of the team also value the role of social work in mental health. Two decades ago, Toseland and colleagues (1986) interviewed members of interdisciplinary mental health teams who represented seven different professions, and social workers were reported as having a high degree of influence, second only to psychiatrists.

Interestingly, much of the literature on interprofessional teams focuses on the challenges various professions experience in working together (Faulkner Schofield and Amodeo, 1999; Reese and Sontag, 2001). Challenges identified include lack of knowledge of the expertise of other professions; role blurring; conflicts arising from differences in professional values and theory bases; lack of respect; and power differentials. It is useful for social workers to be aware that these challenges are experienced by all professional groups involved in the team and are by no means unique to social work. Further, social work group skills can be highly effective in assisting the team during times of crisis or conflict to come to effective resolutions that are in the best interests of clients and client groups.

An Ethical Framework for Social Work in Mental Health

Social work practice in Canada must be conducted in accordance with the Canadian Association of Social Workers' *Code of Ethics* (CASW, 2005). Six core areas of social work values are considered:

1. *Respect for the inherent dignity and worth of persons.* In mental health practice, this principle requires that social workers battle issues of stigma in mental health and show respect for clients regardless of the challenges they are encountering. This value also requires that social workers respect and advocate for client self-determination and their right to make choices based on voluntary and informed consent. As will be noted in Chapters 2 and 3 on mental health policy and legislation, client freedom of choice is sometimes limited by other factors. Social workers have an obligation to be informed of the legislated circumstances of such limitations and need to provide full information regarding options to clients and their families.
2. *Pursuit of social justice.* Social workers advocate for equal access to public services, treatments, and resources for their clients. Because individuals with mental health challenges are sometimes disadvantaged with regard to self-advocacy, this is of particular importance.
3. *Service to humanity.* Social workers place the needs of clients above self-interest when working in a professional capacity and work to promote justice. Social workers seek a greater good in working with disadvantaged clients and groups.
4. *Integrity in professional practice.* Social workers promote social work values in the organizations in which they work. They are honest, reliable, and diligent in their practice and set professional boundaries for the best interest of the client.
5. *Confidentiality.* Social workers respect the privacy and confidentiality of clients and only disclose information when there is consent or when legislation requires disclosure. As such, social workers must be very aware of the legislative requirements related to disclosure in the interests of client safety and public safety (see Chapters 3 and 12).
6. *Competence in professional practice.* Social workers provide the highest-quality service possible and continuously strive to increase their knowledge and skills. They contribute to the development of the professional knowledge base through research and to the training of others in the profession.

Social work practice in mental health, as in other areas of practice, therefore, has a broad ethical base that incorporates core values such as justice, respect for dignity, and an obligation to work with disadvantaged groups. This has implications for the nature of practice and the theories and values on which it is based. Social workers also have an obligation to ensure confidentiality and integrity and thus must be aware of the policy and legal framework in which they work. Finally, social workers have an obligation to ensure that they practise competently, based on established knowledge. This requires social workers to remain current about best practices and research that would support competent practice.

A Recovery Model for Mental Health and Social Work Values

Traditionally, the dominant model of mental health focused on a deficit-based approach that had clear assumptions about normality and pathology (Williams and Collins, 1999). Overall, treatment programs and policies were designed around the assumption of **chronicity**, that is, people having a persistent and long-lasting condition (Carpenter, 2002), and mental health facilities were thought to be required to provide long-term care (as described in Chapter 2). Psychosocial programs focused on areas of family dysfunction, poor social supports, life skill deficits, educational/vocational problems, and non-compliance with treatment. Program success was thus measured in terms of whether the program was able to prevent relapse and readmission, while ignoring the experiences of people dealing with mental health problems in their daily lives (Williams and Collins, 1999). However, practitioners and policy-makers have now progressed in putting consumer choice and recovery at the forefront of mental health policy. This has contributed to a **recovery model** for mental health practice and an inherent belief that individuals can and do recover from severe mental illness, with hope playing an integral part in the recovery process (Carpenter, 2002; Salyers and Tsemberis, 2007). Deegan (1996), one of the early proponents of the recovery model, describes the model as a conspiracy of hope—a refusal to succumb to the images of despair often associated with a diagnosis of mental illness. In its report on this model, the US-based President's New Freedom Commission on Mental Health (2003: 1) began with the statement: "We envision a future when everyone with a mental illness will recover . . . a future when everyone with a mental illness at any stage of life has access to effective treatment and supports—essentials for living, working, learning and participating fully in the community." The Mental Health Commission of Canada acknowledges that recovery can be viewed from a variety of perspectives, ranging from complete freedom from all symptoms of the illness to the ability to live a satisfying life within the limitations caused by illness. Indeed, this differentiation is important. A meta-analysis of studies on recovery from schizophrenia, for instance, found that 20 per cent of individuals attained "complete recovery" while another 20 per cent attained "social recovery" (Warner, 2009). The Mental Health Commission suggests the key components of recovery can be summarized as follows:

- Finding, maintaining, and repairing hope: believing in oneself; having a sense of being able to accomplish things; being optimistic about the future.
- Re-establishing a positive identity: finding a new identity that incorporates illness but retains a core, positive sense of self.
- Building a meaningful life: making sense of illness; finding a meaning in life, despite illness; being engaged in life and involved in the community.
- Taking responsibility and control: feeling in control of illness and in control of life (MHCC, 2009: 28).

The recovery model is based on several fundamental components: self-direction, individualized and person-centred approaches, empowerment, **holistic** views, non-linearity, a strengths-based focus, peer support, respect, responsibility, and hope (Sowers, 2005). In this model, the mental health professional works in full partnership with clients and families, developing individualized treatment plans in which consumers choose what treatment will be provided, by whom, and when. Recovery itself is not viewed as an end, but as a process that will have ups and downs, successes and setbacks (Carpenter, 2002). The recovery model is premised on the value that everyone has growth potential and services need to focus on enhancing growth and improving progress (Farkas et al., 2005). Finally, the recovery model is premised on the belief that a broad set of systems must work together to create opportunities for growth, which includes integrated services and a broad range of community supports to optimize social, educational, vocational, income, and housing opportunities. The principles espoused by the consumer (or client) advocates in this area are highly consistent with social work practice (Deegan, 1996; CMHA, 2008):

- Positive relationships and the support of others are central to recovery and independence.
- Meaningful daily activity, that is, being able to live, work, and play in our communities, helps develop self-respect, maximizes strength, and promotes health.
- Spirituality assists with mobilizing the capacity for inner healing.
- Personal growth involves a process of overcoming disability despite its continued presence.

- Medications are one tool among many that people can use in their recovery process; people can move from *taking* medications to *using* them as part of their recovery process.
- People need opportunities to learn a variety of skills that will assist them in managing their lives and symptoms; mental health professionals must ensure that skill-building opportunities exist.
- Self-determination is a desired outcome—creating an internal locus of control, personal efficacy, power, and responsibility.

A model for social work in mental health must incorporate the concept of recovery and include realistic optimism for the future of clients. Such a model carries with it the expectation of improvement in functioning and the active involvement of the client in working towards that (Williams and Collins, 1999). This model captures the ethics and values of social work and provides an important role for social workers in mental health, both in relation to their clients and families and in relation to others on the mental health team. Indeed, research provides evidence that mental health social workers in Canada do adopt the principles of the recovery model. In the survey conducted by O'Brien and Calderwood (2010), 90 per cent of respondents indicated that they included the client's perspective in treatment planning. In open-ended questions, social workers in the study suggested that the "unique contribution of social work to the mental health field was its client-focused, client-driven recovery, strengths, human rights, empowerment, and person-in-environment perspectives" (328).

Psychiatric Medications and Social Work Practice

As indicated in the aspects of the preceding recovery model, medications are frequently included as one aspect of mental health care. In mental health practice, there are six primary groups of medications: anti-psychotics that are used to treat psychoses, schizophrenia, and mania; mood stabilizers and antidepressants that are used primarily to treat bipolar disorder and depression; anxiolytics for reduction of anxiety; stimulants; and hypnotics for assisting with sleep. Although people experiencing any mental health problem may be prescribed medication, people suffering from certain problems, such as schizophrenia or bipolar disorder, will almost always be prescribed medication. Therefore, social workers in mental health will undoubtedly have clients who are taking **psychotropic medications** or are in the process of deciding whether to take this medication.

Bentley, Walsh, and Farmer (2005) conducted a random sample survey of 994 members of the US NASW to examine the roles and activities of social workers with respect to psychiatric medications. Eighty per cent of those responding indicated that they very frequently or often discussed a client's feelings about taking medication; 91 per cent indicated that they felt competent to do this; and 96 per cent felt this was an appropriate role for social workers. Other activities frequently engaged in by social workers in this study included making referrals to physicians for medication assessment (71.9 per cent); discussing with clients the desired combined effects of medication and psychosocial treatment (70.1 per cent); discussing a medication problem with a client (61.2 per cent); discussing the pros and cons of taking medication (51.6 per cent); and discussing adverse side effects (51.4 per cent). Based on this research, Bentley and Walsh (2006) suggested that social workers in mental health be prepared to ask and reflect on the following questions when working with clients on medication: Why is medication (and specifically this medication) being prescribed for my client? What are the desired effects and what are the possible negative effects? Is there a long-range plan for this medication? When will it be altered, discontinued? How might the client's use of this medication affect other interventions that I am providing? And most importantly, what are my client's views about taking medication?

A growing body of literature addresses the meanings that clients ascribe to medications. This is critical for our work with clients for a number of reasons. First, the response of any person to medication is complex, and in addition to biology, psychological and social factors play a significant role in the outcome of psychopharmacological treatments. For instance, in one review, placebo effects were postulated to account for over 75 per cent of the efficacy of antidepressant medications (Mintz, 2005). A meta-analysis, of 96 studies examining placebo response in antidepressant trials from 1980 to 2005, although somewhat controversial, suggested that the placebo effect accounts for 68 per cent of drug response (Rief et al., 2009). People differ in their beliefs about the nature and uses of medication, but also in the degree to which they believe that they are sensitive or susceptible to the effects of medication—both the positive and adverse effects (Horne et al., 2004). There is a complex interaction between these pre-existing beliefs or expectancies and medication response. Other psychological factors influencing response to medication include readiness for change, a person's general sense of control and specific sense of control over taking the medication, and the client's alliance with the person prescribing the medication (Bradley, 2003; Floersch, 2003). Longhofer and colleagues (2003), in interviewing 90 adults who were being treated for schizophrenia or schizoaffective disease, demonstrated that clients had very individualized views about the causal effects of the medication and often suggested that the effects of the medication were mediated by other factors in their environment—such as the current state of their significant relationships. Similarly, in reporting on research involving youth who were on psychiatric medications, Floersch described the divergent ways in which the effects were interpreted. He concluded that social workers committed to the concept of self-determination must ask clients about their experiences on medications and encourage self-monitoring and self-assessment as keys to medication management and decision-making.

Social workers in mental health will inevitably be working with clients who are prescribed medication. Therefore, they must possess knowledge about commonly used medications and their effects in order to work effectively with clients. Social workers must also be aware that clients will have diverse views and beliefs about medication that may or may not be consistent with the worker's own views. With these factors in mind, the social worker's role with clients on medications can include several elements:

- Social workers can explore with clients and their families the meanings they ascribe to medications and how the use of medications may impact their self-image or the view that others may have of them (Bradley, 2003).
- Social workers can provide clients and families with sources of information about medications, including their purpose, effectiveness, and side effects.
- Based on an understanding of both the meaning that the client ascribes and the benefits and negative aspects of medication, social workers can assist clients in making informed decisions about their own treatment and recovery plan.
- Social workers can assist clients and families to advocate for themselves with respect to questions or concerns around medications, or can advocate for clients directly by consulting and collaborating with other members of the team. For instance, if the client finds the medications helpful to some degree, but is troubled by some side effects, what might be done to alter the medication regime so that it does not interfere with life goals?

Evidence-Based Social Work: An Ethical Responsibility?

Laura Myers and Bruce Thyer (1997) raised the controversial question "Should social work clients have the right to effective treatment?" They argued that providing effective treatments is an ethical responsibility of social workers and that education programs and codes of ethics for social workers should reflect this ethical duty. Their position was not widely accepted at the time and critiques of the position voiced many concerns. The **evidence-based practice** (known as EBP) model, originally developed in medicine, was viewed by some as inconsistent with values of social workers, in particular with the profession's mission, values, and diverse service populations. Evidence-based practice was viewed by some as reductionist, undermining one of social work's most distinctive strengths, that is, the holistic view of a person in the environment (Witkin, 1998). It was seen to be a cookbook approach that involved extracting best practices from the scientific literature and simplistically applying them to clients without regard to who the clients are, their personal motivations and goals, or other potentially complicating life situations (Regehr et al., 2007). Critics also feared that evidence-based practice ignores the social worker's expertise, experience, and judgement, and may "undermine traditional professional practice" (Webb, 2001: 58). Concerned social work writers linked the increasing emphasis on accountability and evidence-based practice to economic and resource issues and raised concerns about whether evidence-based practice is necessarily in the best interests of clients or whether it is merely a means for cost containment. Similar concerns have been raised in medicine (Porta, 2004; Saarni and Gylling, 2004). Although these criticisms may be true to a greater or lesser extent, many factors make evidence-based practice consistent with good social work practice: (1) the obligation to provide our clients with services that are most likely to assist them and least likely to cause harm; (2) the obligation to provide informed consent; and (3) current legal definitions regarding expertise and competence.

Although social workers have always strived to provide the best interventions for clients, dominant treatment methods have at times been detrimental. One clear example of this is the role social workers played in the removal of Aboriginal children from their homes to be placed in residential schools in Canada. It has been observed that social workers were some of the strongest supporters of the residential school system, and when a joint House of Commons and Senate committee recommended closure of all residential schools in 1948, the social work profession joined with the churches in lobbying against such action. Social workers sat on admissions committees for the residential schools; in Saskatchewan, by the 1960s more than 80 per cent of Aboriginal children who were in residential schools had been placed there by social workers (Blackstock et al., 2007). The negative aspects of residential schools, including abuse, inadequate education, and shockingly high death rates, are now well known.

A second example of harmful practice is in the area of family interventions with schizophrenia. In the 1950s, as part of a trend to look for family problems as the cause of mental health problems, communications within the family and family dynamics were targeted as the cause of schizophrenia. This led to coining the term "**schizophrenogenic** mother" (Bateson et al., 1956; Sluzki et al., 1967). Eventually these concepts led to an entire form of therapy—strategic family therapy—focused on changing family interactions and in particular the mother's behaviour, thereby hypothetically curing schizophrenia or at least reducing relapse (Haley, 1976). More recently, however, increased knowledge regarding the biological basis for the disease (see Chapter 7) has discredited this theory as mother-blaming without justification. Nevertheless, many social workers attended major training events in which the model was taught, and large numbers of well-meaning social workers then imposed the model on families. Although not all areas of practice have been subject to research, both qualitative and quantitative data are available on client experiences and the outcomes of many forms of intervention. Any intervention must be subject to the individual scrutiny of social workers. Has the intervention been tested and does it work? Are clients satisfied with the intervention? If no data are available, how intrusive is the intervention and what are the possible negative effects that may result in using this intervention?

A second issue surrounds ethical obligations to obtain informed consent. The notion of **informed consent** is consistent with the long-standing commitment of social work to the value of self-determination, which is the right of clients to participate fully in decisions made about them. The doctrine of informed consent in its most expansive form can be said to have two goals: (1) to promote individual autonomy; and (2) to encourage rational decision-making. Valid informed consent has five elements (Regehr and Antle, 1997):

1. The information provided is adequate for clients to be able to weigh the risks and benefits of the proposed action.
2. Clients have been told the foreseeable risks and benefits of the proposed action.
3. Clients are competent to provide consent.
4. Consent is given voluntarily and without coercive influence.
5. Clients have been told they have the right to refuse or withdraw consent.

Early legal decisions regarding disclosure of information to patients maintained that valid consent was based on the "reasonable physician" standard, that is, information that the average, reasonable physician felt was adequate and appropriate in order for a patient to make a decision about whether to consent to any given treatment. In the United States and Canada, this was replaced by the "reasonable patient" standard (*Canterbury v. Spence*, 1972; *Hopp v. Lepp*, 1980). As a result, disclosure now must include all information that an objective, reasonable person, in the patient's situation, would consider important in reaching a decision to accept or refuse the proposed treatment, including all *material* risks of that treatment and the risks of available options. However, in the absence of evidence, can we, as social workers, describe the possible risks and benefits to a client? Clearly, we were not able to do this in the cases of "schizophrenogenic mothers" and Aboriginal children admitted to residential schools.

Legal definitions regarding expertise and competent practice have changed dramatically in recent years. Since 1923 the standard for expertise in the courts in the United States (and by default in Canada) was based on the concept of general acceptance (*Frye v. United States*, 1923); that is, is the method of treatment "generally accepted" by members of the profession. In 1993, the US Supreme Court ruled on an important case regarding the admissibility of expert evidence (*Daubert v. Merrell Dow Pharmaceuticals*, 1993). The Court cited four factors to assess whether a particular test used to support expert evidence has a reliable foundation: (1) whether the theory or technique can and has been tested; (2) whether the theory or technique has been subject to peer review and publication; (3) whether the error or potential rate of error has been identified and whether standards exist; and (4) whether this theory or technique has been generally accepted. In 2000, the Supreme Court of Canada explicitly adopted the criteria in *Daubert v. Merrell Dow Pharmaceuticals* in the case of *R. v. J. (J.-L.)* (1999). These changes in law clearly suggest that the courts require social workers and all other expert witnesses to take into consideration all materials, guided by the available evidence in their field of inquiry.

How can we institute a model of evidence-based social work that balances the multiple dimensions of social work values and responsibilities? Evidence-based practice in medicine originally was defined as "the conscientious, explicit and judicious use of current evidence in making decisions about the care of individual patients" (Sackett et al., 1996: 71). More simply defined, it is the use of treatments for which there is sufficiently persuasive evidence that they will attain the desired outcomes (Rosen and Proctor, 2002). Proctor and Rosen (2004) suggest that evidence-based practice has three assertions: (1) intervention decisions should be based on empirical research; (2) critical assessment of empirically supported interventions must be conducted to determine their fit to and appropriateness for the practice situation at hand; and (3) interventions should be subject to regular monitoring and the course of treatment revised based on outcome evaluation. Bellamy and colleagues (2011: 137) add that EBP "includes a philosophical orientation that values client-centered practice, transparency, critical evaluation of practice, [and] a commitment to lifelong professional learning."

In general, decision-making that uses evidenced-based methods is achieved in a series of steps (Wilson et al., 1995; Gibbs and Gambrill, 2002). The first step is to evaluate the problem to be addressed and formulate answerable questions; for example, what is the best way to assist an individual with these characteristics who suffers from depression? The next step is to gather and critically evaluate the evidence available. A decision needs to be made about which intervention strategy is the best approach. Finally, it is necessary to monitor and evaluate the outcome of the intervention. However, EBP does not advocate an approach where the social worker imposes her or his assessment of most effective practices on the client. Rather, EBP can be understood to be a "bottom-up approach" in which social workers integrate evidence into practice in partnership with clients (Bellamy et al., 2011).

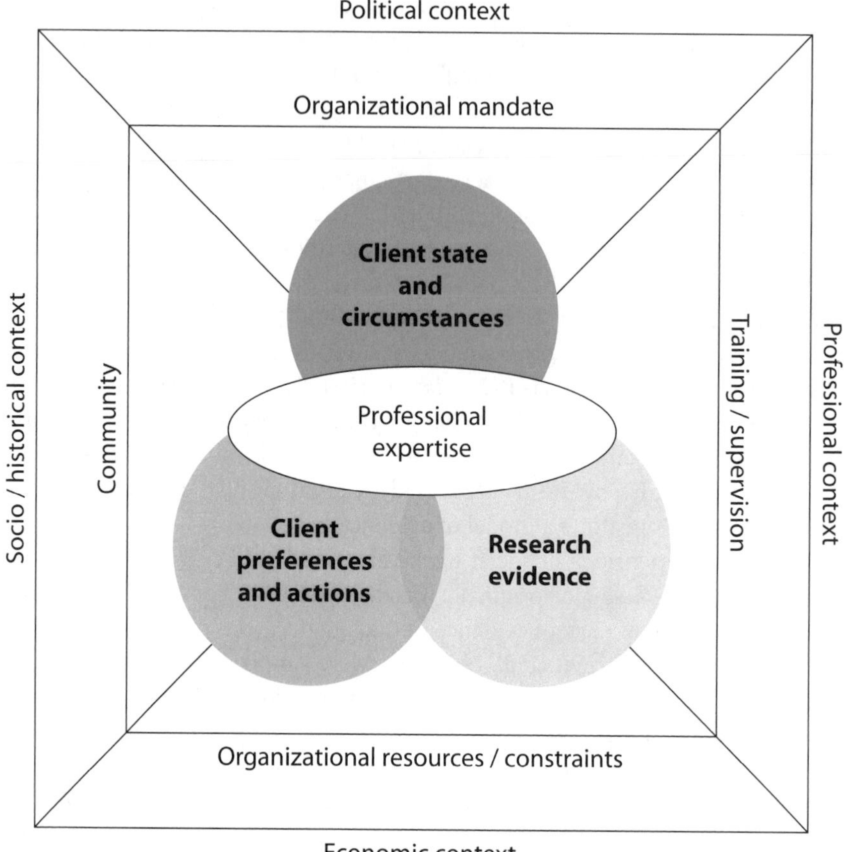

Figure 1.1 A Comprehensive Model of Evidence-Based Practice

Source: Regehr, Stern, and Shlonsky (2007).

Regehr, Stern, and Shlonsky (2007) provide a model for deciding which intervention to implement. This model includes: (1) client wishes (whether an individual, family, group, or community); (2) practitioner expertise (whether a clinician, manager, or policy-maker); (3) agency mandate and constraints; and (4) the broader ecological context. This model is shown in Figure 1.1.

Regehr and colleagues argue that evidence-based practice, by definition, facilitates the very best qualities of social work when a social worker involves clients in a collaborative process to consider the available evidence or lack of evidence. The practitioner fosters self-determination as the client is empowered to contribute to an informed decision about treatment planning in light of his or her goals, values, and situation; at the same time, the practitioner must take into consideration his or her own skills, resources, and agency context.

Although less has been written about evidence-based practice at the policy level, the basic tenets remain the same, with social work professional values underpinning a process that encourages transparency and collaborative decision-making while recognizing the existing economic and political exigencies.

This type of approach to evidence-based practice supports the notion of other writers that a recovery orientation and evidence-based practice are not opposed to one another (Sowers, 2005). Farkas and colleagues (2005) argue for the integration of evidence-based practice into recovery programs. Their focus is recovery programs based on the notion that individuals and families can move beyond mental illness and lead meaningful lives in their own communities. They identify four key components: (1) person orientation (a focus on the individual, not the disease); (2) person involvement (people's right to full partnership treatment/program planning, implementation, and evaluation); (3) self-determination/choice (regarding goals, outcomes, and preferred services); and (4) growth potential (a focus on the potential to recover). These authors contend that evidence shows that client outcomes improve when clients have opportunities for meaningful involvement, as opposed to when they are coerced into receiving treatment. Further, involving clients in the process of quality assurance and evaluation increases the validity of research findings regarding efficacy of interventions. However, at times, the basic premises of specific evidence-based approaches may need to be examined. For instance, Assertive Community Treatment, an evidence-based model described in Chapter 7 and used with individuals who suffer from schizophrenia, has particular elements that could undermine the recovery model. As one example, the unlimited time in which services are offered, if presented in a rigid manner, may suggest that clients cannot manage without support. Further, team members' involvement in readmission to hospital may undermine self-determination of clients (Salyers and Tsemberis, 2007). Thus, in order to integrate the evidence-based approach with a recovery model that incorporates elements of consumer choice, processes may need to be adapted or modified. This must be conducted at the policy level, the organizational and programmatic level, and at the direct practice level.

Multiple Levels of Influence: A Social Work Perspective in Mental Health Practice

The unique perspective of social work in the practice of mental health focuses on multiple levels of influence. Social workers have key roles to play in assisting individuals and their families adapt to and overcome challenges associated with mental illness. As members of interprofessional health teams, social workers seek to assist others in understanding the social and community context in which mental illness occurs and the way in which these larger systems contribute to the development of illness and exacerbate or ameliorate the challenges in adapting to illness. As experts in family processes, social workers assist families to deal with issues of grief and loss associated with mental health conditions and to develop creative ways to manage change and support affected family members. In addition, social workers assist individuals who are experiencing mental health problems to evaluate the challenges they face and the opportunities available to them and to facilitate the processes of making choices, dealing with adversity, and, when possible, recovering from illness. Further, social workers participate in the modification and development of relevant and effective programs, service systems, and policies in the areas of mental health and health.

To do this, social workers must be knowledgeable in a broad span of issues. This book is intended to provide a foundation for social work practice in mental health. Chapters 2 and 3 consider the policy and legislative framework in which mental health programs are developed and mental health practice occurs. This larger framework creates both opportunities and limitations for clients; only with a thorough understanding can social workers articulate the systemic challenges that clients face and advocate for change. Mental health law deals with highly complex issues related to treatment of individuals who may not have the ability to make decisions about their own care or who may be a danger to themselves or others. Legislation in this area covers such issues as decisions regarding consent to treatment, **substitute decision-making**, and involuntary commitment. Social workers are called upon to instruct patients regarding their rights; instruct families regarding their ability to ensure that treatment is or is not provided to an ill loved one; provide assessments regarding the potential consequences of treatment decisions for provincial review boards; and provide assessments regarding the capacity to consent. Each of these roles requires an understanding of the laws pertaining to consent and treatment, essential elements of consent and capacity, and the process of review through provincially appointed boards.

Social work assessments in mental health address biological factors; individual cognitive and psychodynamic factors; family systems issues; cultural, religious, and community considerations; and the socio-political and legislative environment in which mental health problems are experienced. In addition, social workers working in the area of mental health must be familiar with the *Diagnostic and Statistical Manual of Mental Disorders* (DSM) in order to communicate effectively with others on the multidisciplinary team (APA, 2013). Further, social workers must be familiar with mental status examinations and suicide risk assessments as critical components of mental health assessment. Knowledge of the DSM does not imply uncritical acceptance of all aspects of the manual and the framework on which it is based. However, as we discuss in Chapter 4, critical analysis should be based on a thorough understanding of the text. In this way, if social workers disagree with formulations provided by other members of the health-care team, they are able to present their points in a credible manner, based on knowledge of the concepts used by others and expertise in other ways of formulating the issues.

Finally, each type of mental health problem presents with a different symptom picture, a different etiology, and different challenges for individual clients and their families. As a result, the most effective treatment approaches vary widely from one mental health problem to another.

Each chapter on specific mental health problems begins with case examples that illustrate the lived experience of individuals. Next, each chapter addresses the research and literature on the nature of the problem, its presentation and prevalence. Finally, evidence-based treatments, which include community-based interventions, family interventions, group interventions, individual interventions, and medication, are reviewed. In each of these categories of mental health challenges, this book advocates that optimal social work practice in mental health involves a biopsychosocial approach to assessment and intervention that is based on the best current available evidence.

Summary

Social workers bring to the practice of mental health a broad perspective that includes an awareness of biological, psychological, and social influences on mental health and well-being. The unique contributions that they bring to the multidisciplinary team, however, are related to the focus on how these factors intersect with other issues in the person's life. This includes the family and social environment in which the client lives; opportunities and challenges that exist within the community; systemic forms of oppression that influence the individual, including factors affected by race, gender, sexual orientation, ability, and social class; and social policies that influence choices. Social work interventions are based on this broad awareness.

Social work practice is governed by ethical principles, which are codified in our *Code of Ethics*. These ethical principles require that we are respectful of all persons with whom we work; that we serve humanity through the pursuit of social justice; that we practise with integrity, including ensuring that our clients have a right to privacy and confidentiality; and that we practise competently and provide the best-quality services available. These best-quality services must be based on a combination of the best available knowledge in the area, professional expertise, and judgement, a consideration of the agency and external context, and, above all, client values and consent.

Discussion Questions

1. What is the unique role of social work in mental health practice?
2. What are the possible positive and negative aspects of using an evidence-based approach to social work practice in mental health?
3. What should the role of social work be with respect to medications?
4. How does the recovery model fit with social work values and ethics?
5. Are there inherent conflicts between the recovery model and evidence-based practice?

Suggested Readings and Websites

Canadian Association of Social Workers. 2005. *Code of Ethics.* Ottawa: CASW. At: www.casw-acts.ca/en/what-social-work/casw-code-ethics. The *Code of Ethics* issued in 2005 is the ethical framework within which all social workers in Canada must practice. A companion *Guidelines for Ethical Practice* can be found at the same website.

Health Canada. 2002. *A Report on Mental Illnesses in Canada.* Ottawa. At: www.cmha.ca/bins/content_page.asp?cid=4-42-215. This report provides an overview of the incidence and costs of mental health problems in Canada.

Mental Health Commission of Canada. 2009. *Toward Recovery and Well-Being: A Framework for a Mental Health Strategy for Canada.* At: www.mentalhealthcommission.ca/English/Pages/Reports.aspx. This report is based on an extensive consultation process and outlines key goals for an integrated mental health strategy for Canada.

2 A Policy Framework for Mental Health Practice in Canada

Learning Objectives:

- To provide an overview of the legislative framework for developing mental health policy in Canada.
- To provide an overview of health policy in Canada.
- To describe the history and development of mental health policy in Canada.

Background

The policy and legal framework within which mental health practice exists in Canada is multi-layered. The Canadian constitution defines the powers of government. The Canadian Charter of Rights and Freedoms protects the fundamental rights of Canadians. Federal and provincial legislatures make, alter, and repeal laws, and judiciary and administrative bodies (such as mental health review boards) interpret and apply the law (Regehr and Kanani, 2010). Broadly speaking, social policy refers to legislation that provides overarching principles about values held by society and consequently the delivery of social programs. National policies regarding health and mental health (which falls under health policy) address such issues as payment for services and access to services. By failing to meet these federally prescribed policy requirements, provincial governments can be denied federal transfer payments in the area of health. Specific provincial legislation and case law govern actual practices in the delivery of mental health services such as involuntary commitment and treatment. These issues are discussed in Chapter 3 on mental health legislation.

Canada's democratic parliamentary system is derived from the British system of governance. Canada's first constitution, the British North America Act (BNA Act), was enacted in 1867. This Act (now known as the Constitution Act, 1867) provided for the division of legislative and economic powers between the federal government and the provinces. The federal government has jurisdiction to make laws concerning Canada as a whole, including trade, immigration, national defence, and criminal justice. Health care, education, employment programs, and the administration of social welfare programs are among the policy areas defined as provincial responsibilities (Thomlison and Bradshaw, 2002; Regehr and Kanani, 2010). This division was wise in a large country such as Canada in which regions were geographically isolated from one another. Local legislators would presumably be more knowledgeable about the particular needs of people in their region and be better able to oversee the administration of services. However, taxation power was placed largely in the hands of the federal government, thus ensuring federal influence over health care and mental health care, based on the ability to allocate resources.

The Constitution Act, 1867 further set out the basic principles of democratic government and defined the three branches of government: (1) the executive, which includes the prime minister and other ministers, which is responsible for administering and enforcing laws and which answers to the legislature; (2) the legislature, which has the power to make, alter, and appeal laws; and (3) the judiciary, which interprets and applies the law (see Figure 2.1).

In 1982, the Canada Act came into force by which British parliament agreed to surrender the power to makes changes to the Canadian constitution to Canadian parliament. Coinciding with the Canada Act, the Constitution Act, 1982 was passed, a fundamental component of which was the Canadian Charter of Rights and Freedoms. The Charter enshrines protection of the primary human rights of Canadians in the constitution (Regehr and Kanani, 2010). Specifically, section 1 of the Charter "guarantees the rights and freedoms set out in it subject only to such reasonable limits prescribed by law as can be demonstrably justified in a free and democratic society." The Charter takes precedence over all federal and provincial legislation, and consequently no

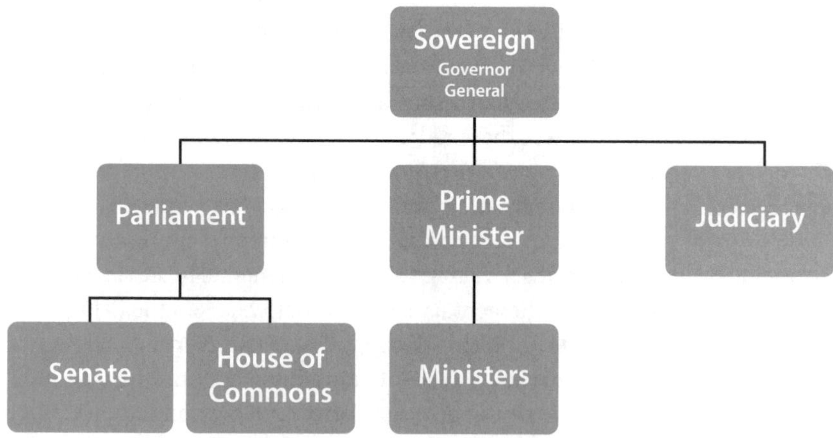

Figure 2.1 The Three Branches of Government in Canada

Canadian law or government may violate the guaranteed rights of Canadians under the Charter unless these rights threaten a free and democratic society. This requires balancing the rights of the individual against the common good. The Charter (s. 2) identifies the following fundamental freedoms for all Canadians:

(a) freedom of conscience and religion;
(b) freedom of thought, belief, opinion and expression, including freedom of the press and other media of communication;
(c) freedom of peaceful assembly; and
(d) freedom of association.

When considering the manner in which policy and service responsibility in health and mental health is divided between the provincial and federal governments, it is not surprising that conflicts erupt. In June 2004, the Supreme Court of Canada heard an appeal in the case of *Auton (Guardian ad litem of) v. British Columbia (Attorney General)* that questioned whether the BC government's refusal to fund a particular type of autism therapy was contrary to the Charter. The case involved four children with autism whose parents sought funding for an intensive applied behaviour analysis (ABA) therapy known as Lovaas therapy, which cost between $45,000 and $60,000 per year per child. Although the provincial government did fund some programs for children with autism through the Ministry of Health, the Ministry of Children and Families, and the Ministry of Education, it did not fund ABA therapy for a number of reasons, including the high cost of the therapy and the controversy surrounding the treatment's success. This treatment was funded in some other provinces to varying degrees, but in British Columbia the cost was borne by the families. The case was first heard in the Supreme Court of British Columbia, which found the province liable for the costs of services under the Charter of Rights and Freedoms. The case was appealed by the Attorney General of British Columbia to the Supreme Court of Canada, where a unanimous judgement allowed the BC attorney general's appeal and declared that the province did not have to fund this service. The decision, written by Chief Justice Beverley McLachlin, determined that a province's public health plan under the Canada Health Act (1985) is not required to provide a particular health treatment outside the "core" services administered by doctors and hospitals (*Auton v. British Columbia*, 2004).

A second example of possible controversy occurred in the case of Jordan River Anderson. Under Canadian policy, the health care of Aboriginal persons is a federal responsibility; however, all health-care services are provided by provincial governments. The issue then arises, how can Aboriginal persons be assured of health care when their coverage is at question? The following description of this case is found on the First Nations Child and Family Caring Society of Canada webpage (2008).

> Jordan was a young First Nations child who was born with complex medical needs. As his family did not have access to the supports needed to care for him at their home on reserve they made the difficult decision to place Jordan in child welfare care shortly after birth. Jordan remained in hospital for the first two years of his life as his medical condition stabilized. During this time the First Nations child and family service agency, First Nations community, and family worked together to locate a medically trained foster home and to raise money to refit a van for Jordan's safe transportation. Shortly after Jordan's second birthday, doctors said he could go to a family home. This decision should have been a time of celebration but for federal and provincial governments it was a time to begin arguing over which department would pay for Jordan's at-home care. The jurisdictional dispute would last over two years during which time Jordan remained unnecessarily in hospital. The disputed costs ranged from some higher cost items such as renovations to the home for a wheelchair ramp to low-cost items such as showerheads. The community initially tried to mediate a solution between the governments but when this failed they turned to legal action. Shortly after Jordan's fourth birthday in hospital, the jurisdictional dispute was settled but not in time for Jordan who sadly passed away before he could live in a family home.

Stemming from this tragic situation, "Jordan's Principle" was established. Under Jordan's Principle, if a jurisdictional dispute arises between two government parties or between two ministries of the same government regarding payment for services guaranteed to First Nations children, the agency first contacted must pay for the services without delay or disruption. After the care of the child is assured, the paying government can seek recompense through jurisdictional dispute mechanisms. In short, this principle states, first address the medical needs of the child and then, and only then, worry about payment. On 12 December 2007 Jordan's Principle was passed unanimously in the House of Commons. One month later Premier Gordon Campbell announced that the BC government supports Jordan's Principle, recognizing the culture and traditions of First Nations children, and promised to work in co-operation with First Nations across the province to bring it into effect in British Columbia.

From these two case examples, it is evident that overall guidelines provided by the federal government regarding the administration of health care in the provinces do not always provide straightforward answers and that the interpretation of responsibilities will vary significantly based on fiscal—and not clinical—considerations. When considering the issue of mental health policy and other social welfare concerns, competing demands arise. Delaney

(2009) recognizes that we strive for a **pluralistic society** in Canada, which benefits from many diverse viewpoints that contribute to our view of the common good. Although pluralism has many benefits, such as a valuing of diverse cultures, religious views, sexual orientations, and a multi-party system, it also poses challenges in the development of social welfare policy. A major challenge is that pluralism encourages competition for political dominance of various world views on such issues as social welfare policy. These diverse opinions may or may not support the notion of publicly funded programs and services in many areas that include mental health and addictions (Delaney, 2009). Further, these different views vary in their perception of the degree to which rights and the well-being of the individual are subjugated to, or supersede, communal rights and well-being. These issues come into sharp relief in Chapter 3 when we discuss mental health law and provisions for involuntary detainment and treatment for individuals with mental health problems.

Health Policy in Canada

Mental health in Canada falls under the umbrella of health policy and services. Andreae (2002) identifies seven core values of Canadians related to health and health care consistent with Canadian values regarding mental health and mental health care. He divides Canadian values in this realm into two aspects, essential values and instrumental values. Essential values are: (1) equity, including the equal opportunity to achieve health and well-being and equal opportunity to receive health-care services according to their needs; (2) quality, including both a right to a high quality of life and a high quality of health care; and (3) informed choice, involving the ability of all Canadians to choose health options based on best available information. Instrumental values are: (1) the right to live in a healthy social, economic, and natural environment; (2) accountability in the health-care system; (3) efficiency in the use of resources; and (4) citizen participation and citizen decision-making in their own health care and the health care of family members. These values are reflected to greater or lesser extents as we review the history of health care and mental health legislation in Canada.

Early health legislation in Canada related to public health measures in regard to communicable diseases. For instance, in 1832 the Upper Canada Sanitary Commission and Board of Health issued a directive related to quarantine of immigrants infected with cholera (Hick, 2006). In Canada's early days, health care was provided on a fee-for-service basis, leaving those who had no resources without access to health treatment. In the early to mid-1900s, insurance plans began to come into effect, including a payroll deduction plan for miners in Nova Scotia and Ontario. Hospitals and medical associations also developed plans in Ontario, Manitoba, and Nova Scotia. In 1939, Manitoba formed the first Canadian Blue Cross health insurance plan for those who could afford to pay premiums. In the 1920s, workers' groups in British Columbia and Alberta pushed for universal health-care coverage but were unsuccessful. The Great Depression, which left many destitute, became a catalyst for more widespread pressure to enact universal health care. Issues raised were that private insurance schemes were available only to those who could pay premiums or had employers who would pay premiums and that individuals with serious health problems did not qualify for coverage. In 1947 Saskatchewan instituted the first public insurance plan for hospital coverage. The federal government, in 1957, passed the Hospital Insurance and Diagnostic Services Act whereby Ottawa agreed to finance 50 per cent of the cost of provincial hospital care; notably, this excluded mental health care. By 1961 all the provinces and territories had signed agreements regarding federal cost-sharing for hospital care (Government of Canada, 2008).

In 1961, under the leadership of Premier Tommy Douglas, the government of Saskatchewan began Canada's first universal health care system (Nelson, 2006). That same year, the federal government established the Royal Commission on Health Services, chaired by Justice Emmett Hall, to study and report on the health care needs of Canadians. The 1964–5 Royal Commission on Health Services report recommended a comprehensive and universal medicare system for all Canadians, including the coverage of physician care and prescription drugs. This proposal had massive grassroots support, particularly from women's groups and organized labour (Hick, 2006). In 1966, the federal government passed the Medical Care Act that extended access to government-funded health care to all Canadians. Because health care is a provincial area of jurisdiction the government of Canada entered into negotiations with each province individually. By 1972, each province had established its own system of free access to physician services and the federal government shared in the funding (Government of Canada, 2008). In 1979, a second Hall Commission was asked to study the operation and financing of health care in Canada and recommended the abolition of extra-billing and user fees. Then, in 1984, the federal government passed the Canada Health Act, which outlined principles for funding health care in Canada. To qualify for federal health-care funding, the insurance plan of the province must meet the five criteria, as shown in Box 2.1.

In 2000, the Standing Senate Committee on Social Affairs, Science and Technology, chaired by Senator Michael Kirby, began a review of health care in Canada that took two years and heard more than 400 witnesses. The report, *The Health of Canadians—The Federal Role*, released in October 2002, became popularly known as the Kirby Report. This report stressed the need for co-operation among stakeholders to reduce problems of maldistribution, undersupply, and jurisdictional competition in the area of health. It focused on three key areas:

Box 2.1 Principles of the Canada Health Act

- *Public administration:* The health-care insurance plan is to be administered and operated on a non-profit basis by a public authority, responsible to the provincial/territorial government and subject to audits of its accounts and financial transactions.
- *Comprehensiveness:* The health insurance plans of the provinces and territories must guarantee all insured health services and, where permitted, services rendered by other health-care practitioners.
- *Universality:* One hundred per cent of the insured residents of a province or territory must be entitled to the insured health services provided by the plans on uniform terms and conditions.
- *Portability:* Residents moving from one province or territory to another must continue to be covered for insured health-care services by the "home" province until the new province or territory of residence assumes health-care coverage. Residents temporarily absent from the country must also continue to be covered for insured health-care services.
- *Accessibility:* The health insurance plans of the provinces and territories must provide reasonable access to insured health-care services on uniform terms and conditions, unprecluded, unimpeded, either directly or indirectly, by charges (user charges or extra-billing) or other means (age, health status, or financial circumstances).

Source: Health Canada 2002.

adequate human resources, appropriate public funding, and systemic reform to delivery and funding of services. The recommendations of the report included:

- enactment of a health-care guarantee that would reduce wait times and ensure that patients get services within a specified period of time (the penalty for exceeding wait times was to be the requirement of the province to pay for treatment in another jurisdiction);
- expansion of public health insurance to cover catastrophic drug costs and homecare costs;
- an increase in the federal contribution to developing health-care technology, evaluating system performance and outcomes, and wellness and illness prevention;
- additional federal revenue for health care and additional federal investment in health care;
- changes to health human resources that would include: restructuring of the hospital/physician relationship; ensuring an adequate supply of graduates in various health fields; facilitating the movement of health-care professionals across provinces through co-ordination of licensing and immigration requirements; increasing the supply of health professionals from under-represented groups such as Aboriginal people; increasing the supply of health professionals in under-serviced regions.

Several of these recommendations, particularly those related to human resources in health, have been enacted. For instance, changes were made so that licensing bodies for health professions, including social work, must establish means for allowing practitioners to transfer their licensure from one Canadian province to another. To this end, in March 2007 the 10 provinces entered into a Mutual Recognition Agreement on Labour Mobility for Social Workers in Canada that establishes the conditions under which a social worker registered in one Canadian jurisdiction can have his/her qualifications recognized in another Canadian jurisdiction that is a party to the agreement (Regehr and Kanani, 2010).

Before the Kirby Report was even released, Allan Rock, federal minister of health in 2001, identified a need for review of health care in Canada, and subsequently Prime Minister Jean Chrétien formed a commission led by Roy Romanow that resulted in the report *Building on Values: The Future of Health Care in Canada*. According to Romanow:

> My recommendations are premised on three overarching themes. **First**, that we require strong leadership and improved governance to keep Medicare a national asset. **Second**, that we need to make the system more responsive and efficient as well as more accountable to Canadians. And **third**, that we need to make strategic investments over the short term to address priority concerns, as well as over the long term to place the system on a more sustainable footing. (Government of Canada, 2002)

Thus, while the Romanow Report upheld Canadian values about universal health care, particularly in the realm of catastrophic illness, Romanow also recognized the need for accountability and cost containment. This is in large part due to the fact that increasing proportions of provincial budgets are spent on health care. For instance, in Ontario, the top government expenditures were transportation and infrastructure in the 1940s and education in the late 1950s and early 1960s, but by the late 1960s, this moved to health care. By the early 1990s health care consumed 34 per cent of Ontario's budget (McNeill and Nicholas, 2009). This amount continues to rise. Ontario reported in 2012: "Today, health care consumes 42 cents of every dollar spent on provincial programs. Without a change of course, health spending would eat up 70 per cent of the provincial budget within 12 years" (Government of Ontario, 2012). Similarly, Alberta Health (2012) reported that funding for health and wellness was $16 billion in 2012–13, an increase of 7.9 per cent over the previous year. This represents 39 per cent of total government spending. In part, this increase is related to increased costs of health care. For instance, while Canadians over the age of 65 comprise 14 per cent of the population, they consume 44 per cent of all health-care dollars (CIHI, 2010). As the baby boom continues to age, this expenditure is expected to grow. Another cause of the increased expenditure at the provincial level was related to decreased federal funding, which fell from 42 to 10 per cent between the mid-1970s and 2000 (Nelson, 2006). Clearly, such growth in cost at provincial levels is unsustainable and thus we are now in a period of cost containment. The new mantra is "bending the cost curve." Of concern is that when expenditures to health are cut, mental health care is often one area that is hardest hit.

Despite significant investments in health care, it is clear that provision of funds for programs that deal with physical and mental illness alone will never be adequate. In 1999, Health Canada released a report entitled *Toward a Healthy Future: Second Report on the Health of Canadians*. This report focuses on the determinants of health, which in large part are social determinants. According to the report, the principal factors influencing the health of Canadians are: income and social status; social support networks; education; employment/working conditions; social environments; physical environments; personal health practices and coping skills; healthy child development; biology and genetic endowment; health services; gender; and culture (Public Health Agency Canada, 2008). These factors are described in greater detail in Table 2.1. What is evident here is that factors that can be influenced by social work intervention are key determinants of health and mental health status.

Although health-care legislation also encompasses mental health, legitimate pressing concerns such as access to cancer treatments, waiting lists for

Table 2.1 Social Determinants of Health for Canadians

Income and Social Status	• Evidence clearly points to an association between social and economic status and health and access to health care. Only 47 per cent of Canadians in the lowest income bracket rate their health as very good or excellent, compared with 73 per cent of Canadians in the highest income group (Health Canada, 1999).
Social Support Networks	• Access to strong social support networks is associated with better health. Low levels of social support have been associated with increased mortality in a wide range of illnesses and increased morbidity in mental health.
Education and Literacy	• Increased education is associated with increased access to healthy environments. For instance, the number of lost work days decreases with increasing education (Health Canada, 1999). • Education level is associated with access to health care and mental health professionals in Canada. That is, more highly educated people are more likely to access psychiatrists, psychologists, social workers, and family physicians (Steele et al., 2007).

continued

Table 2.1 Continued

Employment and Working Conditions	• A major review done for the World Health Organization found that high levels of unemployment and economic instability in a society cause significant mental health problems and adverse effects on the physical health of unemployed individuals, their families, and their communities.
Social Environments	• Social exclusion caused by racism and other factors affects both health and mental health. Members of racialized groups have differential access to economic resources, housing, and employment; consequently, this has a significant impact on health and mental health status. • Factors such as child abuse and intimate partner violence are significantly associated with health and mental health status.
Physical Environments	• Contaminants in air, water, food, and soil can cause a variety of adverse health effects, including cancer, birth defects, respiratory illness, and gastrointestinal ailments. • First Nations members who live in northern communities characterized by unsafe water, inadequate housing, and other deficits have significantly higher rates of mental health concerns and suicide. Infant mortality rates among First Nations people in 1994 were still twice as high as among the Canadian population as a whole.
Healthy Child Development	• In utero care can have long-standing effects due to the impact on neurological development. For instance, approximately 3,000 children are born each year in Canada with fetal alcohol spectrum disorder resulting in lifelong problems with cognition, kidney disorders, and mental health.
Access to Health Care	• Where access to health and mental health care is limited, such as in northern and rural communities, or where access is limited by other factors, such as language or social exclusion, health and mental health suffer.
Personal Health Practices and Coping	• High-risk behaviour and substance abuse are related to health and mental health outcomes. • Opportunities to learn positive coping, problem-solving, and stress reduction strategies are related to better health and mental health outcomes.

Source: Public Health Agency of Canada (2008)

life-saving surgery, and child health issues frequently take precedence over mental health, which tends to be more chronic and less dramatic than other issues in the public view. Further, stigma associated with mental health issues has tended to keep them out of the central focus. Therefore, the call for provincial and national action plans on mental health and mental illness is relatively recent.

Mental Health Policy in Canada: History and Reform

In the initial stages of Canada's development as a nation, people with significant mental health problems were left to fend for themselves and when they became troublesome or dangerous, they were placed in jails (BC Mental Health and Addiction Services, 2008). The records of the colony of Vancouver Island, for instance, noted few cases of "insanity," and these cases were either cared for by friends and family or sent home to their countries of origin (Yearwood-Lee, 2008). The first hospital devoted to people with mental health problems in Canada opened in New Brunswick in 1836, followed shortly by 10 other mental health institutions throughout the country (Nelson, 2006).

William Lyon Mackenzie was appointed to head a committee in 1830 charged with investigating the conditions of the jails in Upper Canada. Finding that people suffering from mental health problems were confined to cells and sleeping on straw in a dungeon, the committee argued for more humane treatment of **lunatics**. This recommendation led to legislation in 1830 and 1833 that provided for the development of lunatic asylums in Upper Canada (Edginton, 2002). In 1850, the Toronto Lunatic Asylum (popularly known simply as 999 Queen Street) was opened on a 27-acre site at 999 Queen Street West. Today, this site, with an address of 1001 Queen Street West, is the location of the Centre for Addiction and Mental Health. Once this asylum opened, it quickly became filled to capacity with 500 patients (Duffin, 2000). Over half of those admitted came from local jails, and most were destitute. Dr S.D. Clarke, the medical director of the Kingston Asylum (for whom the Clarke Institute was later named), lamented that psychiatric institutions had become a means for society to deal with the poor and were in effect large boarding homes. By 1894 the Toronto Lunatic Asylum had opened workshops as part of its "moral treatment," and in 1904 the average working patient was employed 297 days per year.

In British Columbia, the gold rush of 1858 resulted in a dramatic increase and shift in the population. The rise in population also meant a greater number of people suffering from mental illnesses. As in other parts of the country, these people were often housed in jail cells (Yearwood-Lee, 2008). Public outcry grew, and in 1864 British Columbia opened an infirmary for women in Victoria, which had among its patients "lunatics." In 1872 the first BC asylum for the insane opened in the Victoria area in the former quarantine hospital, but within six years it became overcrowded and the 36 residents were moved to a new facility in New Westminster. By 1899 the number of residents exceeded three hundred. Patients included not only those with mental illnesses but also people with various disabilities. The principle causes of insanity were seen to be heredity, intemperance, syphilis, and masturbation (BC Mental Health and

Addiction Services, 2008). Treatments focused on containment and moral interventions such as manual labour as a means of treatment. Indeed, using mostly patient labour, in 1905 the province constructed a new hospital site, Colony Farm, which later supplied food to the Provincial Hospital for the Insane. A1904 report stated: "By so doing a vast saving can be effected in the general economy of the institution, as well as much health and pleasant occupation secured to the patients" (Yearwood-Lee, 2008: 3). This later became the new Hospital for the Mind in 1913 and housed 453 male patients. In later years buildings were added for female patients and the elderly. Later named Essondale, in the 1960s this facility became known as Riverview Hospital. In 1919 a hospital for the "criminally insane" had been opened in Saanich to afford much-needed relief to the "overcrowded wards at New Westminster and Essondale, although this relief has almost been lost sight of in the increased admissions to these places" (Yearwood-Lee, 2008: 3).

Reports on the facilities in British Columbia were troubling. A *Royal Commission Report on the Asylum for the Insane* in 1894 cited problems with cruelty and oppression whereby patients were tightly clinched in straitjackets, handcuffed, and dunked in vats of cold water with their hands and feet bound. The superintendent resigned after the report was released. In 1900 a select committee report was published on the Provincial Lunatic Asylum. This report indicated that the asylum was in very good order, but identified a concern that 25 Chinese patients who were unfit for work were in the asylum and recommended they be returned to China to lessen the financial burden on the provincial government. This sentiment continued over the years and 65 Chinese patients were repatriated in 1935 (Yearwood-Lee, 2008).

In the late-nineteenth century and early part of the twentieth century, mental health was underscored by a belief in "moral management." For instance, Gradby Farrant, the director of the Colquitz Mental Home in British Columbia between 1920 and 1933, was renowned for cajoling residents to "reclaim their sanity and humanity and partake in the restorative activities of physical labour" (Menzies, 1995: 278). He decried public ignorance about the insane and dismissed in outrage attendants caught brutalizing clients. The institution was open to a wide range of community groups including concert bands and orchestras, members of benevolent societies, the clergy, the Salvation Army, and the YWCA. At the same time two divergent models for understanding and treating mental illness came into being and attained precedence. The first was **psychoanalysis**, developed by Sigmund Freud in his 1900 book, *The Interpretation of Dreams*. By 1911 the American Psychoanalytic Association had been founded by eight people, two of whom were from Canada. The second model was based on **neuropsychiatry**, in large part due to the discovery of the causes for syphilis and viral encephalitis. The biological model spawned a number of treatments including **insulin shock therapy** in the 1930s, electroconvulsive shock therapy (ECT) that began in the 1940s, and **prefrontal lobotomies** in the 1930s and 1940s (Duffin, 2000).

It was not until the discovery of **phenothiazines** (major tranquilizers for the treatment of psychosis) and lithium (for the treatment of **mania**) in the early 1950s that mental health treatment and consequently mental health policy took an abrupt shift. The first social worker was hired by the Toronto Psychiatric Hospital (the renamed Toronto Lunatic Asylum) in 1947; a second was hired shortly thereafter. Mora Skelton (1996) recalls:

> Modest forerunners of the new look in psychiatric treatment in Ontario, we were relegated to two tiny cubbyholes on the third floor, reached by a winding wooden stair. The fire department decreed that there must be a fire escape for the third floor, but there was no way of adding one it seemed. A strong young man arrived with a rope, knotted at intervals, to be dangled from the third floor window in case of fire. However, while demonstrating how easy it would be for us and our clients to climb down to the ground outside, that strong young man fell and broke his arm. Helen and I coiled the rope in a corner and prayed for rain.

The 1960s were heralded as the period of deinstitutionalization not only in Canada, but across the world (Shera et al., 2002). A community-based mental health-care centre was established in Burnaby, BC, in 1957 (Yearwood-Lee, 2008). A report released that year by Mental Health Services indicated that this centre was aiming to treat individuals with mental health problems in the early stages of their illness, thereby preventing admissions to inpatient care. In 1959, proposals were drafted to the Ontario Ministry of Health for community-based treatment and the establishment of psychiatric beds in general hospitals (Hartford et al., 2003). As a result of the high cost of inpatient psychiatric treatment, the ability of new medications to relieve psychotic symptoms, and a belief in the benefits of community-based treatment over institutional care, a revolution in mental health care began. The goal was to provide services outside the hospital so that hospital care would only occur when there were acute treatment needs.

Between 1965 and 1981, the number of beds in provincial psychiatric hospitals across Canada dropped by 70 per cent from 69,128 to 20,301 (Nelson, 2006). Some of the "deinstitutionalized" patients, specifically the elderly and those with developmental delays, went to newly established homes for special care or private nursing homes. Others were absorbed by an increase in psychiatric beds in the general hospital system. Most, however, went into the community. Although the deinstitutionalization plan was to flow money to community-based programs, only a small proportion actually did. By the late 1970s there was a shortage of housing and support systems, and many of these formerly hospitalized patients found themselves in poor-quality, unregulated boarding homes. Psychiatric ghettos developed in areas of all Canada's major cities. Welfare payments for disability received by patients were often taken and "managed" by boarding home operators, leaving those with serious mental illnesses impoverished. After-care programs were limited and often consisted only of medication (Hartford et al., 2003; Nelson, 2006). Community care became community neglect. A study conducted in 1981 demonstrated that of those discharged from provincial psychiatric hospitals, one-third were readmitted within six months because community supports did not exist (Goering et al., 1984).

In the 1980s it was clear that deinstitutionalization without adequate community resources doomed people with mental health problems to the revolving door of hospital care. That is, people would become ill in the community, be admitted to hospital for stabilization and short-term care, then be discharged to inadequate supports, income, and housing, and within a short period of time would again reach a crisis state requiring hospitalization. Thus, provinces across Canada embarked on an agenda of mental health reform. Plans arising from this reform had several components, including the increased investment in community-based services and the shifting of focus on existing community-based services from those highly motivated for treatment (sometimes called the worried well) to individuals with serious mental illness, which was determined by diagnosis, disability, and the duration of the illness. This focus was important to ensure that the seriously mentally ill did, in fact, have access to mental health services. A 1991 report by a BC Royal Commission noted that the shift away from institutional treatment was not part of a comprehensive policy and that the mentally ill were simply being moved into communities that were unable and unprepared to provide adequate support. Further, Offord and colleagues (1994) reported that 42 per cent of people seeking mental health treatment in Ontario did not suffer from a mental disorder. Thus, the dollars that did exist for community-based care were being directed to those with the lowest level of need.

Another aspect of mental health reform involved consumer partnerships in which individuals who had experienced the mental health-care system as patients were to be provided with opportunities for input into the planning and administration of programs. Consumers were encouraged to join boards of directors of institutions and community services and provide a different viewpoint; however, the system was not always receptive to this involvement and provisions to allow for meaningful involvement of consumers were not always instituted. Simultaneously, consumer self-help groups were established, resulting in more concerted efforts among consumers to advocate for rights and programs. Policy shifts related to funding began to occur across the country. During the late 1980s, all provinces spent 68 per cent of their mental health budgets on institutionally based care (with the exception of Saskatchewan, at 48 per cent). Between the 1980s and 1998 provincial spending on community mental health increased by a factor of 13 (Nelson, 2006). Supportive housing programs, assertive community treatment programs, consumer support programs, and drop-in centres for persons with mental health problems were established.

Calls continued for deinstitutionalization despite considerable shifts during the 1980s. For instance, in Ontario the influential Graham Report set the target that by 2003 the number of psychiatric beds in Ontario (including both provincial psychiatric hospitals and general hospitals) should be 30 per 100,000 population (Ontario Ministry of Health, 1991). This was down from 219 per 100,000 in 1965 and 58 per 100,000 in 1992. Further, Ontario was to spend 60 per cent of its mental health budget on community care by 2003, compared to 20 per cent in 1992 (Hartford et al., 2003). Although theoretically this sounded very attractive, significant concerns were raised about the viability of such a radical decline in in-patient beds without demonstrable evidence of success of the model. For instance, evidence from the United States demonstrated a direct link between deinstitutionalization and homelessness (Lamb, 1998) and with increases in the number of mentally ill persons in jails (Lamb and Weinberger, 1998), a process some have called **transinstitutionalization**. Using US data from 1928 to 2000, Harcourt (2000) demonstrates a remarkable stability in institutionalization rates when institutionalization in both psychiatric and correctional facilities is considered. In Canada there is similar concern about the prevalence of mental illness in prisons. A BC study reported that male inmates had exponentially higher rates of schizophrenia (1.5 vs 0.5 per cent), anxiety disorder (18.3 vs 8.7 per cent), and mood disorder (30.2 vs 7.1 per cent) than men in the community (*Canadian Journal of Public Health*, 2004). More recently, the 2010–11 annual report of the Canadian federal Office of the Correctional Investigator suggested that 50 per cent of female inmates and 38 per cent of male inmates in federal institutions had mental health symptoms on admission (Sapers, 2011).

In short, the promised money for programs had not found its way to the community. Mental health spending relative to health spending in Ontario declined between 1989 and 2005 and targets for community mental health spending relative to institutional spending had not been met (Lurie, 2005). Lurie more recently stated that the mental health share of health-care funding has continued to decline. In Ontario alone in 2012, 42,000 people were on waiting lists for supportive housing and 16,000 were on waiting lists for case management services (Lurie, 2012).

In 2002, the Ministry of Health and Long-Term Care in Ontario (2002) released *The Time Is Now: Themes and Recommendations for Mental Health Reform in Ontario*, which described the results of nine regional task forces on mental health. The report adopted the following mission: "To urgently seed and develop the social wisdom throughout structures, institutions and communities of Ontario for normalizing mental illness, eliminating its stigma, and creating an impetus for innovating the whole spectrum of care to restore hope and realize recovery with dignity." The report was based on a philosophy that recovery (as defined by the individual, not service delivery professionals and systems) is possible for all people suffering from mental illness. In the end it concluded that:

- The Ontario mental health system was fragmented, with many services and supports operating independently of one another.
- The needs of people with mental illness were not being met equitably across the province and that disparities existed related to regional, cultural, and gender differences.
- There is a need for increased community-based services to address housing, education, employment, and income security.
- The system was lacking accountability and performance indicators.

The report suggested reform in a number of areas, including: putting the consumer at the centre of mental health planning; increasing equity and access; increasing accountability and research; undertaking broad-based public education; enhancing supports to families; and increasing services related to housing, income, and employment. Clearly, despite numerous attempts at mental health reform, many struggles continued to exist in the delivery of services to best meet the needs of people with serious mental illnesses.

According to *Out of the Shadows at Last*, the first national report on mental health in Canada released in 2006, Canada was the only country in the **G8** group of countries that did not have a national strategy on mental health (Standing Committee, 2006). Consequently, in 2007, the prime minister announced the creation of the first Mental Health Commission of Canada, headed by Michael Kirby. The Commission had three strategic initiatives: (1) develop a national mental health strategy; (2) conduct a 10-year anti-stigma campaign; and (3) build a national knowledge exchange centre. The national mental health strategy is intended to provide guidelines for mental health services in each province, guided by the conceptual model provided in Figure 2.2. That is, it is based on the notion that comprehensive mental health programming must incorporate elements aimed at the social dimensions of mental health described earlier in this chapter, including programs aimed at housing, education, and employment as well as programs enhancing social supports from family, friends, and others.

A second aspect of the *Out of the Shadows at Last* report is the campaign against stigma (Kirby, 2008). One of the reasons previous attempts at mental

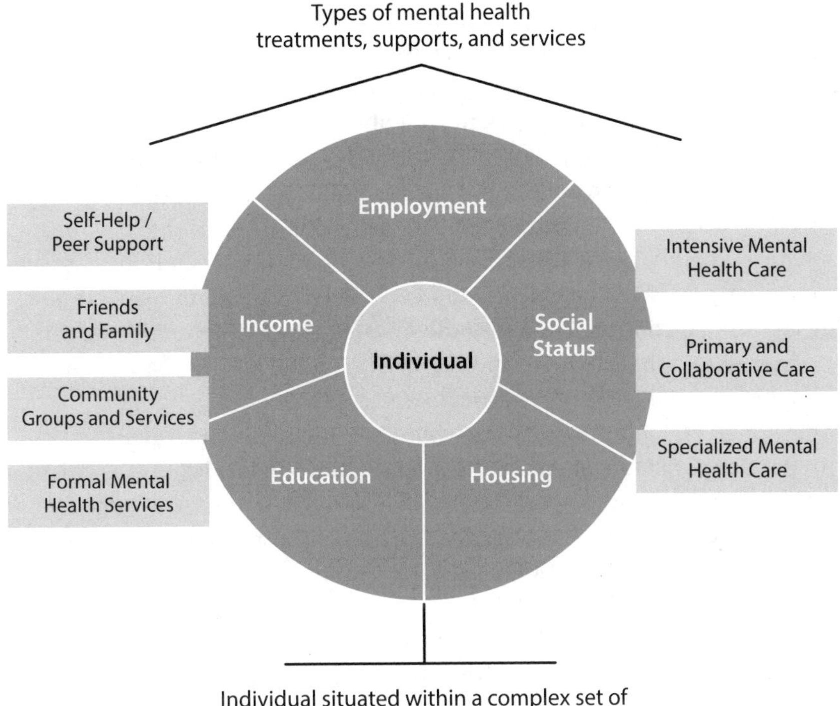

Figure 2.2 Standing Committee

Source: The Standing Senate Committee on Social Affairs, Science and Technology, 2006.

health reform have failed is reluctance in the community to acknowledge mental illness and accept those with mental health problems as citizens who can actively engage as contributing members of society. The Canadian Alliance on Mental Illness and Mental Health (2006), a coalition of non-governmental organizations and professional bodies, including the Canadian Association of Social Workers, reports that many people in Canada, including many health-care professionals, have negative views of people suffering from mental illnesses, causing stigma not only at the societal level but also at the health-care provider level. In the United States, nationally representative surveys have tracked public attitudes about mental illness since the 1950s. In the 1950s the public viewed mental illness as a stigmatized condition and held unscientific understandings of mental illness. By 1996, it was discovered that the public had a better understanding of mental illness and could differentiate between types of mental illness with some accuracy, but social stigma remained essentially unchanged. In this survey, mental illness was more likely to be associated with violence than in the 1950s, with 31 per cent of the respondents mentioning violence in their descriptions of mental illness (Link et al., 1999).

Further, individuals suffering from mental illnesses experience self-stigma that limits their participation in society and often their willingness to seek assistance (Corrigan et al., 2011). In fact, nearly two-thirds of those suffering from mental illnesses do not seek treatment (Regier et al., 1993).

Finally, the third aspect of the *Out of the Shadows at Last* report was to promote knowledge exchange. The fragmentation of our mental health systems has contributed to fragmented data-gathering. There is no co-ordinated system to identify needs for service, there is no clear measure of the prevalence of mental health problems, and consequently it is impossible to identify factors that contribute to morbidity (Canadian Alliance on Mental Illness and Mental Health, 2006). The formation of a central knowledge exchange on mental health will facilitate evidence-based approaches to policy and practice with the aim of enhancing services while ensuring cost-effectiveness.

Building from *Out of the Shadows at Last*, the Mental Health Commission of Canada released *Changing Directions, Changing Lives: A Mental Health Strategy for Canada* in 2012. Described as a blueprint for change, this strategy has six strategic directions (Mental Health Commission of Canada, 2012: 4):

1. Promote mental health across the lifespan in homes, schools, and workplaces, and prevent mental illness and suicide wherever possible.
2. Foster recovery and well-being for people of all ages living with mental health problems and illnesses, and uphold their rights.
3. Provide access to the right combination of services, treatments, and supports, when and where people need them.
4. Reduce disparities in risk factors and access to mental health services, and strengthen the response to the needs of diverse communities and northerners.
5. Work with First Nations, Inuit, and Métis to address their mental health needs, acknowledging their distinct circumstances, rights, and cultures.
6. Mobilize leadership, improve knowledge, and foster collaboration at all levels.

Within these strategic directions priorities include: awareness and prevention; recovery models that actively involve those with mental health problems; co-ordinated community-based treatments; improved living and working conditions; access to services by minority and disadvantaged groups; improved data collection and knowledge exchange. Individual provinces began moving forward with consultation processes to develop their own mental health strategies. Nova Scotia, for instance, announced public consultations beginning in 2011 by an oversight committee co-chaired by Professor Michael Ungar of the School of Social Work at Dalhousie University and Joyce McDonald of the

Canadian Mental Health Association. Clearly, social workers have important roles to play in operationalizing, implementing, and delivering this national strategy.

Summary

Mental health legislation and health legislation in Canada are complex and are driven by many factors, including societal views about health and mental health, prosperity of the nation, and political priorities. Over the past 200 years, treatment of and services for those with mental health problems have shifted dramatically from community neglect and family-based care, to institutionalization of those with mental illnesses, and now again to a community focus. However, it is not clear that current strategies for community-based care will meet their objectives. At present, poverty, inadequate housing, and lack of support services inhibit recovery and health. A multi-pronged approach that focuses on the social determinants of mental health is still a goal to be achieved.

Discussion Questions

1. What could the role of an individual social worker or social work as a profession be in cases such as that of Jordan River Anderson?
2. How can social workers use the social determinants of health in their practice with regard to mental health?
3. In what ways does national policy impact the mental health of Canadians and social work practice in mental health?

Suggested Readings and Websites

Mental Health Commission of Canada. 2012. *Changing Directions, Changing Lives: A Mental Health Strategy for Canada*. Calgary. At: strategy.mentalhealthcommission.ca/download/. This report outlines the first national mental health strategy for Canada and sets the priorities for policy, services, and funding.

Standing Senate Committee on Social Affairs, Science and Technology. 2002. *The Health of Canadians—The Federal Role*. Ottawa: Senate of Canada. At: www.parl.gc.ca/Content/SEN/Committee/372/SOCI/rep/repoct02vol6-e.htm. This report outlines the role of the federal government with respect to health care, identifies overall objectives, discusses the issue of funding, and affirms the overall commitment to universal health care in Canada.

Standing Senate Committee on Social Affairs, Science and Technology. 2006. *Out of the Shadows at Last: Transforming Mental Health, Mental Illness and Addiction Services in Canada*. Ottawa: Senate of Canada. At: www.parl.gc.ca/Content/SEN/Committee/391/soci/rep/rep02may06-e.htm Reports the results of an extensive consultation process, identifies the state of mental health and mental health treatment in Canada, and makes recommendations for a national strategy.

3 Mental Health Law in Canada[1]

Learning Objectives

- To present the history of mental health law in Canada.
- To discuss grounds for involuntary admission to hospital.
- To examine issues of consent in mental health treatment.
- To discuss issues related to financial competence.
- To identify professional duties to warn and protect.
- To outline the limitations to confidentiality of mental health treatment records.

Case Example

Dimitri is a 30-year-old architect who has been married for almost two years. Lara, his wife, was attracted to Dimitri due to his boundless exuberance, creativity, and zest for life. He had great plans for the future, was the life of any party, and colleagues marvelled at his ability to generate new projects almost overnight. Lara was swept off her feet by his flamboyant romantic gestures, and they were married within a few months of knowing each other. Recently, however, Dimitri's behaviour has been become erratic. He is unable to sleep, pacing through the night or suddenly leaving in the middle of the night to go running or to attend an after-hours club. He quit his job because he felt others did not fully appreciate his visionary abilities and superior talents, announcing that he was going to start his own architectural firm. Lara later discovered that he had remortgaged the house without her knowledge, had put the money down on a large space for a new office, and made advance payments to contractors. When she questioned him about this he became hostile, claiming that she had no faith in him, and left the house in a rage. His agitation and irritability continued to increase. Most recently, he became enraged with a neighbour who had parked his car on the street in a spot that Dimitri viewed to be his own. He went to the neighbour's home, shouting

[1]Sections of this chapter are reprinted from Regehr and Kanani, 2010.

profanities and threatening to have his "mafia contractor" friends kill the neighbour if he did not move his car.

Lara contacted Dimitri's parents, who are quite elderly and live in another province. They indicated that he had been hospitalized in the past for both depressive and manic episodes, but they did not tell Lara earlier as they believed that marriage would settle him down. He is presently not taking medication and is refusing hospitalization. Lara is seeking the assistance of the mental health system.

The ability of mental health professionals to address the concerns of Lara while respecting Dimitri's rights is governed by mental health legislation. The role of the social worker in these cases is frequently to provide information to both families and clients about the options available to them and to ensure that all parties are aware of their rights.

Mental Health Law

Mental health legislation in Canada, as in other parts of the world, attempts to balance three things: the **civil liberties** of individuals to live as they choose; the responsibility of society to ensure the safety and well-being of individuals who can't understand the consequences of their choices because of diminished capacity; and the responsibility of a society to ensure that the choices and behaviour of one individual do not compromise the safety and security of others (Regehr and Kanani, 2010). As we see in the case of Dimitri, families and others close to an individual suffering from a mental disorder often approach social workers and other mental health practitioners seeking advice on how to obtain treatment for the person even when that individual does not believe that he or she requires treatment. At times families are seeking to have the person admitted to hospital against his or her will, or wish to find means to ensure that their loved one will remain in treatment when in the community, in order to ensure that the person does not relapse. This pressure to ensure that people in need of assistance are not abandoned by the system must be balanced with an individual's right to determine whether or not he or she will accept treatment. Strong opinions are expressed on both sides of the issue. Psychiatric survivor groups have focused on abuses they endured as a result of involuntary admission and argue for its abolition (Capponi, 2003). Others, such as Hershel Hardin (1993), a member of the Vancouver Civil Liberties Association and a parent of a person with schizophrenia, contend that civil liberties are not respected when people are denied involuntary treatment and left as prisoners of their illnesses. More recently, Erin Hawkes wrote in an editorial about her struggle with schizophrenia and her experience with involuntary admission. She described the auditory hallucinations telling her to die and her delusions that she must take her own life to fulfill a deep meaning. She concluded that "being involuntarily hospitalized and medicated against my will saved me from my suicidal self" (Hawkes, 2012: A16).

The history of mental health reform in Ontario provides an example of the struggles society has attempted to resolve through legislation. In 1813 the British House of Commons passed the Country Asylums Act, which gave local authorities the power to establish mental health institutions. In these institutions, medical superintendents controlled all aspects of the institution with the exception of admissions and discharges, which were regulated by the courts (Bay, 2004). The first mental health legislation in Ontario was enacted in 1871 and was entitled "An Act respecting Asylums for the Insane." This Act was intended to address the rights of individuals residing in the "Provincial Lunatic Asylum in Toronto, the Lunatic Asylum in London, and any other public asylums." The Act indicated that no person could be confined in an asylum except under an order of the lieutenant-governor and a certificate of three medical professionals verified by the mayor or reeve. The medical professionals were required to certify that they had examined the patient and "after due enquiry into all the necessary facts relating to his case, found him to be a lunatic. . . . Such certificate shall be a sufficient authority to any person to convey the lunatic to any of the said asylums, and to the authorities thereof to detain him so long as he continues to be insane." These provisions were essential because **detainment** was tantamount to a life sentence. Asylums provided primarily custodial care, staffing and financing were sparse, and the etiology of mental health problems and avenues of treatment were largely unknown (Regehr and Kanani, 2010).

More than 60 years later, the Mental Hospitals Act, 1935, while clearly specifying a process for involuntary admission of "mentally ill and mentally defective persons," remained relatively vague regarding the criteria for admission under involuntary conditions. Nevertheless, this Act removed the courts from the decision regarding admission, which then allowed involuntary admission based on the authorization of two physicians. This was also the first Act to allow for the fact that a patient may recover and therefore the first to deal with the issue of release from hospital. In part this may have been due to the development of pharmacological treatments for mental illness. However, this legislation coincided with an era of community psychiatry that continued to rise in the 1940s. Mental health institutions were viewed by some as causing, not relieving, mental health problems and the goal became deinstitutionalization (Martin and Cheung, 1985). Following this trend, the revisions of the 1967 Mental Health Act sought to limit the role of medicine and reduced the grounds for involuntary admission to any person who would not enter a hospital voluntarily and suffered "from mental disorder of a nature or degree so as to require hospitalization in the interests of his own safety or the safety of others." These revisions to mental health legislation occurred at a time of growing distrust in the medical profession (Goffman, 1961; Szasz, 1963) and during an era of legislative activism in the interests of social reform (Bagby, 1987). As time progressed, there was a belief that the term "safety" was too broad and open to interpretation, resulting in further limitation of the concept of safety in the 1978 Act. This legislation restricted the notion of safety to the likelihood of *serious bodily harm* to self or others or *imminent and serious impairment* due to lack of competence to care for self. Nonetheless, concerns continued regarding the civil rights of people in mental health facilities and whether processes were in place to ensure proper procedures. Thus, the 1984 Act required that all certificates of involuntary admission be reviewed by the officer in charge of the facility and that the physician complete a form notifying the area director of legal aid that a certificate had been completed so that a lawyer could instruct the patient about his or her right to appeal. In 1987 the Act was again modified and the initial period of involuntary admission was reduced from five days to three. Over the course of more than 100 years in Ontario, then, there were attempts to refine legislation to limit the possibility of abuse of power and increase the rights of those suffering from mental health problems. Paradoxically, however, this at times increases burdens and risks to families and to the community.

Involuntary Admission to Hospital

One of the central issues related to mental health legislation over the years relates to involuntary hospitalization and treatment. The criteria for involuntary admission are similar throughout Canada, but some regional differences do exist (see Table 3.1). Generally, danger is the primary criterion for involuntary admission. For example, Manitoba requires that:

> After examining a person for whom an application has been made under subsection 8(1) and assessing his or her mental condition, the psychiatrist may admit the person to the facility as an involuntary patient if he or she is of the opinion that the person
>
> (a) is suffering from a mental disorder;
>
> (b) because of the mental disorder,
>
> (i) is likely to cause serious harm to himself or herself or to another person, or to suffer substantial mental or physical deterioration if not detained in a facility, and
>
> (ii) needs continuing treatment that can reasonably be provided only in a facility; and
>
> (c) cannot be admitted as a voluntary patient because he or she refuses or is not mentally competent to consent to a voluntary admission.

The terminology used to define "danger" varies across Canada: Manitoba, as stated above, uses the term "serious harm"; Quebec uses "grave and imminent danger to himself or others"; the phrasing in New Brunswick is "imminent physical or psychological harm"; and British Columbia refers to "protection of the person or others" (see Table 3.1). Regardless of the exact terminology, the courts have attributed broad interpretations to the harm considered. For example, the Ontario term "serious bodily harm" is being increasingly interpreted to include both physical and emotional harm (Hiltz and Szigeti, 2004). Similarly, a PEI court included in the concepts of harm and safety the alleviation of distressing physical, mental, or psychiatric symptoms (Regehr and Kanani, 2010).

In most **jurisdictions** impairment is another means for involuntary admission. Alberta added this criterion in 2009 and now requires that the person is "likely to suffer substantial mental or physical deterioration or serious physical impairment." Most other provinces limit this criterion to "substantial mental or physical deterioration," although the Northwest Territories and Nunavut further limit it to "imminent and serious bodily impairment." Quebec and New Brunswick do not have provisions to admit someone involuntarily due to impairment or deterioration.

Additional criteria for involuntary admissions are found in some jurisdictions: British Columbia, Saskatchewan, and Manitoba require that the patient needs treatment. Saskatchewan adds that the person must be incapable of making independent treatment decisions. In other parts of Canada, the person can be competent to make treatment decisions, yet present a risk due to mental illness. Gutheil (1986) highlighted the paradox of separating the decisions regarding hospitalization and treatment, noting that dangerousness was the criteria for involuntary admission, yet mental health facilities are not permitted to provide involuntary treatment that would reduce the risk of danger. The case of *Starson v. Swayze* described below demonstrates the possible consequences of this separation.

Specific definitions of what constitutes a mental disorder vary. Ontario, Nova Scotia, and Newfoundland have relatively broad definitions that may include developmental disabilities or anti-social personality disorder. Nova Scotia specifically includes drug and alcohol addiction in the definition. New Brunswick specifies the definition of mental disorder as substantial disorder of thought, mood, perception, orientation, or memory that grossly impairs a person's: (a) behaviour; (b) judgement; (c) capacity to recognize reality; or (d) ability to meet the ordinary demands of life. Alberta, Saskatchewan, Manitoba, PEI, and the territories similarly limit the definition to substantial disorders that grossly or seriously impair functioning (Gray et al., 2000). Therefore, in those jurisdictions, the dangerous behaviour that the person is exhibiting must be due to factors such as psychosis or serious depression, not anti-social personality disorder or substance use.

Table 3.1 Mental Health Legislation in Canada

Province/Territory	Governing Mental Health Legislation	Involuntary Admission: Harm Criteria	Involuntary Admission: Impairment Criteria	Consent and Advance Directives Legislation	Substitute Decision-Making
British Columbia	Mental Health Act, R.S.B.C. 1996	Protection of the person or others, broadly defined	Substantial mental or physical deterioration	The Health Care (Consent) and Care Facility (Admission) Act, R.S.B.C. 1996, 2000 Adult Guardianship and Planning Statutes Amendment Acts, S.B.C. 2007	Adult Guardianship and Planning Statutes Amendment Act, S.B.C. 2007
Alberta	Mental Health Amendment Act, 2007	Likely to cause harm to themselves or others	Likely to suffer substantial mental or physical deterioration or serious physical impairment	Personal Directives Act, R.S.A. 2000	Powers of Attorney Act, R.S.A. 2000 Adult Guardianship and Trusteeship Act, 2008
Saskatchewan	Mental Health Services Act, S.S. 1984–85–86	Harm to self or others	Substantial mental or physical deterioration	Health Care Directives and Substitute Health Care Decision Makers Act, S.S. 1997	Powers of Attorney Act, S.S. 2002 Adult Guardianship and Co-decision-making Act, S.S. 2000
Manitoba	Mental Health Act, C.C.S.M., 1998	Serious harm to himself or herself or another person	Substantial mental or physical deterioration	Health Care Directives Act, C.C.S.M. 1992	The Powers of Attorney Act, C.C.S.M. 1998 Vulnerable Persons Living with a Mental Disability Act, C.C.S.M. 1993

Ontario	Mental Health Act, R.S.O. 1990, 2010	Serious bodily harm to the person or to another person	Substantial mental or physical deterioration of the person or serious physical impairment	The Health Care Consent Act, S.O. 1996	Substitute Decisions Act, S.O. 1992 Public Guardian and Trustee Act, R.S.O. 1990
Quebec	An Act Respecting Health Services and Social Services, R.S.Q c. S-42	Grave and immediate danger to himself or others	None	An Act Respecting the Protectiion of persons whose mental state presents a danger to themselves or others, S.Q. 1997, 2002 Civil Code of Quebec S.Q. 1991	Public Curator Act, S.Q. 1989
New Brunswick	Mental Health Act, R.S.N.B. 1973, 2010	Imminent physical or psychological harm	None	Infirm Persons Act, R.S.N.B. 1973, 2000	Property Act, R.S.N.B. 1973 Infirm Persons Act, R.S.N.B. 1973, 2000
Nova Scotia	Hospitals Act, R.S.N.S. 1989	Serious harm to himself or herself or towards another	Serious physical impair-ment or serious mental deterioration, or both	Involuntary Psychiatric Treatment Act, S.N.S. 2005	Incompetent Persons Act, R.S.N.S. 1989 Public Trustee Act, R.S.N.S. 1989

Continued

Table 3.1 Continued

Province/Territory	Governing Mental Health Legislation	Involuntary Admission: Harm Criteria	Involuntary Admission: Impairment Criteria	Consent and Advance Directives Legislation	Substitute Decision-Making
Newfoundland and Labrador	Mental Health Care and Treatment Act, S.N.L. 2006	Harm to himself or herself or to others	Substantial mental or physical deterioration or serious physical impairment	Advance Health Care Directives Act, R.S.N.L. 1995	Enduring Powers of Attorney Act, R.S.N.L. 1990 Mentally Disabled Persons Estates Act, R.S.N.L. 1990 Public Trustee Act, S.N.L. 2009
Prince Edward Island	Mental Health Act, R.S.P.E.I. 1988, 2010	Person's own safety of the safety of others	None	Consent to Treatment and Health Care Directive Act, R.S.P.E.I. 1988, 2010	Powers of Attorney Act, R.S.P.E.I. 1988 Trustee Act, R.S.P.E.I. 1988 Public Trustee Act, R.S.P.E.I. 1988 Adult Protection Act, R.S.P.E.I. 1988

Northwest Territories and Nunavut	Mental Health Act, R.S.N.W.T. 1988, 2003	Serious bodily harm to himself or herself	Imminent and serious bodily impairment	Personal Directives Act, S.N.W.T. 2005	Powers of Attorney Act, S.N.W.T. 2001 Guardianship and Trusteeship Act, S.N.W.T. 1994
Yukon	Mental Health Act, R.S.Y. 2002	Serious bodily harm to the person or to another person	Impending serious mental or physical impairment	Health Act, R.S.Y. 2002 Care Consent Act, S.Y. 2003	Enduring Power of Attorney Act, R.S.Y. 2002 Decision-Making Support and Protection to Adults Act, S.Y. 2003

Throughout Canada, a person can be admitted involuntarily to a psychiatric facility by the following means:

- A physician may complete an application for psychiatric assessment and the individual will then be transported to the psychiatric facility for assessment, if necessary by the police.
- A judge can order a person with an apparent mental health disorder to be taken by the police to a mental health facility for psychiatric assessment.
- Family members or concerned community mental health workers can swear before a justice of the peace (a position that can generally be found in any provincial court) that a person with an apparent mental disorder is behaving in a manner that may meet the criteria for harm or danger. The justice of the peace, having heard the evidence, may then issue an order that instructs the police to assist with transporting the individual to a psychiatric facility where a physician can complete an application for psychiatric assessment.
- A police officer may apprehend a person who is believed to meet the criteria under mental health legislation and transport him or her to a psychiatric facility for assessment. Police have specific guidelines for action depending on the circumstances (Hoffman and Putnam, 2004).

In these circumstances, some jurisdictions allow the individual to be detained in an approved psychiatric facility for a specified number of hours or days for the purpose of a psychiatric assessment to determine whether involuntary admission is warranted. It is important to recognize that while an individual is under detention for assessment he or she is not a patient of the psychiatric facility. Involuntary admission at law only occurs after the psychiatric assessment is completed and it has been determined that the individual meets the requisite criteria. Thus, in each of these cases, physicians must carry out independent assessments to determine whether the person indeed meets the criteria for involuntary admission. For practical purposes (specifically, the lack of physicians) the Northwest Territories also allows psychologists to complete certificates for involuntary admission and the Yukon legislation provides that nurses can perform this task.

In most jurisdictions, once it has been determined through the psychiatric assessment that the requisite criteria for involuntary admission are fulfilled, the physician files a certificate for involuntary admission with the director in charge of the facility, who, as a check and balance, reviews the same to ensure compliance with the legal requirements. In New Brunswick the final sign-off is provided by a tribunal, in Quebec by a judge, and in the Northwest Territories by a minister of the government. The time period for which a person can be required to remain in hospital following involuntary admission is specified under each provincial and territorial Act.

Under the Canadian Charter of Rights and Freedoms, involuntary patients must: (1) be informed promptly of the reasons for detention; (2) be given the opportunity to retain or instruct counsel without delay; (3) have the validity of the detention reviewed and determined. In some jurisdictions involuntary admissions may be challenged before review boards or panels, whereas in other jurisdictions **recourse** is only through the courts. In Ontario's mental health legislation, for instance, patients are provided with information through a patient advocate or rights adviser and given a mechanism for appeal through the **Consent and Capacity Board** and thence, secondarily, through the courts. In addition to the involuntary patient, any other person on his or her behalf, the minister of health, or the official in charge of the psychiatric facility where the patient is detained may bring applications to the Consent and Capacity Board to review whether the legislative criteria for involuntary admission have been met (Hiltz and Szigeti, 2004). Further, court actions for malicious prosecution and false imprisonment have also been brought against mental health facilities. For instance, in the BC case of *Ketchum v. Hislop* (1984), the patient was awarded damages for procedural irregularities and the fact that the statutory requirements for admission had not been met. This occurred despite the fact that the court found that the patient both needed and benefited from treatment (Schneider, 1988).

If individuals are willing to be admitted voluntarily (that is, are capable of consent and do consent to admission) or can be admitted as informal patients (that is, are not capable of consent but consent is obtained from a substitute decision-maker), then involuntary admission is not appropriate. In contrast to patients who have been admitted involuntarily, individuals who have been admitted voluntarily have the legal right to leave the psychiatric facility at any time. In practice, this right is often illusory. If, at the time a patient wishes to leave, a psychiatric assessment reveals that the criteria for involuntary admission are met, the physician may simply detain the individual under the appropriate section of the Mental Health Act (Hiltz and Szigeti, 2004).

This issue was recently tested by the case of *Ahmed v. Stefaniu* (Glancy and Glancy, 2008). In this case, William Johannes was involuntarily admitted to hospital after his sister, Roslyn Knipe, with whom he resided, contacted her family practitioner stating that her brother, who suffered from severe paranoia, had threatened to kill her. Mr Johannes appealed his involuntary admission to the Ontario Consent and Capacity Review Board, which concluded that without treatment there was a likelihood that he would continue to deteriorate and cause harm to others. While in hospital, Mr Johannes assaulted other patients, threatened staff, physically fought with staff, and walked around the unit naked. Over the next two months he was seen by several consultants and the opinion was that he was beginning to settle and become less threatening. One evening, after threatening a nurse, Mr Johannes was assessed by Dr Stefaniu. She did not find him to be psychotic and noted that he denied any intention to harm anyone and further that he claimed to have faked his symptoms. She concluded that he no longer met the criteria for being an involuntary patient and because Mr Johannes refused to remain in hospital on a voluntary basis, he was discharged to his sister's apartment. On 24 January 1997, 50 days after his discharge, Mr Johannes killed his sister. His brother-in-law, Mr Ahmed, and Ahmed's two daughters commenced legal action against Dr Stefaniu alleging professional negligence. Dr Stefaniu was found negligent in that she failed to meet the standard of care when she made the decision to change Mr Johannes's status to that of a voluntary patient. The case was appealed in 2006, but the appeal court dismissed the appeal and upheld the original verdict. Dr Stefaniu was held accountable for Ms Knipe's death. This decision could potentially have a chilling effect on mental health practitioners and may cause physicians to err on the side of safety when making the decision to keep people in hospital on an involuntary basis.

As indicated earlier in this chapter, there has been substantial legislative reform with regard to mental health, with each subsequent revision further defining the grounds for involuntary admission, the length of involuntary admission, and the scope of control over clients by those working in psychiatric institutions. It appears that these changes have been substantive, but in practice, have the legislative reforms actually changed the procedures for involuntary admission? Page (1980) examined involuntary admission certificates following changes in the Ontario Mental Health Acts in 1967, 1970, and 1978 and reported no changes in the reasons provided in practice for involuntary admissions after each of the legislative revisions. Bagby (1987) and Martin and Cheung (1985) similarly concluded that changes in mental health legislation in Ontario did not have the effect of reducing involuntary admissions (see Figure 3.1). It is not clear as yet what the impact of the legal decision in *Ahmed v. Stefaniu* will have on decisions regarding involuntary admissions.

Despite legal decisions and legislative reforms, experimental analyses indicate that dangerousness and the presence of psychiatric illness are the key factors in the decision to admit patients under involuntary conditions (Bagby et al., 1991). This would suggest that other factors are at play in maintaining the admission rate despite legislative reform. One such factor is that doctors and judges continue to use a "common-sense" perspective to assess the risk that a person with an acute mental illness may present to self and family (Gray et al., 2000). Further, families and others are thought to adapt to restrictive legislative criteria by exaggerating the elements of danger and violence in order to obtain treatment. This creates a tension between the letter of the law

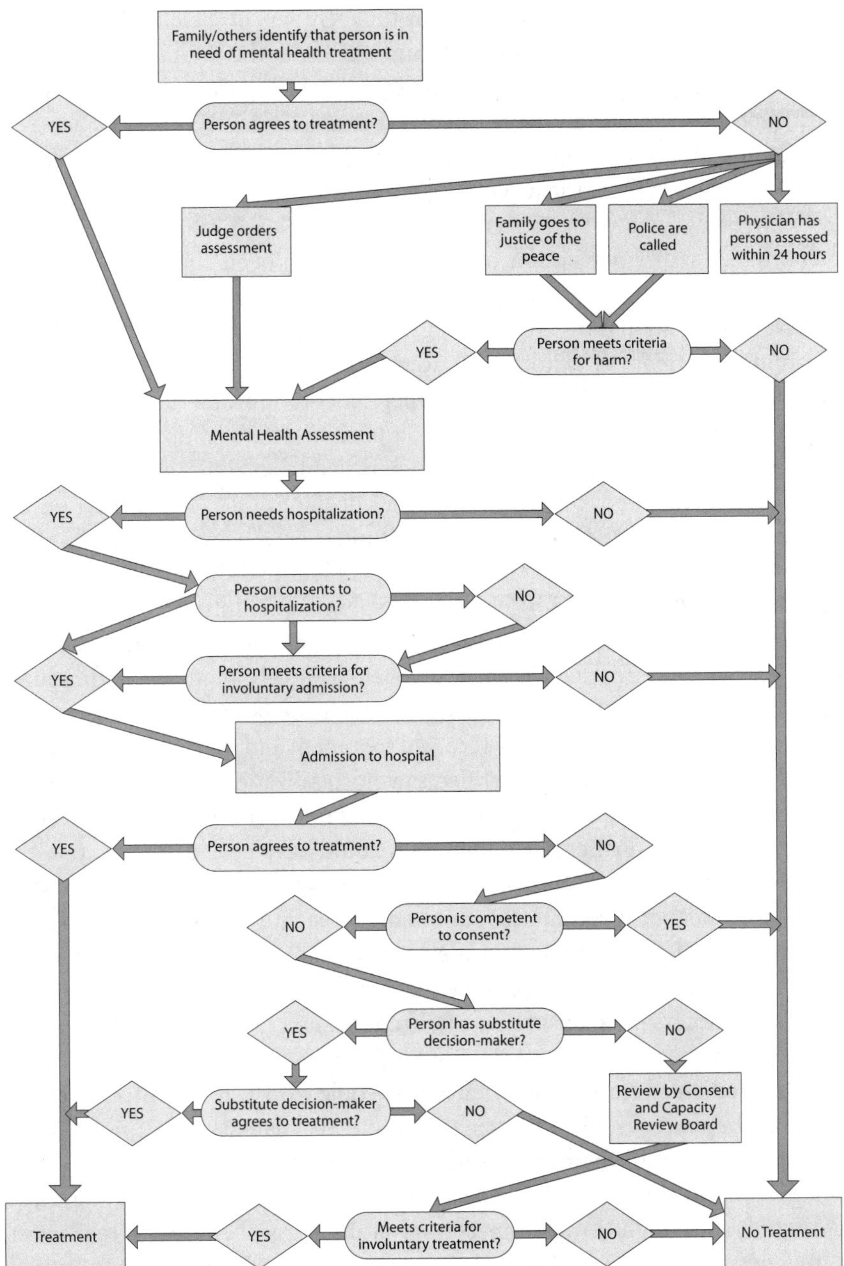

Figure 3.1 Pathways to Treatment in Ontario

and what is perceived as morally right by the members of society (Appelbaum, 1994). Similar histories across Canada and the rest of the Western world demonstrate the close connection between mental health legislation and prevailing societal values. Despite all the legislative changes, however, the application of legislation remains relatively stable since practitioners must always respond to the lived experiences of those with mental illnesses.

One of the central concerns for social workers and other mental health practitioners is the perception of clients who have been subject to involuntary admission. Not surprisingly, research has demonstrated that client views on involuntary admission are variable. Sheehan and Burns (2011) found that involuntary patients in Oxford, UK, were almost twice as likely as voluntary patients (89 per cent as opposed to 49 per cent) to indicate that they experienced **coercion** as inpatients. However, a positive relationship with the therapist was associated with lower levels of perceived coercion. In another study conducted in England, 59 people who had been admitted to hospital on an involuntary basis participated in in-depth interviews between three months and one year after discharge. The researchers identified three distinct groups of respondents: people who felt their involuntary admission was justified (50 per cent); people who felt it was unjustified (30 per cent); and those who were ambivalent (20 per cent). Those who felt positively about their admission believed that coercion was necessary given their mental state at the time and that hospitalization ensured they received treatment and averted further harm. People who thought it was unjustified saw hospitalization as an infringement on their autonomy. Those who were ambivalent now believed that they needed treatment to avert further harm, but felt it could have been achieved in a less coercive manner (Katsakou et al., 2011). These same researchers interviewed family members of involuntarily admitted people and discovered the following themes: relief that the family member had been admitted to hospital; a sense of frustration that services had not been able to respond earlier and that a crisis was necessary to ensure hospitalization; and concern about the burden of caregiving they experienced (Jankovic, 2011).

Researchers in Ireland interviewed 68 people who were admitted involuntarily at the end of their admission and one year later. Interestingly, while 72 per cent believed their admission was necessary at the time of their discharge, only 60 per cent believed so a year later. On the other hand, one-third of those who thought it was unnecessary at discharge, believed in retrospect it was necessary one year later. Those who saw admission as necessary had a greater understanding of the nature of their illness and perceived that the process of involuntary admission was procedurally fair (O'Donoghue et al., 2011). Thus, while involuntary admission is used as a measure of last resort, focusing social worker interventions on working effectively with both clients and their families to provide education about the legal processes, maintaining a good therapeutic alliance, and enhancing the sense of client choice within constraints can lessen the possibility of the negative impact.

Consent to Psychiatric Treatment

It is enshrined in Canadian law and in the ethical guidelines of each health discipline that before a practitioner can provide health care for a person, she or he must receive the authorization of that person. Individuals generally have the right to permit or refuse treatment. This principle has been enunciated by the Supreme Court of Canada as follows:

> every patient has a right to bodily integrity. This encompasses the right to determine what medical procedures will be accepted and the extent to which they will be accepted. Everyone has the right to decide what is to be done with one's own body. This includes the right to be free from medical treatment to which the individual does not consent. This concept of individual autonomy is fundamental to the common law. (*Ciarlariello v. Schacter* [1993] at 135)

Prior to the 1960s the capacity to consent to treatment by the patient and the authority of hospital personnel to treat someone were not viewed as separate from the authority to hospitalize and detain against someone's will. That is, any person admitted to hospital against his or her will could be treated without consent. This was in large part because admission to hospital was based on the presumption of need for treatment. For example, the 1980 Alberta Mental Health Act specifically stated that a physician may treat a patient once a conveyance and examination certificate had been issued. Similar provisions were found in Newfoundland, Saskatchewan, and New Brunswick. Legislation in British Columbia allowed for the person in charge of the mental health facility to sign consent-to-treatment forms for an involuntary patient (Gordon and Verdun-Jones, 1983). However, the emergence of legislation regarding consent has distinguished involuntary admission from the right to consent to treatment once in the hospital (Gray et al., 2000). Every province now has consent legislation that makes it clear that a health-care professional cannot administer treatment to an individual without valid consent. For instance, the Consent to Treatment and Health Care Directives Act (1996, c. 10, s. 4) of Prince Edward Island states:

> Every patient who is capable of giving or refusing consent to treatment has the right
>
> (a) to give consent or to refuse consent on any grounds, including moral or religious grounds, even if the refusal will result in death;

(b) to select a particular form of treatment from among those proposed by a health practitioner on any grounds, including moral or religious grounds;
(c) to be assisted by an associate; and
(d) to be involved to the greatest degree practicable in case planning and decision making.

When valid consent cannot be obtained from an individual, alternative authority for consent must be sought.

There are two forms of consent: express and implied. Express consent is the oral or written expression of consent, for example, by the patient stating, "I would like you to remove this wart from my finger." In contrast, implied consent is derived when consent can be implied from the action or inaction of an individual. For example, consent for obtaining a blood sample is implied by the action of rolling up one's sleeve and presenting one's arm (Etchells et al., 1996). Consent to treatment must be obtained before the treatment begins. Further, once consent is provided it can be withdrawn. As stated by the Supreme Court of Canada: "an individual's right to determine what medical procedures will be accepted must include the right to stop the procedure" (*Ciarlariello v. Schacter*, 1993). If consent has been withdrawn, medical personnel are obligated to stop the procedure, although they must ensure that they do so at a stage where the patient's safety is not in jeopardy. Any treatment provided without consent may result in criminal charges of assault or civil actions of negligence or battery (the unlawful application of force to another person) (Morris et al., 1999; Rozovsky, 2003). No intent to harm is necessary for a finding of battery; the lack of consent to the named intervention will be sufficient to establish the liability of the practitioner.

Elements of Consent to Treatment

It is not sufficient for a practitioner simply to obtain consent. In order for a practitioner to rely on the consent obtained, the practitioner must ensure that the consent is valid (see Box 3.1 for elements of consent). For consent to be valid the person must have the capacity to consent; consent must be informed; and consent must be voluntary (Antle and Regehr, 2003). Treatment can be provided without consent in an emergency if a person for whom the treatment is proposed is incapable of consenting and the delay in consulting with a substitute decision-maker would result in prolonged suffering or put the patient at risk of sustaining serious bodily harm if treatment is not administered promptly. This type of situation is most easily understood in medical situations. For example, in the Nova Scotia case of *Marshall v. Curry* (1933), a surgeon performed an unauthorized procedure during surgery and the court found "where an emergency which could not have been anticipated arises . . . it is the surgeon's duty to act in order to save the life or preserve the health of the patient, and . . . in the honest execution of that duty he should not be exposed to legal liability." It is more difficult to determine the issue of emergency in mental health situations. For instance, it may be determined that it is an emergency situation when a psychotic individual is behaving in a violent manner that threatens the safety of staff—in which case he or she may be treated with medications or placed in physical restraints.

Capacity to Consent

In order to have the capacity to consent, people must be able to understand information that is provided to them and how that information applies to their specific situation. The PEI Act, for example, states that a patient is capable to consent to treatment if he or she is able: (a) to understand the information that is relevant to making a decision concerning the treatment; (b) to understand that the information applies to his or her particular situation; (c) to understand that the patient has the right to make a decision; and (d) to appreciate the reasonably foreseeable consequences of a decision or lack of a decision.

Controversy arises, however, over the concept of "understanding," an issue addressed by the Supreme Court of Canada in *Starson v. Swayze* (2003). Scott Starson (born Scott Schutzman) challenged a Capacity and Consent Board of Ontario decision, which ruled that he was incapable of refusing mental health treatment. Starson had been found not criminally responsible due to mental disorder of criminal charges related to uttering threats, and as a result he was ordered to be confined at the Centre for Addiction and Mental Health. He did not believe that he suffered from bipolar affective disorder, despite repeated hospitalizations in Canada and the United States over an 18 month period. As a result, he refused all treatment while confined to hospital. The Supreme Court decision was split, but it nevertheless concluded that while Starson's decision may not have been rational, "unwise choices are permitted" under law and people have the right to "act unreasonably" (Sklar, 2007). Three years later, Chief Justice McLachlin referred in a speech to the fact that Starson was still hospitalized, noting the cruel paradox that his right to refuse treatment resulted in his loss of liberty as he remained a danger and could not be released.

The case of Starson highlights a particular challenge whereby individuals may have the right to refuse medication, but by virtue of the danger they present as a result of their illness they do not have the right to leave hospital and return to the community. Gutheil (1980) referred to this situation decades ago as "rotting with your rights on." Kress (2006: 573), in exploring this issue, identifies a group of patients who are not compliant to treatment until they are "substantially healthier than being barely not mentally ill or barely not dangerous." He underscores the problem of restricting liberty through civil commitment while not compelling treatment. Mela (2012), a psychiatrist in Saskatchewan, argues that choice is dependent on insight and that as we become increasingly aware of the neuro-biological basis for mental illness, we need to consider the influence of brain functioning on the exercise of choice.

Capacity is not static or all-encompassing, but it is specific to a particular procedure and particular time frame. Thus, a person may be incapable of consenting to some treatments but able to consent to others. For example, a person may be able to consent to a procedure such as blood work but not to cardiac surgery (Nelson, 2002). In addition, consent is fluid. A person may be able to consent to a particular procedure at one time but not able to consent to the same procedure at another time.

Where a minor has the capacity to consent, the views of the minor should be given due consideration. The UN Convention on the Rights of the Child (1990: Article 12) provides that "parties shall assure to the child who is capable of forming his or her own views the right to express these views freely in all matters affecting the child, the views of the child being given due weight in accordance with the age and maturity of the child." Although each province and territory in Canada identifies a certain age at which an individual may be presumed capable of giving and refusing consent, age itself is not the governing criterion for determining if an individual has the capacity to consent (Morris et al., 1999). Rather, when a minor is capable of understanding and appreciating the nature and consequences of a specified treatment or procedure, he or she may be capable of providing consent. Issues to be considered under Canadian law are the degree to which the young person is emancipated from his or her family (Sneiderman et al., 2003; Downie et al., 2002) and his or her level of maturity. Nevertheless, despite the legal rules and precedent-setting cases regarding a minor's capacity to consent, there is variation across institutions as to whether emphasis is placed on the rights of the mature minor or on parental involvement in decision-making (Rozovsky, 2003). Even where minors have the capacity to consent, there are often concerns that children's wishes are not respected. A British study of a child and adolescent mental health unit, for instance, revealed that in four of 42 consecutive cases children were unaware of their appointments and 14 of 42 came unwillingly (Paul et al., 2000).

Social work ethical guidelines in Canada and the United States, until very recently, have remained surprisingly silent regarding the issue of the capacity of children to consent, only addressing children in relation to the social worker's duty to protect vulnerable clients from harm (Antle and Regehr, 2003). However, because social workers are frequently in situations where they are working with both the child and the family, there is an obligation to ensure that children are informed about what is going to happen to them, that they have an opportunity to express their views, and that parents consider these views when making decisions regarding treatment and consent. The Canadian Association of Social Workers guidelines on informed consent and confidentiality (2007) states: "Social workers who have children as clients must determine the child's capacity to consent and explain to the child (where appropriate), and to the child's parents/guardians (where appropriate), the nature of the social worker's relationship to the child and others involved in the child's care." Where children do not have the legal capacity to provide consent, the practice of obtaining assent is becoming increasingly common, whereby children are asked to express their agreement with the treatment plan verbally or in writing. Although this is not legally binding, it does provide a formal way of ensuring that the child feels respected and that her or his views are clearly documented.

Consent Must Be Informed

Consent or refusal to consent must be offered by an individual based on information provided by the practitioner about the benefits and potential risks of the course of treatment. Clearly, in any treatment decision, there are a vast array of possible outcomes, some highly unlikely; disclosure of each and every one could result in information overload and impair the ability to make a decision. In *Reibl v. Hughes* (1980), the Supreme Court of Canada stated that practitioners have a duty to disclose "all material risks." In addition, the legislation in some jurisdictions defines specific information required to be disclosed, including the nature of the treatment, the expected benefits, the material risks, the material side effects, alternative courses of action, and the likely consequences of not having the treatment. Further, details of who will be participating in the procedure, including student interns, should also be provided (Dykeman, 2000).

However, in some situations an individual may be harmed by receiving the full scope and depth of disclosure as outlined above. In *Reibl v. Hughes* (1980: 13) the Supreme Court stated: "[I]t may be the case that a particular patient may, because of emotional factors, be unable to cope with facts relevant to recommended surgery or treatment and the doctor may, in such a case, be justified in withholding or generalizing information as to which he would otherwise be required to be more specific." Therefore, if a health-care provider believes the person's mental health would be compromised or emotional state would be significantly affected, the professional may limit the information provided to the patient. Dickens (2002) cautions, however, that this does not imply that the obligation to provide information is erased. Health-care professionals may need to consider alternative means to ensure that information is conveyed to the patient in a manner that is less distressing.

Consent Must Be Voluntary

An individual's decision to consent or refuse consent must be free of coercion or undue influence. Such influence may include financial incentives,

Box 3.1 Elements of Consent

- *A person must have the capacity to consent.*
  – A person's ability to consent must not be impeded by mental health, health, or maturation.
- *Consent must be informed.*
  – Information must be available about all risks and benefits of treatment.
  – Information must also be available about risks of no treatment.
- *Consent must be voluntary.*
  – It must be free of overt or implied consequences for consent or non-consent.

unnecessary fear, or influence created by the therapeutic alliance between the patient and the health-care provider (Regehr and Antle, 1997). Information must not be presented in a manner that induces unnecessary fear in the patient—for instance, "You must do this or die." In addition, it is important that practitioners be keenly aware that in some circumstances the power of the therapeutic alliance can induce a person to suspend critical judgement in an effort to please the practitioner. For instance, if a surgeon is seeking consent for a procedure, the patient may feel that refusing consent will displease the doctor and indicate that he or she does not trust the doctor's skill. If a social worker is seeking consent, the person may feel that refusal could result in a withdrawal of social support.

Some jurisdictions have mechanisms for appealing decisions dealing with capacity and consent of an individual, through boards or panels, whereas in other jurisdictions recourse is only through the courts. Ontario, for instance, has a Consent and Capacity Board and BC has a Health Care and Care Facility Review Board. These boards review care decisions made by a substitute decision-maker (which can include a designated family member or the health-care facility), and can either confirm the decision or make alternative decisions regarding care. In doing so they must consider the patient's pre-expressed wishes, the patient's values, and the patient's best interest. In Alberta, if two physicians complete a form (Form 11 under the Mental Health Act) indicating that a patient is incompetent to provide consent, treatment can be administered without consent. However, the patient does have the right to appeal this decision to a review board and treatment will be suspended until the appeal is heard (Alberta Mental Health Act, 2000).

Advanced Directives

The prior wishes of a patient who is deemed to be incapable of consent are central to the decision-making regarding involuntary treatment. In the case of *Sevels v. Cameron* (1995), a patient suffering from schizophrenia expressed a wish, while competent, not to be treated with neuroleptic medication, a request with which the substitute decision-maker and treating health team was forced to comply. The judge stated: "[W]ishes are not a mere factor in best interests. They are the expression of the right of individuals to determine what will be done with their bodies." One way in which clients can express this wish is through an advanced directive.

An **advanced directive** is written while a person is competent to specify what decisions should be made about treatment if she or he becomes incapable of delivering consent. At times, people with severe mental disorders may be incapable of fully appreciating and weighing the relative risks and benefits of treatment options versus no treatment. At other times, these same people may clearly understand these issues and, after careful consideration, have a preferred course of action (Appelbaum, 1991). When patients remain in control of the content of advanced directives, they can increase their sense of autonomy and decrease the sense of coercion associated with emergency mental health treatment (Ritchie et al., 1998). Manitoba, in 1992, was the first province to specify a role for advanced directives in mental health legislation (Ambrosini and Crocker, 2007). This legislation binds the substitute decision-maker to following the directive unless the expressed wishes endanger the physical or mental health or safety of the patient or another person. A **Ulysses Contract**, named after the classical hero, is often included in a mental health advanced directive. Ulysses, who knew he would be unable to resist the call of the sirens that would lead to the destruction of his ship, ordered that he be tied to the mast and be disregarded when he begged to respond. Under this contract, a person may request detainment or restraint and may waive the right of appeal of involuntary admission and treatment (Bay et al., 1996).

Substitute Decision-Makers

If the individual does not have an advanced directive for treatment being considered, an alternative decision-maker will need to be identified for the individual. A person may designate a **power of attorney** (person granted authority to act on behalf of the grantor) for personal care prior to becoming incapable of consenting. If there is no power of attorney in place, then the decision-maker will be an individual or entity identified under the law. Substitute decision-makers are entitled to all information regarding the treatment of the person's care that may be relevant to the decision. In making decisions they must consider the patient's best interests as well as the wishes expressed by the patient when he or she was competent (Vayda and Satterfield, 1997).

Even if treatment is authorized for an incompetent patient, based on the necessary considerations and following the required procedures, certain treatments are still excluded; for instance, Saskatchewan and Ontario exclude psychosurgery. In addition, the Manitoba Vulnerable Persons Living with a Mental Disability Act of 1993 specifically excludes from the decision-making authority of a substitute decision-maker any research and sterilization not medically necessary. Other interventions, such as restraint and seclusion also remain controversial.

Community Treatment Orders

In response to legislative restrictions on involuntary admission to hospital and the move to deinstitutionalize those with serious mental health problems, there has been a recent movement to community-based treatment. In 1995, Brian Smith, a popular sportscaster in Ottawa, was shot and killed by a man who was suffering from paranoid schizophrenia but had refused treatment. A coroner's inquest was conducted and recommended changes to mental health legislation in Ontario that, when introduced in the legislature in December 2000, received the support of all parties (*Burlington Post*, 2001). Known as Brian's Law, this legislation made two major changes to the Ontario Mental Health Act and the Health Care Consent Act. First, it deleted the word *imminent* from the criteria of "imminent and serious bodily harm," allowing for earlier intervention. Second, it created community treatment orders (CTOs) by which a person may choose to comply with treatment in the community instead of being involuntarily admitted to a hospital (Ministry of Health and Long-Term Care, 2000). These changes to Ontario legislation are an excellent example of the influence of high-profile cases and public pressure on public policy.

Orders for community mental health treatment (known as "leash laws" by opponents) represent one of the most controversial issues in mental health law. Under these laws, a person who suffers from a serious mental disorder may agree to a plan of community-based treatment. This action is less restrictive than being detained in a psychiatric facility, but once the patient agrees to the order he or she will be required to comply with its terms and may be returned to the issuing physician for examination if there are reasonable grounds to suspect non-compliance (Hiltz and Szigeti, 2004). In the United States, which has a longer history of outpatient commitment, various measures are used as leverage to encourage compliance, for instance, access to welfare funds and housing or avoidance of hospitalization and jail (Monahan et al., 2001). In Canada, community treatment orders were first introduced in Saskatchewan in 1994; most recently, Alberta adopted them in 2010. Other provinces (Manitoba, British Columbia, and PEI) have adopted similar measures in the form of leave certificates (Trueman, 2003). In 2005, Nova Scotia enacted the Involuntary Psychiatric Treatment Act with the aim that "treatment and related services are to be offered in the least-restrictive manner and environment with the goal of having the person continue to live in the community or return to the person's home surroundings at the earliest possible time." This Act specifies:

> A psychiatrist may issue a community treatment order respecting a person where the criteria in clause (3)(a) exist.
>
> (3) A community treatment order must
>
> (a) state that the psychiatrist has examined the person named in the community treatment order within the immediately preceding seventy-two hours and that, on the basis of the examination and any other pertinent facts regarding the person or the person's condition that have been communicated to the psychiatrist, the psychiatrist is of the opinion that
>
> (i) the person has a mental disorder for which the person is in need of treatment or care and supervision in the community and the treatment and care can be provided in the community,
>
> (ii) the person, as a result of the mental disorder,
>
> (A) is threatening or attempting to cause serious harm to himself or herself or has recently done so, has recently caused serious harm to himself or herself, is seriously harming or is threatening serious harm towards another person or has recently done so, or
>
> (B) is likely to suffer serious physical impairment or serious mental deterioration, or both,
>
> (iii) as a result of the mental disorder, the person does not have the full capacity to make treatment decisions,
>
> (iv) during the immediately preceding two-year period, the person
>
> (A) has been detained in a psychiatric facility for a total of sixty days or longer,
>
> (B) has been detained in a psychiatric facility on two or more separate occasions, or
>
> (C) has previously been the subject of a community treatment order, and
>
> (v) the services that the person requires in order to reside in the community
>
> (A) exist in the community,
>
> (B) are available to the person, and
>
> (C) will be provided to the person.

Ontario instituted CTOs in 2000 as "part of the government's plan to create a comprehensive, balanced and effective system of mental health services that provides a continuum of community-based, outpatient and inpatient care" (Ministry of Health and Long-Term Care, 2000). The goal is to eliminate the revolving-door syndrome, where individuals improve while in the hospital only to relapse after discharge because they don't take their medication. Alberta, in a brochure for consumers of mental health services, offers the following explanation: "A community treatment order (CTO) under the Mental Health Act is a tool intended to assist you in complying with treatment while in the community. Your community treatment order is a treatment and care plan that outlines care specific to your needs, and may include (but is not limited to) medications you must take and appointments you must attend with care providers" (Alberta Health, 2012). However, some argue that the prospect of "being forcibly taken to a physician for examination, which may lead to an involuntary admission, simply for failing to take medication as prescribed, is often very troubling" (Hiltz and Szigeti, 2004: 273).

What is the effect of legislation permitting community treatment orders? Saskatchewan enacted CTOs in 1994, and thus has the longest history of using them in Canada. The first study on their use was conducted by O'Reilly et al. (2000), who found that although psychiatrists view the orders positively, they rarely use them. For example, in the 21 months from April 1996 to December 1997, only 96 orders (each valid for three months, after which they must be renewed) were issued in a population of approximately 1 million people. These findings were similar to those of earlier studies conducted in the United States (Torrey and Kaplan, 1995). O'Brien and Farrell (2005; O'Brien et al., 2009) collected data on patients who were issued CTOs at the Royal Ottawa Hospital. They determined that patients on CTOs had a significant decrease in both the number and length of admissions to hospital and a concomitant increase in access to and participation in community support services, including supportive housing. None of the patients in their study chose to contest the CTO despite being provided information regarding their right to do so. A study conducted in Quebec over a nine-year period similarly revealed decreased rates and length of hospitalizations, which were sustained even after the CTOs had expired (Nakhost, Perry & Frank, 2012). In a review of international studies on the effectiveness of CTOs published in the *Canadian Journal of Psychiatry*, Swartz and Swanson (2004) conclude that CTOs are effective provided that they are of sufficient duration and are used in conjunction with a wide range of community support services.

A different question relates to client views of community treatment orders. Schwartz and colleagues report the results of a study designed and conducted by four social work students at Carleton University in which six clients were interviewed regarding their personal experiences with CTOs. Participants identified that they were placed on CTOs primarily because they were not taking medication and were not caring for themselves. Clients did express negative feelings about being labelled, stigmatized, and controlled by the CTO. In addition, however, they noted positive outcomes in terms of support systems and improved mental health. One participant stated that "It changed my whole life around. I went from being a paranoid freak, to a well-groomed individual." Nevertheless, CTOs remain highly controversial and social workers with clients on CTOs must work to ensure that clients remain involved in planning their care and choosing the course of their treatment (Schwartz et al., 2010).

Protection of Financial Security

Incapacity to manage finances is certainly not a ground for involuntary admission to hospital, regardless of whether mental health problems impair judgement, but it is often a concern of family members seeking to have someone admitted against his or her will. Each jurisdiction has a mechanism to declare persons incapable of managing their own funds and have them managed by another authorized individual. In 1927, Ontario's Hospitals for the Insane Act provided a role for the **public trustee** to act as "committee of the estate" for a person confined in a psychiatric hospital who had no other person to act as trustee. Interestingly, under this Act the power to appoint a trustee for persons in Saskatchewan and Manitoba also resided with the lieutenant-governor in council of Ontario. A more recent example is the Incompetent Person's Act (1989) of Nova Scotia. The Ontario Substitute Decisions Act provides a mechanism by which someone can grant an individual power of attorney for property when that person is capable, in anticipation of the possibility that she or he may become incapable of managing personal finances. This form is often completed when preparing a last will and testament. Someone who is paid to provide health, social, or housing care cannot be designated as a power of attorney. In Ontario, under the Mental Health Act, a physician must assess financial competence upon admission to a psychiatric facility. However, the Act does not cover certificates of financial incompetence for those who are not inpatients (Lieff and Fish, 1996). According to the Ontario Court of Appeal, the test for financial competence includes:

- the ability to understand the nature of the financial decision and the choices available;
- the ability to understand his or her relationship to the parties to and potential beneficiaries of the transactions; and
- the ability to appreciate the consequences of making the decision.

A person who is incapable of providing consent to medical treatment may be equally incapable to manage his or her financial affairs, but is not necessarily so. A power of attorney for personal care does not encompass financial matters and is entirely distinct from a power of attorney for finances. Further, the substitute decision-maker for health care does not automatically become the decision-maker for financial issues.

Ideally, a person, while competent, has considered that there may be times of inability to manage personal financial affairs because of vacation or illness and thus has assigned a financial power of attorney. As discussed earlier in this chapter, a power of attorney is the authority given by one person to another to act on his or her behalf. The authority can be comprehensive, or relate to certain specified acts or types of decisions (Fowler, 2004). If a power of attorney has not been signed while the person is competent, upon loss of capacity an application can be made to the court designating someone known to the patient or the public trustee to assume the financial responsibilities of the individual. Note that when a family member or friend seeks authority to manage the finances for a person, after the person is no longer capable of granting such authority on his or her own, the court process is lengthy and contains many steps: (1) a notice of application; (2) an **affidavit** of the applicant; (3) management plans that demonstrate the best interest of the incapable person; (4) medical affidavits (Schnurr, 2004). The public trustee may or may not be involved in this process, depending on the jurisdiction. In Saskatchewan, for instance, the public trustee is charged with investigating all applications with respect to property decision-making involving those who are mentally incompetent. The public trustee may inform all other relatives about the application. In addition, the property decision-maker must provide the public trustee with an annual accounting and inventory of the person's property (Government of Saskatchewan, 2002).

The public guardian and trustee in each jurisdiction is an independent and impartial public official and is an officer of the court. The public guardian and trustee of British Columbia, for instance, "operates under provincial law to protect the legal rights and financial interests of children, to provide assistance to adults who need support for financial and personal decision-making, and to administer the estates of deceased and missing persons where there is no one else able to do so" (www.trustee.bc.ca). Application for the public guardian and trustee to assume responsibility requires documentation and a procedure specified by each province, verifying the incapability of the individual to manage his or her own affairs. At times, less formal options are available; for example, Alberta offers informal trusteeship to incapable parties who only require assistance with the handling of monthly government cheques, through which trusteeship arrangements are made with the government departments issuing the cheques.

The Duty to Warn and Protect

The duty to warn and protect applies when a social worker has reason to believe that a client will cause serious harm to another person. This concept of a duty to warn others has a long tradition in the United States, where it was highlighted and clarified by the famous *Tarasoff* decision (*Tarasoff v. Regents of University of California*) in California in 1976. In that case a patient told his treating psychologist that he intended to kill his former girlfriend, Ms Tarasoff. The therapist, concluding that the patient was dangerous, contacted the campus police but did not warn the intended victim. Ms Tarasoff was subsequently killed and her family sued the therapist. Despite defence arguments that the duty to warn violated the accepted ethical obligation to maintain confidentiality, the courts ruled in the plaintiff's favour. The court concluded that the confidentiality obligation to a patient ends when public peril begins. While the *Tarasoff* decision, requiring a duty to warn and protect third parties, did not apply in Canadian jurisdictions, it was generally assumed that Canadian courts would offer a similar decision should the issue arise (CASW, 2005). Nevertheless, mental health practitioners continued to question their responsibilities because no provincial or federal statutes (except in Quebec) require or permit therapists to report clients who threaten to seriously harm a member of the public (Carlisle, 1996).

The Supreme Court of Canada clarified this issue in the 1999 case of *Smith v. Jones* (Chaimowitz et al., 2000). In the course of a forensic psychiatric examination of Mr Jones, Dr Smith became concerned that Mr Jones would carry out his fantasies to kidnap, rape, and kill prostitutes. Dr Smith notified defence counsel of his concerns, who requested that Dr Smith keep this confidential under solicitor–client privilege. Dr Smith began civil action to allow for disclosure. After a series of appeal processes through the BC courts, the Supreme Court of Canada ruled that danger of serious harm to the public overrules solicitor–client privilege, the highest privilege recognized by the courts. As such, the duty to protect now exists when the following three elements are in place: (1) in the event that risk to a clearly identified person or group of persons is determined; (2) when risk of harm includes bodily injury, death, or serious psychological harm; and (3) when there is an element of imminence, creating a sense of urgency (Chaimowitz and Glancy, 2002).

From a practice perspective, what must a social worker do when caught between the duty to warn and protect and the duty of confidentiality? Appelbaum (1985) recommends a three-part approach: (1) assessing danger; (2) selecting a course of action; and (3) implementing and monitoring. First, during the clinical interview, the social worker assesses the risk that this person may present. This involves a thorough assessment, good note-taking, and possible consultation with other professionals, particularly if the social worker is not experienced or skilled in this area. Second, once a determination has been made that the person is dangerous, the social worker needs to determine if he or she suffers from a mental disorder that may qualify for certification under mental health legislation. If the social worker believes the person suffers from a mental disorder and has agreed to assessment, the social worker must ensure transport of the person to a hospital or physician for assessment regarding voluntary or involuntary hospitalization. If the social worker believes that the person does not suffer from a mental disorder or refuses assessment and there is an identifiable victim and a reasonable belief that imminent harm may be suffered by such a victim, the social worker must warn the intended victim and law enforcement agencies. The third part of the approach requires monitoring the situation on an ongoing basis and ensuring that the intervention is effective. That is, the duty to protect does not end once someone has taken that person for assessment by a physician (Regehr and Kanani, 2010). As noted earlier in this chapter, however, there is no guarantee that the person will be admitted to hospital or will remain in hospital until the risk is eliminated. Therefore, ongoing monitoring is a duty.

Mental Health Records

Confidentiality is central to the provision of health and mental health services. It is embedded in the right to privacy that is articulated in the *Universal Declaration of Human Rights* (UN, 1948) and the *International Covenant of Civil and Political Rights*. Although the Canadian Association of Social Workers *Code of Ethics* requires that "social workers respect the importance of the trust and confidence placed in the professional relationship by clients and members of the public" (CASW, 2005: 7), the code does identify several exceptions to the rule of confidentiality. These include written authorization by the client, information required by a statute or order of a court of competent jurisdiction, or a threat of harm to self or others. (Issues related to the duty to protect are discussed in greater detail in Chapters 5 and 11.) Although these standards for practice appear clear, their actual application creates a number of dilemmas for social workers. Legislative enactments and court decisions have muddied the waters further regarding what information is confidential and what information the social work practitioner ought to reveal (Glancy et al., 1998; Regehr et al., 1997).

In addition to the ethical confidentiality obligations, social workers will be subject to legislation specific to confidentiality and privacy that govern the collection, maintenance, use, and disclosure of information. Canada has two federal privacy laws, the Privacy Act and the Personal Information Protection and Electronic Documents Act. The Privacy Act, which took effect in 1983, imposes obligations on federal government departments and agencies to respect privacy rights by limiting the collection, use, and disclosure of personal information. The Personal Information Protection and Electronic Documents Act sets out ground rules for how private-sector organizations may collect, use, or disclose personal information in the course of commercial activities.

The provinces and territories have also enacted legislation governing the collection, use, and disclosure of personal information. These Acts prescribe the circumstances under which practitioners may grant access to or disclose information to the individual from whom it was collected and/or other third parties. Further, social workers should be aware that they may also be subject to various provincial statutes governing confidentiality, access, use, and disclosure in their specific areas of practice, including legislation on provincial education, child and family services, hospitals, and mental health (Solomon and Visser, 2005).

For social workers working within organizations, specific policies regarding privacy of information should have been developed by the organization in compliance with the requirements of applicable legislation. Social workers not working in organizations, however, are required to develop their own privacy policies, practices, and procedures in accordance with the law. The Ontario College of Social Workers and Social Service Workers Privacy Toolkit (OCSWSSW, 2005) is recommended as an excellent resource for this purpose.

Client Access to Records

As stated above, privacy legislation allows client access to information by various stipulated means. This legislation reinforces an earlier judgement of the Supreme Court of Canada (McInerney v. MacDonald, 1992) that established the right of clients to have access to all mental health and medical records regarding their care. This includes not only records compiled in the treatment facility to which the request for access is directed, but also all records obtained from other facilities following the signed consent of the client. If a treating professional has reason to believe that access to the information contained in a clinical record may be harmful to the client or a third party (such as a family member who has provided information), she or he may, as defined by legislation, be able to deny the request for access or apply to the court to deny the request for access. For instance, under the Ontario Mental Health Act, if the record is compiled in a mental health facility, the attending physician may block access to all or part of the record if he or she states in writing that in his/her opinion that disclosure will be harmful. However, if the potentially dangerous information is contained in records that have been forwarded to another facility subsequent to a signed release of information form, the worker who authored the records may not be informed that the information is to be released and therefore may not have the opportunity to make application to have the information kept private.

While initially viewed with alarm by practitioners, client access to records is now seen by some as having benefits. For instance, clients are given the opportunity to correct or amend erroneous records. Further, when aware that clients will access records, social workers tend to ensure that records are better organized, shorter, more factual, and more goal-oriented (Gelman, 1992). It has also been suggested that involving clients in the production of case records can be an effective tool in the treatment process (Badding, 1989).

Access to Records in Criminal and Civil Cases

Access to the treatment records of victims has been the centre of considerable controversy (Regehr et al., 1997). In criminal court proceedings, arguments have focused on balancing the legal rights of the defendant, particularly in sexual assault trials, with the privacy rights of the victim. As a result of the vocal concerns of therapists and other victim advocacy groups, changes to the **Criminal Code** have placed restrictions on access to victims' treatment records (Statutes of Canada, 1997). Although subsequent court decisions challenged the legislation on the basis that it violated the Charter of Rights and Freedoms, these provisions were recently upheld by the Supreme Court of Canada (*R. v. Mills*, 1997). Nevertheless, if victim records are determined to be relevant to the case, they can become a part of the criminal trial.

In the case of civil litigation, individuals who initiate legal proceedings that put their treatment, medical condition, or health in issue are viewed as waiving the right to confidentiality and implicitly consenting to the disclosure of confidential information relevant to the action (*P. [L.M.] v. F. [D.]*, 1994). Thus, the defendant in a civil action generally has access to records of the complainant's care. This has significant implications in cases where victims choose to sue their abusers. In addition, access to records may also be granted in family law disputes. For example, during a custody dispute, a husband requested that the psychiatric records of his wife be disclosed to support his claim that she could not care for children (*Gibbs v. Gibbs*, 1985). The court concluded that the potential harm to the children was the greater risk and thus ordered disclosure of records despite her doctor's conclusion that it would likely be harmful to her. The demand for clinical records generally comes in the form of a **subpoena**. The development of law in this area arose in the context of high-profile sexual assault cases (*R. v. O'Connor*, 1995; *R. v. Mills*, 1997) and subsequently resulted in changes to the Criminal Code.

Today, professionals whose records are subject to subpoena have standing in criminal proceedings and a right to object to the order to produce confidential files. For example, in criminal cases involving sexual assault or similar charges, the accused may apply to the judge trying the case for the production of clinical records and set out the grounds on which the records are relevant to an issue at trial or to the competence of a witness to testify. Seven days' notice of the application must be served on the prosecutor, the complainant, or witness, and the record-holder. An in-camera hearing is held at which the record-keeper may appear and make submissions. Following this, the judge may order production of the record if he or she deems it necessary in the interest of justice.

In doing so, the judge is mandated to take into consideration a number of defined factors, including the salutary and deleterious effects on the accused's right to make full answer and defence, the right to privacy and personal dignity of the complainant or witness, society's interest in encouraging the reporting of sexual offences, society's interest in encouraging treatment for complainants of sexual offences, and the effect of the determination on the integrity of the trial process (Glancy et al., 1998). If the judge orders production of the record, he or she has the discretion to impose conditions in order to ensure, to the greatest extent possible, the privacy of the complainant or witness. These conditions can include that the record be edited as directed by the judge, that a copy of the record rather than the original be produced, that the record be viewed only at the offices of the court and that the contents not be disclosed, and that names and addresses regarding any person be severed from the record.

Despite the fact that subpoenas represent significant risk to the privacy of the client and inconvenience to the social worker who is receiving it, serious sanctions can be imposed by the courts if a subpoena is ignored. However, a subpoena is not a licence to breach client confidentiality (College of Physicians and Surgeons of Nova Scotia, 2006) and it does not grant the social worker permission to speak to a lawyer, police officer, or anyone else about the content of the records or any aspect of the client's treatment.

Possible Social Work Interventions in the Case Example

Social work interventions in the situation of Dimitri and Lara described at the beginning of the chapter fall into two broad categories, information and advocacy. Lara is approaching the social worker seeking assistance with hospitalization at a time when Dimitri is acutely ill. The social worker's role therefore is to provide information regarding: Dimitri's rights to determine his own treatment direction; and the circumstances and mechanisms under mental health legislation in which family members may be able to obtain assistance with involuntary admission or treatment (assuming Dimitri does not have an advanced directive or has not designated a substitute decision-maker). In general, the grounds for involuntary admission will be limited to the issue of safety as defined by the specific provincial legislation (Table 3.1). The social worker can assist Lara to link with the necessary resources, such as the justice of the peace or medical practitioners who may be able to assess Dimitri at home. Further, the social worker can discuss with Lara means of ensuring her safety should she become concerned that Dimitri's anger may result in violence.

The social worker may also have the opportunity to work with Dimitri when he is not acutely ill and when he is able to make competent decisions about his care. Dimitri can be assisted to consider which treatment options are consistent with his values and are, in his opinion, in his best interest. He can also be encouraged to write an advanced directive or designate a family member or friend who is respectful of his wishes and will make decisions regarding his care that are consistent with his values should he be incapable of providing consent. Should Dimitri be admitted to hospital on an involuntary basis or be ordered to receive treatment, the social worker should inform him of his rights and ensure that he has access to advocacy services.

Summary

Mental health legislation in Canada impacts social work practice in mental health in two key areas. First, mental health legislation sets clear guidelines regarding issues of consent to treatment and in which circumstances individuals can be hospitalized and treated against their will. Social workers must be knowledgeable about these issues so they can advise individuals with mental health problems and their families about their rights and options. Second, mental health legislation governs access to treatment records. Social workers must be aware of the limits of confidentiality of the records that they produce and the means of protecting the confidentiality of clients with whom we work.

Discussion Questions

1. How is advising family members of means to obtain involuntary admission and treatment for an ill relative consistent with or contrary to social work values?
2. What is a social worker's role with regard to issues of consent to treatment?
3. What are the ethical issues involved in community treatment orders?
4. How can social workers balance obligations regarding confidentiality with mandated requirements regarding access to records?

Suggested Readings and Websites

Canadian Association of Social Workers. 2007. *Informed Consent and Confidentiality: CASW Guidelines*. Ottawa: Canadian Association of Social Workers. Practice guidelines that provide useful and concrete advice to social work practitioners.

Evans, K. 2012. "Consent: A Guide for Canadian Physicians," Canadian Medical Protection Association. At: www.cmpa-acpm.ca/cmpapd04/docs/resource_files/ml_guides/consent_guide/com_cg_informedconsent-e.cfm. Although directed specifically towards physicians, this website provides useful information on issues related to consent and confidentiality, and is a valuable source for social workers.

Ontario College of Social Workers and Social Service Workers. 2005. *Privacy Toolkit for Social Workers and Social Service Workers: Guide to the Personal Health Information Protection Act, 2004 (PHIPA)*. Toronto: OCSWSSW. At: www.ocswssw.org/sections/pdf/PHIPA_Toolkit_Final_Web.pdf. Although privacy legislation is provincial, the decision trees and strategies for addressing privacy issues provided in this guide can easily be applied to provinces other than Ontario.

4 Social Work Assessment in Mental Health

Learning Objectives

- To discuss the nature and importance of assessment in mental health social work practice.
- To consider assessment within a cultural context.
- To present a framework for social work assessment and formulation.
- To present a framework for conducting mental status examinations.
- To examine issues related to classification and diagnosis of mental health problems.

Regardless of context, assessment is key to social work practice and is the foundation upon which effective and evidence-based intervention can be built. Intervention without assessment runs the risk of being misguided, ineffective, and **iatrogenic**. A social worker seeks to understand the multiple factors influencing the situation at hand, the stakeholders involved, the history leading to the current state of affairs, and the possible solutions that might be available (see Box 4.1). In the organizational context, this is often referred to as a **SWOT analysis,** which refers to consideration of strengths, weaknesses within the organizations, and the opportunities and threats in the environment in which the organization exists. In clinical contexts, the assessment considers the intersection between the person who is identified as needing assistance in some form and the individual's environment. Although similarities exist in the assessment process within the various domains in which social workers practice, such as child welfare, health care, and settlement services to immigrants and refugees, there are also differences. In mental health social work practice social workers are required to be skilled in standard psychosocial assessments, which will be familiar across all domains of practice. In addition, however, social workers in mental health must be capable of performing mental status examinations to assess the nature and severity of a mental health problem from which a person may be suffering. Social workers must also be familiar with the classification of mental health problems as specified by the

Box 4.1 Social Work Defined

"The social work profession promotes social change, problem solving in human relationships and the empowerment and liberation of people to enhance well-being. Utilising theories of human behaviour and social systems, social work intervenes at the points where people interact with their environments. . . . Social work bases its methodology on a systematic body of evidence-based knowledge derived from research and practice evaluation, including local and indigenous knowledge specific to its context. It recognises the complexity of interactions between human beings and their environment, and the capacity of people both to be affected by and to alter the multiple influences upon them including bio-psychosocial factors."

Source: International Federation of Social Work (2013).

Diagnostic and Statistical Manual of Mental Disorders to communicate effectively with other members of the interdisciplinary team. This chapter outlines the standard social work assessment, the mental status examination, and the classification of mental disorders standardized by the DSM.

A social work assessment in mental health brings a unique perspective to the multidisciplinary team. The social worker considers challenges, strengths, supports, and barriers at multiple levels that affect the experiences of a person suffering from a mental health problem and the choices available to him or her (see Figure 4.1). At the *individual level*, the person comes with biological, psychological, and interpersonal strengths and challenges that have been influenced by the individual's unique genetic endowments and environmental experiences. At the *familial level*, characteristics of individual family members, the structure of the family, and relationships between family members have a tremendous impact on challenges experienced by people suffering from mental health problems and on the resources available to them for coping with crisis and difficulty. The *community context* includes the availability of resources in terms of formal services and informal supports. It also includes the cultural context in which this person resides, such as the cohesion of the community and attitudes towards mental health concerns. Further, it is important to consider whether this person and/or the family members experience exclusion on the basis of any factors such as race, religion, sexual orientation, or social class. Finally, at the *societal level*, policies and practices are in place that limit or enhance opportunities. What is the immigration status of this person and does it influence access to services and entitlements? Are there affordable housing options for this person and his/her family? How do legislative frameworks influence the ability to obtain or refuse treatment?

Blackstock (2009) highlights how the multiple influences model (often referred to as the ecological model), while attempting to integrate a broader

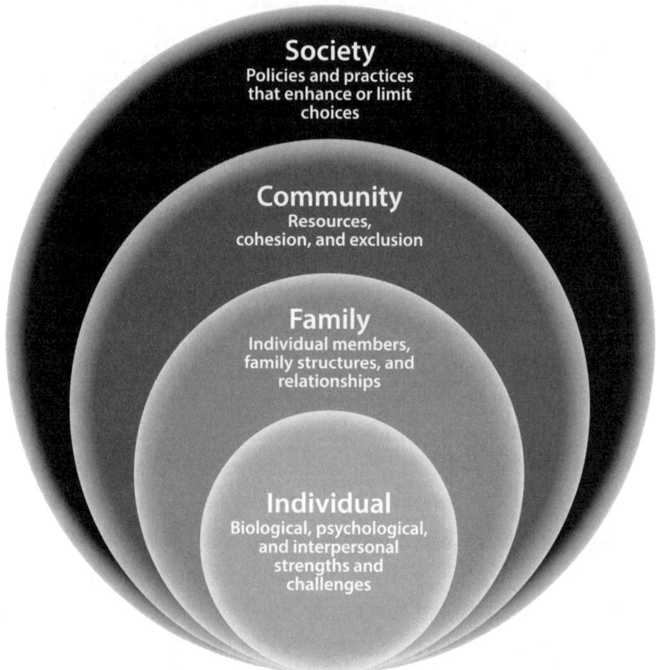

Figure 4.1 Multiple Levels of Influence in Social Work Assessments

perspective into the assessment process, continues to focus on the individual. This focus can be a mismatch with the world view of the client. When working with Aboriginal clients, for instance, the view focuses on the interconnection of experience and knowledge over the span of generations. Blackstock notes that within social work, ecological theory is generally believed to apply well to work with Aboriginal peoples because of the perspective that the individual is nestled within his or her community and societal context, as shown in Figure 4.1. Yet, such an approach continues to ignore that within Aboriginal **epistemology**, or knowledge, "the child, family, community, and world are wholly affected by four interconnected dimensions of knowledge—emotional, spiritual, cognitive, and physical—informed by ancestral knowledge, which is to be passed to future generations in perpetuity." These four interconnected themes are demonstrated in Figure 4.2. From this perspective, the multiple levels of influence model in Figure 4.1 is transformed from a series of concentric circles demonstrating the manner in which the individual is embedded within his/her culture to a series of interconnected circles. The social work assessment must therefore consider the world view of the client and his or her cultural group and ensure that the assessment takes into account this unique perspective.

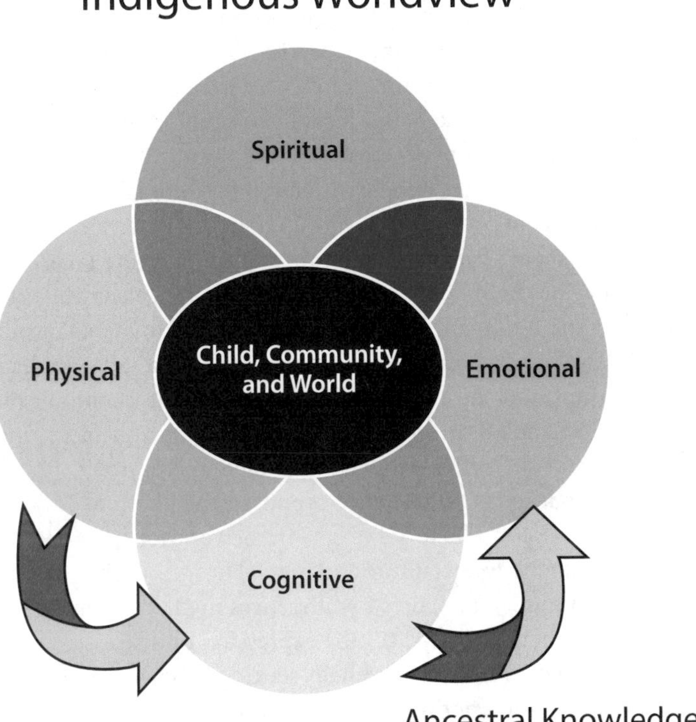

Figure 4.2 Applying an Aboriginal Framework to Social Work

Sources: Blackstock (2009a, 2000b).

Assessment within a Cultural Context

The mental health system and social work practice within it are without question heavily influenced by broader social, political, and economic structures in society (Bhugra and Bhui, 2001). Social work assessments in mental health must therefore be conducted in a manner that recognizes the social and cultural context in which the assessment occurs. The availability of services and access to mainstream health systems are dependent on political and economic structures that subtly or not so subtly exclude members of groups defined by ability, ethnicity, race, gender, social class, and sexual orientation. For instance, while new immigrants to Canada have better overall health and fewer chronic conditions than their Canadian-born counterparts, once exposed to the social, physical, and economic stressors of the new society, their health status becomes equal to that of other Canadians (Setia et al., 2011). One explanation for the change in health status of immigrant groups is unequal access to health care due to a wide variety of factors, including personal and cultural beliefs, linguistic barriers, and systemic barriers (Department of Health, 2003; Lai, 2004; Hwang et al., 2008). Immigrants who have been in the country for less than five years are less likely to access health care (Bierman et al., 2012), although this equalizes by the time people have been in Canada for 10 years (Setia et al., 2011). In addition, people with lower levels of income, lower proficiency in English, and of certain ethnic groups (such as Aboriginal Canadians) are more likely to report barriers to finding appropriate care (Bierman et al., 2012). After entering the mental health system, difference continues to influence assessment and treatment. The assessment process in mental health relies heavily on observation and assessment of behaviours and judgements regarding the perceptions and the means of expression of the client, all of which result in a final formulation of the challenges this person faces, including whether or not he or she suffers from a major mental illness.

Hwang and colleagues (2008) have proposed the Cultural Influences on Mental Health (CIMH) model to serve as a framework for understanding the complex intersection between culture and mental health. Within this model, it is proposed that culture contributes to differences in (1) the prevalence, etiology, and course of mental illness; (2) the expression of distress; (3) diagnosis and assessment; (4) coping styles and help-seeking behaviour; and (5) appropriate treatment and intervention. Various aspects of their model are outlined below.

Cultural Influences in the Prevalence, Etiology, and Course of Mental Illness

Culture frequently influences life experiences, including such things as exposure to trauma and exposure to stress. For instance, refugees often enter Canada having experienced a variety of traumatic events, including war, genocide, violence, famine, and political persecution. Groups exposed to such violence have increased rates of post-traumatic stress and depression, as evidenced by studies conducted with people from Southeast Asia, Africa, Bosnia, and Kurdistan (Hwang et al., 2008). In addition to the traumatic circumstances that contributed to a decision to leave the home country, the journey to Canada may be life-threatening. Primarily during the 1980s, people leaving Vietnam or other parts of Southeast Asia often travelled to North America by boat in perilous conditions, which included unseaworthy vessels, insufficient stocks of food and water, violent storms, and pirates (Gong-Guy et al., 1991). Refugees may have spent time in camps throughout the world that were similarly characterized by overcrowding, scarce resources, inadequate housing and sanitation, rape, and violence. Undoubtedly, all these experiences contribute to increased risk of mental health issues and to the development of views of people in authority (such as mental health professionals) that will affect their willingness to access services. Regardless of immigration status, those entering a new country frequently experience acculturation stresses, including adaptation to a new environment, loss of social supports, and barriers to employment, education, services, and housing.

Whether they are new to the country or their ancestors lived on this continent long before the arrival of Europeans, as in the case of Aboriginal Canadians, racialized individuals and those with other forms of difference experience discrimination at both interpersonal and systemic levels. Such experiences influence the development of mental health and other problems. A history of state treatment of Aboriginal peoples provided by the Royal Commission on Aboriginal Peoples (1996a) provides an arresting account of the process of colonization, including the development of the residential school system as early as 1874, all of which has contributed to increased risk for Aboriginal peoples on many adverse social indicators. In 2006, the reported median income for Aboriginal Canadians was $18,962, fully 30 per cent lower than the national median of $27,097 (Wilson and MacDonald, 2010). Unemployment rates of Aboriginal peoples have long been considerably higher than those of the non-Aboriginal population, and this disparity increased following the economic downturn of 2008–10 (Usalcas, 2011). The death rate for Aboriginal persons between 25 and 44 years of age is five times higher than the general rate and the life expectancy for both Aboriginal men and women is 6.7 years lower than for non-Aboriginals (Health Canada, 2011). Aboriginal women experience violence at disturbingly high rates (Goel, 2000; Bohn, 2003), the overall mortality rate resulting from violence being three times higher for Aboriginal women than for non-Aboriginal women (NWAC, 2004). Aboriginal people comprised 4.3 per cent of the nation's population according to the 2011 census, yet they account for approximately 21 per cent of Canada's federal offender population (Office of the Correctional Investigator, 2012). This is more prevalent in some provinces; for instance, in Manitoba Aboriginal people constitute approximately 12 per cent of the population, yet a decade ago they accounted for over one-half of the 1,600 people incarcerated on any given day of the year in correctional institutions (Aboriginal Justice Implementation Commission, 2004). Clearly, these social factors intersect with the development of mental health concerns and must be taken into account in our assessment of risk and needs.

Cultural Differences in the Expression of Distress

Expressions of distress vary widely across cultures. Somatization, or the degree to which a person describes distress in physical terms, is one type of expression of distress that is highly influenced by cultural norms. Research suggests, for instance, that people from Asian cultures are more likely to describe symptoms of distress as physical, such as gastric distress, headaches, or body pain, whereas people from Western cultures are more likely to state that they are sad, depressed, or experiencing some other emotional disturbance (Hwang et al., 2008). Early studies reported by Hwang and colleagues found that 88 per cent of Chinese psychiatric patients versus 20 per cent of American-born psychiatric patients reported no typical psychiatric complaints, rather focusing solely on physical concerns, and that nearly 70 per cent of Taiwanese patients had predominantly physical complaints. Ryder and colleagues (2008) confirm that people presenting with distress in China are more likely to report considerably higher rates of somatic symptoms than patients in Canada. However, this study suggests that this is due to an overemphasis in Western cultures on personal experiences and emotional distress rather than an Asian overemphasis on somatic distress. These authors concluded that Western **psychologization** may be more of a cultural phenomenon than Asian **somatization**.

Cultural Influences on Diagnosis and Assessment

Canadian philosopher Ian Hacking (1998) suggests that an interactional effect between expert knowledge, social structures, and human behaviour results in certain types of mental diagnoses. He provides an historical analysis of diagnoses that emerge in a particular context, become prevalent, and then die out. Using the example of "the mad traveller," a fugue state that occurred among men of a certain social class beginning in France in the late 1800s, he examines the factors that resulted in this briefly popular diagnosis.

In present-day society, there are clear differences in rates of diagnosis of certain illnesses between various groups. For instance, research consistently finds that individuals of African and Afro-Caribbean backgrounds, particularly males, are more likely to be diagnosed with schizophrenia in Western countries than are individuals of other races (Fearon et al., 2006; Selten et al., 2007; Gara et al., 2012). Suggested explanations for this include: bias of mental health professionals; the effects of disadvantage and adversity related to systemic racism (Luhrmann, 2007); and increased risk caused by migration and social policies that make it difficult for families to immigrate together (Morgan et al., 2007). The migration theory is supported by research with other groups. For instance, high rates of psychotic illness and schizophrenia diagnosis in immigrant groups in the United States who originated in Western Europe have been associated with migration and neighbourhood density (Veling et al., 2008). Disparities in diagnosis between groups, based on race, also occur in other diagnostic categories. Some studies point to higher rates of diagnoses of depression among people of Chinese origin in North America, while others suggest lower rates (Hwang et al., 2008).

Differential diagnosis rates begin in childhood. Aboriginal children, for instance, have been found to demonstrate higher rates of attention deficit hyperactivity disorder on standardized testing instruments (Baydala et al., 2006). In a study of 406 children presenting with mental health problems, African-American children were more likely to receive a diagnosis of conduct disorder than white children (15.7 per cent versus 6.7 per cent), but were 5.1 times less likely to receive a diagnosis of autism than white children (Mandell et al., 2007). Other authors have suggested that the incidence of autism in African-American children is the same as in other ethno-racial groups, but later diagnosis results in the need for more intensive and longer intervention (Gourdine et al., 2011). Further, later diagnosis may lead to higher incidence of conduct problems. In summary, there is an awareness that diagnosis and culture are linked, but research on incidence rates and causes of differential rates of diagnosis is far from conclusive. In view of these issues, the latest edition of the DSM (APA, 2013) provides an outline for a cultural formulation and an approach to assessment using a Cultural Formulation Interview.

Cultural Influences on Help-Seeking

Culture is a central contributor to public **stigma** surrounding mental illness (the negative responses a person experiences in interactions with others in the community) and to self-stigma (internalized negative and self-defeating thoughts and emotions regarding mental illness) (Abdullah and Brown, 2011). Public stigma and internalized beliefs in turn affect help seeking behaviour. Individuals who believe their distress is physically based will more likely seek assistance from medical practitioners than from a professional who focuses on psychological or interpersonal factors. Further, stigma related to mental illness may cause many people to avoid mental health services. For example, Abdullah and Brown suggest that Latino individuals in the US report that stigma is a reason for not taking antidepressant medication. They cite research evidence that taking medication is contrary to cultural expectations of resilience, machismo (the strength of men), and marianismo (the nurturing self-sacrifice of women). Gong-Guy et al. (1991) report that refugees from Southeast Asia associate mental health treatment only with severe pathology requiring permanent institutionalization. Thus, they indicate that in these groups all interventions are highly stigmatized and treatments are to be shunned. Other beliefs include that mental illness in the family affects marriageability of other family members due to inheritability of illnesses or a belief that illness is related to past family transgressions. Cultural beliefs may therefore dissuade the use of mental health services and move people to informal supports, spiritual leaders, or indigenous healers (Hwang et al., 2008).

Assessment and Gender

Key to assessment and treatment in social work is the knowledge that mental health and mental illness, at least to some degree, are experienced differently by men and women. Johnson and Stewart (2010: 17) note: "Gender influences all aspects of psychopathology including the stressors and exposures that influence the onset of the disease, how symptoms are expressed, whether clients/patients seek care, and how they are treated by the mental health system." One obvious way in which gender influences mental health is biological, including biological stressors caused by reproduction and hormonal variations. Gender-based stressors also include such factors as violence exposure, financial resources or lack thereof, and opportunities. The Canadian Institutes of Health Research (CIHR) Institute for Gender Health describes the intersection of violence, gender, and health. It reports that injury and violence account for 1.45 per cent of the burden of disease in the developed world and 15.2 per cent in the developing world. Approximately 20 per cent of the women in the world report a history of physical or sexual abuse (CIHR, 2013). According to the 2004 Canadian General Social Survey, 7 per cent of women and 6 per cent of men reported experiencing violence at the hands of a current or previous partner in the past five years (Canadian Centre for Justice Statistics, 2005). Further, women in Canada have historically had less access to higher education and occupational opportunities and concomitant lower levels of income. Recently, however, young men in Canada are significantly less likely to attend university than young women. Across Canada, 58 per cent of students enrolled in university programs were women in 2008–9. In some programs the gender gap is much more pronounced. For instance, in 2002 the percentage of women in enrolled in the University of Montreal medical school hit 80 per cent (Drolet, 2007). The long-term impacts of this and other social changes on mental health are yet to be seen.

Diagnosis varies considerably with gender. Schizophrenia, for instance, is more likely to be diagnosed in men than women. The POWER project identifies that women in developed countries are twice as likely to suffer from depression as men. Further, women are more likely to express depression through symptoms of anxiety and disturbances in appetite and sleep. Men are more likely to engage in alcohol and substance abuse, which are often associated with depression (Bierman et al., 2012). While women have higher rates of suicide attempts, men are more likely to die from suicide. Clearly, we need to try to understand the nature of these gender differences and ensure that both advocacy initiatives and intervention strategies address these concerns.

Social Work Assessment

According to Gold (2002), assessment is an essential part of social work practice at all levels of intervention, including individuals, families groups, organizations, and communities. In each case the assessment involves two components, data collection and data analysis. In a social work assessment, data are generally collected from a range of sources. These include information the individual presents and information from family or significant people in the person's life, as well as from other professionals involved with the person, records available from health-care or social service organizations, and social policies and organizational practices that may create or hinder choices available to the person being assessed.

In mental health social work assessments, the worker begins with a standard model of social work assessment that considers key aspects of the person's current situation and history. The format of the assessment interview varies in its structure depending on the nature of the assessment situation. Assessment interviews conducted in an emergency situation will understandably be brief and focus quickly on key points. Assessments conducted with individuals with whom the social worker will have multiple contacts occur at a slower pace and are more comprehensive. Any assessment, regardless of the nature, is dependent on the worker establishing some type of working alliance with the client so that the client trusts that the information he or she is about to provide is going to be used in his or her best interests and will be kept in confidence. Thus, an assessment interview should begin with the worker introducing himself or herself, identifying his or her role in the organization, and identifying the purpose of this meeting. It is also necessary to identify the limits of confidentiality of information obtained in the interview. For instance, a social worker in a hospital will be sharing the information with other members of the interprofessional team, and this should be made explicit. A social worker in private practice is bound to confidentiality unless the client consents to release of information or unless information is revealed that suggests that the client is at risk of harm to him/herself or others, or must be disclosed in certain circumstances.

The written format of a social work assessment follows an outline similar to that in Box 4.2. The manner and order in which this information is collected, however, will vary somewhat because clients will generally tell their stories in the way that makes the most sense to them. The social worker asks open-ended questions, directing the interview to areas that have not yet been covered. Overly rigid adherence to an interview guideline will often result in missing important information. The assessment usually begins with the social worker asking why the client is here or, if he or she is not here voluntarily, why others might have thought assessment and/or treatment is needed. The corresponding written format begins with a description of the presenting problem from the perspective of the referral source, the perspective of the client, and the perspective of the client's family if they were involved in the assessment process or have provided information in advance. As indicated in Box 4.2, other information collected includes a description of the client's personal history, psychiatric history, family members and others important in the client's life, current life situation, treatment history, and other professionals or agencies that may currently be involved with the client.

Once the social worker has asked all the questions that seem pertinent, it is important to end the interview by asking the client whether there is any question or area that has been missed. The authors learned from experience how critical this question is. At the conclusion of a two-and-a-half-hour interview with the family of a young offender who required a mental health assessment, the mother and father were asked whether there was anything that had been missed. The mother responded that it was probably important to note

Box 4.2 The Social Work Assessment

Identifying data
Presenting problem
- Information obtained from referral sources and other professionals
- A summary of the problem as viewed by the client and family

Personal history
- Developmental history: any critical health events in gestation or early years; pace of development and educational attainment
- Relationship history
- Educational and employment history

Mental health history
- Course of the present problem: What symptoms or problems have been experienced? When did they emerge? How long have they been a problem? Are they constant or fluctuating?
- Previous treatment: other therapy, hospitalizations, medications. Have any diagnoses been shared with the client or family member?

Family constellation
- Brief description of members of the nuclear family: current relationship with the client; current social situation in terms of relationship status, occupation, etc.; any history of mental health, substance abuse, or legal problems
- All other significant family members (biological or family of choice) involved in the client's life

that she and her husband were not really the young man's parents. He was actually the child of their daughter but because she was so young at the time of the birth, they took the baby as their own and referred to his birth mother as his sister. The client had never been told this information. The interview then took another half-hour while additional missed information regarding this story was obtained.

At the conclusion of an assessment interview, the social worker should summarize the information collected to ensure this is how the client understands the situation. Where possible, an agreement can be made with the client about next steps. Where an agreement is not possible, for instance, when the social worker believes the client needs treatment but the client does not agree, or when a safety issue exists, the social worker should inform the client about what is to happen next. One might say, "I would like you to wait while I consult with (my colleagues, the Children's Aid Society, the psychiatrist) to determine how best to help you."

Most of the components of a written social work assessment can be understood in terms of stating the "facts" of the case as presented by various sources.

Cultural/spiritual/social context

- Cultural identity: degree of identification with cultural group; cultural influences on problem identification/formation
- Religious affiliations
- Spiritual beliefs that influence client's view of the issues and solutions
- Social inclusion/exclusion

Current situation

- Present concerns about health/mental health; current treatment including medications
- Living situation, income, employment, legal status, immigration status
- Current relationships

Mental status

- To be completed if there are any indicators of mental status issues during the interview

Suicide risk

- To be completed if there are any indicators of suicidal thought or self-harm during the interview

Formulation

- Predisposing factors: why this person? Vulnerabilities/history/stressors
- Precipitating factors: why now? Major stresses/critical events
- Perpetuating factors: what maintains the problem? Social-environmental factors/ health/substance use/personality
- Protective factors: what are the strengths? Supports/successes/abilities
- Plan: where do we go from here? Client wishes/intervention/referral/advocacy

These facts should be presented without prejudice or opinion. Thus, in describing the family, the social worker may indicate that the client states that she has a dysfunctional relationship with her mother. However, the social worker should not conclude in this section that the client *does* have a dysfunctional relationship. Rather, the social worker could record that the mother seems to have negative views about her daughter and record examples of comments made that would reflect this statement. Statements should include comments like "according to X . . ."and "Y believes that . . . ."

The formulation is the place where the social worker synthesizes the data and draws conclusions about the case based on his or her expert opinion (see Box 4.2). In the formulation, the social worker considers the factors that *predispose* the client to experiencing the current problems, including the individual's vulnerabilities and history, and the developmental stressors he/she has encountered. This may include, for example, a family history of mental illness, deprivation or abuse in childhood, or a history of convulsions in childhood. Next, the social worker identifies what *precipitated* the current crisis and caused the client to come for treatment at this time. The precipitating factors may be relational, environmental, maturational, physical, or psychological. For instance, a client with a history of sexual trauma may arrive at a social worker's office years after the event but her distress might have been triggered by entering into a relationship, having a daughter reach puberty, or being confronted with an assault on someone else. Often the problem with which a client presents is *perpetuated* by other factors such as substance abuse, being in a violent relationship, poverty, or being barred from critical life goals by public policies such as in the case of an internationally educated professional who is depressed because he or she is barred from obtaining work commensurate with his or her education and experience. *Protective* factors refer to the strengths and supports that a person has. A social worker could refer to the tremendous resilience this person has shown in the face of adversity and the manner in which she or he has creatively dealt with roadblocks. In addition, spiritual beliefs and the faith community may be strong protective factors. Finally, the *plan* emanates from the formulation and represents a combination of the social worker's recommendations and the client's views about what is acceptable and feasible.

Weerasekera (1993) provides an excellent overview of the multi-perspective model of formulation (see Table 4.1). Within this model, both individual factors and systemic factors that contribute to the problem are considered. At the individual level, biological factors can include genetic predispositions, current physical health, or neurological issues. Cognitive factors include both cognitive abilities and perceptions and beliefs that the individual holds about the situation. Dynamic factors include psychological distress; present-day relational issues and issues caused by previous life experiences

Table 4.1 The Multi-Perspective Formulation

	Individual Factors				Systemic Factors			
	Biological	Cognitive	Dynamic	Spiritual	Familial	Cultural/ community	Opportunities (education, employment)	Social policy
Predisposing								
Precipitating								
Perpetuating								
Protective								
Plan								

Source: Adapted from Weekasekera (1993).

such as trauma; prior relationships, particularly with family, and ability to maintain current relationships. The spiritual domain includes the spiritual beliefs the individual holds that offer comfort or cause distress. Systemic-level factors consider the opportunities and challenges provided by people and systems that the client encounters. While the cultural and community context can address challenges and supports at the community level, the opportunity structure considers such factors as access to education, employment, affordable housing, and transportation. Finally, the policy domain, among other issues, considers laws that address safety for the client if she or he is a victim of violence, youth criminal justice policies and alternative justice models for troubled young people, or immigration.

Mental Status Examinations

The basic social work assessment is conducted in almost all areas of social work practice. In mental health social work practice, however, an additional task is determining whether a person suffers from symptoms of a mental health problem or major mental illness and the degree to which these symptoms impinge on the individual's life. Examinations of mental state are therefore conducted as a means for determining the presence or absence of signs and symptoms of mental health distress. A standard mental status examination consists of the following elements: appearance, attitude, and behaviour; mood and affect; speech and thought form; speech and thought content; perception; cognition; and insight and judgement (see Box 4.3) (Kendell and Zealley, 1983; Goldberg and Murray, 2006).

Appearance, Attitude, and Behaviour

The first window into the mental state of a client is the manner in which he or she looks and behaves. Obviously, dress and appearance in our society are

Box 4.3 Aspects of a Mental Status Examination

- Appearance, attitude, and behaviour
- Mood and affect
- Speech and thought form
- Speech and thought content
- Perception
- Cognition
- Insight and judgement

highly individual and are influenced by cultural factors (such as garments or accessories worn for religious reasons), by the group or subculture with which one identifies (for instance, goths), and by personal taste. Thus, consideration of appearance must not be directed by a social worker's expectation that an individual's appearance should reflect his or her own style. Aspects to note regarding appearance include whether the person is unkempt, has paid little attention to hygiene, is dressed in a manner inappropriate to the season (such as wearing several layers of heavy clothing in summer), is dressed in an idiosyncratic manner (such as wearing a negligee or evening gown during the day), or has an unusual style of makeup (such as having lipstick smeared on his or her face). Also included in appearance are the person's posture (huddled in a corner, bowed by **melancholia**, or lying across the floor) and facial expressions. A respected geriatric mental health worker used to point out that the mental status examination begins as the worker turns into the street on which the client lives. Is the yard unkempt and strewn with garbage? Is the house in a state of disrepair? Is there aluminum foil obscuring the windows? A lot can be learned by careful observation.

Behaviour and attitude in an emergency room or office setting can often be observed from afar before the interview begins. Is the person able to sit in the waiting room and read a magazine or is he or she pacing back and forth in an agitated manner? How does the person behave towards other people in the surrounding area? Does the person appear frightened? Does the person speak to others in an engaging manner, or does he or she appear hostile or suspicious of others? Are interactions with others appropriate to the current situation? Are there any unusual mannerisms or repetitive gestures? Are any actions speeded up or slowed down? Attitude continues to be assessed as the assessment progresses. How does the person engage with the social worker? Can he or she make eye contact? How does the person understand his or her illness and/or problem?

Mood and Affect

Mood refers to the pervasive emotional state that a person experiences; *affect* refers to the emotions presently being expressed. It has been suggested that weather is to climate zone as affect is to mood. Mood is assessed by asking questions about the depth, duration, and intensity of a particular state and the degree to which this state fluctuates. Terms to describe mood can include: depressed, irritable, stable, dysphoric, expansive, or euphoric. Affect can be **labile** (fluctuating dramatically throughout the duration of the interview). It can be described as constricted, blunted, or flattened when there is a limited range of emotion or no evidence of expressed emotion. Affect can either be appropriate or congruent with the situation or incongruent, for instance, when a person begins to laugh when telling the story of someone who has died.

Speech and Thought Form

In mental health we differentiate the *form* of the speech from the *content*. Speech form and content are carefully examined because they provide a window into the form and content of a person's thoughts. Examination of speech form considers the quantity, rate, and production of speech (Kaplan and Sadock, 1996). Descriptions of speech can include whether it is pressured or speeded up; whether it is slowed down or contains unexpected pauses; whether the speech is clear or slurred; loud or whispered; flows smoothly or is staccato. Does the person use strange words or syntax, rhymes, or puns? Is speech spontaneous, does the person only provide brief answers to direct questions, or does the person not respond at all?

Obviously, in describing speech and thought form, the ability of the person to speak the language of the interviewer must be taken into consideration. Further, cultural and situational factors must be accounted for. If this person has been brought to hospital against his or her will, is not familiar with the surroundings, and does not have English as a first language, that individual's speech will be considerably different from that of an English-speaking person who attended the interview voluntarily with the purpose of seeking assistance. Further, individuals who are very familiar with the mental health system and have had multiple periods of treatment and hospitalization will frequently know the interview format as well as or better than the interviewer and their speech and answers will be consequently affected.

Speech form provides a window into certain aspects of thought form. The following are some examples of disturbances in thought form (Kaplan and Sadock, 1996):

- *Neologism:* new word created by the person, e.g., "modication."
- *Word salad:* incoherent list of words.
- *Circumstantial thinking:* person reaches the final point after including many irrelevant details.
- *Tangential thinking:* person never reaches final point and moves from one topic to another.

- *Perseveration:* person is unable to move away from a particular point or phrase.
- *Echolalia:* person repeats the words of others in a repetitive persistent manner.
- *Loosening of associations:* ideas shift from one to another with no obvious link.
- *Derailment:* sudden deviation from the original point mid-sentence.
- *Flight of ideas:* constant shifting from one idea to another, although there is some vague association between the ideas.
- *Blocking:* abrupt interruption in speech.
- *Clang associations:* rhyming or putting words together that sound similar without an apparent point.

Speech and Thought Content

Although thought content is the specific target of the mental status examination, thought content is only accessed through speech. Thought content can include worries or anxieties from which the person is suffering, fears, ruminations, or suicidal ideas. It can also include delusions, preoccupations, obsessions, or phobias. Delusions are fixed false beliefs that are not consistent with the person's cultural or religious background. Such delusions may include content that is persecutory, grandiose, somatic, or erotic. Specific types of delusions are described in more detail in Chapter 7 in the discussion of schizophrenia and other psychotic illnesses; however, a list of examples follows (Kaplan and Sadock, 1996):

- *Somatic delusions:* false beliefs involving the functioning of the body.
- *Persecutory delusions:* false beliefs that one is being harassed, cheated, or persecuted.
- *Delusions of grandeur:* exaggerated ideas of one's importance.
- *Ideas of reference:* beliefs that events refer to oneself, for instance, that an advertisement on the radio is speaking directly to or referring specifically to the person.
- *Thought withdrawal:* someone or something is stealing the person's thoughts.
- *Thought insertion:* someone is putting thoughts in the person's head.
- *Erotomania:* delusional belief that someone is in love with the person.

Perception

Disturbances of perception include **hallucinations**, **depersonalization**, and **dissociation**. Questions that will allow a person to speak about such perceptual disturbances include: Do you ever hear voices when there is no one around? Do you ever see things that other people do not see? Do you ever have strange sensations in your body? Do you ever feel that you are not really here? Common perceptual disturbances include (Kaplan and Sadock, 1996):

- *Auditory hallucinations:* hearing voices or other sounds not heard by others (this is the most common delusion in psychotic disorders).
- *Visual hallucinations:* seeing things.
- *Olfactory hallucinations:* smelling things (more common in neurological disorders).
- *Tactile hallucinations:* often involving bugs crawling up the skin.
- *Somatic hallucinations:* a false belief that something is happening to the body, such as something is growing in the stomach.
- *Hysterical anesthesia:* loss of feeling in some part of the body with no medical cause.
- *Depersonalization:* sense that the self is unreal, unfamiliar.
- *Derealization:* sense that the environment is strange or unreal.

Cognition

Cognition in a mental state refers to the person's orientation, attention, concentration, and memory (Goldberg and Murray, 2006). Orientation is to the person's ability to identify person, place, and time. It is assessed simply by asking if the person knows where he or she is and how he or she got here, whether the person knows the current date or day of the week, and if he or she knows who the interviewer is. Attention and concentration refer to the degree to which the person is able to concentrate on the interview. Simple tests for attention and concentration can involve asking a person to say the months of the year in reverse order or to subtract serial 7s from 100 (93, 86, 79, 72 . . .). Chapter 10, on neurocognitive disorders, presents examples of simple tests for cognition.

Long-term memory is best assessed by comparing the person's account of his/her life with what others have said. Individuals with certain cognitive difficulties will attempt to cover gaps in their memory by making up stories or facts. This is referred to as **confabulation**. It occurs because the person knows that she or he should be able to come up with the requested information, but, unable to do so, the individual proceeds to fill in missing data as a way of saving face.

Insight and Judgement

Insight is defined by the *Oxford World Dictionary* in general terms as "an accurate and deep understanding" or in psychiatry as the "awareness by a mentally ill person that their mental experiences are not based in external reality." The *Canadian Oxford Dictionary* defines insight as "the capacity to understand hidden truths." In practical terms in the context of mental health, insight is the degree to which the person's understanding of events fits with that of others. For instance, a person can be asked "Why do you think the police arrested you and brought you to hospital?" It is important that **pejorative** opinions do not form the basis of this part of the examination. After all, the person may understand that others believe he or she suffers from schizophrenia and simply not agree with the diagnosis. This may not reflect poor insight but rather could be a carefully considered determination, or it may simply be that the person holds out hope for a different outcome. Judgement refers to the degree to which the person is able to consider the consequences of his or her actions or assess a particular situation.

The *Diagnostic and Statistical Manual*

The *Diagnostic and Statistical Manual of Mental Disorders* has long been a lightning rod within the field of social work regarding how to conceptualize human behaviour (Newman et al., 2007). One frequent concern is the way in which the DSM counteracts the strengths-based perspective of social work, focusing solely on pathology and dysfunction. This pathology is individualized and ignores the larger social context that contributes to distress. Further concern focuses on the use of labelling that can result in stigma, discrimination, and an internalization of the stigmatized identity on people who are given labels of a mental illness (Kutchins and Kirk, 1997). Another concern is the degree to which the use of such an individualized model may absolve social workers of the duty to advocate for social and institutional change (Mitchell, 2003). In addition, critics point to the way in which the social construction of mental illness is reflected in the DSM. This is exemplified by the inclusion of homosexuality in DSM-II.

On the other hand, social work educators have identified positive aspects to the use of the DSM by social workers, including assisting social workers to communicate effectively with others on the interdisciplinary team, organizing thinking, directing research efforts related to mental health, and linking treatment approaches to specific challenges (Newman et al., 2007) (see Table 4.2). Ponniah et al. (2011), for instance, suggest that all empirically supported mental health treatments are based on DSM diagnoses and thus determining a client's diagnosis aids in selecting the most effective treatment. They therefore suggest that clinical acumen in using the DSM leads to better social work interventions and outcomes. Harkness (2011) concurs with the use of DSM diagnosis to select effective care and identified that the iatrogenic effects of misdiagnosis can be catastrophic. On the contrary, a qualitative study conducted with clinical social workers found that respondents tended not to use diagnosis as a means of selecting treatment models; rather, they found the DSM most helpful from an educative perspective and for validation of the client's

Table 4.2 Potential Advantages and Disadvantages of the DSM

Advantages	Disadvantages
• Enhancing interprofessional communication • Organizing thinking • Directing research efforts • Linking treatment to specific challenges • Enhancing evidence-based practice	• Countering strengths-based perspectives of social work • Pathologizing • Individualizing, ignoring social contribution such as oppression, poverty • Stigmatizing/labelling • Socially constructed views of mental illness

experience of suffering, that is, "helping clients make sense of their experiences" (Probst, 2012). These respondents did not see a conflict between the DSM and the person-in-the-environment perspective of social workers, but they did caution that social workers needed to balance the benefits of diagnosis with the potential for stigmatization.

There is no definitive answer to whether the DSM should or should not be embraced by social work as a profession. Nevertheless, social workers in mental health must be aware of the DSM and familiar with its use. A social worker cannot communicate with the interprofessional team in mental health without knowing the language of DSM, even if simply to dispute its use or to disagree with a particular diagnostic category in which a client has been placed. If using the DSM as a tool, social workers must not lose sight of the aspects of the recovery model described in Chapter 1 and ensure that diagnosis does not eliminate hope and that clients are centrally involved in the planning for their treatment and recovery.

History of Classification

Although classification of diseases began as early as 1742 in Europe, the first International Classification of Diseases (ICD) was established in 1855 for the purposes of developing a common language to describe the causes of death. After several revisions, the sixth revision (ICD-6) was adopted by the World Health Organization in 1948 as a means to standardize disease classifications across the world (Dilling, 2000). In the United States, a need was identified to develop a classification system specific to mental illness in the 1800s for the purposes of gathering statistical information. The first US census that attempted to identify the incidence of mental illness was in 1840 and contained one category, idiocy/insanity. Seven categories appeared later in the 1880 census, including mania (elated mood and excessive energy), melancholia (depression), **monomania** (holding a delusional belief), **paresis** (loss of movement), dementia (cognitive deterioration), **dipsomania** (craving for alcohol), and epilepsy (APA, 2000).

In 1952, the American Psychiatric Association published the first edition of the *Diagnostic and Statistical Manual for Mental Disorders* (DSM-I). This edition was developed by a committee of leading clinicians and researchers based on their experience and the current literature on mental illness. The draft was sent to 10 per cent of the membership of the American Psychiatric Association for review, although no results of the survey were reported (Widiger and Clarke, 2000). DSM-I identified two major categories of disorders: disorders caused by or associated with brain tissue function (such as dementia, intoxication, and infection); and psychogenic disorders that did not have a clear physical cause (such as psychotic disorders, neurotic disorders, and personality disorders) (Corcoran and Walsh, 2010).

DSM-II followed in 1968, and was generated in a similar fashion to DSM-I in that it represented the consensus of experts. It contained 10 categories of mental disorder: organic brain syndromes, psychoses, neuroses, personality disorders, somatic disorders, situational disturbances, child and adolescent behaviour disorders, and conditions without psychiatric disorder, which included homosexuality. In the years that followed, the inclusion of homosexuality as a mental disorder received understandable criticism, and in 1974 the membership of the American Psychiatric Association voted to have it removed. In DSM-III the diagnosis was changed to "ego dystonic homosexuality," that is, those who were disturbed by their own homosexual feelings (Corcoran and Walsh, 2010).

DSM-III (1980) was followed by DSM-III-R (1987), which represented a new model for development of diagnostic categories. One aspect was an attempt to use research findings to support the diagnostic validity of all categories of diagnosis. However, this was hampered by the dearth of research literature within the field of psychiatry and other disciplines in mental health, resulting again in a system of categorizing that was reliant primarily on the clinical judgement of the developers. Further, DSM-III first introduced the concept of multi-axial diagnoses by which clinicians considered diagnoses in five domains: clinical or mental disorders; personality disorders and mental retardation; general medical conditions; psychosocial and environmental problems; and **global assessment of functioning (GAF)** (Dilling, 2000).

DSM-IV, which began development in 1988 and was published in 1994, expanded the use of empirical evidence to derive diagnostic categories. This edition was based on 175 literature reviews, 36 studies of diagnostic criteria, and 12 field trials to test the reliability and validity of the classifications. Minor changes were made to DSM-IV, resulting in the revised edition of the manual, DSM-IV-TR, in 2000 (TR refers to text revision).

Planning for DSM-5 (note that the abbreviation no longer uses Roman numerals) began in 1999 with the publication of two documents, *A Research Agenda for DSM-5* and *Age and Gender Considerations in Psychiatric Diagnosis.*

Almost nine years later the DSM-5 task force and 13 diagnostic area working groups were established who were responsible for conducting literature reviews, developing clinical criteria, collecting feedback, and overseeing field trials to determine the reliability and validity of diagnoses (Kraemer et al., 2010). Field trials were conducted at large clinical sites with samples of patients designed to be representative of the patient population (Kraemer et al., 2012). In the end, the goal is to enhance the scientific validity of diagnostic categories and at the same time increase patients' involvement in their own assessment and care through the integration of dimensional assessments (Kuhl et al., 2011).

The Cultural Formulation Interview

A major criticism of previous versions of the DSM was its inattention to cultural issues, specifically "*its limited attention to culturally patterned diversity in phenomenology, risk moderation, and course through excessive reliance on decontextualized epidemiological data*" (Alarcón et al., 2009: 559). Alarcón et al. further noted that if diagnosis fails to attend to socio-cultural factors, including those related to race, ethnicity, gender, sexual orientation, and religion, it risks promoting misdiagnosis, perpetuation of stereotypes, and unequal access to treatment. This concern was particularly acute given global migration and the wide cultural diversity of people seeking mental health services within North America, and given the wide dissemination of the DSM throughout the world. Thus, through the process of developing DSM-5, field trials aimed to include culturally diverse individuals, and feedback was sought at multiple points regarding the impact of socio-cultural factors on diagnosis (Barrera and Jordan, 2011). Arising from this process, DSM-5 introduces for the first time a cultural formulation interview. This interview has four domains (APA, 2013: 752–4):

- *The cultural definition of the problem:* defined as the client's description of the presenting issues from the perspective of his/her world view.
- *Cultural perceptions of the cause, context, and support:* referring to the client's view of what factors contribute to the problems he or she is experiencing.
- *Cultural factors affecting self-coping and past help-seeking:* client views of what has helped in the past and what have been barriers to care.
- *Current help-seeking:* client views on what might facilitate the current treatment and what might interfere with the clinical relationship.

Summary

The social work assessment is critical for informing work with a client or client system. It allows social workers to understand the context in which the individual lives, such as the person's community, society, family, and physical and economic environment. The assessment allows the social worker to determine how the client interprets his or her environment and what influence this interpretation has on well-being. In addition, the assessment allows the social worker to view some of the strengths and challenges inherent in the individual related to the biological self, cognition, personality structure, and ability to relate to the world.

Social work assessment in mental health practice is both similar and different to assessments in other areas of practice. As with other areas of practice, the social worker must be skilled in collecting data relevant to the psychosocial assessment and in analyzing the data for a comprehensive formulation. As with other areas of practice, culture and context are critical to understanding the nature of an individual's stressors and concerns and the culturally bound manner in which a person expresses distress. Finally, mental health practice requires the social worker to be skilled in performing mental status examinations and knowledgeable about the DSM as a form of classification for the purposes of communication. Clearly, social workers in mental health must have specialized knowledge and advanced skills in order to practice effectively.

Discussion Questions

1. How may cultural expressions of distress affect assessment of mental health issues and treatment planning?
2. How may the factors related to the social determinants of health affect an individual's mental health?
3. What unique perspectives may social work bring to mental health assessments that other members of the interdisciplinary team may not?
4. What are the risks of using the DSM as part of a social work assessment?

Suggested Readings and Websites

American Psychiatric Association. 2013. *Diagnostic and Statistical Manual of Mental Disorders*, 5th edn. Washington: APA Press. The DSM system of classification is used worldwide to provide a common language for diagnosis of mental disorder.

Bierman, A., A. Johns, B. Hyndman, C. Mitchell, N. Degani, A. Shack, et al. 2012. "Social Determinants of Health and Populations at Risk," *POWER: Project for Ontario Women's Health Evidence-Based Report*. At: www.powerstudy.ca/. This project reports the health of men and women in Ontario and is intended to support evidence-based treatment and policy-making.

5 Suicide and Self-Harm

Learning Objectives

- To describe the nature and incidence of suicide and self-harm behaviour in Canada.
- To identify factors contributing to suicide risk and self-harm.
- To present a model for risk assessment.
- To discuss ethical and legal issues related to working with suicidal clients.
- To discuss the impact of suicide on families and friends.
- To identify evidenced-based interventions for social work practice with clients who are suicidal or exhibit self-harm behaviours.

Case Example 1

Stanislav, age 17, was brought to the hospital emergency department by friends who were concerned that he was intoxicated, that his affect was fluctuating between angry and tearful, and that he threatened to jump in front of the subway. Stan's parents, who came to Canada from Eastern Europe in 1993, are unaware that he is in the emergency room. Stan did well in high school until the end of Grade 11 when his parents moved from one city to another for the purpose of employment. He reports being a misfit in his new school, being angry, despondent, and on the margins. His grades have dropped, teachers are criticizing poor work habits, and this academic term he is failing half of his subjects. His parents are angry and threaten to kick him out if he does not get his act together. Over the past couple of years Stan has become increasingly aware that he is attracted to men, a fact he cannot share with his devoutly religious parents. Tonight, he had arranged a first date with someone he had met on the Internet but the young man cancelled at the last minute by text message.

Case Example 2

Tina is a 30-year-old woman who has been hospitalized on several occasions for suicide attempts and has worked with a variety of mental health workers in the community. Tina was removed from the home of her mother at the age of 11 and taken into the care of the local child welfare authority. Tina's mother was addicted to cocaine and supported her drug habit through prostitution. Over her young life, Tina suffered physical and sexual abuse at the hands of multiple men who stayed sporadically in her home. While in the care of child welfare services, Tina lived in multiple foster homes, frequently being moved due to her unmanageable behaviour. She now works intermittently as a bartender or waitress. She is in a tumultuous common-law relationship with a man she states works as a "bookie." At times, Tina feels such despair that she will take a razor and make cuts across her wrist, watching the blood drip into the sink. She is embarrassed about the resultant scars and thus always wears long-sleeved clothing. At other times her despair leads her to take overdoses of non-prescription or prescription medication. Two days ago Tina had a fight with her common-law husband, who left the house and has not returned. Tina is convinced he has gone to live with another woman and she has come to the emergency department having consumed a large amount of alcohol, shouting that this is the last straw and she is unable to go on.

Case Example 3

Sue Rodriguez was a 42-year-old woman suffering from amyotrophic lateral sclerosis (ALS, also known as Lou Gehrig's disease). The prognosis for her type of ALS was a steady loss of physical ability, followed by death. Near the end of her life, it was anticipated that she would be conscious and aware of her situation but completely dependent upon the care of others and the support of artificial respiration, hydration, and nutrition. She commenced a court action, asking that the Criminal Code provision prohibiting assisted suicide be declared contrary to the Canadian Charter of Rights and Freedoms (Regehr and Kanani, 2010). She requested that a qualified physician be allowed to set up technological means by which she might end her life by her own hand at the time of her choosing, when she was no longer able to enjoy life. This request was denied. It is uncertain whether her death in 1994 involved assisted suicide or voluntary **euthanasia**, however, no charges have been laid (Special Senate Committee on Euthanasia and Assisted Suicide, 1995).

Case Example 4

In the first five months of 2008, 37 children and 10 adults in Shamattawa First Nation attempted suicide, and 52 others told health-care workers or family they planned to kill themselves (Reynolds, 2008). One year later rates had not improved; in 2009 seven suicides and 110 attempts were reported (CBC, 2010). The problems in this community, located 1,200 kilometres north of Winnipeg, first hit the national press in 2002 when three people committed suicide in the community in one month, bringing the total to 32 in one decade or one out of every 30 people in the 900-person community (CBC, 2002). In the aftermath of the 2002 crisis, government crisis teams were dispatched and federal and provincial governments joined forces to fast-track a $100,000 suicide prevention program in Shamattawa, establishing a new healing centre in the remote community. Evidently little was accomplished. There are lengthy waiting lists for substance-abuse treatment facilities in the North. The only recreational facility in Shamattawa, a drop-in centre, was found to be contaminated by a fuel leak. There are very few employment opportunities. A doctor flies in once a month to provide medical care; a pediatrician and optometrist fly in once a year. In 2008 the one RCMP officer posted to the community was removed when his trailer was set on fire while he slept (CBC, 2010).

Suicide

"The term suicide is applied to all cases of death resulting directly or indirectly from a positive or negative act of the victim himself, which he knows will produce this result" (Durkheim, 1951: 44). The act of suicide or attempted suicide results from the interaction of a variety of personal, interpersonal, historical, and contextual factors (Kirmayer et al., 2007). Suicidal ideation can emerge from extreme personal circumstances, which are either long-standing, such as in the case of chronic illness, or transient, such as in the case of interpersonal loss. Suicide can be culturally congruent and at least tacitly condoned by a community, or can be viewed as a criminal act or a cardinal sin. High suicide rates in a particular community can be the result of poverty, hopelessness, and despair related to historical and contextual factors, as exemplified in the case of suicide in Aboriginal communities.

When assessing and planning social work interventions with individuals who are suicidal, it is important to differentiate among acute suicide risk, chronic suicide risk, and the probability of risk-taking or self-injurious behaviour.

Acute suicide risk refers to a person who at a particular moment in time is experiencing intense wishes to be dead, often related to a particular life event that to the individual is of catastrophic proportions. In general, these feelings are transient and if the acute situation is managed, suicide risk diminishes. It is important to be aware that the perception of loss is entirely personal; thus, for one individual the breakup of a relationship even of short duration may precipitate suicide risk that in another person would seem to be a more minor life setback. People at chronic risk of suicide may also have periods where they become at more acute risk due to a life event or the onset of a particular stage in a long-standing illness.

Chronic suicide risk occurs most commonly in individuals suffering from a long-term health or mental health problem that appears to have no possibility of relief. For these individuals, the future looks bleak and the contemplation of suicide is less impulsive but rather a more reasoned decision arrived at and sometimes sustained over a period of time in which the person has considered other options.

Self-harm or self-injury occurs in some individuals who harm themselves without lethal intent. For instance, a person who repeatedly cuts herself or himself may be attempting to relieve intense personal distress. The self-injurious behaviour results in some relief. However, these individuals remain at high risk of eventual suicide either because they have periods of acute risk related to specific situations or because they accidentally kill themselves while inflicting self-harm.

DSM-5 includes both "suicidal behaviour disorder" and "non-suicidal self-injury" as conditions for further study. That is, these classifications are not for the purpose of clinical diagnosis, but are identified as areas for further research and discussion. The proposed criteria for non-suicidal self-injury includes the criterion that an individual has engaged in intentional self-harm that is likely to cause bleeding, bruising, or pain on five or more days in the past year. The proposed criterion for suicidal behaviour disorder is that an individual has initiated behaviour in the expectation that it would lead to his/her death in the past 24 months. In both cases, the acts are not taken solely for religious or political reasons and do not occur at a time when the person was confused or delirious. It is proposed that these two disorders may occur simultaneously in the same person (APA, 2013).

Incidence and Prevalence

In 2005, 3,743 Canadians died due to suicide, which translates to a rate of 11.6 per 100,000 or 0.011 per cent of the population (Statistics Canada, 2010). Every year, approximately 1 million people die from suicide, resulting in a worldwide mortality rate of 16 per 100,000, or one death every 40 seconds. Suicide is the second leading cause of death for those aged 15 to 19 and is in the top three for people aged 15 to 44. Within this average there is an enormous variation,

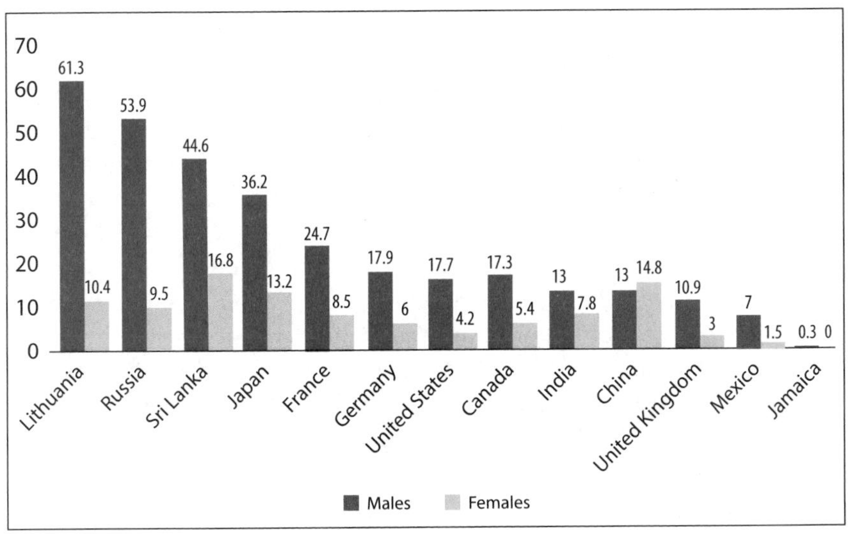

Figure 5.1 Suicide Rates per 100,000 in Selected Countries

Source: Based on data from WHO (2011).

ranging from a suicide rate of 61.3 per 100,000 for males in Lithuania to a rate of 0.3 per 100,000 in Jamaica. In general, rates for males are higher than those for females, with the exception of China where rates for females are higher (WHO, 2011). A comparison of suicide rates in selected countries can be found in Figure 5.1 (note that rates for Africa are unavailable).

In general, the highest rates are found in Eastern Europe and the former USSR region, the lowest rates are found in Central and South America, and moderate rates are found in North America and Southern Europe. Canadian suicide rates are somewhat lower than the international average, at 11.6/100,000. Gender-specific rates are 17.3/100,000 for males and 5.4/100,000 for females. Mental disorders, particularly depression and substance abuse, are estimated to be associated with 90 per cent of all suicide-related deaths in the world.

Suicide among Aboriginal Canadians

While the overall suicide rate in Canada has been declining, the rates in some Aboriginal communities have been rising for the past two decades (Kirmayer et al., 2007). Suicide rates for Inuit youth are 11 times the national average, placing them among the highest in the world (Health Canada, 2006). The suicide rate for female Aboriginal youth is four times higher than that for Canadian females as a whole, and the rate among male Aboriginal youth is 2.6 times higher than the national average (Health Canada, 2005).

Aboriginal youth on reserves are five to six times more likely to die of suicide than youth in other parts of the country. The most common method of suicide is hanging, accounting for almost half of the suicide deaths among First Nations youth, followed by firearms for males (35.3 per cent) and drug overdose for females (30 per cent). While overall increased rates are highly concerning, rates in specific communities are alarming. For instance, in British Columbia, Aboriginal males age 10–19 are eight times and females 20 times more likely to commit suicide than non-Aboriginal youth of the same age (MacNeil, 2008). Pikangikum, a First Nation community in the Sioux Lookout area of Ontario, has the highest suicide rate in the world. Between 1992 and 1995 the suicide rate for males aged 10–19 was over 50 times higher than the national average for youth the same age (Health Canada, 2005). In 2007 alone there were 10 suicides among Pikangikum's 2,400 people—a suicide rate of 417 per 100,000 population (Office of the Chief Coroner, 2011).

Some factors associated with suicide in all youth populations include: mental health problems (depression, substance abuse, anxiety, or conduct problems associated with impulsive and aggressive behaviour); a history of physical or sexual abuse; a friend or family member who has attempted suicide; poor relationships with parents; and poor school attendance or performance. In Aboriginal youth, however, historical government policies that attempted to force acculturation through the residential school system, isolation of communities, inadequate resources, and resultant community **anomie** are additional factors (Kirmayer et al., 2007; MacNeil, 2008). It is suggested that the act of suicide among Aboriginal youth reflects an overwhelming sense of shame and hopelessness within a fractured cultural, economic, and political environment (Ferry, 2000). These youth live in environments that often have inadequate housing, contaminated water and soil, poverty, the presence of drugs and alcohol, and an absolute lack of opportunity. Pikangikum, for instance, is not connected to the provincial electricity grid. Running water and indoor plumbing do not exist in most households. People are faced with poverty, substandard housing, challenges with food and water security, lack of health care, and poor education (Office of the Chief Coroner, 2011). Families in First Nations communities frequently have histories of substance use and mental health challenges. In addition, rates of **fetal alcohol syndrome** (FAS), which increases suicide risk, are consistently higher than the national and international averages. The prevalence of FAS in the United States is estimated to be 1–3 per 1,000 births. While no national average is available in Canada, small isolated Aboriginal communities in BC, Yukon, and Manitoba have estimated rates of 25–190 per 1,000 live births (Chudley et al., 2005). In sum, these environments carry many significant risk factors for suicide and the result is tragedy.

Factors Contributing to Suicide

Social-Environmental Factors

Emile Durkheim, a French sociologist, published his book *Suicide* in 1897. He suggested that suicide was the result of either anomie, in which a person experiences despair due to lack of connection with society and its goals, or altruism, in which the suicidal behaviour is associated with excessive integration into a group, such as in the case of a politically or religiously motivated suicide bomber. Generalized anomie can occur in the wake of some sort of dramatic change in social or economic circumstances, such as after the stock market crash in 1929, or in prolonged periods of cultural despair, such as in the case of Aboriginal communities. The economic crisis of 1997–8, for instance, was associated with higher rates of suicide in East Asian countries that had high rates of unemployment (Chang et al., 2009). Further, widespread focus on suicide within a culture can be associated with higher rates. Media attention to the suicide of a celebrity is associated with an increase in suicides, suggesting both a modelling and acceptance effect (Cheng et al., 2007). Thus, from the social environmental perspective, suicide is understood to arise from a convergence of factors related to the presence or absence of social pressures and opportunities in the interpersonal environment.

Intrapsychic Factors

Freud described suicide as aggression turned inwards. That is, suicide was seen as the result of angry, murderous urges towards another as a result of some form of injury to the self. Indeed, researchers have found that hostility and aggression are linked to suicidal behaviour (Mann et al., 1999; Zhang et al., 2012). Such anger and aggression are often related to personal histories of abuse and neglect. For instance, impulsivity, self-harm behaviours, and suicide attempts are found more commonly in individuals who are survivors of childhood physical and sexual abuse (Carballo et al., 2008). It is hypothesized that growing up in an environment of fear, pain, and unpredictability can lead to disconnection from others and a profound sense of self-blame and self-hatred. These reactions may be turned against the self at times of high stress or distress (Herman, 1992). A further **intrapsychic** factor that has received considerable research support is hopelessness about the future and about one's own ability to change current and future circumstance (Reinecke, 2000). Clearly, this sense of individual hopelessness is often intricately linked to social-environmental factors that oppress individuals and groups, limit choices, and block opportunities. For instance, homosexual youth have significantly higher rates of suicide than heterosexual youth (Miller and Glinski, 2000). From an intrapsychic perspective, therefore, suicide results from a complex and heterogeneous mix of intolerance of negative affect, low frustration tolerance, impulsivity, and intolerable psychic pain (Nierenberg et al., 2008).

Genetic and Neurochemistry Factors

Strong genetic links have been suggested in suicidal behaviour. Adoption studies find a six- to fifteen-fold increase in suicide in biological relatives of adoptees when compared to rates in adoptive families (Brent and Mann, 2005). In twin studies, the **concordance** rate between **dizygotic** (fraternal) twins for both suicidal behaviour and suicide is 0.7 per cent. Among **monozygotic** (identical) twins the concordance rate for suicidal behaviour is 14.9 per cent and for suicide is 23.0 per cent, a remarkably higher rate. Similarly, family proband studies show higher rates of suicide among those who are first-degree relatives of suicide attempters (30.3 per cent) versus those in a control group (3.6 per cent). Researchers have demonstrated that history of suicide and severe mental illness in biological parents had similar effects on offspring regardless of whether they were raised by biological or adoptive parents. These researchers concluded that the main effects of these factors in biological parents are not moderated by the environment in which offspring are raised (von Borczyskowski et al., 2011).

A number of genes may increase vulnerability to suicidal behaviour (Ernst et al., 2009). For instance, a tendency towards suicide is associated with distinct neurotransmitter and receptor profiles (Nierenberg et al., 2008). Specifically, those individuals lacking in one receptor (5-HT_{1b}) are likely to have higher levels of impulsivity, aggression, and substance abuse, all of which contribute to suicide risk (Mann et al., 1999). Further, serotonin deficiency (related to 5-HIAA) has been found in patients suffering from depression who attempted suicide. Other neurotransmitters such as dopamine, adrenaline, noradrenaline, and particularly glutamate and GABA (gamma-aminobutyric acid) have also been associated with suicidal behaviour.

A relatively new and exciting area of study is that of **epigenetics**, which is the study of the manner in which the inherited genes interact with the environment. It has been demonstrated that chemical changes throughout the lifespan (such as DNA methylation) can turn the gene on or off, thereby inhibiting gene transcription (Ernst et al., 2009). That is, environmental and social factors acting on a genetically predisposed individual result in suicide. This may be mediated through certain personality traits such as impulsivity, aggression, or a tendency to poor decision-making (Courtet et al., 2011). Thus, changes in the chemical behaviour of neurotransmitters produce an impulsive aggressive predisposition, which coupled with precipitating social life events may result in suicide.

Self-Harm Behaviour

Deliberate self-harm involves the destruction of body tissue without suicidal intent (Cumming et al., 2006). In general, this behaviour is divided into three categories:

1. *Stereotypic self-harm* involves repeated acts such as head-banging and biting of oneself, often associated with developmental delays, autism, and neurological disorders such as **Tourette's syndrome**.
2. *Moderate self-harm* is the most common form of self-harm and typically involves cutting (as seen in Case Example 2 of Tina) and skin-burning. This type of behaviour is usually associated with borderline personality disorder, dissociative states, complex post-traumatic stress, and eating disorders. Moderate self-harm can be episodic or repetitive.
3. *Major self-harm* is the rarest form of self-harm and is usually associated with psychosis. This results in severe injury such as self-castration or amputation. Often the specific form of mutilation is related to a particular delusion, for instance, that a particular body part is rotting or possessed.

Self-harm behaviours are generally related to impulse control, which, from a biological perspective, is related to lower pre-synaptic serotonin availability. Individuals who repeatedly self-harm may report a reduction in anxiety and psycho-physiological arousal. These individuals will often refer to the act as self-soothing or as resulting in lower levels of psychic pain. It can also be an external representation of internal pain. Alternatively, self-harm can be a form of self-punishment for individuals who experience excessive self-blame. Self-harm behaviours frequently begin in adolescence and end in middle age. Individuals who self-harm are at 66 times the risk of suicide when compared to the general population (Hawton et al., 2003).

Assessment of Suicide Risk

The majority of people who take their own lives have contact with health-care and mental health professionals shortly before their deaths. An Australian study using coroner's data revealed that 79 per cent of people had contact with health-care professionals in the three months before their deaths by suicide (Draper et al., 2008). A review of 40 studies by Luoma et al. (2002) determined that on average 45 per cent of suicide victims had contact with health-care providers one month prior to their death and 20 per cent had contact with mental health professionals in the month prior to death. It is therefore imperative that mental health professionals are skilled at differentiating between those individuals who are at imminent risk of death and require hospitalization and those who are safe in the community.

In assessing suicide risk, the social worker goes through a series of categories of information, attempting to collect data with which to gauge the current level of risk of a lethal attempt (see Box 5.1). Risk factors are perhaps best understood to fall into three main categories: static factors or demographic factors that form the foundation of risk, modifiable or acute factors that are amenable to change, and intent.

Static Factors

One issue to be considered is whether this person is in a group with higher risk of suicide than other groups. Clearly, static factors alone do not lead to suicide, but rather they provide a basis for considering level of risk. For instance, as noted earlier, men are at higher risk of completing suicide in almost every country in the world, although women are at higher risk of attempting suicide or self-harm. Young men and men over the age of 65 are at particular risk. Aboriginal youth are at higher risk than youth in other cultural groups, particularly if living in impoverished or isolated communities. Some occupational groups are at higher risk than others, for instance, doctors and nurses are in the highest-risk occupations (primarily due to access to lethal drugs), followed by manual labourers in low-paid jobs. The lowest-risk occupations are people in the armed forces, architects, schoolteachers, and engineers (Agerbo et al., 2007; Mustard et al., 2010). Unemployed individuals are at highest risk of all (Mustard et al., 2010). Despite being in the higher-risk group however, the majority of people in these demographic groups do not commit or attempt suicide.

Among static factors, a previous suicide attempt is the best predictor of a future suicide or suicide attempt (Mann et al., 1999). Among people with depression who die of suicide, for instance, 40 per cent have made previous attempts (Kaplan and Sadock, 1996). Individuals who engage in self-harm behaviours are at high risk of eventual suicide. These individuals also frequently make multiple suicide attempts that have a low level of possible lethality, often referred to as **parasuicide**. However, those who engage in parasuicidal attempts have a 20 to 47 per cent chance of eventual death from suicide (Cumming et al., 2006) and therefore it is important not to dismiss their suicidal ideation as merely "attention seeking." Critical in the consideration of previous suicide attempts as risk factors for future or current suicide is the degree of impulsivity in the acts and the severity of previous attempts. People who are subject to impulsive behaviour are at higher risk of future attempts and eventual death by suicide. The difficulty for clinicians, however, is determining whether this particular period in time represents a high risk or not, because an impulsive person's risk of suicide can fluctuate very quickly. Despite these high numbers,

Box 5.1 Assessment of Suicide Risk

			Increasing risk ↓
Static Risk Factors	Demographic considerations	• Gender (males are at higher risk) • Age (highest risk for youth between 15 and 24, followed by men over 65) • Upper or lower socio-economic group • Unemployed or retired • Single, widowed, or divorced • Social isolation	
	Past psychiatric history	• The person and his/her family – affective disorders have 15 per cent mortality by suicide – among suicides, 45 to 70 per cent have affective disorders	
Modifiable Risk Factors	Alcohol use	• Alcoholics have 15 per cent eventual mortality rate by suicide • Suicide attempts are preceded by alcohol intake in 50 per cent of men and 50 per cent of women	
	Present mental status	• See mental status exam in Chapter 4 • Severe depression • Hallucinations that command the person to act in a harmful manner	
	Precipitating events	• Recent loss or separation • Is there a clear precipitant? • Can there be some resolution to the problem?	
	Resources	• Limited personal resources • Limited resources within the person's network • No community resources	
Intent	Method or plan	• Abstractly considered suicide • Has given thought to method • Has prepared for suicide – saving pills, purchased gun • Level of intent to die • Lethality of method – drug overdose common in Canada (1/3 suicides, 2/3 attempts)	
	Future plans	• No plans to do something other than suicide today • No longer-term plans	

overall only 20 to 30 per cent of people who eventually kill themselves have made previous attempts; thus, it is important to consider other factors.

The risk of suicide for individuals with histories of mental illness is 3 to 12 times that of the general population. The suicide rate among people suffering from schizophrenia is 12 times that of people in the general population, and it is estimated that 4.9–10 per cent of people with schizophrenia will end their lives by suicide (Cohen et al., 2010). The suicide rate for people with major depression is 20 times the expected rate, with the highest risk occurring in the first few weeks following inpatient treatment (Harris and Barraclough, 1997). Suicide accounts for 19 per cent of deaths in patients with bipolar disorder (Carballo et al., 2008). In addition, certain personality disorders are associated with high rates of suicide. For instance, individuals with borderline personality disorder have a lifetime rate of suicide of between 5 and 10 per cent (McGirr et al., 2009). Level of education and insight are positively associated with higher rates of suicide in people with major mental illness. That is, those with higher levels of education and more insight are at greater risk of suicide (Hor and Taylor, 2010).

Family history of suicide and mental disorder is another important static risk factor. In general, individuals with family histories of suicide are at higher risk of suicidal attempts and completed suicide. This is particularly true in individuals who have a history of childhood physical or sexual abuse (Carballo et al., 2008). It appears that there is a complex interaction between family history of suicide and current suicide risk. One aspect may be genetic, as perhaps evidenced by a tendency towards earlier onset of depression and mania in those who have had a family member suicide or a tendency towards impulsivity and poor decision-making. Not surprisingly, however, individuals with family histories of suicide are found to be more pessimistic about the future (Nierenberg et al., 2008). A further possibility is that if someone in a person's family has committed suicide, the taboo against suicide is somehow lifted and suicide may become a viable option for dealing with intolerable situations and states. In support of this hypothesis, Swanson and Colman (2013) reviewed data from the Canadian National Longitudinal Study of Children and Youth. They discovered that either exposure to a schoolmate's suicide or personally knowing someone who had successfully completed suicide was associated with increased risk of both suicidal ideation and suicide attempts in youth 12–17 years old. Interestingly, among youth that reported a schoolmate's suicide, knowing the deceased personally did not compound the risk of suicide ideation or attempts.

Modifiable Factors

Modifiable factors may place a person at higher risk of suicide at the present time, but with intervention or time, these risk factors may diminish. For instance, alcohol use acts as a disinhibitor with respect to suicide and is associated with depression. Up to 15 per cent of people who abuse alcohol commit suicide (270/100,000 population). About 80 per cent of alcohol-dependent suicides are male. Heroin abusers have a rate of suicide 20 times that of the general public (Kaplan and Sadock, 1996). This factor is modifiable, but not readily, and risk may be higher at times of either intoxication or withdrawal.

Associated with the presence of a mental health problem is current mental status. Those individuals who are severely depressed may focus entirely on suicide and annihilation and be at extremely high risk due to their inability to foresee a future free of depression. Individuals who suffer from command hallucinations aimed at self-destruction, such as voices that tell them they are worthless and should kill themselves, are at very high risk, even in the absence of other risk factors. Hospitalization with the option of medication may be required to reduce the risk associated with acute mental health concerns.

Strengths and resources should also be considered as modifiable factors that increase the safety of a person who is contemplating suicide. In addition to these factors, social workers evaluating for suicide risk must determine whether there is an acute precipitant of the current suicidal ideation and whether this precipitant can be diminished in intensity or resolved. Sometimes reassurance and instilling hope, while allowing time to heal, can be helpful in reducing acute risk.

Intent

Social workers should ask very directly about suicidal ideation and intent. This includes questions related to an exact plan for suicide. Possible questions include the following:

- Are you feeling so badly about the current situation that you have been thinking about hurting yourself? (Easing into the conversation about suicide and self-harm. Clients will frequently ask if you mean would they kill themselves and will assure you that they will not.)
- How would you hurt yourself? (Determining whether this is self-harm behaviour or suicidal behaviour if they have answered the previous question in the affirmative.)
- Do you have access to pills/a gun? How many pills do you have? Where is the gun? (Exploring preparation for the specific method that they have considered. For instance, a person may state that he or she would use a gun for suicide but has no access to firearms. Alternatively, a person may have been saving pills for the occasion.)
- Have you made any other preparations? Or have you thought about what would happen to your kids if you were gone? (Exploring other types of

preparation and planning. For instance, has the person recently written a will?)

- Have you ever hurt yourself before? What did you do to yourself? What happened? Did you get treatment? (Exploring seriousness and impulsiveness of previous attempts or self-harm.)
- Do you know anyone who has committed suicide? What was that like for you? (Exploring family history and attitudes towards suicide.)
- What were you planning to do when you left here today? (Assessing whether the person has other plans for the day, expects to see someone, etc. When the person has no plan at all, this adds to risk.)

In the end, it is difficult to predict suicide because individual risk fluctuates dramatically, particularly in individuals with high levels of impulsive behaviour. If there is any question in the mind of the social worker assessing the client, he or she should seek consultation and not feel obligated to make a decision about risk alone. Clients at high risk are often hospitalized, but in situations where risk can be managed, community-based treatment is usually preferred in order to support individual coping skills.

Suicide Scales for Assessment

Social workers may find it useful to use scales to assist with the assessment of suicide risk. Although there are numerous suicide scales in use, many have very little data supporting their use. A study conducted at the Centre for Addiction and Mental Health compared a variety of scales to clinical assessments. This study determined that six scales identified high-risk patients: the SAD PERSONS Scale, the revised Beck Depression Inventory, the Beck Hopelessness Scale, the Beck Anxiety Inventory, the Beck Scale for Suicidal Ideation, and the High-Risk Construct Scale. Of these, the most accurate were the Beck Scale for Suicidal Ideation (BSS) and the High-Risk Construct Scale (Cochrane-Brink et al., 2000). More recently, the Columbia Suicide Severity Rating Scale (C-SSRS) has been introduced and is in wide use in intervention studies and clinical trials. Further, it provides excellent guidance for clinicians conducting suicide risk interviews (Posner et al., 2011). The C-SSRS is available online and provides online training. Nevertheless, while these scales are important adjuncts to clinical assessment, no scale predicts whether clients will ultimately die of suicide (Harriss and Hawton, 2005). Further, these scales are not accurate enough to suggest that a particular cut-off point should result in hospitalization. Scales, therefore, can be used to ensure that information about risk factors has been gathered in a systematic and thorough manner, but they can only guide the professional judgement of the clinician.

Ethical and Legal Duties in Working with Suicidal Clients

In 2008, Accreditation Canada introduced the following required organizational practice for mental health facilities: "The organization assesses and monitors client risk of suicide." Tests for compliance include that the organization assesses each client for risk of suicide at regular intervals, that the organization identifies clients at risk of suicide, and that the organization addresses immediate safety needs of clients. In both community and institutional health settings, this task often falls to social workers as front-line mental health service providers.

Probably more than in any other clinical situation, a suicidal client forces the social worker to confront complex ethical questions while being faced with urgency, uncertainty, and risk. On one hand, it seems that protecting the lives of individuals is central to social work values; on the other hand, a person contemplating suicide who suffers from a chronic and life-threatening health condition, such as in the case of Sue Rodriguez, may be quite different from the person suffering acute depression who expresses suicidal thoughts. What is a social worker expected to do in these circumstances? In general, there is consensus in the literature that the practitioner is obliged to do absolutely whatever he/she can to help the suicidal client find a way to live. While there may be circumstances where suicide is a reasoned decision, the prevailing opinion is that if it is unclear whether the person can make a rational and autonomous decision, the practitioner should err on the side of caution and intervene. The choice to intervene may provide an opportunity for a second chance and can always be reconsidered and reversed (Mishna et al., 2002).

While the literature on suicide may allow for the possibility of suicide as a rational decision, what about the legal and ethical obligations of social workers? Mishna, Regehr, and Antle (2003), in reviewing the legal obligations of social workers in Canada with respect to suicidal clients, consider two main factors: (1) the standard of care that the practitioner is required to provide; and (2) the duty to disclose confidential information that a client may be suicidal. Physicians have a well-defined duty under the law to try to prevent suicide. If physicians, particularly psychiatrists, do not take adequate measures to protect life or are negligent in meeting the standard of care, they may be held liable (Regehr and Kanani, 2010). Indeed, failing to prevent suicide is a leading reason for malpractice suits against mental health professionals and institutions in the United States (Corey et al., 1998). However, the potential liability of a social worker with regard to a client's suicide is uncharted territory in Canadian law. Although the fact that no social worker has been held civilly liable or criminally responsible for a client's suicide may offer some comfort, it certainly does not guarantee future immunity from liability. To ensure protection from this outcome, social workers must follow standards of care in working with suicidal clients, including performing thorough assessments, providing recommended treatments, and being informed of, and following decisions related to, breach of confidentiality when a client threatens self-harm (Mishna et al., 2003). In terms of social work ethics, the *Code of Ethics* (2005) underlines confidentiality as a central ethical duty, while the *Guidelines for Ethical Practice* of the CASW (2005) state:

> Social workers who have reason to believe that a client intends to harm him/herself are expected to exercise professional judgement regarding their need to take action consistent with their provincial/territorial legislation, standards of practice and workplace policies. Social workers may in this instance take action to prevent client self-harm without the informed consent of the client. In deciding whether to break confidentiality, social workers are guided by the imminence of self-harm, the presence of a mental health condition and prevailing professional standards and practices. (CASW, 2005: Standard 1.6.3)

Social workers must therefore rely on practice guidelines, which call for a good therapeutic alliance, thorough assessment that is carefully documented, and consultation.

The preceding discussion does not fully address the issue of a client with a chronic condition who has determined that suicide is the most reasonable choice, given the person's current condition and the anticipated course of the illness. Mishna, Regehr, and Antle (2003) note that self-determination is central to social work ethics and values and a fundamental human right in Western society. However, there have always been limits to self-determination, especially in situations where a person has diminished capacity for decision-making and consent. This is dealt with in detail in Chapter 3. Thus, a social worker must include consideration of capacity when determining suicide intervention in situations of chronic risk.

It is important to note that while suicide and attempted suicide are not illegal in Canada, assisting with a suicide is a criminal offence. Section 241 of the Criminal Code provides that anyone who: (1) counsels a person to commit suicide; or (2) aids or abets a person to commit suicide, whether suicide ensues or not, is guilty of an indictable offence and liable to imprisonment for a term not exceeding 14 years. Individuals with life-threatening illnesses and their doctors have gone before the courts attempting to establish a constitutional right to assisted suicide; however, despite the efforts of Sue Rodriguez (Case Example 3) the law was upheld by the Supreme Court of Canada in 1993 (Regehr and Kanani, 2010). In continued attempts to challenge the issue, Bill C-562, An Act to amend the Criminal Code (right to die with dignity) was introduced into the House of Commons in 2008 (Tiedemann and Valiquet, 2008) but did not receive assent. On 15 June 2012, the Supreme Court of British Columbia ruled that section 241 of the Criminal Code was unconstitutional in a case brought forward by Gloria Taylor. Like Sue Rodriguez, Ms Taylor suffered from ALS and petitioned the court to allow her to proceed with physician-assisted suicide. Ms Taylor was granted a constitutional amendment to the Criminal Code. The government of Canada was given one year to redraft legislation on physician-assisted suicide (Dhillon, 2012). However, in October 2013 the BC Court of Appeal overturned the ruling and upheld the ban on assisted suicide.

The Impact of Suicide on Family and Friends

Death by suicide results in special issues and challenges for those who are left behind. Parents of those who have committed suicide are first dealing with general issues related to the loss of a child. The loss of a child is seen as a violation of the natural world order and interrupts the continuity of the family and its anticipated future (Maple, 2005). Such a loss can lead to mental health and physical health issues, disrupted marital relations, and increased morbidity, including suicide risk. When the death is caused by suicide, additional factors emerge: (1) the survivors can struggle to find meaning in the death; (2) there are high levels of guilt for not preventing the death; (3) survivors experience a sense of abandonment by the deceased; (4) stigma and absence of social supports; and (5) fear. Parents in particular feel guilt related to their perceived inadequacies as parents and often a sense of moral guilt related to past wrongdoings (Parrish and Tunkle, 2005). Related to this, they may feel fear for their remaining family members, particularly related to future possibilities of mental illness and suicide (Clark and Goldney, 1995). Family members feel isolated, stigmatized, and shunned, and social supports are often not forthcoming. As a result, a conspiracy of silence may emerge and the deceased person is not spoken about, as if to suggest that he or she did not exist. This does not allow for the process of grieving in survivors. Friends and peers of the deceased are often in a state of shock, which in the case of youth is compounded by age-related inexperience and emotions.

Finally, one factor more frequent in suicide-related deaths is the horror of the death scene. Images of the death scene obviously occur when a family member or friend has discovered the deceased; however, this can also occur as a result of imagined scenes based on what has been learned about the death (Clark and Goldney, 1995).

Interventions

Psychosocial interventions for people who are at risk of suicide fall into two main categories: (1) crisis intervention to deal with acute risk; and (2) longer-term treatment such as dialectic behaviour therapy or interpersonal therapy to manage chronic risk and self-harm. The second category of interventions is discussed in Chapter 12 on personality disorders.

Crisis Intervention with Acute Suicide Risk

Crisis intervention is a brief treatment approach based on the premise that support, education, and guidance provided in a timely manner can assist individuals to mobilize their inherent strengths and resources for the purposes of moving towards a speedy resolution of the distress caused by a particular occurrence. Crisis intervention focuses on the resolution of an immediate problem. The goal is to prevent further deterioration and return to at least a pre-crisis level of functioning. In working with suicidal clients, crisis intervention focuses on reducing acute risk through diminishing affective arousal and assisting the client to develop some immediate plans. This model of intervention was originally proposed by Caplan in 1964 and later by Golan in 1978. More recently, Roberts (2000) defined seven stages of crisis intervention:

1. *Planning and conducting a thorough assessment*, including any acute risk of harm to self or others. The assessment process has been described in detail earlier in this chapter.
2. Rapidly *establishing rapport*, demonstrating respect, acceptance, and a non-judgemental attitude. Rapport is established very quickly in a crisis situation through the demonstration of concern for the problems being experienced by the person in distress and a desire to assist with basic needs. Such assistance can include offering food or drink in the emergency room and ensuring the person is comfortable and protected from the chaos that may be characteristic of the environment.
3. *Identifying various dimensions of the current problem*, including the "last straw" of precipitating events. As discussed in Chapter 4 on assessment, the social worker attempts to quickly identify the biopsychosocial domains of the current problem. What are the underlying struggles this person encounters? What has led up to the current crisis? In general, the social worker should be prepared for the fact that the client in crisis will present a wide range of problems, including those that have been continuing for some time and those that are new. The social worker needs to be careful not to become overwhelmed and, rather, as the interview continues, begin to organize the problems in his or her own mind according to those that are static, those that are modifiable over a longer period of time, and those that are more immediately modifiable and therefore will reduce risk.

4. Active listening while *exploring* and describing previous *coping strategies* and *successes and resources* available. The social worker using a crisis intervention approach seeks to discover the personal strengths of the client as well as those within that individual's social network. Who could help the client if he or she needed help? How has the person coped in the past? If the client describes positive coping, reinforce those abilities and celebrate those successes. For instance, while a client might not identify this as a particular success, the social worker may remark, "I see you as someone with tremendous strengths and resources based on the fact that you managed to complete high school despite all the challenges that were thrown your way." Recognize that even if the client is able to accept the positive reinforcement, he or she may not be able to handle the stresses in this particular day and may need further intervention.
5. Generating and exploring *alternative strategies* for managing the problem. Once the client has laid out the problems he or she is encountering, the social worker summarizes the issues for the client. For instance, "I can see that you are managing many problems. Some of these have been going on for a long time, such as your relationship with your mom, your problems in school. . . . On top of all of that, in the last two days X has happened." The social worker then suggests that some of the issues can't be dealt with right now, but that a referral for future counselling is certainly possible. However, it does seem that together the client and the social worker might be able to come up with some ideas to manage the most recent problems over the next couple of days. At this point the social worker searches for possible solutions by gently exploring alternatives with the client. At any point, the social worker has to be prepared to change tactics and move from a community-based approach to other measures such as hospitalization if the client does not appear to be able to engage in problem-solving and suicide risk remains high.
6. Developing and formulating an *action plan* with the client. Once alternatives have been explored, the social worker and the client move to an immediate action plan. Generally, both the client and the social worker have some responsibilities in the plan. The social worker may undertake to contact a parent, friend, or other support person who can assist the person. The social worker may also undertake to do some advocacy work with a professor, landlord, or source of funding to reduce some systemic pressures on the client. The social worker may arrange a shelter bed and provide a taxi for the client to get there. The client also agrees to undertake some tasks such as discussing his/her concerns with a particular person or following through on a task that he or she has been avoiding. In formulating the action plan, the social worker will often provide notes to the client with necessary phone numbers or steps to be followed.

7. Establishing *follow-up* plans. Follow-up plans tend to be short-term in crisis intervention. For instance, a client can agree to visit or phone the social worker the next day. Follow-up plans can also be longer term in nature, although it is important to note that quite commonly clients who attend crisis services do not follow through with referrals to longer-term services. It is hypothesized that this may be due to the fact that he or she is a crisis-oriented person who does not engage in longer-term strategies, or that crisis intervention performed correctly and at the ideal time creates change in and of itself and no further assistance is needed. That is, in a time of acute stress a client benefitted from the opportunity to sort through difficulties with someone qualified and motivated to help. All follow-up plans with people who are potential suicide risks must include strategies and options should the person feel that he or she is at acute risk of suicide and needs immediate assistance. Such options include suicide hotlines and hospital emergency departments.

Some practitioners and treatment centres employ no-suicide contracts, whereby the client undertakes to promise the therapist, or even sign a document, that he or she will not attempt suicide. There is no empirical support for the effectiveness of such contracts in reducing suicidal behaviour (Reinecke, 2000). Some have suggested that this is simply an approach that reduces therapist anxiety and may in fact cause a breach in the therapeutic alliance if the client does not follow the contract and makes an attempt.

While limited research has considered the efficacy of the crisis intervention model, a study in England and Wales assessing the impact of various interventions on suicide revealed that instituting 24-hour crisis services was the factor associated with the greatest reduction in suicide rates (While et al., 2012).

Hospitalization for Acute Risk

Where suicide risk is particularly high and outpatient treatment is unable to ensure safety, hospitalization may be required. In general, hospitalization is viewed as a short-term measure to treat an acute psychiatric illness, such as depression, or to get someone who is a chronic risk through a particularly difficult time. This is discussed further in Chapter 12 on personality disorder.

Counselling Interventions for Self-Harm and Fluctuating Risk

Although crisis intervention is useful in times of acute suicidal risk, individuals who have long histories of abuse and neglect that later result in self-harm behaviours and chronic fluctuating suicide risk require longer-term counselling interventions. These interventions are discussed in more detail in the chapters on trauma and grief (Chapter 6) and on personality disturbance (Chapter 12). In general however, the approach includes: providing support and validation; providing stability; containing distress; and working through and managing crises. In addition, two particular forms of longer-term intervention—dialectic behaviour therapy (DBT) and interpersonal therapy (IP)—have been shown to be effective. These are discussed in Chapter 12.

Pharmacological Intervention for Suicide Risk

The essential principle of treatment in this area of suicide risk is careful assessment and treatment of the underlying disorder. Most commonly, this involves treatment of a depression or mania, schizophrenia, borderline personality disorder, or substance abuse (see later chapters for more information). Suicide and self-harm are commonly associated with all of these mental health problems and should always be part of the initial and ongoing assessment. This suggests that psychopharmacological options (such as SSRIs, clozapine, or lithium carbonate) may be of help in conjunction with psychosocial treatments in clients who are suicidal (Cardish, 2007; Mamo, 2007).

In the treatment of depression, one study demonstrated a clear relationship between the number of prescriptions for selective serotonin reuptake inhibitors (SSRIs) and serotonin norepinephrine reuptake inhibitors (SNRIs) dispensed in a given area and time period and suicide rates (Gibbons et al., 2005). That is, as prescriptions increase, suicide rates decrease. A study looking at national suicide mortality files in the US between 1990 and 2000 demonstrated a similar association in youth suicide rates (Olfson et al., 2003). Although this fact may be true on a population basis, in Chapter 6 we discuss how risk of suicide may increase on an individual basis in the initial stages of recovery. Therefore, careful monitoring and supervision with regular follow-up is essential.

A body of research has established that decreased serotonergic activity is associated with suicidal behaviour (Mann et al., 1999). Studies emanating from this work support the use of lithium carbonate (Bocchetta et al., 2007) and clozapine (Cardish, 2007; Mamo, 2007) in decreasing suicide rates. This is especially effective in those suffering from mood disorders but also applies across the diagnostic spectrum.

Social Work Interventions with Families and Communities after Suicide

Family interventions following suicide can take several forms, including work with individuals who are most affected, work with couples struggling in the aftermath of losing a child, meetings with the family as a group, and support groups of suicide survivors. In general the intervention must include several elements (Kaslow and Aronson, 2004):

- demonstrating compassion, acceptance, and gaining trust;
- shifting flexibly between a supportive, educative, and counselling stance;
- assessment of each member of the family to determine his/her unique needs and risks;
- addressing issues of blame, stigma, shame, guilt, and fear.

In order to do this, the social worker must examine his or her own reactions to suicide and be prepared for being exposed to painful emotions and distressing information.

Support groups for survivors of suicide can be of benefit to bereaved individuals to share experiences of stigma and isolation (Parrish and Tunkle, 2005). Hopmeyer and Werk (1994) conducted a study comparing five types of bereavement groups in Montreal. Aspects of group intervention that family survivors of suicide reported as most helpful included: (1) sharing similar experiences; (2) gaining comfort and reassurance; (3) learning new skills for coping; (4) sharing with others what they had learned; and (5) gaining assistance for their depression.

Suicide does not occur in equal rates in all communities, and, as noted earlier in this chapter, when suicide rates are high in a particular community the impact is felt well beyond the individual families. As a result, community-based interventions are necessary to fully address the after-effects of suicide and the ongoing risks. A community-based program for families following suicide was initiated in a high-risk neighbourhood in Galway, Ireland. This project emerged because of the realization that suicide was a common issue within the community, resulting in many bereaved families, and the community support programs felt ill-equipped to deal with the problem. This family support program was embedded in the ecological perspective and focused on the impact of suicide on all aspects of the system and the possibilities of support from multiple levels. The program was planned through a community development process. The final program began with the distribution of cards to all households in the community. These cards described issues related to suicide and supports available. An information night was held for all community members and a video was made to encourage discussion and impart information. The model emphasized the supports needed by the extended family, friends, neighbours, and the community in general and identified not only formal services but also informal mechanisms for assistance (Forde and Devaney, 2006).

There have been many diverse approaches to working with Aboriginal communities in Canada where the tragedy of suicide permeates (Leenaars, 2000). Such approaches are vital because the causes of suicide in these communities are related to mental health, health, and substance use problems that stem from poverty, marginalization, and oppression (Kirmayer et al.,

2003). One aspect of a comprehensive community approach involves re-articulating tradition through reconciliation and renewal. The Aboriginal Healing Foundation, which was established in 1998, has focused on developing community-based services, workshops and gatherings, cultural activities, and training and educational programs. Another aspect has been focusing on youth identity and community empowerment. This has involved including youth in decision-making processes and the development of community services. Mental health programs are being directed towards the mental health and cultural identity of young people. At the larger level, self-governance models are being implemented to allow for local control over social services, education, and resources, with the aim of building community capacity and addressing issues of despair and hopelessness.

Possible Social Work Interventions in the Case Examples

Case Example 1: Stanislav

Stanislav is suffering from acute suicide risk as a result of situational factors. He feels isolated from his family and peers, is having difficulty in school, is exploring his sexuality, and feels rejected by someone with whom he wished to develop an intimate relationship. The following could be aspects of a sound social work intervention.

- The first step with Stan will be to conduct a thorough assessment to determine if other underlying factors are affecting a suicidal ideation; for instance, does he suffer from depression, has he previously had suicidal thoughts, and/or has anyone in his family suffered from depression or attempted or committed suicide? If these are additional risk factors, a consultation for mental health problems may be in order.
- A further aspect of the assessment will be determining the degree of present risk. Does he have a plan and how serious are his intentions?
- Next, the social worker will move into crisis intervention strategies. What solutions might Stan consider for the problem? Will Stan allow the social worker to intervene with his school to get assistance? Is there an LGBTQ group that may be welcoming of him? Will Stan allow the social worker to be in contact with his family and if so is the family likely to be supportive?
- Upon working out a strategy, the social worker will assess whether the suicide risk remains acute. If so, Stan may need to be taken to hospital for assessment. If not, a follow-up interview and plan can be established should he become acutely distressed again.

Case Example 2: Tina

Tina has a tragic life history that has led to ongoing distress manifested in self-harm behaviours and recurrent suicidal risk. The emergency room social worker will probably take some of the following steps to intervention.

- The social worker will begin by allowing Tina to describe her story and the factors that led to this acute situation today. It is possible that as a result of the support and empathy of the social worker, Tina will begin to feel better.
- The social worker will determine if Tina is presently seeing a mental health professional and what the plan is for their work together. The social worker may, with Tina's consent, call that therapist to discuss possible plans.
- The social worker will attempt to use problem-solving approaches with Tina in order to see if the current crisis can be abated. For instance, are there social supports that can be drawn upon to assist at this time of crisis? Does Tina have some self-care or self-soothing strategies she has used in the past that may work at this time?
- If Tina's agitation and risk do not remit, she may need a brief period of hospitalization to help her through the crisis period. The social worker will then have to seek consultation on this matter with someone who has admitting privileges (often a physician).

Case Example 3: Sue

The case of Sue is not one in which there has been a rash decision to commit suicide. Instead, Sue explored all options and determined that, rather than die in a painful and debilitating manner, she would prefer to have control over her own death. The social worker must consider the following issues.

- A social worker cannot counsel suicide or assist with suicide regardless of his or her moral beliefs about the subject.
- A social worker must assess whether the client is competent to make decisions about his or her own future and whether he or she suffers from a mental health problem (such as depression) that is influencing judgement.
- The social worker should continue to provide support and counselling, assisting with any factors that are making life more difficult in order to reduce stress and social isolation. That is, any factors that may contribute to suicide risk should be diminished or eliminated if at all possible. The social worker must be careful not to give up.

- On the other hand, it has been suggested that in the case of chronic and unremitting mental or physical illness, a social worker's conviction that suicide can and must be prevented may reflect an avoidance of the ethical dilemma and responsibility (Mishna et al., 2002). That is, the continuation of enforced treatment may only intensify the unbearable pain and distress for the suicidal individual. Narveson (1986: 107) writes that the intervention may be "what the professional insists is 'treatment,' and what the subject regards as, simply, a refined variety of torture." Some writers suggest that if a practitioner is able to empathically hear the client's unbearable suffering and death wishes, this may build trust in the relationship with the therapist. They speculate that, paradoxically, this may foster some hope in the clients (Nelson, 1984). Thus, listening to the client as he or she discusses the pain may in fact diminish risk.

Case Example 4: Shamattawa First Nation

In the case of Shamattawa First Nation, while suicide unquestionably affects individuals and their families, the causes of suicide are not individual. Rather, they reflect the results of systemic oppression, abuse, and neglect. Social work interventions therefore must be much broader than individualized interventions described in the previous cases.

- All strategies for community interventions in the prevention of suicide and in the recovery of suicide must emanate from the community itself and not be imposed from the outside.
- Social services must be designed by the local community in collaboration with social workers in a way that meets the needs of their members.
- Social workers can work with communities around issues of reconciliation and self-governance in order to restore cultural identity and a common sense of purpose and future.

Summary

All social workers working in the area of mental health will be faced with clients who are at risk of suicide. The despair that individuals suffering from major mental disorders experience at various times in the course of their illnesses may lead to suicidal thoughts and attempts. The emotional roller coaster and recurring interpersonal crises that individuals with personality disorders encounter can lead to fluctuating or chronic risk of self-harm and suicidal behaviour. The average person encountering a life crisis or significant loss may uncharacteristically consider suicide at a particularly bleak time. Further, individuals who are members of certain groups that are plagued with disadvantage and substance use may have learned that suicide is a viable alternative. It is essential that social workers develop skills in the assessment of suicide risk and in intervention with people who are experiencing acute risk. Work with suicidal clients is generally stressful and often fraught with ethical dilemmas. Social workers and others involved with suicidal clients must ensure that they have a good team of colleagues within their own discipline and within the interdisciplinary team to consult in order to make reasoned and competent judgements and to ensure that they can obtain professional support when the stress of this work takes its toll.

Discussion Questions

1. What is the obligation of social workers to intervene in cases of acute suicide risk?
2. Do social workers have the same obligations in cases of suicide decisions arising from chronic illness as they do in acute suicide risk?
3. What moral and religious values may influence the work of social workers with clients who are contemplating suicide? Do these values conflict with ethical and legal guidelines?
4. What reactions may social workers have to clients who engage in self-harm behaviours and how might these reactions affect the therapeutic relationship?

Suggested Readings and Websites

Kirmayer, L., G. Brass, T. Holton, K. Paul, C. Simpson, and C. Tait. 2007. *Suicide among Aboriginal People in Canada*. Ottawa: Aboriginal Healing Foundation. This report reviews research on suicide among Aboriginal people in Canada in order to better understand the origins of suicide and to identify effective interventions and strategies of prevention.

Perlman, C., E. Neufeld, L. Martin, M. Goy, and J. Hirdes. 2011. *Suicide Risk Assessment Inventory: A Resource Guide for Canadian Health Care Organizations*. Toronto: Ontario Hospital Association and Canadian Patient Safety Institute. At: www.oha.com/KnowledgeCentre/Library/Pages/Guides.aspx. This guide helps health care organizations understand and standardize suicide risk assessment principles, processes, and tools.

Social Workers. "Help Starts Here: Suicide Prevention." At: www.helpstartshere.org/mind-and-spirit/suicide-prevention. This website includes a collection of resources that examine suicide risk factors and intervention strategies particularly among teens and LGBTQ youth.

World Health Organization. 2007. "Suicide Prevention." At: www.who.int/mental_health/prevention/suicide/suicideprevent/en/. This article discusses suicide prevention, including effective intervention strategies as well as challenges and obstacles, and provides links to further resources.

6 Trauma and Traumatic Grief

Learning Objectives

- To describe trauma response as a continuum of distress.
- To describe factors that contribute to trauma response.
- To discuss the intersections between trauma and grief reactions.
- To identify evidence-based approaches to working with individuals suffering from trauma and grief.

Case Example 1

Jasmine is a 23-year-old student living in residence at university. She was shy in high school and never dated. While at university Jasmine was raped. She describes her experience as follows:

> It was January and I was finishing my last year. I lived in a co-op residence. And I had lots of wonderful friends there. And there was this one guy who lived three doors down from me. He was really screwed up, into drugs, alcohol. He was majorly mixed up. And I wanted to help him. And we became friends. We talked a lot. I remember he told me that I looked just like his ex-financée who had dumped him and that he would do anything to hurt her. I thought he meant just emotionally. Well, that one night he kept calling me her name, the night he raped me. I don't think he knew it was me. But I'm not excusing him. He was drunk and on cocaine, may not even know what he did. He pounded on my door at two a.m. He needed someone to talk to. . . . No one else around. . . . Swearing. . . . Calling me a tease. . . . Calling every name in the book. . . . Pinned in a low chair. . . . Ripped nightgown. . . . Forced oral sex which I've never done, never wanted to do, and then he raped me. He didn't beat me or anything. The verbal abuse was a horrible violation. I should have screamed, but I didn't. In the past when was drinking he got very aggressive with other people. So I thought I better watch it.

> . . . .Afterwards, he left. I went to the shower and scrubbed myself for an hour. I just felt so dirty. I hoped someone would come in, but on the other hand I didn't want anyone to. I was convinced it was my fault. That maybe he was right, maybe I was giving off signals. But then I really didn't think I did. And I sort of thought that if I did, then that's his problem. I was really convinced that I should die. That I asked for it. . . . I didn't want to tell my parents because I was worried that they would take me out of there and I didn't want to leave. I was really worried that I was pregnant. What would I do? I was terrified that he would get me again. I saw him every day and he acted like nothing happened. I did tell his best friend, who was also my friend. But he just said I must be wrong. He asked, are you sure it was rape?

As a result of this experience, Jasmine began to have nightmares of being assaulted and became extremely fearful. In addition to locking her dorm room when she was in there, she would wedge a chair in front of the door. She did not like to go out at night and made excuses about her workload to explain why she did not attend parties. She tried to arrange to walk to all classes and the library with friends, which she realized they thought was odd because she had not shared with them about the rape. Jasmine felt highly anxious, she had trouble concentrating on her work, and felt tearful and sad all the time. Somehow, however, she managed to complete the year and graduate, but with much lower grades than she had achieved in the past.

Case Example 2

At 12:06 a.m. on 23 October 2011, police in Grande Prairie, Alberta, were called to the scene of a collision between a pickup truck driven by a 21-year-old man and a car carrying five teenagers. The five young men, aged 15 and 16, were students at the Grande Prairie Composite High School and members of the school's football team. Four died at the scene from injuries sustained in the crash. The fifth, Zachary Judd, age 15, was airlifted to Edmonton with critical injuries. On the day Matthew Deller, Vincent Stover, Walter Borden-Wilkins, and Tanner Hildebrand were laid to rest, Zachary remained in a medically induced coma; he later regained consciousness and began a prolonged rehabilitation process. Brenden Holubowich, 21, was charged with impaired driving causing death and failure to remain at the scene (CBC News, 2011; Wittmeier, 2011).

The Nature and Prevalence of Trauma Reactions

Trauma has become part of the common lexicon of our society. Many commonplace events are referred to as traumatizing and a wide variety of reactions are referred to as traumatic stress. For social workers in mental health, it is important to differentiate between traumatic stress as a clinical diagnosis and other types of stress or crisis reactions; this helps to predict the course of the distress and to plan the interventions most likely to result in positive outcomes. In this chapter we are conceptualizing trauma response to fall on a continuum that includes crisis, acute stress, post-traumatic stress, complex post-traumatic stress, and personality disturbance, as shown in Figure 6.1. Personality disturbances are covered in extensive detail in Chapter 12.

Individual response to distressing events is highly varied. Several studies have demonstrated that rates of trauma exposure over the life course are between 60 and 80 per cent, but rates of experiencing **post-traumatic stress disorder (PTSD)** are only 5 to 8 per cent (Ozer and Weiss, 2004; Kessler et al., 2005; Koenen, 2006; Bonanno et al., 2007). A nationally representative study of almost 3,000 Canadians revealed that 75.9 per cent reported lifetime exposure to one or more traumatic events such as sexual assault or a life-threatening motor vehicle accident. Despite high rates of exposure, the lifetime prevalence rate for post-traumatic stress was 9.2 per cent (5.3 per cent in men and 12.8 per cent in women) the current (point) prevalence rate was 2.4 per cent (Van Ameringen et al., 2008). Populations exposed to particular traumatizing events provide another interesting viewpoint on the development of post-traumatic stress. For instance, 9.4 per cent of Israelis who had been directly exposed to a terrorist attack (Bleich et al., 2003) and 18 per cent of a sample of US Latinos who had experienced political violence in their homeland (Eisenman et al., 2003) met the criteria for PTSD. On the basis of these findings Shalev (2002)

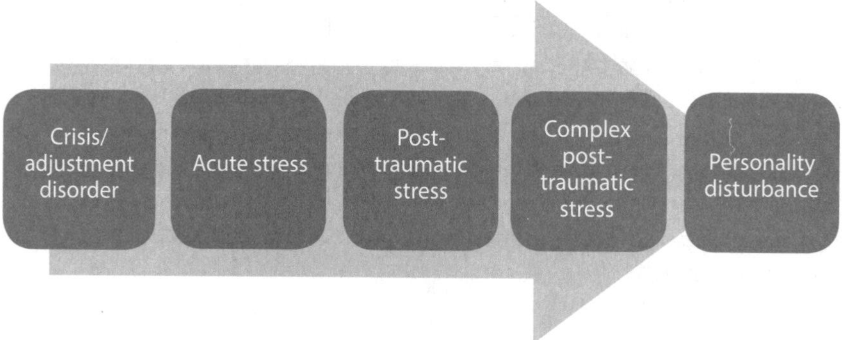

Figure 6.1 Continuum of Trauma Reactions

suggested that "traumatic events" are more appropriately called "potentially traumatizing events." Several factors combine to help us understand the intensity, nature, and duration of symptoms and responses to stressful or traumatic events; these include the nature of traumatic exposure, the recovery environment, individual history and coping, and individual peritraumatic response.

Nature of Trauma Exposure

The most intuitive contributor to post-traumatic reactions is the nature of the trauma exposure. One aspect of this is the *dosage* or *level* of trauma exposure, which in several studies has been found to correlate with the development of post-traumatic distress (Resnick et al., 1992; Mollica et al., 1998; Marmar et al., 1999; Brewin et al., 2000). For instance, emergency responders (Bryant and Harvey, 1996) and war veterans (Orcutt et al., 2002), who experienced higher levels of exposure, report higher rates of PTSD. Similarly, Mollica and colleagues (1998) found a relationship between the degree of post-traumatic stress and the degree of violent exposure experienced by both Vietnamese and Cambodian survivors of mass violence and torture. Blanchard et al. (1995) demonstrated that survivors of motor vehicle accidents had higher levels of trauma symptoms if they had greater injuries or were at greater risk of death.

Other authors argue, however, that the dose-effect model is inadequate in explaining post-traumatic stress reactions and that other event-related factors are more important in differentiating the degree of suffering a person experiences after traumatic exposure (Yehuda and McFarlane, 1995; Bowman, 1999). For instance, the degree to which an event is *intentional* rather than an act of God and is *personalized* to the individual affects the development of PTSD (Briere, 2000). High rates of PTSD in victims of sexual assault demonstrate the importance of these factors. In one study, 94 per cent of rape victims met the criteria for PTSD a week after the rape occurred, 65 per cent did at four weeks post-rape, and 47 per cent did at 12 weeks post-rape (Rothbaum et al., 1992). Another crucial event factor in trauma response is **secondary loss** experienced by victims (Brewin et al., 2000; Green et al., 2001; Hobfoll, 2001). For example, individuals who lost their homes and experienced ongoing difficulty securing housing after Hurricane Katrina, which devastated New Orleans and the surrounding Gulf coast in August 2005, were more likely to have prolonged symptoms of PTSD (McLaughlin et al., 2011).

Environmental Supports and Attitudes

Related to the nature of trauma exposure is the degree of support available to people after the traumatic event. Of the multiple factors that mediate distress secondary to traumatic exposure, higher levels of social support are consistently found to be associated with lower degrees of post-traumatic symptoms and depression (Brewin et al., 2000; Ozer et al., 2003; Regehr, 2009; Trickey et al., 2012). Other environmental influences include community resources and the community response to the event. In the case of sexual violence, community attitudes to violence and victims of sexual assault and abuse, court and police response, and the availability of counselling and other supports can have a profound impact on response and recovery (Regehr et al., 2008).

Individual Experiences and Coping

Social support and interactions with the environment are not independent of the person seeking assistance. Rather, the ability to garner support from others and cope individually stems from previous life experiences that either build or undermine **resilience** (Rutter, 1993; Bowman, 1999) and from the capacity to reach out to others in time of need. For instance, traumatic exposures in childhood may result in subsequent vulnerability to post-traumatic stress (Brewin et al., 2000; Ozer et al., 2003) through undermining of coping abilities. In research conducted with women who were raped, individuals with positive early life experiences were more able to mobilize adaptive coping mechanisms, thereby diminishing the impact of the sexual assault experience. In contrast, women with disruptive or traumatic early life experiences had negative views of themselves and others, which were reinforced by the rape and subsequently interfered with their ability to activate coping mechanisms (Regehr and Marziali, 1999; Regehr et al., 1999). These coping mechanisms contribute significantly to the development or amelioration of trauma-related symptoms (LeBlanc et al., 2008). Other individual factors include biological predeterminants and concurrent mental health problems (Yehuda, 1999, 2002; Ozer et al., 2003; Trickey et al., 2012).

It has been suggested that while vulnerabilities and resilience capacity do not predict the occurrence of acute distress, they are important in inhibiting its resolution or the amelioration of symptoms (Kardiner, 1941). Thus, while the severity of the stressor (or dosage) may be the primary determinant of acute trauma symptoms, prior life experiences and pre-existing personality factors are presumed to be primary contributors to the development of chronic trauma symptomatology (McFarlane and Yehuda, 1996).

Peritraumatic Distress Responses

Recent research has suggested that psychological appraisal of the event and psychological and biological response in the acute situation best predict the longer-term severity of post-traumatic distress. In two **meta-analyses** of predictors of PTSD, *perceived life threat* during the traumatic exposure was strongly associated with the development of PTSD (Ozer et al., 2003; Trickey et al.,

2012). Peritraumatic distress refers to the reactions to this appraisal of risk. This type of distress is linked to persistent symptoms of PTSD (Thomas et al., 2012). Psychological aspects of peritraumatic distress include fear, helplessness, and horror; physiological aspects include trembling, sweating, and tachycardia (Vaiva et al., 2003). Immediate treatment of these symptoms can lead to better outcomes in those exposed to traumatic events (Vaiva, et al., 2003).

Genetics and Biology

Yehuda et al. (2011: 67) note that "for at least two decades after the diagnosis of PTSD was established in 1980, it would have been unheard of to propose that genes might be involved in the etiology or pathogenesis of this condition." Rather, the concept of PTSD was founded on the notion of normal and expected reactions to horrifying events. Nevertheless, the repeated observation that PTSD is not an inevitable outcome of traumatic exposure, combined with studies of identical twins demonstrating higher concordance rates, has led to a burgeoning of research on biological correlates of trauma response.

There has long been an awareness that exposure to an event that elicits attributions of fear or danger results in neurophysiological changes that enhance the capability for fight or flight (van der Kolk, 1997; Yehuda, 1999). These biological responses generally return to normal levels within a period of hours. As stated above, failure to modulate the neurobiological stress response in the early stages after traumatic exposure (that is, during the period of peritraumatic distress) may contribute to the development of chronic symptoms. In individuals suffering from post-traumatic stress, several biological alterations remain, including: an exaggerated startle response that does not diminish; increased activation of the amygdala, a part of the brain involved in processing fear (Antai-Otong, 2007); abnormal secretion of **cortisol** from the adrenal glands, thus affecting the processing of fear (Yehuda, 2002; Shea et al., 2004); increased dopamine and decreased serotonin, which contribute to arousal and intrusion symptoms (Sherin and Nemeroff, 2011); and reduced size of the hippocampus, a part of the brain involved in learning and memory (Morgan et al., 2001; Lindauer et al., 2006). Sherin and Nemeroff (2011) provide an outstanding summary of the neurobiological impact of trauma, some aspects of which can be found in Table 6.1.

In summary, although many studies have supported the view that the intensity of the trauma has a bearing on the severity and chronicity of trauma symptoms, it is becoming increasingly clear that trauma exposure and distress do not have a simple cause–effect relationship. Rather, traumatic events may act as precipitants, the severity of response to which is determined by individual differences and the environment in which the affected person finds himself or herself (Regehr and Bober, 2005).

Table 6.1 Biological Correlates of Trauma Response

Neuroendocrine	
Hypothalamic-pituitary-adrenal Hypothalamic-pituitary-thyroid	• Changed cortisone levels affect fear processing • Abnormal thyroid levels increase anxiety
Neurochemical	
Catecholamines Serotonin	• Increased dopamine interferes with fear conditioning • Increased norepinephrine results in increased arousal, blood pressure, and startle reflex • Decreased 5-HT increases vigilance, startle reflex, and memory intrusion
Neuroanatomical	
Hippocampus Amygdala	• Reduced volume alters stress response through memory-processing deficits • Increased acivity promotes hypervigilance

Source: Adapted from Sherin and Nemeroff (2011: 265) © 2011 LLS.

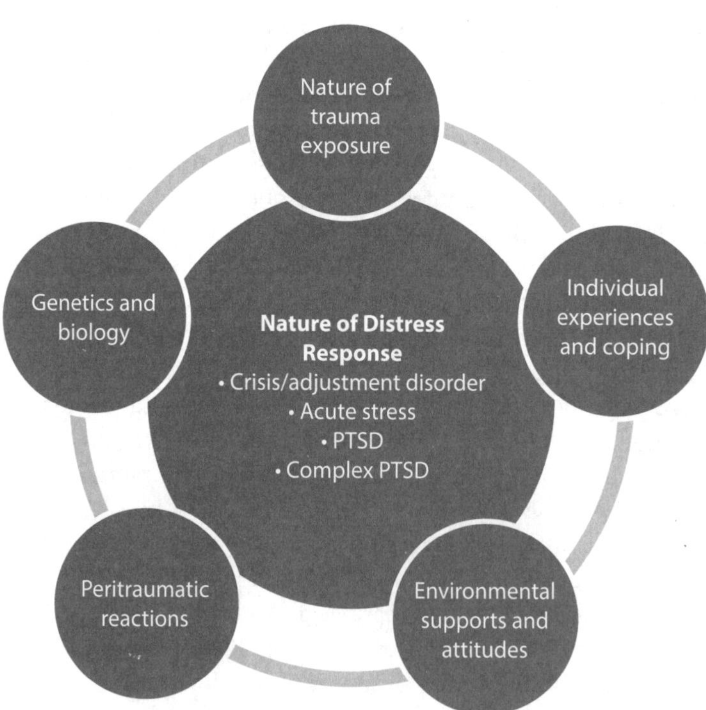

Figure 6.2 Factors Contributing to Distress Response

Types of Trauma Response

Crisis Response and Adjustment Disorder

A crisis is "a period of psychological disequilibrium, experienced as a result of a hazardous event or situation that constitutes a significant problem that cannot be remedied by using familiar coping strategies. A crisis occurs when a person faces an obstacle to important life goals that generally seems insurmountable through the use of customary habits and coping patterns" (Roberts, 2000: 7). As a result of exposure to crisis-producing events, people may feel a sense of disorganization, confusion, anxiety, shock, disbelief, or helplessness that may increase as usual coping mechanisms do not work (Regehr and Bober, 2005).

Two primary types of events can result in a crisis response: (1) situational and (2) developmental. *Situational crises* were first described and documented in 1944 with the early work of Lindemann following a 1942 fire in the Coconut Grove nightclub in Boston in which close to 500 people died. Lindemann observed and documented the reactions of 101 survivors, which included bodily (somatic) responses, preoccupation with horrifying images, feelings of guilt, anger, and functional impairments. Situational crises are now understood to span a wide range of events, including diagnosis of a life-threatening or serious illness, job loss, or divorce and separation. Caplan (1964) built on the work of Lindemann and expanded crisis theory to include the concept of *developmental crises*, which occur naturally in the course of the lifespan. Developmental crises can include the birth or adoption of a child, adolescence, marriage, and retirement. He suggested that the adaptation required by even expected events can tax an individual's coping resources and lead to crisis response. Crises are commonly viewed to have a number of characteristics, as listed in Box 6.1.

Crisis response occurs in five stages. It begins with a pre-crisis **equilibrium** phase, followed by the impact phase (when the crisis event occurs), a crisis phase, a resolution phase, and a post-crisis phase. The crisis phase has two elements: (a) confusion and disorganization during which functional level declines and the person experiences symptoms of anxiety, fear, and helplessness; and (b) trial-and-error reorganization, during which the person attempts various strategies to improve the situation and manage his/her emotional and physical responses. Some of these strategies work and others do not. During the resolution phase, the person regains control over his or her emotions and works towards a solution to the crisis situation. Finally, in the post-crisis stage the person arrives at what is the new equilibrium. This new equilibrium may be at the same level of functioning that the person had prior to the crisis. However, the crisis may have also resulted in new learning and new insights and result in a higher level of functioning, or the person may have become depleted and now be at a lower level of functioning. This variable outcome has led to the common statement that the Chinese symbol for crisis is made

Box 6.1 Characteristics of Crisis

- *Crisis events are perceived as sudden.* Although one anticipates the birth of a baby, the changes in sleeping schedules, lifestyle, and relationships within the family feel sudden and unexpected, and suddenly undermine an individual's sense of competence.
- *Crises overwhelm an individual's customary coping strategies.* The diagnosis of a chronic illness can be devastating for one individual, yet another may take it in stride and proceed to make required changes to his or her lifestyle.
- *Crises are time-limited, lasting one day to four to six weeks.* Crisis response is characterized by a heightened level of arousal and distress that produces discomfort. In the normal course of events, individuals adapt their coping strategies to match the situation and mobilize social supports to assist.
- *Crises may lead to dangerous or self-defeating or self-destructive behaviour.* In times of disequilibrium, people may experience suicidal thoughts or may express their distress by lashing out at others and undermining social support networks.
- *Response to crisis events can potentially be an opportunity for growth.* The concept of post-traumatic growth is based on the observation that adverse events can ultimately lead to positive outcomes in the individual (Tedeschi et al., 1998).

up of two symbols representing challenge and opportunity, although linguists dispute this colloquial belief.

At times, crisis responses do not resolve and the individual may continue to experience distress, which, depending on the severity, may be diagnosed as an adjustment disorder (APA, 2013: 286). Adjustment disorders are characterized by marked distress that appears to be "out of proportion to the severity or intensity of the stressor, taking into account the external context and cultural factors that might influence symptom severity and presentation." In addition, adjustment disorders may be characterized by impairment in social and/or occupational functioning.

Acute Stress and Post-Traumatic Stress

Parallels between the description of psychological trauma in classic literary texts and present-day formulations demonstrate the remarkable centrality of trauma as part of the human condition. Shay (1994) explores the parallels between the depiction of Achilles, a soldier in the Greek war against Troy, recounted in Homer's *Iliad*, and the experiences of combat veterans who had returned from the Vietnam War. In the play *Titus Andronicus*, Shakespeare describes in gruesome detail the rape and mutilation of Lavinia and the impact of the attack on those around her (Regehr and Regehr, 2012). In recognition of this enduring theme, psychiatrist Pierre Janet wrote in 1919: "All famous moralists of olden days drew attention to the ways in which certain happenings would leave indelible and distressing memories—memories to which the sufferer was continually returning, and by which he was tormented by day and by night" (quoted in van der Kolk, Weiseath, and van der Hart, 1989: 1530).

Robert Burton's *The Anatomy of Melancholy*, first published in 1621, described the impact of "perturbations" as follows: "a cruel torture of the soul, inexplicable grief, poisoned worm, consuming body and soul, and gnawing at the very heart, a perpetual executioner, perpetual night, heating worse than fire and a battle that has no end. It crucifies worse than any tyrant; no torture, no strappado, no bodily punishment is like unto it" (Burton, 1651: 162). By the late 1800s and early 1900s, the impact of traumatic exposure was described as an interaction between the psyche and physical ailments. Herbert William Page (1883: 147), in his *Injuries of the Spine and Spinal Cord, without Apparent Mechanical Lesion and Nervous Shock*, observes that "The incidents indeed of almost every railway collision are quite sufficient—even if no bodily injury is inflicted—to produce a very serious effect upon the mind, and to be the means of bringing about a state of collapse from fright, and from fright only." Around the same time, references to combat-related traumatic responses include the development of syndromes such as **irritable heart**, described by DaCosta in 1871 (Oppenheimer and Rothschild, 1918). In 1915, functional (non-physical) heart disorders resulted in 15,000 admissions to hospital of military personnel (Jones, 2006). **Shell shock** in World War I soldiers involved tremor, restricted movement, and nervous exhaustion, which they believed to be caused by the concussive or toxic effects of artillery fire, but are now believed to have been a psychological response (Jones, 2006). In addition, **neuraesthenia** was a prevalent neurological condition described as "an ensemble of phenomena which result from the non-adoptation [*sic*] of the individual to a continuous emotive cause and the struggle of the individual for this adaptation" (Mott, 1918: 127). Mott reflects that this term not only rendered mental disorder acceptable, but allowed for compensation under the UK Employer's Liability Act.

Interest in the effects of psychological trauma on individuals subsided after the end of the Great War and did not resurface again until the mid-1970s. At that time two social factors brought issues of trauma into the forefront. The first was the return of US soldiers from Vietnam whose horrifying experiences left them scarred and unable to integrate back into society. The second was the political focus of the women's movement on rape and a growing awareness of its aftermath, resulting in the concept of "rape trauma syndrome" (Burgess and Holstrum, 1974). Together, the pressures arising from the needs of these two highly divergent groups of sufferers resulted in official recognition of post-traumatic stress disorder in the third edition of the *Diagnostic and Statistical Manual* (DSM-III) in 1980.

Acute stress and *post-traumatic stress*, as defined in DSM-5 (APA, 2013), have similar etiologies and symptom patterns. The major difference is that acute stress symptoms occur between three days and one month after a traumatic event, whereas in post-traumatic stress symptoms must last for more than one month. For both acute stress and post-traumatic stress, an individual must be exposed to actual or threatened death, serious injury, or sexual violation either directly, by witnessing events as they occur to others, by learning that such an event occurred to a close friend or family member, or by repeated exposure to adverse details of traumatic events (such as by a police officer or therapist). Symptoms of both acute stress and post-traumatic stress fall into three clusters. **Intrusion symptoms** include recurrent thoughts, nightmares, and feelings as if the event were reoccurring, and intense psychological and/or physiological distress at exposure to cues that retrigger the event. **Avoidance symptoms** include efforts to avoid thoughts or stimuli that are reminiscent of the event, avoiding people and places that cause distress, an inability to recall important aspects of the event, restricted affect, and feelings of detachment. **Arousal symptoms** include difficulty falling or staying asleep, emotional outbursts, difficulty concentrating, hyper-vigilance, and exaggerated startle response. Biological correlates of these reactions include increased heart rate, skin conductance, and blood pressure (Pole, 2007). In addition, acute stress is characterized by a fourth cluster of symptoms. **Dissociative symptoms**, now referred to as "negative alterations in cognition and mood," include persistent inability to experience positive emotions, an altered sense of reality, an inability to remember important aspects of the event, markedly diminished interest, and feelings of detachment from others.

Complex Post-Traumatic Stress

Judith Lewis Herman, in her groundbreaking book *Trauma and Recovery* (1992), identified that the concept of post-traumatic stress was inadequate in describing the reactions of individuals who were survivors of prolonged and extreme trauma and abuse situations. Such situations include survivors of horrific childhood abuse, women in long-term abusive relationships, concentration camp survivors, and prisoners of war. Post-traumatic stress according to the criteria in the DSM is attributed to survivors of circumscribed traumatic events, that is, those that have a clear beginning and end. Herman argued that survivors of prolonged abuse develop characteristic personality changes that affect both their sense of identity and their ability to form and sustain interpersonal relationships. As a result, she proposed a new diagnosis, complex post-traumatic stress. Elements of complex post-traumatic stress are as follows:

- *a history of subjection to totalitarian control over a long period of time*;
- *alterations in affect regulation*, including **dysphoria**, chronic suicidal thoughts, self-injury, explosive anger, and compulsive or extremely inhibited sexuality;

- *alterations in consciousness* such as dissociative episodes, depersonalization, reliving the experience;
- *alterations in self-perception*, including shame, guilt, self-blame, and a sense of being completely different from others;
- *alterations in perceptions of the perpetrator*, such as ascribing unrealistic power to the perpetrator, idealizing the perpetrator, or rationalizing the abusive behaviour;
- *alterations in relations with others*, including isolation and withdrawal, distrust or overtrusting behaviour, and disruption in relationships;
- *alterations in systems of meaning*, such as loss of faith, hopelessness, and despair (Herman, 1992: 121).

Intersections between Grief and Trauma

What is clear from the case example describing the death of four teenagers and critical injury of a fifth at the beginning of this chapter is that grief and trauma often do not occur independently of one another. Perplexingly, however, grief and trauma have emerged as two separate theoretical models, with two divergent models of intervention, generally addressed by two different groups of professionals. Grief theory has focused on mourning and bereavement, either relating to the loss of a loved one or in anticipation of one's own imminent death. Issues considered are relationships with others and the process of detaching oneself from those lost. Recommended treatments focus on remembering, working through feelings, and attaining a new understanding of oneself in relationship to others. Trauma research and theory, as discussed above, have long considered both the psychological and physiological dimensions of terror and its aftermath. Distressing memories and physiological reactions are viewed as symptoms of a disorder. Treatment is aimed primarily at symptom management and eradicating intrusive images of the traumatic event (Regehr and Sussman, 2004).

Because virtually all humans can be expected to experience significant loss at some time in their lives, grief is viewed as a normal, albeit distressing, process. High levels of emotion are experienced, but are viewed as having a clearly defined goal, that is, helping the bereaved to abandon the commitment to the relationship to the deceased (Freud, 1957 [1917]). Movement towards resolution is conceptualized to occur in stages or phases during which individuals complete a series of mourning tasks. One of the first and most influential writers in this area was Elisabeth Kübler-Ross, who in her famous text *On Death and Dying* (1969) identified five stages of grief: denial, anger, bargaining, depression, and acceptance. Dr Kübler-Ross's conceptualization of loss arose out of her work in Switzerland with terminally ill patients who were anticipating death. It has since been expanded to apply to a wide variety

Table 6.2 Types of Trauma Response

Type	Causes	Time Frame	Reactions
Crisis If unresolved can become **Adjustment Disorder**	• Unexpected event that overwhelms coping ability	• Crisis: 4–6 weeks • Adjustment disorder: Indefinite	• Helpless/overwhelmed • Impaired decision-making • Heightened anxiety • Impaired functioning
Acute Stress	• Exposure to actual or threatened death, serious injury, or sexual violation	• 3 days to 1 month after event	• Numbing/**derealization**/depersonalization/amnesia • Intrusion: nightmares, flashbacks • Avoidance: dissociation, restricted activities • Arousal symptoms: sleeplessness, hypervigilance
Post-Traumatic Stress	• Exposure to actual or threatened death, serious injury, or sexual violation	• More than 1 month after the event • Acute <3 months • Chronic >3 months	• Intrusion: nightmares, flashbacks • Arousal symptoms: sleeplessness, hypervigilance • Negative alterations in cognitions and mood
Complext Post-Secondary Traumatic Stress	• History of prolonged, totalitarian control (POW, severe childhood abuse)	• Indefinite	• Alterations in affect regulation • Alterations in self-perception • Alterations in consciousness • Disturbed relationships • Alterations in systems of meaning
Personality Disturbance (see Chapter 12)	• Childhood abuse? • Parental neglet? • Societal structures that cannot make up for parental pathology?	• Indefinite	• Unstable self-image • Impulsivity/self-mutilation • Affective instability (intense anger) • Transient paranoid ideation

of forms of loss. Central to this stages-of-death-and-grief model, however, is the understanding that grieving and the experience of loss are highly individualized and that not everyone will pass through each stage; that the order in which people experience these stages may vary; and that people can become stuck in any one stage.

- *Denial* involves a conscious or unconscious process of refusing to accept that the loss has occurred or is about to occur.
- *Anger* is the externalization of grief. People may be angry at the lost loved one for abandoning them (if he had taken better care of his health, he would not have died). The anger can also be directed at people who might have saved the person, such as the health-care team, at the self for not doing more to help, or at random others who are not involved in the loss at all but are perceived as not fully appreciating the extent of the loss.
- *Bargaining* is typically thought to occur in the anticipation of death whereby a person bargains with God. (I will become a better person if this death does not occur.)
- *Depression* occurs when the extent of the loss is fully realized by the person.
- *Acceptance* is the time when the person is able to move forward with other life tasks despite the loss (Kübler-Ross, 1969).

Subsequent authors have suggested other sets of stages related to the grieving process; in general, however, three stages, typically lasting one to two years in total, are conceptualized. These have been summarized by Regehr and Sussman (2004):

- *Acute grief* occurs in the first six to eight weeks following death. This stage is characterized by numbness, frequently yearning for the deceased, and denial of the reality of the loss (Worden, 1991; Humphrey and Zimpfer, 1996).
- *Disorganization* is a sense of despair and functional impairment lasting several months (Schuter and Zisook, 1993).
- *Reorganization* happens when the intensity of emotion begins to subside and the bereaved individual learns to function in an environment without the deceased and to come to a new sense of the lost relationship (Bowlby, 1980; Worden, 1991).

Although grief theory and trauma theory have differing perspectives on the etiology and outcome of tragic events, clearly bereavement and trauma are not mutually exclusive. Prigerson and colleagues (1999) have proposed a diagnosis of *traumatic grief*, based on post-traumatic stress criteria. Their model has two central elements: (1) the death of a significant other and the response to this event involve a distressing, intrusive preoccupation with the deceased person (e.g., yearning, longing, or searching for the deceased); (2) marked and persistent symptoms include efforts to avoid reminders of the deceased, feelings of purposelessness and futility about the future, a sense of numbness or detachment resulting from the loss, feeling shocked, stunned, or dazed by the loss, disbelief, feeling that life is empty and unfulfilling and meaningless, and a shattered world view.

Evidence reveals that people who experience prolonged, complicated, or traumatic grief often experience concurrent mental health problems (such as depression, anxiety, and suicidal thoughts), social and occupational impairment, and stress related medical disorders (Boelen et al., 2003; Bryant, 2012). Regehr and Sussman (2004) propose a model for understanding the development of traumatic grief (Figure 6.3). One factor in this model is the *enormity*

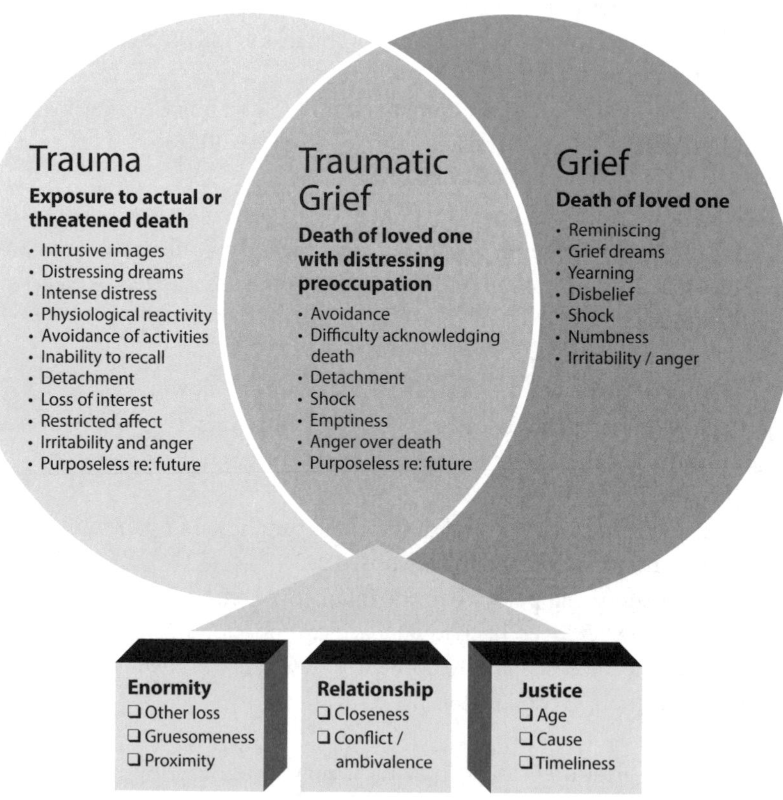

Figure 6.3 Intersections between Grief and Trauma

Source: From Regehr and Sussman (2004).

Table 6.3 Psychosocial Interventions for Trauma

Type of Trauma Response	Interventions
Crisis	*Crisis intervention* (Chapter 5) • Organize issues • Support coping • Reinforce strengths • Aid with decision-making • Assess risk
Acute Stress	*Supportive counselling* • Reinforce strengths • Support coping *Psycho-education* • Information • Normalization *Symptom management with cognitive-behavioural therapy (CBT)* • Distraction • Avoidance • Relaxation • Exercise
Post-Traumatic Stress	*Symptom management with CBT* • Relaxation • Thought-stopping • Desensitization? *Psychotherapy* • Resuming lost activity/relationships • Meaning–making • Remembering?
Complex Post-Traumatic Stress	*Symptom management with CBT* *Interpersonal therapy* (Chapter 7) • Establishing safety • Remembrance and mourning • Reconnection
Personality Disturbance	*Symptom management with CBT* *Interpersonal therapy or dialectic behaviour* therapy (Chapter 12) • Do no harm (avoid iatrogenic effects) • Reduce chaos, be clear about limits • Avoid prolonged hospitalization • Shift focus away from suicidal or self-destructive behaviour • Focus on here and now—avoid explorations and interpretations of previous life events
Traumatic Grief	*Symptom management with CBT* *Psychotherapy* • Exploring relationship issues • Problem-solving • Enhancing ability to engage in social relations

of the event, including such aspects as the degree of loss (Najarian et al., 2001; Norris et al., 2002), and the gruesomeness of the events leading to death (Stroebe et al., 2001). Violent death from accident or homicide, for instance, has been associated with bereavement that is complicated by PTSD and depression (Thompson et al., 1998; Kaltman and Bonanno, 2003). A second factor is the nature of *relationship* with the person or person(s) lost. This includes both the perceived degree of closeness and the nature of the attachment with respect to such factors as conflict and ambivalence (Shear et al., 2007). Finally, traumatic grief can be fuelled by a sense of *injustice* regarding community and legal response to the event (Rock, 1998; Armour, 2002), and whether or not the death seemed timely (that is, the age of the deceased and whether the death was expected).

Interventions

Not all people confronted with traumatic events will seek or require intervention. For instance, in one study, only 16 per cent of those who lost a family member to homicide sought treatment (Freedy et al., 1994). While it may be tempting to attribute this absence of treatment-seeking to negative causes such as denial or avoidance, it may also demonstrate that individuals have a remarkable capacity to deal with the aftermath of tragedy. Interventions following traumatic exposure or loss must be highly sensitive to the needs of clients and respectful of individual coping styles. For instance, denial and avoidance in the early stages after a horrifying or disturbing event may be highly adaptive. In this instance, avoiding emotional triggers can reduce intrusive thoughts and mediate emotional response in order to restore coping capacity and facilitate processing of painful memories (Shear, 2010). In a review conducted by Regehr and Sussman (2004) it appeared that denial was equally effective to intervention in the case of normal bereavement, suggesting that the reflex response of health-care professionals to refer people to bereavement groups after a loss may not be useful to many people. This is not to suggest that social workers cannot be helpful to individuals who encounter loss and trauma, but rather that interventions must be carefully considered.

In considering the evidentiary base of interventions for post-traumatic responses, one of the challenges in conducting research in this area is the degree to which symptoms spontaneously remit. The DSM, in fact, differentiates between acute stress and post-traumatic stress due to the fact that symptoms do tend to diminish on their own after a traumatic event, as shown by Rothbaum et al. (1992) in their study of rape victims and PTSD, discussed earlier in this chapter. Thus, while hundreds of original reports describe the effectiveness of treatments for individuals who have been exposed to traumatic events, the vast majority are not empirically based studies (Solomon and Johnson, 2002).

The natural diminishing of symptoms of PTSD requires that controlled studies be considered when discussing efficacy. While many excellent reviews and meta-analyses exist of the research related to treatment efficacy for traumatized individuals, it is generally acknowledged that only cognitive-behavioural and psychopharmacological methods have been subject to rigorous evaluation with controlled trials (Ehlers and Clark, 2003; Bisson et al., 2007). Hence, while other models are discussed in this chapter, social workers must be cautious to ensure that clients are experiencing their assistance as helpful.

In the case of crisis or in the early phases following a traumatic event or traumatic loss, crisis intervention is the most common approach because it focuses on assisting people to mobilize their strengths, make decisions, and take action to move forward (see Chapter 5). Good empirical evidence supports trauma-focused cognitive-behavioural strategies for symptom management and regaining a sense of cognitive control in the initial stages following the trauma exposure (Agorastos et al., 2011) and as symptoms persist (Bisson et al., 2007). At later stages psychotherapy, dialectic behaviour therapy (see Chapter 12), or interpersonal therapy (see Chapter 8) can also assist in managing depression and anxiety, integrating the trauma into a sense of self and enhancing the ability to relate to others.

Cognitive-Behavioural Approaches to Symptom Management in Trauma Response

A number of reviews of the effectiveness of cognitive-behavioural therapy (CBT) for post-traumatic stress conclude that CBT is effective in reducing the severity of post-traumatic stress symptoms in individuals who have experienced a wide range of traumatic events and in individuals who suffer from both acute and chronic symptoms (Rothbaum and Foa, 1996; Follette et al., 1998; Harvey et al., 2003; Bradley et al., 2005; Bisson et al., 2007). Further, CBT has been demonstrated to have superior effects over supportive treatment in the treatment of post-traumatic stress in a number of controlled studies (Regehr et al., 2012).

Cognitive-behavioural therapies come in a variety of forms. Exposure therapy is based on the notion that the common strategy of avoiding trauma-related memories and cues interferes with emotional processing of the event by reinforcing erroneous cognitions and fears. During imagining and in vivo exposure and recounting of the event, individuals are assisted to manage the resulting anxiety and allow distress to habituate. Stress inoculation training, based on social learning theory, teaches individuals to manage fear and anxiety through cognitive-behavioural techniques. Cognitive therapy assists individuals to identify trauma-related dysfunctional beliefs that influence response to stimuli and subsequent physiological and psychological distress. Some have provided evidence that exposure therapy in combination with stress inoculation training or cognitive therapy yields the most positive results (Hembree and Foa, 2003); others have provided evidence that inoculation does not necessarily enhance other cognitive methods and that, provided alone, they are equally effective (Tarrier et al., 1999; Harvey et al., 2003). It is important to note that people with personality disturbances, current life crises, and self-harm behaviours are most often screened out of participation in exposure methods. Thus, this model of treatment should be used only when a sound therapeutic alliance has been formed and a thorough assessment has been completed to ensure that clients have the capacity to manage the increased arousal that occurs during the treatment (Calhoun and Atkeson, 1991). Individuals in this type of treatment group should be assessed to have the capacity to tolerate high anxiety arousal, have no active suicidal ideation, no comorbid substance abuse, and, most importantly, no current life crises (Foy et al., 2000). If they are equally effective, CBT methods without exposure may yield a lower risk of iatrogenic effects.

Group treatment methods are less clear-cut. One form of group treatment is the single session debriefing model that has been the subject of much controversy regarding efficacy. In general, however, findings suggest that when used with professionals exposed to trauma in the context of their jobs, people find them helpful and supportive, but they do not relieve trauma symptoms and may in fact exacerbate them (Regehr, 2001; Agorastos et al., 2011). When applied to victims of trauma, however, the results are more concerning. Mayou, Ehlers, and Hobbs (2000) randomly assigned traffic accident victims to psychological debriefing or no treatment groups. At four months post-injury they reported that the psychological debriefing was ineffective, and at three years the intervention group remained significantly more symptomatic. They concluded that patients who initially had high intrusion and avoidance symptoms remained symptomatic if they received intervention but recovered if they did not receive intervention. Bisson et al. (1997) reported that burn victims who received debriefings had significantly higher rates of anxiety, depression, and PTSD 13 months following their injury than did burn victims who did not have debriefings. It has been suggested that the exposure elements of this group intervention are responsible for the iatrogenic effects in victims.

Longer-term group models using CBT have more promising results. Foy and colleagues (2000) reviewed six studies of CBT group treatment with trauma survivors (three wait-list control studies and three single-group pretest–posttest studies) and indicate that all showed positive outcomes on PTSD symptom measures. Reported effect sizes ranged from 0.33 to 1.09 with a mean of 0.68. Larger treatment effects were reported for avoidance symptoms than intrusion symptoms.

Therefore, although treatment approaches described in the literature for resolving trauma are diverse, evidence suggests that cognitive-behavioural methods are effective in symptom reduction. Several different models of CBT exist, some that focus on cognitive restructuring, some on symptom management, and some on exposure to traumatic imagery followed by anxiety management. Evidence indicates that each method can be effective; however, there is concern that exposure therapy may increase distress and increase treatment dropout in high-risk groups. Pharmacological treatment for individuals with extremely high levels of distress should also be considered.

While most models of CBT involve a structured process, some single CBT-based strategies can be of assistance to individuals who are attempting to manage symptoms of post-traumatic stress. Structured breathing exercises can be extremely helpful in assisting individuals in reducing autonomic arousal. Social workers can learn these techniques and become proficient enough to teach others through yoga classes or relaxation therapy tapes. Individuals with traumatic stress frequently awaken at night having had a nightmare. When they awaken, their heart is racing, they are sweating, and they are unable to fall back asleep. People who have this experience will then frequently lie awake for hours with recurrent thoughts of the event circling around in their minds. Social workers can discuss several options for people who experience this. One option is to get up and write down the repetitive thoughts, say them into a tape recorder, or speak to someone at a distress centre. After the person has expressed the intrusive thoughts or images, they are likely to diminish for the time being. Another option is distraction through watching TV, going for a walk (if it is safe and the person is comfortable), reading a book, or doing some low-impact activity. Once the high-anxiety symptoms are reduced and the thoughts diminished, the person is more likely to be able to return to sleep, although she or he may need to repeat the regular bedtime routine before going back to sleep. A further technique is to assist the person to identify ways to reduce arousal and the re-stimulation of traumatic response through avoidance of certain places or stimuli (for instance, violent movies). While this may not be a long-term solution, it can assist people to regain a sense of control in the immediate situation. If the fears and thoughts persist beyond the time of acute stress disorder (four weeks), then other longer-term CBT approaches may be in order.

Approaches to Traumatic Grief

Mancini, Griffin, and Bonanno (2012) recently reviewed meta-analytic studies of grief therapy for adults and children. A key conclusion of their analysis is that grief treatment is not appropriate for all people who have lost a significant person in their lives. General psychotherapy approaches have been found to be unhelpful for the majority of those suffering loss, and grief treatments can indeed lead to a deterioration of functioning in some individuals (Regehr and Sussman, 2004). Thus, grief treatments should be reserved for individuals with prolonged or complicated bereavement. CBT aimed at cognitive restructuring and symptom management appears to be effective for individuals with traumatic loss (Boelen et al., 2007); however, if the treatment includes exposure therapy, some individuals suffering from traumatic loss may experience increased distress (Shear et al., 2001).

The following is a summary of findings related to treatment approaches to traumatic grief (Regehr and Sussman, 2004).

- Not all people who have experienced traumatic loss require treatment.
- Those with unresolved relationship issues towards the deceased may benefit from relational-based therapy.
- Those with unresolved relationship issues towards others may benefit more from therapy aimed at providing immediate support and problem-solving rather than interpretation and conflict exploration.
- CBT aimed at cognitive restructuring and symptom management appears to be effective for those experiencing distressing intrusion and arousal symptoms.
- Those with traumatic loss may experience increased distress in exposure therapy.

Pharmacological Treatment for Trauma and Grief

Although psychosocial therapies are generally considered the treatment of choice, research demonstrating that traumatic exposure can affect neurotransmitters and hormones has led to the conclusion that medication may be helpful for some individuals (Cooper et al., 2005; Stein et al., 2005). Certainly, medications may be prescribed for people suffering the after-effects of both trauma and grief. As a result, social workers should be aware of medications that their clients may be taking. The social worker can discuss the impact these medications may have on the symptoms the client is experiencing and encourage the client to discuss this with her or his physician.

Antidepressants are the most studied and most used treatments for post-traumatic stress (Antai-Otong, 2007). SSRIs (see Chapters 7 and 8 for more discussion) are often used, based on findings of low serotonin metabolites (5-HIAA) in **cerebrospinal fluid** in individuals with post-traumatic stress, particularly those people who have impulsivity problems and repeated episodes of self-harm as a result of complex post-traumatic stress (Schoenfeld et al., 2004; Stein et al., 2005). Several studies have suggested that these medications alleviate intrusion, avoidance, and arousal symptoms. Older antidepressants such as the tricyclics have been shown to have positive effects especially on symptoms of panic.

Biomedical research has established that post-traumatic stress is likely also associated with increased levels of norepinephrine (noradrenaline) in certain parts of the brain that deal with the emotional pathways (Schoenfeld et al., 2004). This can contribute to experiences of anxiety associated with re-experiencing, hyper-arousal, and numbing symptoms. The benzodiazepines (e.g., Valium) are perhaps the most often used and most often requested medications in the treatment of post-traumatic stress as a result of the belief that they will decrease these symptoms of stress and anxiety. Paradoxically, little evidence supports the efficacy of these agents; they carry the risk of abuse and dependency, and have been found to interfere with psychosocial treatments (Bernardy et al., 2012). On the other hand, recent studies have established that beta-adrenergic blockers such as propranolol can help alleviate the symptoms of hyper-arousal, avoidance, and perhaps re-experiencing in both adults and children. In fact, the administration of adrenergic blockers within hours of the trauma and over the next 10 days can significantly decrease the development of post-traumatic stress as measured after one month. Prazosin, another blocker of adrenergic action (alpha-1), has been found to be helpful especially in reducing sleep disturbance and nightmares (Calohan et al., 2010).

Possible Social Work Interventions in the Case Examples

Case Example 1: Jasmine

Jasmine is suffering from symptoms of either acute stress or post-traumatic stress (depending on the duration of the symptoms). Social work interventions with someone experiencing the aftermath of this type of horrifying event vary, based on the timing of the intervention.

- In the early stages, the social worker will provide crisis intervention. This will entail assisting to deal with the immediate aftermath and any issues she may have to face, for instance, reporting to police, if this is her choice. The social worker will reinforce her strengths and coping and help her to draw upon appropriate social supports.
- In the days and weeks that follow, the social worker will explore and normalize symptoms that Jasmine is experiencing and assist her to manage her distressing symptoms (intrusion, arousal, and avoidance) through techniques that will help her feel more in control.
- If Jasmine wishes to discuss the rape, the thoughts and images that intrude upon her, or the impact she feels this has had or may continue to have on her life, the social worker will be open to this. However, if Jasmine prefers to cope by avoiding memories and discussions related to the rape, the social worker should respect this.

- If the symptoms persist for longer periods of time, the social worker can discuss treatment alternatives with Jasmine, such as exposure therapy or psychotherapy and then engage in these treatments if the social worker is qualified to do so.

Case Example 2: The Grande Prairie Football Team

The loss of a young child or a teenager frequently leads to profound grief. When this loss is compounded by other factors, such as the injustice and horror associated with the death, family members and others may experience traumatic grief.

- Immediately after a death, family members have a great number of practical matters to deal with, at a time when they are often shocked, overwhelmed, and unable to focus. Thus, social work skills in crisis intervention and relating with various organizations and agents can be an invaluable support. Families must make funeral arrangements, deal with autopsies, death certificates, insurance, and sometimes the police, at the same time as providing supports for surviving children.
- In addition to assisting with resources, managing various systems, and mobilizing social supports, social workers can provide supportive counselling and an opportunity to talk and begin to understand for family members and friends of the deceased who are experiencing more profound reactions.
- Community-based interventions are also likely necessary. Social workers in the school and community should assess which individuals may be at risk of severe reactions and provide services as necessary. In addition, community-based interventions can focus on shared events for remembrance and mourning.

Summary

While response to distressing and horrifying life events has increasingly been categorized as post-traumatic stress disorder by the public and practitioners alike, reactions to these events can take many forms, ranging from crisis response to acute stress disorder, post-traumatic stress, complex post-traumatic stress and personality disorder, and traumatic grief. The severity of the response is based on a combination of event factors, individual factors, and the nature of the recovery environment. Intervention approaches must be tailored to the specific needs of the client and that person's ability to tolerate distress. Although some methods of intervention can be highly effective for some, they can be iatrogenic to others.

Discussion Questions

1. Why can it be important to differentiate between types of traumatic response?
2. How can interventions contribute to increased distress and symptoms in people experiencing trauma?
3. What types of systemic interventions might social workers consider when working with traumatized populations and how may this help ameliorate distress and symptoms?

Suggested Readings and Websites

Herman, J. 1992. *Trauma and Recovery*. New York: Basic Books. This now classic book outlines the concept of complex post-traumatic stress disorder and the means for intervening with those who suffer from it.

Sherin, J., and C. Nemeroff. 2011. "State of the Art: Post-traumatic Stress Disorder: The Neurobiological Impact of Psychological Trauma," *Dialogues in Clinical Neuroscience* 13, 3: 263–78. This outstanding article summarizes current knowledge regarding the neurobiological aspects of trauma.

Social Workers. "Help Starts Here: Grief and Loss." At: www.helpstartshere.org/mind-and-spirit/grief-and-loss. An excellent resource for the general public regarding normal grief reactions and how social workers might help those who are bereaved.

7 Schizophrenia and Related Psychotic Illnesses

Learning Objectives

- To present multiple factors contributing to the development of schizophrenia.
- To introduce recent findings regarding the neurobiology of schizophrenia.
- To discuss symptoms and challenges associated with schizophrenia.
- To describe other forms of psychotic illness.
- To present evidence-based psychosocial interventions that promote recovery.
- To introduce the psychopharmacological interventions as a part of recovery.

Case Example

Steven is a 20-year-old university student in environmental studies. He was admitted to the psychiatric unit of the university teaching hospital suffering from symptoms of acute psychosis, including auditory hallucinations, paranoid thinking, and disordered speech.

Steven, an only child, was born at 31 weeks gestation and as a result of immature lungs remained in hospital for two months after birth. Throughout childhood he was smaller than other children and was prone to frequent chest infections. When ill he required a ventilation tent to assist with breathing. Despite these challenges Steven learned to walk and talk at a normal rate and excelled in school. However, he had difficulty making friends and was perceived to be awkward in social interactions. During his high school years he rarely socialized with others and, instead, remained focused on his studies. He was very anxious about performing well in school and managed his anxiety by over-preparing for every test or assignment. Steven's sole recreational activity was playing video games.

At age 17, Steven began to hear voices on occasion, which he believed to be angels directing him how to behave. As a member of a religious family he did not share this with others, but yet was not particularly concerned that this was abnormal. In his final year of high school, he became concerned that other students were trying to steal his work through his computer and were watching him through his video games. He became increasingly concerned about this and developed elaborate systems to stop people from spying on him. His focused attention to school work resulted in admission to university with a scholarship. He left home to attend university in a city a one-hour drive from his family home. Living in university residence during his first year created considerable anxiety for Steven and thus he attended a local mental health clinic where he was given medications to manage anxiety. He elected not to return home during the summer and rented a basement apartment near the university, telling his parents he was taking summer courses. During this time he became increasingly paranoid and the voices became more insistent—no longer helpful angels, but now the voice of the devil. By the fall of second year Steven felt out of control; he attended class but was unable to understand the work or complete any readings. One day in November, Steven began smashing video surveillance cameras and computer screens in the university library. University police brought him to hospital.

The Nature of Schizophrenia

Schizophrenia is a major mental illness that, according to the World Health Organization, affects 24 million people worldwide (WHO, 2012). The illness is characterized by two types of symptoms: *positive* psychotic symptoms include thought disorder, hallucinations, delusions, and paranoia; *negative* functioning symptoms include impairment in emotional range, energy, and enjoyment of activities. In order for a diagnosis to be made, the positive symptoms must persist for at least one month and be accompanied by severe impairment in vocational functioning, interpersonal relations, and/or self-care that persists for more than six months. Schizophrenia has a profound impact on those who suffer from it and on others who are close to them. The illness tends to affect many aspects of the individual's functioning, including their ability to relate to others and to integrate into society. Typically, the course of the illness has been viewed to be chronic and the **prognosis** relatively hopeless.

Indeed, it has been largely in response to characterizations of schizophrenia and its course that the recovery movement and the recovery model described in Chapter 1 have emerged. In support of the premises of the recovery approach and its focus on hope for the future of people with schizophrenia, recent longitudinal studies have suggested that many persons do improve or recover from the illness (Thara, 2004). Although biological factors associated with the illness significantly influence difficulties with functioning, the expectations of chronicity and social decline held by mental health professionals, the general public, and ultimately patients and their families also contribute to the challenges faced by people with this illness (Williams and Collins, 2002). As a result, social workers have critical roles to play in assisting individuals with schizophrenia and others in their lives to overcome these challenges and attain the most positive outcomes possible.

Incidence and Prevalence of Schizophrenia

Epidemiological studies of any illness frequently result in a wide variety of estimates of prevalence and incidence of illnesses. In part this is because of differences in diagnostic practices related to both the variations in the illness and the lack of standardized methods for ensuring consistency. As well, it is partly due to different sampling methods and the degree to which the population selected is truly representative of the larger society. Prevalence is defined as the number of cases per 1,000 people in the general population in a given time or over a defined time period. Meta-analyses of studies conclude that the prevalence of schizophrenia in North America is between 1.4 and 7.2 per 1,000. The incidence of schizophrenia, defined as the number of new cases in a population per 1,000 people in a given time period, is generally considered to be between 0.17 and 0.54 per annum (Picchioni and Murray, 2007). The reason why the prevalence of schizophrenia is so much higher than the incidence is that this is an illness that generally starts in early adulthood and often becomes chronic. Schizophrenia is responsible for 1.1 per cent of "total disability adjusted life years" worldwide and 2.8 per cent of the "years lived with disability" worldwide (Jablensky, 2000). People diagnosed with schizophrenia are estimated to make up about half of all patients in psychiatric hospitals and may occupy as many as one-quarter of the world's hospital beds. Nevertheless, WHO (2012) suggests that 50 per cent of people across the world who suffer from schizophrenia are not receiving treatment; 90 per cent of people with untreated schizophrenia live in developing countries. WHO pilot programs in India, Iran, Pakistan, and Tanzania are working to provide services for people with schizophrenia and their families through primary health-care systems. In 1996 the total direct cost of schizophrenia in Canada (including health-care costs, administrative costs of income assistance plans, value of lost productivity, and incarceration costs attributable to schizophrenia) was estimated to be $2.35 billion. The indirect costs of schizophrenia are estimated to account for another $2 billion yearly (Public Health Agency of Canada, 2002).

Schizophrenia is more common and has an earlier age of onset in men than women, with a ratio of 1.4 to 1. Likely due to neurodevelopmental and social differences, it is also more serious, has greater incidence of negative symptoms, and is less amenable to treatment in men (Abel et al., 2010). Regional differences have been found in the incidence and prevalence in schizophrenia.

Asian and Scandinavian countries report lower rates than other parts of the world (Goldner et al., 2002); Hutterites and certain Pacific island populations are reported to have particularly low rates (Jablensky, 2000). The prevalence of schizophrenia is higher in urban populations than in rural populations and small towns.

Factors Contributing to the Development of Schizophrenia

As with all mental health problems, the etiology of schizophrenia is far from definitively known. A variety of causes have been posited and investigated, which includes genetic predispositions and neurobiology, substance abuse, and family/environmental influences.

Social and Family Influences

The relatively high prevalence of schizophrenia in urban centres has been the subject of considerable debate and research. Earlier theories for this difference focused on geographic drift, specifically that people who do not fit into smaller homogeneous populations leave or are driven out and move to larger urban centres. Thus, these theorists suggested that rates in cities are an artifact of the illness, not the cause. Faris and Dunham (1939), for instance, in noting higher rates of people diagnosed with schizophrenia in urban areas, especially in low socio-economic groups, coined the term *social drift*. They suggested that people with schizophrenia drift down the socio-economic ladder to inner-city centres where transient and socially mobile populations exist. Hollingshead and Redlich (1954), in an early body of research that helped to delineate some social factors associated with schizophrenia, discovered that the fathers of those with schizophrenia were likely of a higher socio-economic group than the clients themselves, suggesting that the clients had "drifted" down the social scale, probably because of their illness. More recent analyses of the rural and urban incidence of schizophrenia suggest that urban environments are associated with increased social, environmental, developmental, and genetic risks for schizophrenia (Krabbendam and van Os, 2005).

In the 1950s the trend was to look for family problems as the cause of all illnesses. Schizophrenia was no different in this regard and many authors focused on problems in communication within the family and family dynamics as causes for schizophrenia. This led to the labelling of the mother as schizophrenigenic, that is, a mother who caused schizophrenia in her offspring generally by creating a **double bind** (Bateson et al., 1956; Sluzki et al., 1967). The double bind is described as a situation where a person is faced with two conflicting demands by someone who has a close and powerful relationship with the individual. The power of the double bind is that the conflicting message is not overt and the consequence of either choice is likely the withdrawal of love. Eventually, these concepts led to an entire form of therapy, strategic family therapy, which focused on changing the mother's behaviour and family interactions, thereby curing schizophrenia or at least reducing relapse (Haley, 1976). More recently, however, increased knowledge regarding the biological basis for the disease has discredited this theory as mother-blaming without justification.

Substance Use

A significant risk factor for the development of schizophrenia is early drug use. It has long been known that cocaine, **amphetamines**, and other hallucinogens may precipitate schizophrenia, especially in vulnerable individuals. There is an emerging literature on the use of cannabis and its effects on the risk of schizophrenia. Recent research suggests that at an individual level, cannabis use increases the risk of schizophrenia twofold. At the population level, it has been estimated that the elimination of cannabis use would reduce the incidence of schizophrenia by 8 per cent (Arseneault et al., 2004). Although this conclusion may not be widely accepted by laypersons who support the use of cannabis, these studies have been replicated and controlled for a number of confounding factors, including the possibility that those developing schizophrenia may use drugs to alleviate its symptoms. Drug use alone does not cause schizophrenia; rather, it interacts with genetic and other risk factors to increase the probability of schizophrenia developing. **Co-morbid** substance use also influences the course of the illness in that those who abuse substances have higher relapse rates, greater numbers of psychotic symptoms, increased violence, increased homelessness, and decreased compliance with treatment (Dixon, 1999; Levy et al., 2012).

Biological Factors

While all mental health problems have a complex set of biological, psychological, and social factors that contribute to their development and continuation, some have clearer evidence of a biological basis than others. Recent biological and neurological research has pointed to the important influence of these factors in schizophrenia. This is significant for social workers because it provides an alternative understanding of factors contributing to schizophrenia that moves away from a model that blames the illness either on families and the family environment or on personality traits or deficits in the individual. For example, some of the symptoms associated with schizophrenia can be viewed by others as laziness, lack of motivation, or obstreperousness. Providing families and individuals with information about biological contributors gives them information about potential challenges and allows them to develop a plan towards recovery.

Genetics

Genetic studies, including family studies, adoption studies, twin studies, and now more sophisticated gene-mapping, definitively demonstrate biological contributors to schizophrenia. One method for considering the contribution of genes is to compare the lifetime risk in the general population to that in first-degree relatives of people with schizophrenia. The lifetime risk for schizophrenia in the general population is just below 1 per cent; this risk is increased to 6.5 per cent in first-degree relatives of people with schizophrenia (Kendler et al., 1993). Monozygotic twins who share the same genetic structure have a concordance rate of schizophrenia of approximately 40 per cent (Cardno et al., 1999). It appears that multiple genes are involved and that each has a small but additive effect. If a person inherits several risk genes, he or she is particularly susceptible to this illness (Owens and Johnstone, 2006). The fact that the concordance rate in monozygotic twins is 40 per cent, but not 100 per cent, suggests that an interaction with the environment is necessary in even the most strongly genetically disposed individuals.

Obstetrical Complications

Another significant risk factor in the development of schizophrenia is the presence of obstetrical complications. These complications include hypoxia (being deprived of oxygen), prematurity, and low birth weight. People born in the winter months are more likely to develop schizophrenia due to the increased incidence of prenatal maternal infections (Murray and Castle, 2000). Prenatal rubella, for instance, has been found to be associated with a ten- to twentyfold increase in risk of developing schizophrenia (Brown, 2006). Early insults to the brain, particularly in the second trimester of pregnancy, influence prenatal neurodevelopment and have been linked to structural brain abnormalities in schizophrenia (Gogtay et al., 2011).

Neurobiology

Increasingly, the attention regarding the etiology and progression of schizophrenia is focused on neurobiology and neurotransmission. A **neuron** is a nerve cell that sends and receives electrical signals over long distances within the body. Communication of information between neurons is accomplished by movement of chemicals across a small gap called the synapse. These chemicals, called **neurotransmitters**, are released from one neuron at the presynaptic nerve terminal. Neurotransmitters then cross the synapse, where they may be accepted by the next neuron at a specialized site called a receptor. The action that follows activation of a receptor site may be either excitatory or inhibitory. Neurotransmitters are therefore the intracellular messengers in the body. The quantity of transmitters available may determine a given function of the brain. It is generally considered that some kind of change in the availability of neurotransmitters occurs in schizophrenia. It is not clear whether this change is a cause or a consequence of a structural brain abnormality.

Dopamine is one of the neurotransmitters identified as critical in schizophrenia. The original theory, known as the "Dopamine Hypothesis," was based on four empirical studies that supported a link between schizophrenia and dopamine activity (Owen and Simpson, 1995). The hypothesis states that the brain of a person with schizophrenia produces more dopamine than is the norm, and this increased dopamine is believed to be responsible for the symptoms of the disease. Knowledge in this field has exploded, however, and it may be that the original theory is somewhat of an oversimplification. There is much debate in the scientific community as to the exact mechanism by which altered dopamine levels contribute to schizophrenia. It is now believed that other neurotransmitters, as well as a number of other complicated compounds such as second messengers, transduction systems, and effector enzymes, all play a role.

Dopamine is secreted by only a small proportion of neurons. However, it seems to have an effect on a large number of neurons. Over the past 50 years it has been noted that drugs that increase dopamine (agonists) or decrease dopamine (antagonists) modulate psychotic symptoms. In particular, the antipsychotic medications block dopamine receptors and decrease psychotic symptoms. Amphetamine, which is a dopamine agonist and therefore increases available dopamine, can induce psychotic symptoms. **Positron emission tomography** (PET) is a nuclear medicine technique that provides a three-dimensional image of the chemical processes in the body. Studies using PET technology have generally supported the dopamine theory, demonstrating an increase in dopamine receptors and a decrease in other receptors, such as some serotonin receptors, in people who have schizophrenia.

Another way of studying the brain is by measuring brain waves using **electro encephalogram** (EEG) technology. Sophisticated EEG studies have shown differences in brain-wave activity in people with schizophrenia. This may be related to the finding that people suffering from schizophrenia have an increased rate of eye-movement abnormalities, especially affecting what is known as *smooth pursuit tracking* or the ability to follow an object with one's eyes. Kraepelin (1904), in his careful observations of a number of people with schizophrenia in the late nineteenth century, described a type of attentional abnormality. In a recent trend to look at intellectual impairment in schizophrenia, his observations have been proven remarkably accurate and it is now established that many people with schizophrenia have differences in their ability to concentrate, process information, and lay down memory. In a fascinating study, Walker and colleagues (1994) looked at home movies of people who were later diagnosed as suffering from schizophrenia and had blind raters compare these persons with controls. The raters could reliably predict those who later developed schizophrenia by minor abnormalities in their movements and socialization, suggesting support for the neurobiological model for understanding the illness.

Recent use of **magnetic resonance imaging (MRI)** scans, a magnetic imaging technique that produces a three-dimensional image of the structure of the body, has improved upon older evidence, which was based on **computerized axial tomography (CAT)** scans, a process using a computer to take pictures of the body through "slices" that can be then put together to gain an accurate picture of what is going on in the body three-dimensionally. MRI studies have demonstrated characteristic findings that may contribute to our understanding of the development of schizophrenia. In particular, there is evidence of increased ventricles or spaces in the brain of those suffering from schizophrenia. This is likely a result of a loss of tissue in the cortex of the brain, especially in certain areas such as medial temporal structures. Post-mortem studies have attempted to clarify these findings. **Gliosis** is an abnormality of brain neurons that is generally considered a sign of past inflammation caused by infection or other types of brain injury. This abnormality has been found to be common in certain types of schizophrenia, where there are other **neurodevelopmental** abnormalities. It can also be tentatively concluded from these findings that the process begins in the first or second trimester of pregnancy.

Taking all these findings together, researchers generally consider that a "neurodevelopmental model" of schizophrenia is the best model available. The theory begins with a number of genes that exert small but significant effects on making the individual vulnerable. In early development, perhaps as early in some cases as the first trimester of pregnancy, there may be an environmental insult such as an infection, an immune disorder, or a metabolic disorder, which affects the brain and causes a susceptibility that remains hidden or dormant. In addition, brain abnormalities also may remain undiscovered. Later, however, in adolescence or early adulthood, various environmental or biological factors may trigger the illness. As a result, people may develop schizophrenia, as in the case example of Steven earlier in this chapter, or may develop other similar mental health problems such as a schizophreniform disorder, which is discussed later.

Course of Illness

As noted earlier, until quite recently schizophrenia was considered fundamentally a chronic condition with progressive deterioration. The traditional view was that there are three phases of schizophrenia: it begins with an early deteriorating course that may last for 5 to 10 years; this is followed by 10 years of a middle phase where the client may be somewhat stabilized but suffers regular relapses, often requiring admission to hospital, and experiences marked impairment in social and occupational functioning; finally, the disease is described as gradually improving over the next 10 years, although with continuing functional deficits. Recent longitudinal research, however, has ameliorated this dire prognosis. Current reviews of longitudinal studies that cover the course of the illness over 5 to 30 years suggest that the outcome of the schizophrenic disorders varies and that somewhere between 21 and 57 per cent of people with this illness show improvement or recovery (Jobe and Harrow, 2005).

A number of factors are associated with more positive outcomes of the illness. The time between the first onset of psychotic symptoms and the initiation of treatment, for instance, is directly associated with the response to treatment and outcome. That is, earlier onset and a long duration of untreated psychosis in the initial stages predict a poor response. Early detection and immediate treatment is therefore critical. A number of studies have suggested that early intervention and engagement in high-risk populations even before the onset of psychotic symptoms could delay or prevent the onset of psychosis (Malla et al., 2005; Hegelstadt et al., 2012). Other factors associated with more positive outcomes include a previously well-adjusted personality, having close friends, having an acute onset versus a slow and progressive onset, abstaining from drug use, being married, and being female (Jablensky et al., 1980; Compton et al., 2005; Nordt et al., 2007). Finally, from a recovery perspective, hope and active engagement of the client in the process of treatment planning, intervention, and recovery lead to more positive outcomes.

Symptoms and Challenges

Schizophrenia is an illness that most commonly presents in early adulthood, especially in first-year university or college. It is thought that the challenges of adolescence and possibly moving away from home to university represent significant environmental stresses that may precipitate the illness in those who are predisposed. In general, the onset of the first symptoms comes as a complete surprise to family members and it is only in later interviews that the characteristic changes that may have been present as early as childhood are retrospectively confirmed. This time of onset is highly troublesome for those diagnosed and for their families. It appears to all that the young person is on his or her way, having been accepted to university with the opportunity to seek new adventures and make new friends. Parents believe that they have successfully launched their offspring and dream about the future to which their child will aspire. Contact between the parent and child becomes more limited, which is socially appropriate for this life phase, but results in the young person becoming more isolated and in parents being unable to note early changes in behaviour or mood. Often, therefore, early symptoms of the illness are not detected by others. The young person who is beginning to suffer from symptoms is uncertain what is happening. He or she begins to feel highly anxious, which is attributed to the stresses of workload. Concentration is affected, and he or she begins to have sleep disturbances, which may be either the inability to sleep or excessive sleeping. The young person begins to avoid social contact in an effort to contain symptoms. As time progresses he or she begins to have active symptoms of schizophrenia, including hallucinations and delusions. In others, the presentation is more **insidious**, evidencing a gradual change in personality. Sometimes, following an extended period of this insidious onset, the acute phase may suddenly appear, often precipitated by a stressful life event such as the breakup of a relationship, immigration, or moving away from home.

Positive or Psychotic Symptoms

Symptoms of schizophrenia are divided into "positive" and "negative" symptoms. Positive symptoms are those that are imposed on the person and include hallucinations, delusions, disorganized thinking, and disorganized behaviour. Negative symptoms are those that are taken away from the person and include flattening of affect, poverty of speech, lack of motivation, lack of interest, and social isolation. (For a full description and definitions of these symptoms, see Chapter 4.) The most common presentation of schizophrenia is the onset of auditory hallucinations, often accompanied by bizarre delusions. As discussed in Chapter 4, a hallucination is defined as a sensory perception that has the compelling sense of reality of a true perception but that occurs without external stimulation of the relevant sensory organ. The auditory hallucinations experienced by people with schizophrenia often involve voices that comment on the actions of the person or read his or her thoughts out loud. These voices are experienced as a real perception to the individual and therefore can be quite distressing. The voices are distracting, drowning out other sounds in the world, such as the voices of others. The voices are preoccupying and the client often searches for a meaning or a cause of these troubling symptoms. Sometimes clients act on directives issued by voices, occasionally resulting in violence, especially towards those close to them. This is more of a risk if the hallucination is accompanied by a delusion supporting it.

A delusion is defined as false belief based on incorrect inferences about external reality that is firmly sustained despite what almost everyone else believes and despite what constitutes incontrovertible and obvious proof or evidence to the contrary (APA, 2000). Characteristic delusions of schizophrenia may involve the belief that the client is being hypnotized or controlled by foreign influences. Another characteristic delusion in schizophrenia is the firmly held belief that someone is putting thoughts in one's head (thought insertion) or taking thoughts out of one's head (thought withdrawal) or broadcasting them out loud (thought broadcasting). Sometimes the delusions are bizarre, involving such things as aliens, space, or the CIA: for instance, the belief that a microchip has been implanted in a tooth and this serves as a monitoring and controlling device.

In clinical assessment, the form or flow of speech and thought is distinguished from the content. The content of thought may reveal bizarre delusions, as indicated above. The rate and flow of speech betrays the cognitive processing of the individual. In some clients with schizophrenia, "derailment" and "tangentiality" of thought may be observed whereby a person begins with a preliminary idea and then goes off on a tangent. Sometimes sudden ideas or words are inappropriately inserted into a sentence. Sometimes words that are idiosyncratic to the client (neologisms) are used.

Negative Symptoms and Social Implications

The so-called negative symptoms of the illness, which include lack of motivation, lack of volition or will, and a blunting of affective reactivity, are often observed in the longer-term course of the illness. Such symptoms are related to the significant impairment in social functioning that has been recognized as a cardinal problem of schizophrenia. The negative symptoms, with resultant interpersonal deficits, in addition to neurocognitive impairment, are together linked to the poor outcome of this disorder.

Williams and Collins (2002) do an outstanding job of identifying issues experienced by clients with schizophrenia through the use of a qualitative study. A central issue for clients in this study was the manner in which the illness made them feel alienated from their friends and family. In part, this stemmed from disagreements in defining the problems that the person was experiencing and subsequent disagreements on the need for assistance. This can be intensified if family members or others resort to the use of mental health legislation to force treatment. In part it stemmed from the inability to connect with others because of impairments caused by symptoms; subsequently, the reactions of others to their moods and behaviour caused clients to feel different. A second theme was the fear of being dependent throughout their lives, particularly on family members. Another was the sense that the person had lost everything that he or she once had, such as income, the ability to pursue education, a sense of competence, and previously held social roles. Finally, the social stigma associated with mental illness is acutely felt by those who suffer from schizophrenia. The view that others have of them further impedes the ability to develop and sustain social networks and social supports and leads to discrimination in a wide variety of settings.

Issues for Families

Family members also experience significant challenges in dealing with a loved one who suffers from schizophrenia. Muhlbauer (2002) uses a qualitative study to document the experiences of families who have a member with schizophrenia. She describes five phases for families (Box 7.1) and uses the imagery of a storm at sea to describe their experiences of distress. Distress experienced by family members is related to a number of issues, a central one of which relates to the increased responsibility for care and support placed on families as a consequence of reduced investment in hospital-based care (Chan, 2010). Families are thus confronted with stigma on a daily basis. Further, although the acute psychotic symptoms are without doubt upsetting for families to witness, the negative symptoms are often described as the most difficult to manage for families (Magliano et al., 2005; Perlick et al., 2006). Families often attribute these negative symptoms, such as lack of ambition or social isolation, as volitional on the part of the client. As a result, families may be highly critical of people with schizophrenia and try to push them to be more active and engaged, resulting in a cycle of blame and conflict (Chan, 2010).

Although families are significantly affected by schizophrenia across cultures, cultural differences in family-related expectations and interaction

Box 7.1 Phases of Family Response to Schizophrenia

Phase 1 Development of awareness: storm warnings	• recognition of the problem • increased concerns • escalating but ineffective efforts to obtain assistance
Phase 2 Crisis: confronting the storm	• exacerbation of prolems beyond the family's ability to control • abrupt confrontation with the mental health system—problems communicating • tremendous emotional distress
Phase 3 Cycle of instability: adrift on perilous seas	• instaility and recurrent crises • anger, grief, loss • searching for explanation and knowledge • dissatisfaction with mentall health system • stigma
Phase 4 Movement towards stability: realigning the internal compass	• finding ways to regain control • managing feelings of guilt and helplessness • changing expectations • struggling with setting limits • developing symptom–management techniques
Phase 5 Continuum of stability: mastering navigational skills	• developing workable care patterns • refining symptom management • using support systems

Source: Adapted from Muhlbauer (2002).

patterns may also have an influence (Snowdon, 2007). That is, families from some collectivist cultures are less likely to seek the support of the formal mental health system and are more likely to have the family member with schizophrenia living with them. In addition, the stigma associated with schizophrenia that is pervasive in many societies can be more salient in some cultural contexts (Gong-Guy et al., 1991; Hwang et al., 2008).

Other Related Psychotic Disorders

Several other psychotic disorders are within the schizophrenia spectrum and may often be mistaken for schizophrenia. These include delusional disorder, brief psychotic disorder, schizophreniform disorder, and schizoaffective disorder. Each contains some elements associated with schizophrenia but does not contain all the elements. It is not possible to diagnose schizophrenia definitively at the time a person first presents with symptoms because the diagnosis requires the persistence of positive symptoms for at least one month and continuous signs of the disturbance must persist for at least six months. Thus, usually people with schizophrenia may first be diagnosed as delusional or suffering from a brief psychotic episode because it is unclear whether the symptoms they are experiencing are one-time-only problems, whether they will recur later, or whether they will develop into a more serious illness such as schizophrenia or a mood disorder. A social worker's role at this point, therefore, is to educate and instill a sense of hope, but also to discuss the possibility of recurrence and make plans with the client and his or her family should symptoms recur.

The other forms of psychotic illnesses related to schizophrenia are listed below. DSM-5 lists these in a gradient from least to most severe.

- *Delusional disorder:* If delusional symptoms are confined to a single theme without other psychotic symptoms, this most likely suggests the diagnosis of a delusional disorder.
- *Brief psychotic disorder:* This is defined as the sudden onset of at least one of the previously mentioned psychotic symptoms such as delusions, hallucinations, or disorganized speech or behaviour. In many cases the symptoms appear to be precipitated by a significant life event, such as the breakup of a relationship or the loss of a job. In some cases, however, there is no apparent precipitation. The psychosis is by definition short-lived, lasting at least one day and less than one month.
- *Schizophreniform disorder:* If a person is suffering from delusions accompanied by hallucinations, the initial diagnosis is likely of a schizophreniform disorder. If the total course of the illness continues over six months, then this leads to the diagnosis of schizophrenia.

- *Schizoaffective disorder:* If the symptoms occur at the same time as a severe depression or mania and a period of delusions and hallucinations lasts for at least two weeks in the absence of these affective symptoms, then a diagnosis of schizoaffective disorder may be made. Generally speaking, it is considered that this suggests a better prognosis than a diagnosis of schizophrenia.

The Recovery Model and Schizophrenia

The development of the recovery model was precipitated largely by concerns regarding the negative beliefs about prognosis and chronicity that pervaded mental health services concerning schizophrenia—beliefs that spread to clients, families, and the general community. New treatment models led to recent research that refutes the belief that a diagnosis of schizophrenia means that there is no hope of recovery. As well, the recovery model was developed to counteract treatment decisions made by members of the interdisciplinary team without the input of the client; in this view, the role of the client and his/her family was to passively accept services rather than be active participants and decision-makers in the treatment and recovery process. The recovery model is a treatment concept where services are offered so that consumers (or clients) have primary control over decisions about their own care, building on their strengths and empowering themselves. Andresen and colleagues (2003) use a recovery model lens to define five stages of recovery from schizophrenia, as depicted in Figure 7.1.

Social workers practising within the recovery model apply the principles of hope and self-determination at all levels of practice when working with people suffering from schizophrenia. At the direct-service level, they help individuals build positive relationships with others, develop meaningful daily activities, find a sense of purpose, and seek to attain personal growth (CMHA, 2008). Specifically, social workers provide individuals and families with information

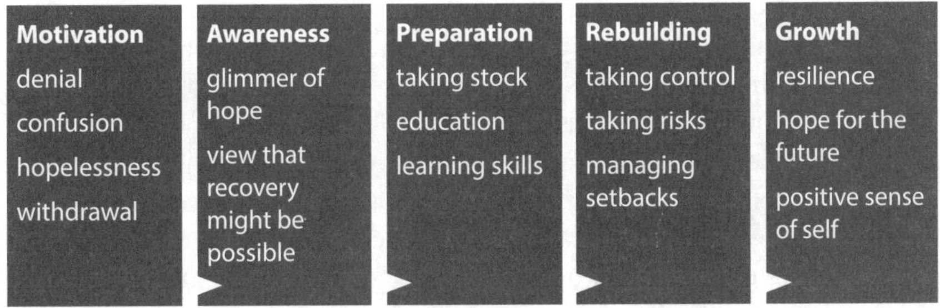

Figure 7.1 Stages of Recovery from Schizophrenia

Source: Adapted from data from Andresen et al. (2003).

about the challenges associated with the illness and factors associated with recovery. They can then help them make informed decisions about their own treatment and recovery plan (Carpenter, 2002). Social workers assist clients to identify their inherent strengths and empower them to build on their capacities. They also connect clients with helpful community resources and support their use.

At the larger-system levels, social workers advocate for funding and develop community-based programs that support recovery. These include educational programs, employment assistance programs, supportive housing programs, and opportunities for social contacts. Social workers can also support the development of client-operated services that offer mutual aid and meaningful employment. The Raging Spoon in Toronto (Raging Spoon, 2008) is such a program. The Raging Spoon was initiated by a group of psychiatric consumer/survivors who came together with the notion of developing a business. The business started out primarily as a café and has now evolved into a large catering business. Over the years, the Raging Spoon has employed approximately 150 different consumer/survivors who might otherwise, without its assistance, have been unable to find steady employment. As another example, a partnership between the Rotman School of Management at the University of Toronto and the Centre for Addiction and Mental Health provides micro loans and mentoring for clients who wish to develop their own businesses (Goar, 2012). Finally, social workers can provide public education to address issues of stigma and to promote the concept of recovery.

Psychosocial Interventions That Promote Recovery

Social work interventions generally focus on assisting the individual to deal with the psychological sequelae of the illness, helping the individual create opportunities to improve social functioning and meet life goals, and working with families to optimize their functioning and their ability to provide social supports. The first task in working with clients towards recovery is to develop a trusting working relationship or therapeutic alliance. One of the inherent difficulties in working with individuals with schizophrenia, particularly those with paranoid delusions, is that they have difficulty trusting others or connecting with them. Therefore, development of collaborative relationships between social workers and clients may take extended periods of time and require persistence and flexibility. In addition to the effects of the illness that influence goal-directedness, clients with schizophrenia may be suspicious of the motives of the social worker or other members of the interdisciplinary team and may feel alienated from the treatment plan. As a consequence, they may frequently miss appointments or fail to "follow through" on agreed goals or tasks (Coodin et al., 2004).

The recovery model offers some suggestions for developing a strong working relationship between the social worker and the client. First, the social worker must engage the client and his or her family in what Deegan (1996) refers to as the conspiracy of hope: although some aspects of the illness may seem overwhelming, there is always the opportunity for positive change and growth. Second, the social worker using the recovery model works in full partnership with clients and families to develop individualized treatment plans where consumers choose what treatment will be provided, by whom, and when (Farkas et al., 2005). Finally, the recovery model is premised on the belief that a broad set of systems must work together to create opportunities for growth that include integrated services and a broad range of community supports to optimize social, educational, vocational, income, and housing opportunities (Sowers, 2005). Social workers, in their roles as brokers of services and advocates for clients and families, must ensure that services are co-ordinated. Social workers can engender trust in clients by working towards the success of these goals.

The rest of this section focuses on three evidence-based interventions commonly used by social workers in mental health that are consistent with a recovery model: (1) assertive community treatment (ACT); (2) psychoeducational interventions with families; and (3) cognitive-behavioural treatment for schizophrenia.

Assertive Community Treatment (ACT)

For several years now there has been a shift away from traditional hospital-based care to community-based alternatives for severely mentally ill individuals. One of the most widely studied of these is assertive community treatment. The key elements of this approach include a multidisciplinary team that is on call 24 hours a day, in vivo treatment (in the person's own environment), and instruction and assistance with basic living skills (LaFave et al., 1996). This model provides flexible, individually tailored treatments, linkages among agencies serving the client, and client involvement in service planning (Bachrach, 1993). The ACT approach is based on the belief that all citizens, including those challenged by the most severe and persistent mental illnesses, have a right to live a decent and satisfying life in the community (Test, 2002). Unique aspects of the ACT model are:

- All psychosocial services are provided directly by ACT team members rather than being provided by other organizations and brokered by the team.
- The ACT team is mobile and provides services in the community where the client actually is.
- Services are highly individualized to each client's concerns.

- Staff is available 24 hours per day, 7 days per week.
- Services are not time-limited and continue as long as the client needs and wants them.
- The ACT team works to adapt the environment to the client's needs, rather than requiring the client to adapt to the rules of the program.

The ACT team assists clients to get housing, financial resources, employment, and health and dental care. The ACT team provides supportive counselling, medications, treatment for substance use, education about symptom management, crisis support, and brief hospitalization as required.

Since the initial demonstration study by Stein and Test in 1980, outcome studies of individuals with schizophrenia and other related disorders have demonstrated reduced rates of hospitalization, increased medication compliance, better quality of life, and decreased legal problems (LaFave et al., 1996). According to a review by Salyers and Tsemberis (2007), despite some changes to the model over the past 30 years, ACT teams have remained effective in their mission of reducing inpatient stay and increasing the likelihood of remaining in the community despite failed economic, social, housing, and mental health policies that have resulted in people with psychiatric disabilities being in disproportionately high numbers in shelters, emergency rooms, jails, and living on the street. Further, they have been very effective in reducing homelessness among people with chronic illness (Nelson et al., 2007).

It is also important to note that the usefulness of ACT has been established with individuals of racialized groups who suffer from severe and persistent mental illness. A study conducted by Mount Sinai Hospital and Hong Fook Mental Health Association in Toronto identified that the functional impairment of minority clients suffering from schizophrenia is compounded by stressors related to migration and acculturation, language difficulties, socio-economic disadvantage, inadequate housing, lack of access to services, and discrimination. An ACT team was therefore developed that targeted the Chinese (which represented 46 per cent of the client group), Tamil (20 per cent of the clients), Vietnamese (18 per cent of the clients), Afro-Caribbean (13 per cent of the clients), and other communities. At the one-year follow-up, significant reductions were found in hospitalization rates and severity of symptoms (Yang et al., 2005).

Psychoeducational Family Interventions

A second area of psychosocial treatment is aimed at members of the social support system of the person with schizophrenia. As noted earlier, family members and others close to the client experience a wide range of emotions and frustrations as a result of being confronted with the symptoms of the illness, the course of recovery, and a mental health system that all too often does not meet expectations. The theoretical basis for this model of intervention is that families can provide a good buffer for the negative impact of schizophrenia, and consequently those individuals with strong social supports tend to see more positive outcomes. Yet, families are frequently managing highly distressing and disruptive behaviour in the ill person with little support or training, and this can result in a range of stress-related reactions (Chen and Lukens, 2011). Further, families are struggling to provide care in a legal environment where access to information about their loved one's condition is limited by privacy legislation (Chan and O'Brien, 2011).

The most common approach to assisting others in the client's life is to provide psychoeducational individual and group interventions. These are aimed at educating families about aspects of the illness, teaching family members communication and problem-solving skills to deal with specific psychotic symptoms, and providing support and individual treatment for family members as required (Neill, 1994). Support groups, in particular, have been found to help family members overcome experiences of stigma, reduce feelings of isolation and burden, understand and accept the disease, and enhance problem-solving abilities in such divergent cultures as Croatia (Gruber et al., 2006), China (Chien et al., 2006), Sweden (Berglund et al., 2003), and the United Kingdom (Kuipers, 2006).

Although all these resources are important for family members dealing with a person with schizophrenia, an additional issue is the potential for physical risk should the individual become delusional about a family member. Thus, family members must also be taught to identify paranoid delusions, to take delusions seriously, and to develop a safety plan for themselves.

Cognitive-Behavioural Treatment

Contrary to earlier views, new research suggests that various modes of psychotherapy may be helpful in the treatment of schizophrenia and other psychotic disorders. Cognitive-behavioural treatment (CBT) is one model that has been more recently applied to schizophrenia. As discussed in more detail in Chapter 8, CBT is based on the premise that as a result of life experiences, individuals develop a series of complex cognitive structures that affect the processing of information about self and others. Called self-schemas, these cognitive structures are attempts by the individual to organize and summarize his or her own motivations, feelings, and behaviour as well as the motivations, feelings, and behaviour of others. Self-schemas govern how interpersonal information is attended to and perceived, which affects are experienced, and which memories are evoked (Horowitz, 1991). Self-schemas are also likely to be self-confirming in that judgements of others affect interpersonal responses. For instance, if an individual believes others will reject him, he will approach the interaction with anger and hostility, thereby increasing the chance of rejection by others.

This theory has been applied to the area of paranoid thinking. Kinderman and Bentall (1996) have suggested that paranoid individuals have discrepancies between their self-perceptions and how they believe their parents perceive them. In Kinderman and Bentall's model, which is substantiated by an emerging body of research, persecutory beliefs are seen as a product of cognitive processes that attribute meaning to events and interpersonal encounters in an attempt to maintain a positive view of self. For instance, the individual may believe "I am not a failure; other people maliciously stop me from succeeding."

In CBT, a client is taught to examine and then change the attributional processes that lead to emotional upset stemming from his or her delusions. Chadwick and Trower (1996) suggest a three-stage model of intervention. First, the therapist introduces the cognitive model and challenges the negative self-evaluative belief. Following this, the therapist teaches the client to challenge the negative self-evaluation. Third, the client is taught to rationally challenge the delusion. In an elegant experimental design, Chadwick and Trower demonstrate that delusions can be significantly ameliorated by cognitive intervention. Contrary to prevailing theories that the patient's self-esteem would be destroyed by the challenge to the delusions—because the delusion is seen to bolster self-esteem—self-esteem and depression scores seemed to improve during the therapy. These authors caution that specific delusions require specific treatment and this model, although illustrative, cannot be used for all types of delusions.

CBT, combined with medication, has been found to be effective in reducing psychotic symptoms, preventing relapses, increasing adherence to treatment, and increasing social adjustment in people with schizophrenia (Hogarty, 1997; Dickerson, 2000; Bradshaw, 2003). Of particular interest is that CBT was found in one study to be effective in 50 per cent of medication-resistant psychotic patients (Kuipers et al., 1997). The authors concluded that CBT may well specifically target delusional thinking. From a recovery perspective, cognitive therapy is based on a partnership between the client and the therapist and on working together to empower clients to control self-defeating beliefs and behaviours. Unfortunately, while there has been some initial hope that CBT may prevent the transition to psychosis for those in prodromal stages, a recent multi-site randomized controlled trial (RCT) has not supported this contention (Morrison et al., 2012).

Pharmacological Interventions as Part of Recovery

The biological basis of schizophrenia means that in almost all cases, medication is a primary form of intervention, augmented by psychosocial approaches. The goals of medication are to control acute symptoms of psychosis and, to a lesser degree, to reduce the negative symptoms in order to allow the client the opportunity to achieve life goals without constantly fighting the symptoms of the illness. The growing body of research has demonstrated that early intervention and treatment, resulting in early engagement and lesser time untreated, can result in better psychosocial and psychological outcomes at 2, 5, and 10 years (Hegelstadt et al., 2012). Some programs have even attempted to intervene in high-risk individuals, prior to the onset of psychotic symptoms, with encouraging results, although it is unclear whether the risk and cost of this produce demonstrably better outcomes at this stage (Malla and Pelosi, 2010).

The advent of antipsychotic or **neuroleptic** medications in the 1950s heralded a marked change to the course of schizophrenia, dramatically and significantly improving the outcome. Whereas early medications were very broad in their span of influence, affecting many parts of the brain and resulting in many side effects, newer medications have benefited from neurological research and are more targeted. Clients in general report increased symptom control and decreased side effects related to the newer medications than those they were prescribed years earlier. Nevertheless, side effects continue to be problematic. In addition, clients frequently experience the medication as an abdication of personal control, that is, complying with the demands of others and relying on pharmacology to control emotions and behaviour (Cohen, 2002). Further, anyone who has tried to comply with a prescription for antibiotics is well aware that adherence to long-term medication regimes is very difficult, particularly for someone suffering from cognitive symptoms.

As indicated in Chapter 1, an aspect of the recovery model is the realization that medications are one tool among many used in the recovery process; people can move from *taking* medications to *using* them as part of their recovery process. Therefore, social workers need to be aware of both the benefits and the downsides to assist clients in making decisions about taking medication and to support them in maintaining a medication regime.

Acute Phase

In the acute phase of schizophrenia, the goal of medication is to facilitate a reduction in active psychotic symptoms and ensure that the client is not a danger to others or at risk of serious physical impairment to her- or himself. In most cases, clients will be required to consent to medication in this phase; in certain circumstances where a client is not competent to consent, medication can be administered without consent (see Chapter 3).

Antipsychotic drugs are divided broadly into two classes, but individual drugs in each class vary considerably (Bezchlibnyk-Butler and Jeffries, 2005). The easiest terms to use in this classification are: (1) the conventional antipsychotics (see Table 7.1); and (2) the second-generation antipsychotics (see Table 7.2).

Table 7.1 Conventional Antipsychotic Medication

Generic name	Trade name	Daily dosage	Pros	Cons
Chlorpromazine	Largactil	75–100 mg	The standard conventional treatment	Risk of extrapyramidal side effects or EPS (i.e., movement disorders such as tardive dyskinesia, tremors, dystonia, Parkinsonism, etc.)
Haloperidol	Haldol	2–100 mg	High potency	Drowsiness, weight gain
Trifluoperazine	Stelazine	5–40 mg	High potency	Drowsiness, weight gain
Perphenazine	Trilafon	12–65 mg	Medium potency	Drowsiness, weight gain
Pimozide	Orap	2–20 mg	May be specific for delusional disorders	Drowsness, weight gain
Loxapine	Loxepac	60–100 mg	In between the first and second generations	Moderate side effect profile
Fluphenazine decanoate	Modecate	12.5–100 mg every 2–3 weeks	Injection every 2–4 weeks	Risk of EPS, drowsiness, weight gain
Flupenthixol decanoate	Fluanxol	20–80 mg	Injections every 2–4 weeks	Risk of EPS, less drowsiness, less weight gain

The conventional antipsychotics are sometimes referred to as neuroleptics. They were first found to have antipsychotic activities in the 1950s, and a number of different drugs have been added to this class since then. The mode of action is likely related to the ability to block dopamine D2 receptors. It should be noted that it takes a few days or weeks to achieve this effect.

One of the major problems of these agents is that dopamine receptors are also found in a pathway in the brain called the **nigrostriatal pathway**, which is related to neuromuscular control of a number of parts of the body (see Figure 9.1). Inadvertent effects on this brain pathway therefore often cause troublesome side effects known as extrapyramidal side effects (EPS), which means that these bundles of neurons run outside of (extra) the pyramidal system in the brain. These side effects include acute **dystonia**, which occurs within hours or days of treatment in about 10 per cent of clients, most particularly young men. Characteristically, people with dystonia have muscle spasms, experienced as cramps in the muscles of the neck, tongue, eyes, or sometimes arms. These

Table 7.2 Second-Generation Antipsychotic Medication

Generic name	Trade name	Daily dosage	Pros	Cons
Risperidone	Risperdal	1–10 mg	Low EPS, available as long-acting injection	Sexual side effects, weight gain, drowsiness, increased salivation
Clozapine	Clozaril	300–900 mg	Most effective agent ↓ aggression	Weight gain, seizures. agranulocytosis, drooling
Quetiapine	Seroquel	25–100 mg	↓ Anxiety, depression, well liked by clients	Weight gain (moderate), drowsiness
Olanzapine	Zyprexa (Zydis)	5–20 mg	↓ Anxiety, depression, well liked by clients	Weight gain
Aripiprazole	Abilify	10–30 mg	Less weight gain, less EPS/TD, especially good for anxiety	
Ziprasidone	Zeldox	20–160 mg	Less weight gain, less EPS/TD	Not for those with heart problems
Paliperidone	Invega	3–12 mg	Similar to Risperidone but does not interact with other drugs that go through the liver	Sexual side effects
Asenapine	Saphris	10–20 mm	Less weight gain	New to Canada

cramps are very uncomfortable, distressing, and sometimes frightening. A slightly longer-term effect is referred to as pseudo-Parkinsonism. The client presents with symptoms that mimic Parkinson's disease, including a shuffling gait, drooling, tremors, and blank facial expression. Most at risk are women over the age of 40.

Another troubling side effect is called **akathisia**. This is a subjective feeling of muscular agitation frequently accompanied by pacing. It is often distressing for the individual, who sometimes becomes angry and even violent as a result of the symptoms. A number of drugs have been used to treat these troubling side effects. There is no consensus in the field about whether these drugs should be given routinely to prevent side effects or only after the person develops the side effects. The most common anti-side effect medication is **benztropine** (Cogentin), which may be given by injection in acute circumstances or orally for longer-term use. Unfortunately, the medications developed to counteract side effects have significant side effects themselves, which include dry mouth, blurred vision, constipation, and sexual dysfunction.

Perhaps the most serious side effect of the conventional antipsychotics is **tardive dyskinesia**. This is a disorder of movement that may occur after chronic treatment with medications. The client presents with various repetitive non-goal-directed movements often involving the mouth and tongue, as well as grimacing. There are also odd movements of the fingers, toes, and limbs. Sometimes they can be so severe as to affect walking, breathing, eating, and talking. This disorder occurs in 20 per cent of clients treated with these medications for more than one year; thereafter, there may be another increase of up to 5 per cent each year. Clients receiving treatment for a long period of time should be continually monitored for the disorder. Tardive dyskinesia tends to be chronic but may spontaneously improve in some clients. Recently, the outlook has improved because second-generation antipsychotics appear to rarely lead to and even to suppress the disorder. There is no doubt that the second-generation antipsychotics are associated with a much lower risk of this serious and troublesome disorder.

Neuroleptic malignant syndrome (NMS) is another major side effect of neuroleptic medication. It is uncommon but may lead to death. If this syndrome develops it is a medical emergency and the client should be hospitalized. The features include hyperthermia, muscular rigidity, and an increase in pulse and blood pressure. A blood test of a particular enzyme called creatinine phosphokinase (CPK) can help diagnose the condition. The second-generation antipsychotics (see Table 7.2) are characterized by the fact that they show a lesser propensity to cause extrapyramidal or neuromuscular side effects. They have a higher ratio of serotonin (5-HT_{2A}) compared with dopamine (D2) blockade. This is referred to as the 5HT/DA ratio. Generally, they are more efficacious in treating psychotic symptoms (Leucht et al., 2009). It has also been suggested that they improve cognitive function that subsequently improves prognosis, and that they may improve negative symptoms, which are important in social and occupational functioning. Second generation antipsychotics, and to a certain extent the conventional antipsychotics, also may have antidepressant, **anxiolytic** (anti-anxiety), and anti-aggressive actions. Clozapine (Clozaril) has been clearly proven to be the most effective antipsychotic and probably the most effective in treating negative symptoms. However, it has a number of troubling side effects. In particular, it causes agranulocytosis in 1 to 2 per cent of treated patients. In this condition, the person does not have white blood cells to resist infections and this can therefore result in death. Therefore, the client needs to have a white blood cell count every week for the first six months of treatment when this side effect is the most common. The use of this drug requires a commitment from the client and the treatment team.

A lot of attention has been drawn to one troublesome aspect of treatment with antipsychotics: the development of **dysmetabolic syndrome** (Consensus Panel, 2004). This is characterized by weight gain, accompanied by elevated cholesterol, lipids, and triglycerides, as well as by insulin resistance that may lead to diabetes. Diabetes has been linked with schizophrenia for nearly 100 years. Research has also noted the link between both conventional antipsychotics and with second generation antipsychotics and diabetes. For this reason, clients should be reminded about diet and exercise and encouraged to follow a healthy lifestyle. The choice of medication should be determined by the risk of diabetes in each client.

Recovery Phase

The goals of treatment in this phase are to minimize the likelihood of relapse and rehabilitate the client into the community. At this stage medication should be reduced to the lowest effective dose to prevent relapse. Clearly, in reviewing the effects and side effects of medication in the preceding section, clients will need to take into account many factors in their decision to remain on medication for a longer period of time. A significant body of research demonstrates that relapse can be decreased from 72 to 23 per cent by remaining on antipsychotic medication. However, this requires a long-term commitment to medication that may be difficult for many clients to consider. For instance, if the client has had two or more acute episodes it is likely that he or she will need maintenance at the lowest effective dose for at least three years and perhaps a lifetime. Some clients who are committed to taking medication but do not wish to do so on a daily basis may consider changing to a long-acting injectable form of medication (see Table 7.2).

Those who remain on medication for a longer period of time should be encouraged to monitor for weight gain and the possibility of diabetes. Clients taking clozapine may need blood tests on a regular basis. The individual should be encouraged to go for regular assessments for neurological side effects such as tardive dyskinesia. Contingency plans should be made with the person and his/her family for early intervention in case there is an exacerbation of the illness. The goal would be to take action before an acute episode requiring hospitalization occurred.

Possible Social Work Interventions in the Case Example

Steven and his family are entering a new life phase that is probably overshadowed by questions and concerns about what his psychotic illness may mean for the future. The role of the social worker is critical in their recovery at this stage.

- At the individual level, the social worker will develop a relationship with Steven and explore his understanding of his experiences, his reaction to a possible diagnosis, his thoughts about medication, life goals prior to his first symptoms, and his current goals. The social worker can work with Steven to develop a treatment and recovery plan that fits with his goals and strengths.

- Similarly, the social worker can meet with Steven's family members to discuss their concerns, answer questions about the illness, and discuss possible treatment options. Family members may need assistance setting realistic expectations. For instance, if Steven is living at home, what are the expectations for his behaviour and/or activities and are these reasonable? On the other hand, Steven's parents should be made aware of opportunities for recovery and growth and factors that can support this outcome.
- As a member of the interdisciplinary team, the social worker can inform the team of aspects of Steven's social environment that may affect his treatment and prognosis. The social worker can also assist Steven by expressing his choices for future treatment.
- At the community level, the social worker can refer and advocate for Steven to gain access to resources (such as disability insurance) and services (such as employment or housing programs).If Steven elects to return to his university program, the social worker can work with the school to ensure that adequate accommodations are made.
- The social worker may also identify that services in their particular community do not meet some of the needs for young people with serious mental illnesses and work to develop new programs for this population.

Summary

Schizophrenia is perhaps one of the most feared mental disorders in part due to its historical reputation as being chronic and untreatable, and in part due to the profound effect that it can have on individuals suffering from the illness and on their families. As indicated in the case example and throughout this chapter, symptoms can be frightening to those with the illness and their loved ones alike. People feel out of control and unable to manage the presentation and course of the illness. Nevertheless, advancing research and treatment methods show great promise and social workers have key roles to play assisting both clients and families to better understand the illness and to discover means for working towards the best possible outcomes. One of the most positive interventions that a social worker can provide is to instill a sense of hope and confidence that this disease can be managed and that improvement and recovery are possible.

Discussion Questions

1. How may instituting a recovery model change the way in which current mental health treatment programs operate?
2. What impact may social work as a profession have on reducing stigma related to serious mental illness?
3. How may social workers best help families living with schizophrenia?
4. What approaches could a social worker take to develop a collaborative working relationship with a person suffering from schizophrenia?

Suggested Readings and Websites

"Schizophrenia: A Recovery" (14 September 2011). At: www.youtube.com/watch?v=oZud_Q40Vd8&feature=related. This video on YouTube has been produced and uploaded by Johnjusthuman, a young man who describes his journey through illness to recovery.

Social Workers. "Help Starts Here. Schizophrenia: How Social Workers Help." At: www.helpstartshere.org/mind-and-spirit/schizophrenia/about-schizophrenia.html. An easily understandable description of schizophrenia, its impact, and psychosocial treatment models.

8 Depression and Mania

Learning Objectives

- To identify factors contributing to depression and mania.
- To present symptoms and challenges associated with depression and mania.
- To identify varying types of mood disturbance.
- To present evidence-based psychosocial interventions that promote recovery.
- To introduce the psychopharmacological and other biological interventions as a possible part of recovery.

Case Example 1

Bodan is a 58-year-old family lawyer who states that he has suffered from depressed mood since he was a teenager. His father was a strict school principal who believed in corporal punishment, and at the age of 16 Bodan ran away from home, having little contact with his parents since that time. Bodan is quiet, reserved, and has few interests outside of his job. He indicates that he can remember only a few times when he was happy. Last Christmas Bodan's wife left him and his 18-year-old son ran away from home, refusing to contact him. His family doctor feels that he cannot offer sufficient assistance and has referred Bodan to a social worker for assistance.

Case Example 2

Everton is a 32-year-old parking enforcement officer. He recently told his supervisor at work that he was thinking of killing himself and was admitted to an inpatient psychiatric unit. Everton reports that prior to admission to hospital he woke up at four a.m. every morning and could not get back to sleep. For the past month, he states that he felt so tired he could barely make it to work, and on the days that he attended he could not concentrate on his administrative duties. Further, he did not have the will or energy to play in his regular cricket game or attend his son's soccer game. He worries that he is a terrible father and will be unable to provide a positive role model for his son.

Case Example 3

Aruna is a 28-year-old costume designer who has been separated from her husband for 18 months. Her six-year-old daughter spends half the week at Aruna's home and half at the home of her father. One year ago she was prescribed antidepressant medication by her family doctor to treat symptoms of a major depression. Over the last couple of months people at work have noticed that she sometimes makes statements that seem odd and out of context, and is uncharacteristically irritable. Her mother has been concerned that she has had very little contact with her parents of late. Although she has not had any relationships since her marital separation, she recently had dates with two men she met on the Internet and had unprotected sex with both of them. She began to have trouble sleeping and started to drink two or three glasses of wine each night to help her sleep. Last evening she had to go to a warehouse to pick up some costumes for a film shoot and was involved in a motor vehicle accident on a busy highway. The police officer at the accident noted her to be highly labile, alternately praying, crying, and laughing, and running back and forth across the highway in a dangerous manner. He brought her to hospital for assessment.

The Nature of Depression and Mania

Perhaps more than any other symptoms in mental health, disturbances in mood are familiar to us all in one form or another. Mood disturbances span all age groups and all cultures, and extend as far back as recorded history. Hippocrates first described melancholia (now known as depression) as being related to secretion of black bile because of the influence of the planet Saturn. Early English texts, such as Burton's (1621) *The Anatomy of Melancholy*, contributed to European concepts of depression (Akiskal, 2004). In 1904, Kraepelin described manic-depressive illness, which he distinguished from both schizophrenia and depression. He believed that manic-depressive illness was hereditary and was caused by altered physiological functioning as opposed to situational depression, which was caused by a particular event or misfortune (Ingram et al., 1999). This is remarkably similar to current understanding.

Mood disturbances, in particular depressed mood, on the surface are easily understood by everyone. However, in reality the spectrum of mood disorders is much more complex. The term *depression* is used widely by the general public and colloquially encompasses a range of experiences from transient low mood that sometimes accompanies distressing events, to chronic low-level symptoms known as persistent depressive disorder (formerly called dysthymia), as demonstrated in the case of Bodan, to major depressive disorder, such as in the case of Everton. In addition, the spectrum of mood disturbances includes mania, which alternates with depression in bipolar disorder, as demonstrated by the case of Aruna. Mental health researchers and writers have attempted to distinguish these different types of experience. Although there are many ways to conceptualize mood disturbances, the *Diagnostic and Statistical Manual* (DSM-5) (APA, 2013) suggests the following typologies:

- *Major depressive disorder:* the presence of one or more major depressive episodes involving symptoms over a two-week period that represent a change from previous functioning and where there has never been a manic or hypomanic episode. This category is separated into a single episode and recurrent episodes of major depression. Further, clinicians must judge the current severity of the depression from mild to severe and whether or not there are psychotic features.
- *Persistent depressive disorder:* a depressed mood that is not as severe as a major depressive episode but extends over a period of at least two years.
- *Bipolar I disorder:* the presence of one or more manic episodes usually accompanied by major depressive episodes. Mania can be described as excitement manifested by physical or mental hyperactivity, disorganized behaviour, and elevation of mood.
- *Bipolar II disorder:* characterized by major depressive episodes punctuated by at least one hypomanic episode. **Hypomania** is a less severe form of mania that does not cause significant distress or impair one's work, family, or social life.
- *Cyclothymia:* a disorder in which there is a period of at least two years with numerous periods of depressed mood alternating with periods of hypomanic symptoms, but no major episodes of either depression or mania.

Incidence and Prevalence

Canadian studies looking at lifetime incidence of major depression have found that 7.9 to 8.6 per cent of adults over 18 years of age and living in the community met the criteria for a diagnosis of major depression at some time in their lives, and between 3 and 6 per cent of adults will experience dysthymia during their lifetime (Public Health Agency of Canada, 2002). Young people are at particularly high-risk for depression. Eighteen per cent of a random sample of adolescents had experienced at least one episode of depression (Fergusson et al., 2007), while 30.6 per cent of students at one university in the United

States reported moderate depression and an additional 23.2 per cent reported moderately severe or severe depression (Garlow et al., 2008). The lifetime prevalence of bipolar disorder in Canada is 2.2 per cent, which is consistent with studies from other parts of the world that show a lifetime prevalence of approximately 2.4 to 2.8 per cent (Rihmer and Angst, 2005; Eaton et al., 2007). Despite the lower rates of bipolar disorder, the emotional, social, and financial costs to the individual are high, as are the costs to society. A recent study determined the annual economic cost of bipolar disorder in the United States to be $151 billion (Dilsaver, 2011).

Epidemiological studies suggest that incidence rates of depression and bipolar disorder are relatively consistent throughout the world, although there is a tendency for Western nations to have higher rates than nations in East Asia. This is believed to be due to cultural/environmental differences, including psychosocial stresses, consumption of alcohol and drugs, and perhaps family cohesion. Within the United States there are mixed findings related to racial differences in incidence rates for depression, with most large studies showing higher rates among Hispanics than within black and Asian groups and among those of European descent, although other research suggests that the highest rates are among caucasians (Lara-Cinisomo and Griffin, 2007). There is a greater prevalence of mood disturbances in urban areas than in rural areas (Rihmer and Angst, 2005; Romans et al., 2011). Although the causes of regional differences are not entirely clear, they may be related to stresses in the environment, community cohesion, and availability of social supports (Romans et al., 2011), or, as was postulated in Chapter 7 on schizophrenia, social drift. Women are consistently found to have higher rates of depression than men, whereas bipolar disorder occurs in approximately equal rates among men and women (Eaton et al., 2007; Fergusson et al., 2007). The onset of depression and mania is often associated with adverse life events or substance use. Of particular note is the period immediately following childbirth, which is a time of high risk for the onset of both depression and bipolar disorder.

Factors Contributing to Disturbances in Mood

As with other mental health problems, disturbances of mood occur as a result of a complex mix of social/environmental and biological factors. At times, the causation may appear to be primarily related to social/environmental events, perhaps in cases of adjustment disorder with depressed mood. At other times, biological factors may be predominant, such as in bipolar disorder. In most situations, however, the social/environmental and biological factors are intertwined. For instance, seasonal changes can have an influence on mood, yet some individuals are more susceptible than others.

Social and environmental factors

Social Stressors

Depression is highly influenced by the social determinants of health described in Chapter 2. One of these determinants is healthy child development. There is strong support in the research that adverse childhood experiences such as emotional, physical, and sexual abuse predispose the person to later depression. Research has demonstrated that parental mental illness, parental substance abuse, and loss of a mother in childhood are predictors of later depression (Phillips et al., 2005). Other social determinants of health include social support, social environments, and employment and educational environments. Life challenges, particularly those involving loss, such as interpersonal loss, job loss, or a marital separation, may precipitate depression in vulnerable individuals, but notably, these challenges do not affect all individuals in this way (Ingram et al., 1999). Being unemployed, being of lower socio-economic status, and living alone are risk factors for depression (Fergusson et al., 2007). Lara-Cinisomo and Griffin (2007) demonstrated that in the United States, white, single mothers with no education were particularly at risk of depression, especially if they had only adolescent children at home. The authors of this study suggested that this particular group of women had fewer protective factors, including larger extended families that could provide social support. A much earlier study also demonstrated risk more generally in women who were home with children. Brown and Harris (1978) demonstrated that women with three young children at home had increased rates of depression when compared with the general population. Thus, the social/environmental contributors to depression in particular are well documented and important for the consideration of social workers.

Seasonality

Seasonal influences on mood have been well established in the research literature. Epidemiological studies demonstrate that about 90 per cent of people report some seasonal influence on mood, social activity, appetite, weight gain, or energy level. About one-third of those reporting these alterations indicate that they experience seasonal changes as problematic (Oyane et al., 2007), with rates of depression increasing during the months of November to March. It is unclear whether a seasonal pattern is more common in depression or bipolar disorder; however, within bipolar disorder, seasonal variations appear to be more common in bipolar II (depression alternating with hypomania) than bipolar I (depression alternating with mania) (APA, 2000). The seasonal pattern of mood disorders was initially described and named "seasonal affective disorder" by Rosenthal and colleagues in 1984. Subsequently, Kasper and colleagues (1989) identified symptoms that occurred at a lower level and termed this "sub-syndromal seasonal affective disorder."

The seasonal pattern of mood disturbance is so well established that it has been included as an episode specifier in DSM-5. The incidence of a seasonal pattern varies with latitude and is associated with greater fluctuations in hours of daylight in northern latitudes. Other factors include cloudiness, air pollution, and shade from buildings (Danilenko and Levitan, 2012). Women have a higher rate of seasonal patterns related to mood, and younger people appear to be at higher risk of winter depression than older people (APA, 2000).

Substance Abuse

Abuse of drugs and alcohol as well as a variety of medications may contribute to both depression and mania. Shaffer et al. (2006), for instance, noted an increase in the probability of depression of 2.04 in their observational work with substance abusers. A multi-site Canadian study revealed that 49.3 per cent of 679 opiate users met the cutoff for major depressive disorder (Wild et al., 2005). Estimates of the co-occurrence of alcoholism and depression are less specific and range from 15 to 67 per cent (McDowell and Clodfelter, 2001). Among people with bipolar disorder, rates of alcohol abuse range from 21.4 to 54.5 per cent, depending on the age of the sample (Oswald et al., 2007).

Biological Factors

Genetics

Studies that investigate the incidence of mental health problems within families have demonstrated an increased risk of major depression and bipolar disorder in relatives of those suffering from mood disturbances. For instance, offspring of parents with bipolar disorder have a 13.4 times higher risk of developing a bipolar spectrum disorder than the general population when adjusting for factors such as socio-economic status and living with one or both biological parents (Birmaher et al., 2009). Twin studies further support the heritability of bipolar illness by comparing the rate of an illness in monozygotic twins (who have identical genes) to the rates in dizygotic twins (who have only a proportion of their genes in common). In the case of depression and bipolar disorder, monozygotic twins demonstrate a 60 to 90 per cent concordance (Kelsoe, 2005). The comparable concordance rate in dizygotic twins is 12 to 35 per cent. While this indicates a significant genetic component to the development of the disease, it should be noted that there is not 100 per cent concordance even in monozygotic twins, suggesting that environmental and developmental factors also make a significant contribution.

A more sophisticated way of looking at the influence of genetics on the development of any mental health problem is by attempting to isolate specific genes. One possibility is that the transmission is through an **autosomal dominant** gene. That is, in a chromosomal pair, one gene contains the illness and one gene does not, resulting in a 50 per cent chance of passing on the illness.

A second possibility is that there are multiple genes that all exert an effect, suggesting a multi-factor effect. A number of studies have used the very sophisticated methods of genome-wide scans in families that have at least one member with bipolar disorder (Detera-Wadleigh et al., 2007; Nwulia et al., 2007; Vonk et al., 2007). These studies support the hypothesis that a number of genes contribute to an inherited vulnerability to a bipolar disorder. Although it has no practical value as yet, this could be helpful information for the early detection of vulnerabilities to mood disturbances and thus lead to preventative interventions that focus on social and environmental influences in higher-risk individuals.

Neurobiology

As in the case of schizophrenia discussed in Chapter 7, neurotransmitters have been a focus of research related to depression and bipolar disorder. There is considerable evidence that drugs that decrease the monoamine neurotransmitters (specifically noradrenaline, serotonin, and dopamine) tend to cause depression and those that increase the monoamines tend to cause manic-like states. Magnetic resonance imaging has allowed researchers to visually identify these processes. Specifically, MRIs have demonstrated that there is a decrease in the activity of monoamine neurotransmitters in people suffering from depression, and this remits when they are treated with antidepressant medications (Schaefer et al., 2006). Similarly, there is an increase in the activity of the monoamine neurotransmitters, particularly in the **orbitofrontal** cortex, in people with mania (Stahl, 2008) (see Figure 9.1). Position emission tomography (PET) studies have identified abnormalities in anterior and frontal brain structures in individuals with mood disorders, particularly those areas related to the regulation of emotion (Fitzgerald et al., 2006; Hajek et al., 2007). These studies are complemented by neuropsychological testing that has demonstrated disturbances in cognitive functioning and performance in bipolar sufferers (Mur et al., 2007). Some studies have suggested that obstetrical complications may have neurological implications that are subsequently related to depression and bipolar disorder. Although this view has been widely accepted, a recent systematic review has questioned the strength of the evidence (Scott et al., 2006).

Hormones

Hormones appear to have a significant impact on both mania and depression. For instance, a significant body of research has found increased concentrations of cortisol (known as the stress hormone) and cortisol releasing factor (CRH) in the cerebrospinal fluid, saliva, and blood of depressed people (Belmaker and Agam, 2008). This finding supports the association between depression and increased stress in the environment. Thyroid hormones are also implicated in depression. **Hypothyroidism**, or low levels of thyroid hormone (thyroxin), can cause a depressive-like syndrome and is also sometimes found in depression. On the other hand, hyperthyroidism, or high levels of thyroxin, can cause manic-like symptoms.

Combining Social/Environmental and Biological Factors

Consistent with the multiple influences model of assessment described in Figure 4.1, the development of mood disturbances does seem to be a complex interaction between biological vulnerabilities, social/environmental stressors, and personality (including coping styles). A person may inherit a biological vulnerability to either depression or bipolar disorder. Adverse childhood experiences, including neglect and abuse, may increase vulnerabilities. Environmental factors such as poverty, unemployment, or unsafe living conditions create stress and may tax coping skills. If substance abuse is used as a coping mechanism, the risk of mood disturbances increases dramatically. Finally, negative life events, particularly if there are multiple such events, especially including job loss, bereavement, and marital separation, can act as precipitants to depression or mania.

Post-Partum Depression

Post-partum depression is perhaps the best example of the interaction between biological and social factors in the development of depression. Although depression can affect any person at any time, the post-partum period represents a time of particular risk. During the first two weeks after the birth of a child, between 50 and 80 per cent of women experience some degree of depressed mood, often referred to as the "baby blues" (Abrams and Curran, 2007). This is relatively short-lived, lasting three to five days, and is characterized by crying, emotional mood swings, and feelings of anxiety and being overwhelmed. In approximately 10 to13 per cent of women these blues develop into non-psychotic post-partum depression, although rates among low-income urban women can be as high as 26 per cent (Bledsoe and Grote, 2006). Most of these cases go undetected by health-care providers and many go unidentified by the mothers themselves. However, post-partum depression has long-lasting harmful effects on infant and child well-being. In addition, depression occurring during pregnancy, which is reported in 13.5 per cent of women, is linked to dysregulation of hypothalamic-pituitary-adrenal functioning in the fetus, low birth weight, and prematurity. Post-partum psychosis, which is generally considered a major depressive episode with psychotic features or bipolar affective disorder, affects less than 1 per cent of women who give birth.

Risk factors for the development of post-partum depression are: (1) problems with spouse or partner; (2) other stressful negative life events, such as adverse housing conditions; (3) low levels of social support; (4) previous personal psychopathology; and (5) family history of bipolar disorder (Grote and Bledsoe, 2007). Hormonal shifts immediately post-partum, including estrogen, progesterone, and cortisol, are likely also implicated.

Course and Symptoms of Depression and Mania

As we have noted throughout this chapter, mood disturbances cover a range of specific mental health problems, each with its own set of symptoms, course, and challenges. For the sake of simplicity, these can be divided into the depression (unipolar) spectrum of disturbances and bipolar spectrum disturbances.

Depressive Spectrum Disturbances

Depressive spectrum disturbances are outlined in Table 8.1. Everyone can recall a distressing situation related to relationships, career, or other important aspects of life in response to which a wave of depressive affect was experienced. Other individuals may have more persistent symptoms of depressed mood, tearfulness, and hopelessness that are reactive to a specific situation and result in significantly compromised social, occupational, or other functioning.

Table 8.1 Depressive Spectrum Disturbance

Type	Time Frame	Symptoms
Persistent depressive disorder	Occurs more days than than not for at least two years, no more than 2 months without symptoms	• Poor appetitie • Insomnia • Low energy or fatigue • Low self-esteem • Poor concentration • Feelings of hopelessness • No major depression
Major depression • can be single major depressive episode or recurrent • can be experienced in varying levels of severity • in severe cases may include psychotic features	At least five symptoms occurring for at least two two weeks	• Depressed mood for most of the day, nearly every day • Markedly diminished interest in all activities • Significant weight loss or decrease in appetite • Insomnia or hypersomnia • Psychomotor retardation or agitation • Fatigue or loss of energy nearly every day • Feelings of worthlessness • Diminished ability to concentrate • Recurrent thoughts of death

Such an experience represents a severe form of crisis response (described in Chapter 6) and could be classified as *adjustment disorder with depressed mood*. While in the past this type of disturbance was found in DSM under mood disorders, it has now been moved to the section on Trauma and Adjustment Disorders in DSM-5 (APA, 2013).

A more severe form of depression takes the guise of *melancholia*, a two-thousand-year-old term that many people believe is the core symptom of a *major depressive disorder*. The most significant characteristic is a distinct quality of mood, often described as a "fog" or a feeling of "being smothered," or as Winston Churchill described it, the "black dog." The person experiences pervasive hopelessness and an inability to see life beyond this fog. As a result, suicidal thoughts are common and suicide risk is high. Some serious depressive conditions are accompanied by the presence of psychotic features, characterized by the presence of delusions and, more rarely, hallucinations. Usually these are described as mood-congruent, that is, abnormal beliefs or perceptions related to a depressed mood; but occasionally they are mood-incongruent and include delusions of guilt, delusions of being deserving of punishment, and somatic delusions.

Another type of depressive spectrum disorder is *persistent depressive disorder*. It is characterized by mild depression, for more days than not, over a period of at least two years. Individuals have a number of additional symptoms such as appetite and sleep disturbance, low self-esteem, and hopelessness, suggesting that this is a chronic low-grade version of major depression. In this situation, the person feels generally sad and unmotivated for long periods of time. As in the case of Bodan above, such characteristics can have profound effects on personal relationships and achievement of life goals.

Bipolar Spectrum Disturbances

Bipolar mood disturbances include the presence of mania, hypomania, or mania with psychotic features in addition to periods of depression (see Table 8.2). Mania is perhaps the most characteristic of psychiatric disorders and is often easily diagnosed by a characteristic elevated or irritable mood, grandiosity, increased talkativeness, and lack of inhibition. If an individual experiences one or more manic episodes, usually accompanied by major depressive episodes, then the diagnosis of bipolar I disorder is made. Bipolar II is more difficult to diagnose. It is often seen in an individual who suffered from recurrent major depressive episodes and only on careful history taking and observation is at least one hypomanic episode noted, leading to the diagnosis. A more moderate form of this disorder is **cyclothymia**. Cyclothymia is a chronic, fluctuating mood disturbance that involves numerous periods of depressive symptoms (which do not meet the criteria for major depressive episode) and hypomanic symptoms (which do not meet the criteria for mania).

Table 8.2 Bipolar Spectrum Disturbances

Type	Time Frame	Manic Phase Symptoms
Cyclothymia	At least two years of periods of numerous hypomanic symptoms and periods of numerous depressive symptoms; no more than two months wthout symptoms	• Elevated, expansive, or irritable mood • Inflated self-esteem • Decreased need for sleep • More talkative • Racing thoughts • Distractability • Increased activity • Excessive involvement in pleasurable activities
Bipolar I disorder	The occurrence of one or more manic episode (lasting at least one week), often alternating with major depressive episodes	• Abnormally and persistently elevated, expansive, or irritable mood • Inflated self-esteem and gradiosity • Decreased need for sleep (less than three hours) • Racing thoughts • Distractability • Increased activity • Excessive involvement in pleasurable activities • Marked impairment in functioning • Psychotic features
Bipolar II dlsorder	One or more major depressive episodes accompanied by at least one hypomanic episode	See cyclothymia above

Mania generally begins with elevated mood and increased energy. People entering a manic phase feel wonderful. They are happy, productive, more creative; their need for sleep is diminished; their self-esteem is raised; and their sexual interest is elevated. This phase may explain the high incidence of reported bipolar disorder in famous creative people throughout history—Charles Dickens, Ernest Hemingway, Abby Hoffman, Edgar Allan Poe, Virginia Wolfe, and Vincent van Gogh. In Canada, Margaret Trudeau, wife of former Prime Minister Pierre Trudeau and mother of the leader of the Liberal Party, Justin Trudeau, has publicly stated that she has been diagnosed with bipolar disorder. Unfortunately for people suffering from bipolar disorder, the initial stage of **euphoria** does not last and sufferers move into a manic stage.

Mania is the Greek word for madness. It is derived from *mainomai*, which means "to rage" or "be furious". In a manic phase people experience euphoria and indiscriminate enthusiasm. Their self-esteem is significantly elevated and often includes grandiose delusions about their power or even about who they are. For instance, people may believe that they are the monarch or a deity. People in this phase do not sleep and often engage in excessive sexual activity with multiple partners. Their thoughts race, their speech is pressured, and their activity becomes increasingly erratic. It is not uncommon, as a result of the confidence and enthusiasm experienced in this state, that a person enters into business deals that later collapse, or spends all the money he or she has been saving for years. Family members frequently can identify early warning signs that a person is entering a manic phase. However, as a result of the wonderful way the affected person feels, he or she is unlikely to agree to mental health treatment. Commonly, only when the mania gets out of control do hospitalization and treatment occur. It is estimated that 75 per cent of individuals with bipolar disorder will relapse within five years of a manic episode. The risk of suicide is 15 times higher in people with bipolar disorder than in the general population (Rouget and Aubry, 2007).

The Recovery Model and Mood Disturbances

The recovery model has important relevance for individuals suffering from depression and bipolar illness due to the intersection of biological and social/environmental factors. Although a person may have a biological predisposition to develop a mood disturbance in response to stress, by managing the contributing social and environmental factors, episodes of depression or mania can be avoided and the effects of the illness can be mitigated.

Supported self-management (SSM) is a model that is gaining increased attention in working with clients suffering from mood disorders (Lurie, 2012). This model requires a strong collaborative relationship between the client and social worker for the purposes of developing a plan for treatment and recovery. It is premised on the notion that depression and bipolar disorders are chronic, long-term illnesses that require a sustained approach. Thus, the collaborative relationship is likely to continue for a prolonged period of time, with breaks and changes along the way. There will be times when the client with depression appears to lack motivation or insight. At these times the social worker will need to draw on knowledge of the strengths and abilities that the client demonstrates when well and use this information to empower the person and engender hope for the future. Similarly, as a client with bipolar disorder enters a new episode of mania, a strong collaborative alliance can help him or her make decisions in his/her best interest for the long term.

Supported self-management has three main elements (Blisker et al., 2012):

1. A self-management guide that uses **psychoeducation** approaches to inform the client about the nature of the illness and his or her skills for coping. Ongoing education regarding practices to promote stabilization, reduce stress, and avoid situations that may contribute to depression and mania is important. There are many available sources for self-management, including books and interactive websites. One such free site is MoodGym, described further at the end of this chapter.
2. Cognitive-behavioural therapy, including behavioural activation, cognitive structuring, and problem-solving.
3. Coaching clients in the use of the self-management guide.

A further role for social workers is assisting clients to make fully informed decisions about the course of treatment that best meets their needs. Treatment approaches for depression include psychosocial intervention alone, psychosocial intervention plus pharmacotherapy, or, in the case of severe depressive episodes, the adjunctive use of antipsychotic medication and possibly electroconvulsive therapy (ECT). The choice of treatment is matched to the needs of the client at a particular point in time, increasing in intensity as the severity of the episode increases. This process has been referred to as the "stepped-care approach" (Blisker, Goldner & Anderson, 2012). In general, psychosocial approaches alone are recommended in the initial stages or for more mild forms of depression. Here the focus is on the client understanding the intrapsychic, social, and/or environmental issues that affect mood and then working to change these factors. Clients with more severe forms of depression may want to consider medication as a means of lifting mood and providing the energy and ability to deal with psychosocial issues.

Suicide risk is a particularly important issue in the treatment of depression. As suicide risk fluctuates during the illness, frequent suicide risk assessment evaluations should be conducted. Indeed, suicide risk frequently increases during the initial stages of treatment. The exact causes for this are unclear but may be related to the fact that the client has a little more energy in the early stages of treatment than when during severe depression, and this energy may mobilize a suicidal attempt. Biological factors also may precipitate suicidal ideation and attempts in those who have just started antidepressant medications.

Special issues exist from a psychosocial perspective in assisting clients with bipolar disorder. The most important initial factor is to ensure the safety of the client and others, during the periods of both depression and mania. Unsafe sexual encounters, overspending, and grandiose thinking during periods of mania may compromise the client's lifestyle and relationships. Erratic driving and speeding and other lapses in judgement may threaten safety. In a very few cases, the person may become dangerous to others, as a person with mania may become irritable and angry when thwarted in his or her goals. Community-based interventions should include sufficient supports and a contingency plan for emergencies, including the possibility of admission to hospital when there is an acute episode. Clients who suffer from severe episodes should be encouraged to engage in pre-planning while they are stable, examining various treatment approaches that can be used during acute periods and preparing an advanced directive regarding their wishes should they be incapable of consent at some point.

Psychosocial Interventions That Promote Recovery

Psychosocial approaches frequently involve identifying and addressing interpersonal, social, and environmental stressors that may be contributing to the mood disturbance. Specific approaches such as cognitive-behavioural therapy, interpersonal therapy, and psychoeducation have been demonstrated to be effective in aiding the recovery process in mood disturbances.

Psychoeducational Approaches

Psychoeducational approaches are well established with respect to mood disorders, given high rates of relapse among people with bipolar disorder and the influence of psychosocial factors for precipitants in relapse. Psychoeducation provides information on the disorder, its symptoms, and treatment, and the social and family consequences of this mental health problem. It assists clients to recognize **prodromal**, that is, early and non-specific, symptoms of relapse and assists clients to understand the nature of medication and reasons for compliance. The "Canadian Network for Mood and Anxiety Treatments Guidelines for Management of Patients with Bipolar Disorder" recommends psychoeducation as a first-line treatment approach in combination with medication (Yatham et al., 2009). Considerable evidence demonstrates that psychoeducation as an addition to medication significantly reduces the risk of relapse (Rouget and Aubry, 2007; Yatham et al., 2009).

Cognitive-Behavioural Therapy

Cognitive-behavioural therapy (CBT) has become one of the most commonly used models of treatment for social work practitioners and our colleagues in other mental health disciplines. Social workers for some time have reported the use of this methodology with a wide range of client groups, including individuals with personality disturbances (Fisher, 1995; Heller and Northcut, 1996); people suffering from major mental illnesses (Albert, 1994; Jensen, 1994); and chronic pain sufferers (Subramanian, 1991). The techniques of CBT are frequently used with individuals or in group therapy but equally they can be applied to couples or families.

Cognitive-behavioural therapy incorporates cognitive, behavioural, and social learning theory components, to explain functioning as a product of reciprocal interactions between personal and environmental variables. Thus, the applicability of CBT to social work practice is immediately apparent. First, the focus on the individual/environmental interactions is highly consistent with social work theory. That is, individual responses shape the environment and the environment shapes the individual. Second, the emphasis on a collaborative relationship between the therapist and the client is consistent with social work values. In this model, the social worker and the client jointly identify goals for change, work together to understand cognitive structures that perpetuate maladaptive behaviours and emotional responses, and develop a joint strategy for altering both cognitions and behaviour. In addition, the clarity and brevity of this model make it appealing in view of the current push for cost-effective treatment modalities (Regehr, 2000). Finally, unlike many models of treatment, cognitive-behavioural treatment has been extensively researched, resulting in clear evidence of its efficacy in the treatment of depression (Bocking et al., 2005; Coelho et al., 2007; Fournier et al., 2008) and bipolar disorder through controlled trials and systematic reviews (Jones, 2004; Williams et al., 2008; Gregory, 2010). Despite its effectiveness in the acute stages of illness, however, one meta-analysis revealed that approximately half of those individuals who respond to cognitive therapy will relapse within two years if they do not receive some continued treatment (Vittengl et al., 2007).

Beck's (1967) original work in cognitive therapy began with observations of people suffering from depressive illnesses. From these observations, Beck described a triad of depressive cognitions: (1) the self as inadequate; (2) the environment as not reinforcing; and (3) the future as devoid of hope. Clients holding negative cognitions are less likely to engage in behaviours that discount the beliefs. For instance, if one believes one is not intelligent and that others will not offer assistance, one is less likely to enrol in higher education, thereby eliminating the possibility of success in that sphere. Further, if one believes that the future holds no promise, the effort required to attempt new behaviours appears useless. These behavioural responses to the negative beliefs reinforce feelings of worthlessness and intensify depressive feelings. The central tenets of cognitive therapy can thus be summarized as follows:

1. Individuals acquire beliefs or cognitive maps of the world from previous experiences. These beliefs become filters through which all information about subsequent interactions must pass.
2. Beliefs or assumptions that individuals hold about themselves, others, or the world in general may accurately reflect their own skills and abilities and the environment in which they live. At times, however, these beliefs become distorted reflections of reality. Cognitive distortions can then

lead to persistent intrusive thoughts of such things as low self-worth and negative views of others (see Box 8.1).

3. Cognitions influence how someone feels about himself or herself or a situation and how the individual will approach it. The manner in which a person deals with any situation affects the outcome and thereby confirms or modifies existing cognitive structures. As an example, a person who believes he or she will fail a driving test may approach the situation with significant anxiety that impedes performance. Similarly, a person who believes that she or he will be abandoned in interpersonal relationships may approach a new relationship with hostility or overly clinging behaviour, thereby pushing a new partner away.

In CBT, individuals are taught to identify, evaluate, and challenge negative assumptions. These negative beliefs are then reframed in a positive or neutral light. Concurrently, individuals are encouraged to modify their behavioural responses in order to maximize the possibility of positive outcomes. These positive outcomes will modify cognitions and influence affect. A more recent adaptation of CBT, mindfulness-based cognitive therapy (MBCT), involves combining cognitive strategies with meditation (Segal et al., 2002). MBCT teaches people skills that allow them to become more aware of thoughts without judgement, viewing negative thoughts as passing events, not fact. It is suggested that limiting cognitive evaluation and rather experiencing negative thoughts as momentary experiences reduces automatic negative self-evaluation and enhances tolerance for negative emotions (Farb et al., 2012). This model has been subject to rigorous testing with good results of efficacy in both bipolar disorder (Williams et al., 2008; Yatham et al., 2009) and depression (Coelho et al., 2007). Meta-analyses have also demonstrated good effects in post-partum depression (Bledsoe and Grote, 2006) and with university students suffering from anxiety and depression (Regehr et al., 2013).

Interpersonal Therapy

Interpersonal therapy (IPT) is a treatment approach with well-established efficacy that was originally designed for use with people suffering from

Box 8.1 Some Examples of Cognitive Distortions

Catastrophic thinking: Seeing small problems as always the beginning of a disaster.
Filtering: Attending only to negative information and ignoring positives.
Overgeneralization: Seeing one setback as a never-ending pattern of defeat.
Polarization: Viewing others as all good or all bad.

Source: Adapted from Beck et al. (1979).

depression, but which has more recently been modified for use with bipolar disorder (Elkin et al., 1989; Jones, 2004; de Mello et al., 2005). The goals of IPT are to alleviate symptoms of mood disturbance by improving interpersonal functioning and working through problems related to loss, change, isolation, or conflict in relationships that are associated with the onset or perpetuation of depressive symptoms. Therapeutic strategies include clarification of feelings, expectations, and social roles, education, and the development of social competence through problem-solving, role-playing, and communication analysis (Ravitz et al., 2008). Interpersonal therapy is a short-term treatment, typically less than 16 sessions. Its goals are rapid symptom reduction and improved social adjustment. IPT emphasizes the ways in which a person's current relationships and social context cause or maintain symptoms rather than exploring the deep-seated sources of the symptoms.

The theoretical basis of IPT is attachment theory, which focuses on early interpersonal relationships in the development of adult interpersonal interactions. In people with depressive symptoms, improved interpersonal relationships can serve to increase social support and decrease negative experiences and cognitions. This can be particularly true in people with early life histories of abuse and neglect that contribute to later-life depressed mood (Talbot and Gamble, 2007). For this group, IPT can address issues of chronic shame, social withdrawal, and attachment avoidance. In people with bipolar disorder, improved relations with others help to modulate social rhythms, in part through increased openness to feedback from supportive others, when a manic episode is on the horizon (Jones, 2004). IPT does not presume that psychopathology arises exclusively from problems within an interpersonal realm. It does emphasize, however, that these problems occur within an interpersonal context that is often interdependent with the illness process. IPT has demonstrated effectiveness in patients with depression, bipolar disorder, and post-partum depression (Bledsoe and Grote, 2006; Yatham et al., 2009).

Pharmacological and Medical Interventions as Part of Recovery in Depression

Although psychosocial interventions are effective in assisting with many aspects of depression and bipolar disorder, medication and other medical interventions are also frequently used, particularly for severe episodes but also to assist clients in maintaining mood stability. Clients and social workers should be knowledgeable about these various types of treatments to fully engage in discussions and decisions about treatment and recovery planning. Client decisions about treatment should be based on multiple sources of information regarding the benefits and drawbacks of each form of treatment.

Medication

Pharmacological interventions are frequently adjunctive to psychosocial interventions in the treatment of depression but may sometimes be used alone. The efficacy of interventions is important for both practitioners and clients to consider. One excellent source of evaluative data is *The Cochrane Library*, which publishes reviews of the literature that appraise, select, and synthesize high-quality research evidence in a particular domain (see Chapter 1 regarding evidenced-based practice). A wide variety of research studies summarized by Cochrane Reviews support the notion that antidepressant medications are effective in the treatment of depression (Furukawa et al., 2003; Lima et al., 2005; Deshauer et al., 2008). However, in a highly publicized article, Turner et al. (2008) argue that clinicians may be misled by the research on antidepressants because only positive trials of antidepressants are published and that negative trials submitted to the Food and Drug Administration are not published. Blier (2008), by contrast, suggests that the approach of Turner and colleagues is part of a trend that teaches the public to fear antidepressant medication when the major thrust in educating the public should be directed towards fearing depression and its stigma. He argues that antidepressants do work and the risk-benefit ratio of using antidepressants is in favour of their use. In the end, however, each client needs to make this judgement for him/herself.

One of the most important points about the use of pharmacotherapy is that these medications should be used in adequate doses for an adequate period of time before switching to another one. Many of these medications have to be started at lower doses in order to let the patient adapt to the side effects. It is therefore necessary to build up the dose of medication for a period of time. This can be frustrating for someone who wants quick relief for discomfort. However, changing medications too rapidly can be harmful and lead to a longer delay in achieving the right medication in the right dose. Clients on medication should be monitored; after four to eight weeks the situation should be reassessed to determine if there has been an adequate response to medication. If the client is clearly not responding to a given antidepressant despite the fact that he or she is taking the medication as prescribed and the medication has been given at a therapeutic dose for a reasonable length of time, then consideration should be given to switching to a different class of antidepressant.

There are three main eras in the development and use of antidepressants: (1) the monoamine oxidase inhibitors and the tricyclics; (2) the selective serotonin reuptake inhibitors; and (3) the serotonin norepinephrine reuptake inhibitors. The original antidepressants, the monoamine oxidase inhibitors (MAOIs), like many other medications, were discovered serendipitously. Iproniazid, which was widely used as an antibiotic for tuberculosis, was noted to have antidepressant properties. Interestingly, the older textbooks on tuberculosis talk about the euphoria of tuberculosis, probably because sufferers were taking Iproniazid. Iproniazid then became used as the first MAOI antidepressant. The mechanism of action is to block the breakdown of monoamine (called norepinephrine), which is believed to alleviate depression through increasing monoamines. The main problem with these medications, which are still used in certain cases today, is that if they are mixed with any food or a medication that releases norepinephrine, the client can have a dangerous elevation of blood pressure known as the tyramine reaction. As a result, clients on MAOIs must abide to strict diets, avoiding such common foods as aged cheeses, smoked meats or fish, soy, and certain wines and beers. More especially, they have to avoid various drugs such as cold remedies and anesthetics.

Shortly after the discovery of MAOIs, an artificially derived class of drugs was developed that mimicked the chemical structure of MAOIs in that they had three chemical rings. They were thus referred to as the tricyclic antidepressants (TCAs). TCAs were found to be effective in the treatment of depression, and to this day all new antidepressants are compared to the TCAs for efficacy. Despite their efficacy, however, they have a wide range of action in various parts of the body and thus produce a number of unwanted side effects.

Concern about side effects of TCAs led to the development of the selective serotonin reuptake inhibitors (SSRIs) in the late 1980s. Fluoxetine (Prozac) was the first of this group. The advantage of this group of medications was that they *selectively* increased the role of serotonin in the neuroanatomical pathways of emotion. Thus the unwanted side effects of the TCAs were to a great extent avoided. Of course, serotonergic action in and of itself has certain unwanted side effects. Thus, in the late 1990s, in an effort to increase the efficacy of antidepressants, there was a trend back to multiple monoamine blockage, with the hope that many of the unwanted side effects could be avoided. This led to the development of the serotonin norepinephrine reuptake inhibitors (SNRIs). The belief is that since they have two therapeutic mechanisms they may be more efficacious. It is not yet clear whether this is the case, although anecdotal experience and some data seem to confirm this hypothesis (Stahl, 2008). A *Cochrane Review* of 16 randomized controlled trials (RCTs) conducted in 2009 concluded that there is inadequate evidence to support that SNRIs have improved outcomes over TCAs, but argued that some evidence suggests that they are favourable in terms of acceptability and tolerability (Nakagawa et al., 2009). Certain antidepressants, such as trazodone and mirtazapine, are variations on these classifications but are useful in certain circumstances, as outlined in Table 8.3.

Fifty to 85 per cent of clients with a single episode of major depressive disorder will relapse at some stage (APA, 2002). If the client has had two or more episodes, the risk of relapse is 70 to 90 per cent over the next five years (Shiloh

Table 8.3 Medications for Depression

Generic Name (Brand Name)	Class	Dosage	Benefits	Side Effects
MAOIs and Tricyclic Antidepressants				
Phenelzine (Nardil)	MAOI	45–90 mg	Good for atypical depression	Dietary restrictions
Moclobemide (Manerix)	Reversible MAOI	300–600 mg	Good for atypical depression	No dietary restrictions Not available in US
Amitriptyline (Elavil)	Tricyclic	75–300 mg	Good when sleep required/ inexpensive	Troublesome anti-cholinergic side effects
Doxepin (Sinequan)	Tricyclic	75–300 mg		Possible cardio toxicity Cannot be used with glaucoma
Imipramine (Tofranil)				Possibly more response in men Lethal in overdose
Selective Serotonin Reuptake Inhibitors (SSRIs)				
Fluoxetine (Prozac)	SSRI	10–80 mg	The original SSRI No withdrawal symptoms	Long-acting = slow onset and stays in system
Paroxetine (Paxil)	SSRI	10–60 mg	Good for anxiety	Withdrawal symptoms
Fluvoxamine (Luvox)	SSRI	50–300 mg	Good for anxiety	Gastric problems
Sertraline (Zoloft)	SSRI	50–200 mg	Good for anxiety	Gastric problems
Citalopram (Celexa)	SSRI	10–60 mg	Good for anxiety	
Clomipramine (Anafranil)	SSRI	75–300 mg	Good for obsessive-compulsive symptoms	
Escitalopram (Cipralex)	SSRI	10–20 mg	Good for anxiety	
Serotonin Norepinephrine Reuptake Inhibitors (SNRIs)				
Venflaxine (Effexor)	SNRI	75–375 mg	Good for co-morbid anxiety	Gastric side effects
Desvenflaxine (Pristiq)	SNRI	50 mg	Good for anxiety	Gastric side effects
Duloxetine (Cymbalta)	SNRI	30–90 mg	Possibly good for chronic pain/ ADHD symptoms	Few side effects
Mirtazapine (Remeron)	SNRI	15–60 mg	Good when sleep required/ dual action	Weight gain

Table 8.3 *Continued*

Generic Name (Brand Name)	Class	Dosage	Benefits	Side Effects
Other antidepressants				
Trazodone (Desyrel)	5HT Antagonist/ SSRI	150–600 mg	Good for aggression Good when sleep required	Rare but serious priapism
Buproprion (Wellbutrin/ Zyban)	NE-DA reuptake inhibitor	100–450 mg	Does not precipitate mania Good for co-morbid ADHD symptoms No sexual side effects	May precipitate seizures

et al., 2005). As a result, it is often necessary for a client to consider whether he or she will remain on medication for a prolonged period of time (Furukawa et al., 2007). Regardless of whether or not they continue on medication, clients will often need ongoing support. In addition, they should be encouraged to develop a relapse prevention plan and education should focus on early signs of relapse and treatment resources that are available.

Electroconvulsive Therapy

Electroconvulsive therapy (ECT) remains one of the most controversial treatments in psychiatry. Most of us have seen the horrific scenes of ECT being used as a punishment in Hollywood films such as *One Flew Over the Cuckoo's Nest* or, more recently, *The Changeling*. In addition, psychiatric survivor groups have identified ECT as one of the ways in which psychiatry controls and abuses clients (Capponi, 2003). Nevertheless, treatment with ECT continues to be used in severe cases of depression that are not responsive to other forms of treatment. Meta-analyses of ECT have demonstrated that it can be highly effective in treatment of depression (Janicak et al., 1985; Geddes and UK ECT Review Group, 2003; Kho et al., 2005).

The history of ECT as a form of treatment dates back to Paracelsus, who in the fourteenth century used camphor to induce seizures in an effort to relieve suffering caused by melancholia (Prudich, 2005). In 1934, Meduna in Italy used camphor and then insulin coma to treat a catatonic patient with success. By 1938, Bini and Cerletti had devised a method of placing electrodes on the head to induce seizures. ECT became very common in the 1940s as a first-line treatment for psychiatric disorder. At that time there were few if any pharmacological treatments available. In the 1960s and 1970s the first randomized control trials proved its efficacy compared to antipsychotic medication and with sham ECT. Over the years newer techniques have developed, including the use of sophisticated brief anesthetic techniques with muscle relaxants and unilateral electrode placement.

The indication for ECT is generally considered to be treatment-resistant depression. When there is a high risk of suicide or dehydration or in the presence of depressive stupor or catatonia or psychotic depression, it may be considered earlier in the course of treatment. ECT treatment takes about 10 to 15 minutes plus time for preparation and recovery. An IV is inserted into the arm to allow for the administration of anesthetic and muscle relaxant. Heart and blood pressure monitors are secured. A small electrode pad is placed on the person's head. An electric shock is administered that causes a seizure lasting 30 to 60 seconds. The mechanism of action is likely due to an effect on the serotonergic system, although this effect is somewhat different from that of antidepressants in that it seems that the electrical current increases the density of serotonin receptors. There is also some evidence that the pituitary may discharge more hormones as a result of the electrical current-induced seizure, resulting in increased cortisol-releasing factor and therefore increased cortisol (Lisanby, 2007).

The side effects of ECT include the common risks of a general anesthetic, albeit the general anesthetic in ECT is very brief. Other side effects include cardiovascular complications. Since the stimulus is applied very close to the jaw bone, it used to be common for clients to break teeth, but this can be prevented by using a bite block. The most serious and well-publicized sequelae are neurocognitive, particularly in elderly people. It is common for the client to experience brief headaches and occasionally periods of confusion for some hours after the treatment. Many clients experience a brief period of amnesia for events immediately following the treatment. This is referred to as anterograde amnesia. This generally diminishes or is absent two or three weeks after the treatment ends. Some people also experience a memory gap of events prior to the ECT, referred to as **retrograde amnesia**. Generally speaking, these memories return, although some are left with a spotty amnesia. It is known that bilateral electrode placement, a long anesthetic, and pre-existing cognitive problems increase the chances of neurocognitive sequelae. Researchers concur that cognitive side effects can be a problem and are seeking methods to reduce this risk through different types of wave forms and electrode placements (Eschweiler et al., 2007; Loo et al., 2007). Concurrent administration of lithium at the time of the ECT also increases the possibility of confusion and neurocognitive problems.

ECT is the most effective treatment for severe, unremitting depression (Perrin et al, 2012). While there are active opponents of the treatment, there are also those who suffer from severe depression who believe it is a life-saving treatment. As a result, clients who suffer from severe episodic depression should research this treatment when they are stable to make an informed choice about its use should they become severely incapacitated by depression.

Transcranial Magnetic Stimulation (rTMS)

A relatively new technology that holds promise for the treatment of depression is repetitive transcranial magnetic stimulation (rTMS). The first use of electromagnetic brain stimulation was designed as a neurodiagnostic tool in England in 1985. The principle of the treatment is that an electromagnetic coil produces a short-lived electromagnetic field that easily passes through the skull and other tissues. It is believed to exert its action by increasing cortical excitability and therefore has an effect on neurotransmitters, including adrenergic and dopaminergic systems. The treatment is generally administered daily over 10 days and some subjects have reported mild headaches but few other adverse effects.

Systematic reviews of rTMS demonstrate that this approach is superior in its effects to sham treatments for major depression (Lam et al., 2008) and newer RCTs continue to support its use with this population (O'Reardon, 2007; George et al., 2010). Side effects of this intervention are generally reported to be minimal. In contrast to ECT, this treatment has been associated with improvements in cognitive functioning (Allan et al., 2012).

Light Therapy

Some clients experience major depressive episodes in late fall or early winter on a regular basis and are thus viewed as having seasonal affective disorder, discussed earlier in the chapter. This seems more common in northern regions where the days are significantly shorter in winter. Over the past 20 years bright-light therapy has been introduced and has been found to result in significant reductions in the severity of depression symptoms in both seasonal and non-seasonal depression (Golden et al., 2005). The therapy is characterized by regular daily exposure to ultraviolet-filtered visible light. A special light box or visor administers the correct brightness of light for 30 minutes per day. Clients can be told to expose themselves to the light by having the box, for instance, in the kitchen while they have breakfast or by wearing a visor first thing in the morning. Side effects are minimal, although some people report nausea, headache, and nervousness as well as eye irritation. There have been no reports of ocular damage. Initially the therapy should be given for 10 days although it is now thought that maintenance therapy can be continued all winter.

Diet

An emerging area of research is the association between diet and mental health. Jacka and colleagues (2010) found that "Western diets" of processed and fried foods, refined grains, and sugars are associated with higher rates of depression, while "traditional diets" of vegetables, fruit, meat, and fish are associated with lower levels. Studies with other populations confirm this association. Mediterranean dietary patterns that are high in olive oil and transfatty acids have been found to be associated with depression (Sanchez-Villegas et al., 2009). Further, healthy Japanese diets with high intakes of vegetables, fruit, and soy products are associated with lower levels of depression (Nanri et al., 2009). While these findings are preliminary at this point, healthy eating is a non-invasive change that could have an effect on depressive symptoms.

Psychopharmacological Treatment of Mania and Bipolar Disorder

In almost all cases, pharmacological treatment is the primary approach to the treatment of mania, augmented by psychosocial interventions. The goals of pharmacological treatment are (1) to control the symptoms in the acute phase and (2) to help the client remain in a stable state, free of acute episodes. During acute phases, clients are frequently treated with antipsychotic medication. These are discussed in Chapter 7. As well as having mood-stabilizing properties in and of themselves, antipsychotics can be used to ensure that clients finally get some sleep and do not exhaust themselves.

The most common and effective treatment for maintenance of stability in mania and bipolar disorder is the use of lithium carbonate (Yatham et al., 2009). Lithium carbonate is a salt that was serendipitously found to be effective in the treatment of mania when it was used in some experiments on rats. The main side effects include nausea, diarrhea, thirst, and weight gain. While clients at times express fears of brain damage from this medication, recent research has demonstrated that it actually increases growth of grey matter (Bearden et al., 2007). Following extensive research, lithium carbonate has been found to be effective in preventing further manic episodes in 60 to 80 per cent of people, to minimize the risk of further depressive episodes, and to reduce death by suicide in clients with bipolar disorder (Smith et al., 2007). However, clients must be committed to reliably following the medication regime when using lithium, including not forgetting doses and not succumbing to the temptation to take a little extra medication, as there is a small "therapeutic window." The dosage is usually guided by reviewing the results of regular blood tests. Other first-line treatments include Valproic acid and some other anti-epileptic medications, which are effective and have few side effects (Nivoli et al., 2011).

Possible Social Work Interventions in the Case Examples

Case Example 1: Bodan

Bodan is suffering from dysthymic disorder, which is now compounded by acute stress.

- The social worker should conduct a suicide risk assessment as Bodan may feel overwhelmed and perceive that he has no reason to continue living.
- Social work intervention should focus on a problem-solving approach to assist Bodan to build his own resources and develop support systems.
- When his immediate crisis situation is resolved, the social worker and Bodan may decide to embark on cognitive-behaviour therapy to address his lifelong depressive perceptions and determine alternative behavioural strategies. If the social worker is not qualified to use these treatment approaches, appropriate referrals can be made.

Case Example 2: Everton

Everton is suffering from major depression.

- The social worker should complete a psychosocial assessment to determine Everton's current needs and to determine supports he will require upon discharge from hospital.
- With his permission, the social worker may be in contact with his family and employer to assist them in understanding Everton's situation and ease his return to his normal life.
- Cognitive therapy or interpersonal therapy could be useful for Everton, and the social worker should discuss psychosocial treatment options.

Case Example 3: Aruna

Aruna is likely suffering from a manic episode associated with bipolar disorder. If this is the case, the symptoms may worsen before they improve, possibly rendering Aruna a risk to herself or others, and certainly causing distress.

- If Aruna is admitted to hospital, the social worker can work with Aruna to plan her return to the community and her program of recovery. The social worker can also work with family and friends of Aruna to assist them in understanding what has happened and make plans for future support.

- If Aruna is not admitted to hospital, the social worker can work with her, if she agrees, to plan for treatment in the community. Alternatively, if Aruna does not agree to intervention, the social worker may be approached by the family to discuss options to assist Aruna. This may include education about the implications of mental health legislation (see Chapter 3).
- The social worker will need to assess risk to Aruna's child and determine whether a child welfare referral is required.

Summary

Depression and mania fall on a continuum of mood disturbance that ranges from mild symptoms to debilitating illness. The causes of mood disturbances are multifactoral, incorporating a range of biological determinants, early life history factors, and current environmental and social factors. As a result, treatment approaches to mood disturbances are highly divergent. In some situations psychosocial interventions alone are the most effective means for dealing with the problem; at times a combination of biological and psychosocial interventions will be most effective; and in the case of acute manic episodes, medication is likely the first line of intervention. Social workers working with clients with depression or bipolar disorder require highly developed assessment skills in order to determine the nature of the issues the client is dealing with and subsequently to determine whether social work intervention alone is indicated or whether the other members of the interdisciplinary team should be involved.

Discussion Questions

1. How might social workers effectively use supported self-management approaches with clients?
2. How can social workers assist clients and families affected by bipolar disorder?
3. How can the recovery model be applied to work with clients affected by depression or bipolar disorder?
4. A number of controversial medical treatments exist for use with clients suffering from depression. What is the social worker's role with respect to clients using or considering these treatments?

Suggested Readings and Websites

Beck, A., J. Rush, B. Shaw, and G. Emery. 1979. *Cognitive Therapy of Depression.* New York: Guilford Press. This groundbreaking book is the foundation for cognitive therapy and is a must read.

The Mayo Clinic. "Post-Partum Depression." At: www.mayoclinic.com/health/postpartum-depression/DS00546. Given the high rates of depressive symptoms and other mental health concerns in the immediate aftermath of giving birth, this website is vital in that it provides a wealth of information accessible to both practitioners and the public.

Mood Gym. At: www.moodgym.anu.edu.au/welcome. Mood Gym is a free website designed and managed by the Centre for Mental Health Research (CMHR) at the Australian National University. It incorporates psychoeducational material with interactive activities aimed at enhancing coping skills in managing depression.

9 Anxiety

Learning Objectives

- To identify factors contributing to the development of anxiety.
- To identify symptoms and challenges associated with anxiety.
- To identify different types of anxiety disorders.
- To present evidence-based interventions that promote recovery.

Case Example 1

Nico is a 21-year-old student studying electrical engineering who lives at home with his parents. He has arrived at an appointment at University Health Services stating that he suffers from stress that he believes interferes with his work. He explains that he has always felt stressed about school and managed his stress by "being organized," but these strategies are no longer working. Nico adheres to a very strict vegan diet and carefully considers all food he consumes to avoid toxins. He can only eat off glass plates washed in a particular type of detergent. If Nico eats outside his home, he must bring not only his own food but also his own utensils because of fear that dishes or utensils supplied by others may be contaminated. As a result, he does not attend social events.

When doing his school work, Nico goes through elaborate rituals, repeatedly readjusting the lighting, cleaning his work surfaces, and ensuring that his various study tools are positioned in a particular way. If he must get up from his desk for any reason, he must begin the process again. Often Nico becomes so preoccupied with these details that he is unable to focus on the task at hand. He cannot manage group assignments because others do not follow the same routines, and consequently he must consistently request alternative individual assignments. In the past few months, Nico has taken to repeatedly revising all his assignments to improve the quality, in the end missing deadlines because he does not feel the work meets his personal standards.

Case Example 2

Josi is a 33-year-old mother of two children who in the past enjoyed walks in the neighbourhood with her kids, volunteering at their school, and taking the children to programs at the library and community centre. One day two years ago, Josi was shopping at the local mall with a friend when suddenly she experienced a rush of immobilizing anxiety. Her heart started to race; she at first began sweating profusely and then felt as though the blood had drained from her body and began to feel chilled and shaky. She feared that she might be having a heart attack or a stroke. Her friend became extremely concerned and wondered about calling for assistance. Within a few minutes, however, it had passed and Josi was just left feeling frightened and exhausted. Upon returning home, Josi made an appointment with her family doctor, who after a series of medical investigations reported that there was nothing physically wrong with her. Josi resumed all normal activities but continued to be a bit concerned about the event. Two months later, again in a shopping mall, Josi had a similar experience. This time, her doctor informed her that she was having **panic attacks**. Josi decided that she would only go to shopping malls accompanied by her husband or mother because she feared if she were alone or with her children she would not be able to cope. After three additional panic attacks, two of which occurred in the grocery store, Josi decided that she could no longer shop and began finding alternative ways of getting groceries and clothing for her children. As time progressed Josi's panic attacks began to occur in other places, and as a result she has been further limiting her activities. She now arranges for her children to have play dates in her own home so that she will not have to go into public places, and she no longer volunteers in the classroom for fear she will humiliate herself and her children due to a panic attack.

The Nature of Anxiety

Anxiety is common to all humans. It is characterized by two components: (1) a diffuse, unpleasant, and vague experience of apprehension; and (2) physical symptoms such as headache, perspiration, heart palpitations, general restlessness, difficulty sleeping, and gastric discomfort. Anxiety can have an adaptive function, warning the person of impending risk and allowing the person to take remedial action. For instance, in early days, anxiety that the family may starve during a long cold winter could have motivated people to harvest and store extra food. Similarly, now a person who is anxious about a test or upcoming interview may prepare for it and thus both decrease anxiety and increase chances of success. Anxiety becomes problematic when the symptoms are experienced to the extent that they no longer motivate adaptive behaviour but rather impede efforts to rectify the situation. Further, anxiety may not be easily tied to specific events and may instead be a more general sense of unease, discomfort, and foreboding, making it difficult for a person to be able to take actions that will reduce distress.

Incidence and Prevalence

Anxiety states represent the most common of all mental health problems, affecting approximately 12 per cent of Canadians—about 9 per cent of men and 16 per cent of women—during a one-year period. The one-year prevalence in Canada for individual anxiety disorders is as follows: generalized anxiety disorder, 1.1 per cent; specific phobia, 6.2 to 8.0 per cent; social phobia, 6.7 per cent; obsessive compulsive disorder, 1.8 per cent; and panic disorder, 0.7 per cent (Public Health Agency of Canada, 2002). In the United States, the lifetime prevalence of having an anxiety disorder is 28.8 per cent, most often involving social phobia (12.1 per cent) or specific phobias (12.5 per cent).The age of onset for anxiety disorders is lower than for any other disorder, with a median age of 11 years, indicating that anxiety disorders in childhood are a significant issue. This is compared to a median age of onset of 30 years for mood disorders (Kessler et al., 2005).

Stress and anxiety among university students have recently become high-profile concerns. *Maclean's* magazine, for instance, reported that 50 per cent of 1,600 University of Alberta students identified feeling "overwhelming anxiety" in the past year (Lunau, 2012). Similarly, the CBC reported a survey conducted at McMaster University indicating that 88.8 per cent of students reported feeling generally overwhelmed and 50.2 per cent stated that they were overwhelmed with anxiety (Craggs, 2012). A study involving 16,460 undergraduate students in the United Kingdom charted the longitudinal course of anxiety and revealed that undergraduate student anxiety scores peaked in the first term of second year and in the final year (Bewick et al., 2010).

The direct and indirect costs of anxiety disorders in the United States are reported to exceed $40 billion annually (Smoller and Faraone, 2008). In a review conducted by Hoffman and colleagues (2008), generalized anxiety disorder was associated with an average of between 1.5 and 5.4 impairment days in the past month, after adjusting for the presence of other mental health problems and socio-demographic characteristics. In a large general population survey in New York, anxiety disturbances were more common among people who are divorced and unemployed, and were significantly less common in people over the age of 65 than in those who are younger. Further, there was a significant overlap between anxiety and major depression—that is, a large number of people suffer from both (Gwynn et al., 2008).

Causes of Anxiety

As with depression, which is closely linked with anxiety, the causes of anxiety are generally thought to be a complex interaction between biological predispositions and social/environmental factors.

Intrapsychic Factors

Rollo May, in his classic book *The Meaning of Anxiety* (1950), traces descriptions of the intrapsychic experience of anxiety through such writers as Descartes, Kierkegaard, Nietzsche, and Kafka. These writers focus on societal influences that result in a sense of **existential anxiety** in which a person becomes aware of the profound meaninglessness of life and existence. From this perspective, existential anxiety is a fundamental, ontological experience, resulting from the recognition of the inherent uncertainty of the human condition. Kierkegaard suggests that the goal is not to remove anxiety but rather to confront the existential anxiety and move ahead despite it.

Early psychoanalytic theory focused on anxiety related to psychosexual developmental phases. Indeed, Freud's use of the word *angst* (or *fear* in German) is the origin of the current term *anxiety*. **Separation anxiety**, in which a child fears separation from its main attachment figure (traditionally the mother), is central to this theoretical understanding and forms the underpinnings of adult anxiety. The threat in anxiety is differentiated from fear because it is vague and non-specific. It is a threat on a deeper level and attacks the core or essence of personality (May, 1950).

Social-Environmental Factors

High-stress environments can contribute to the development of anxiety. For instance, a child living in a violent household can be in a heightened state of arousal attempting to anticipate when violence might erupt. The chaotic nature of these types of environments often means that the child cannot reliably predict when the violent parent might erupt or when he or she might be kind and nurturing. The child then begins to live life on "pins and needles," carefully attempting to avoid situations that might, in his/her view, cause the anger and violence. Similarly, a person living in economic distress, attempting against all odds to make ends meet, or a person in a high-stress job may begin to feel increasingly anxious as a result of an inability to satisfy the demands made of her or him.

Behavioural theories suggest that anxiety is a learned response to experiences in the environment. According to this theory a person becomes conditioned to respond in a particular way to certain situations. Cognitive theorists add that the anxiety experienced by a person reflects that person's interpretation of the situation, which may or may not be faulty. Thus, a person may have experienced negative interactions with certain people, subsequently generalizing this to all others and therefore responding to situations with anxiety that is not objectively rational. For instance, an individual may have been bullied in high school and as a result developed a rational fear of some people within the school environment. However, that fear may generalize and later the individual may perceive other social situations as dangerous and view him/herself as socially incompetent. As a result, an invitation to a work-related cocktail party causes significant anxiety and avoidance behaviours.

The pattern of behaviour described above is reflected in the notion of self-efficacy or competence as described by social learning theorists. Bandura (1977) suggests that expectations of competence or personal self-efficacy triggered by the contextual factors in any situation arise from diverse sources of information, including judgements of past performance and previous responses from others. These judgements of efficacy in turn affect the outcomes of situations and thereby confirm or modify existing cognitive structures. For example, people who judge themselves to be **inefficacious** in managing potential threats approach such situations anxiously and experience disruptive arousal. This arousal, in turn, negatively impacts on their performance and confirms feelings of inadequacy. Individuals who repeatedly perceive their efforts to be ineffective can develop "learned helplessness" (Seligman and Garber, 1980).

Biological Factors

Biological theories related to anxiety also have a long history. Selye (1936), for instance, focused on biological responses to stress and noted that when acute threats were encountered, biological adaptations served as protective mechanisms. Respiration and blood pressure increased, oxygen and energy shifted to large muscles from the immune, digestive, and reproductive systems that were less essential for immediate survival. This led to the development of his theory of general adaptation syndrome, a three-stage model for stress adaptation involving: (1) alarm and mobilization when the body prepares for action; (2) resistance in which the body's stress response diminishes and returns to normal functioning; and (3) exhaustion, which occurs if stress is unrelenting or repetitive. Thus, anxiety responses such as panic attacks occur when there is a disruption in this process and there is significant autonomic arousal to relatively minor threats.

More recent biological research has determined that the primary region of the brain responsible for processing fearful material is the amygdala, which coordinates the autonomic response to fear (see Figure 9.1). Sensory information reaches the amygdala, which in turn initiates autonomic nervous system responses and behavioural responses. The hypothalamic-pituitary-adrenal (HPA) axis is an interactive system of hormones released in

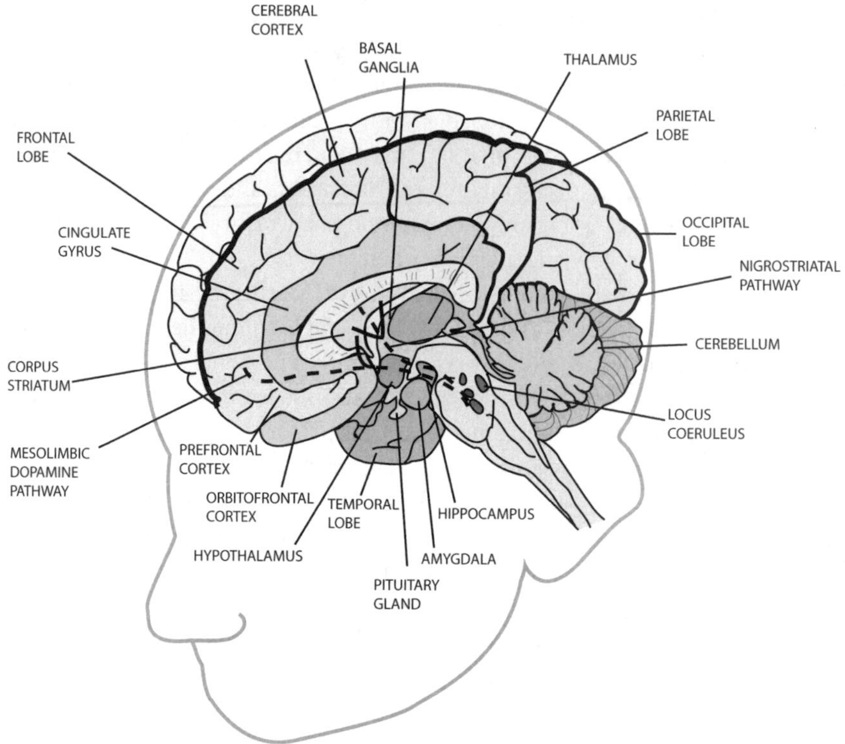

Figure 9.1 The Brain

response to stress. The hypothalamus releases corticotrophin-releasing factor (CRF), prompting the pituitary to release adrenocorticotropin-releasing hormone (ACTH), which in turn stimulates the adrenal cortex to release cortisol. This produces the "flight or fight" response in which the autonomic nervous system regulates such things as heart rate, breathing, dilation of blood vessels, and the emptying of the bowel and bladder. These responses are modulated by the prefrontal cortex of the brain, which assesses the threat cues and determines the actual degree of threat (Mathew et al., 2008). For instance, a loud noise that resembles a gunshot may cause an instant startle reflex and a sudden rise in heart rate. However, when the person then assesses that the noise was caused by a car backfiring, he or she works to calm down rather than run away or fight. Anxiety disorders occur in individuals where this modulating function is impaired by one factor or another, resulting in a more chronic and pervasive fear response (Spiegel and Barlow, 2000; Stahl, 2000; Mojtabai, 2005).

Family and twin studies of panic disorder and phobias have provided consistent evidence that these problems are familial. People with relatives with panic disorder, for instance, have a 5 to 16 per cent increased risk of this particular illness. If a first-degree relative has a panic disorder, the risk of developing one is increased by seven times. Similarly, there is a six to nine times greater risk of developing phobias if one has a first-degree relative with a phobic disorder. Twin studies have reported heritabilities of 0.28 for panic disorders, 0.36 for agoraphobia, 0.10 for social anxiety disorder, and 0.24 for specific phobias.

Compared to other mental health problems such as schizophrenia and bipolar disorder, this rate of heritability of anxiety-related mental health problems is relatively low. Thus, while there is undoubtedly a genetic component, the environmental also appear to have a significant influence. Indeed, a large twin study that considered both diagnosis of panic and phobic disorders and personality factors found that genetic determinants of personality traits accounted for all the genetic influences influencing social phobia and agoraphobia (Smoller et al., 2008). That is, inherited personality characteristics, such as the need for control over situations or being shy, were the genetic factors that predicted social phobia and agoraphobia. Similar results have been found for generalized anxiety disorder, suggesting that the inherited personality traits may predispose the person to an anxiety disturbance, but that the disturbance itself may not be directly inherited (Hettema et al., 2004).

Symptoms and Types of Anxiety Disorders

Anxiety disorders have many common features (see Box 9.1). They generally have three groups of symptoms—physiological, cognitive, and behavioural. The physiological symptoms include a racing heart or palpitations, shallow breathing, trembling, shaking, sweating, dizziness, muscle tension, nausea, and gastric distress. The cognitive symptoms include fearful thoughts, fearful predictions, fearful beliefs, and preoccupation with the potential threat. Behavioural symptoms include both avoidance of situations and stimuli that will trigger the anxiety, as well as safety behaviours such as overpreparation, hiding, rituals, checking, and hypervigilance. As readers will recall from Chapter 6, these symptoms also occur in people with post-traumatic stress disorder. Although acute stress disorder and post-traumatic stress disorder are forms of anxiety, because of the prevalence and unique nature of the stressors that lead to these mental health problems, they have been covered separately in Chapter 6. Further, while this chapter identifies several types of anxiety, there is considerable overlap between each of the types of anxiety and there is controversy in the literature about whether they indeed constitute distinct syndromes. Nevertheless, it is useful for social workers in mental health to know how variations on anxiety are defined.

Box 9.1 Symptoms of Anxiety

Physical
- Racing heart or palpitations
- Shallow breathing
- Trembling, shaking
- Sweating
- Dizziness
- Muscle tension
- Nausea and gastric distress

Cognitive
- Fearful thoughts
- Fearful predictions
- Fearful beliefs
- Preoccupation with the potential threat

Behavioural
- Avoidance of situations and stimuli that will trigger the anxiety
- Overpreparation
- Rituals
- Repeated checking
- Hypervigilance

Source: APA (2013).

Anxiety symptoms are difficult for family and friends to understand and this may compound the distress experienced by sufferers. For instance, other people may become annoyed that the person with social anxiety will not attend a particular event or that a person with panic attacks cannot enter a shopping mall. To others this seems ludicrous and they may believe that just a little willpower will allow the person to overcome the fear or resistance. In addition, anxiety behaviours may be open to ridicule. A person with obsessional traits can be made fun of for his or her constant attention to detail or focus on cleanliness. To the outsider, the person with an anxiety disorder can appear weak, ineffectual, or rigid and therefore not ill. Family members may also feel the burden of stigma. Thus, if an anxious child refuses to go to school, the parents may be criticized by others for not exercising appropriate discipline by forcing the child to go.

Panic Disorder

Panic disorder is often a severe and disabling form of anxiety that is characterized by panic attacks. Panic attacks are defined as sudden, discrete episodes of very intense anxiety accompanied by feelings of impending doom. These attacks develop in a spontaneous manner, which the person initially feels "came out of nowhere" (Cox and Taylor, 1999). They are accompanied by a number of physical symptoms such as intense sweating, palpitations, and dizziness in which the person fears that he or she may faint or have a heart attack. Characteristic symptoms of panic disorder are found in Box 9.2. The most commonly reported symptoms are racing heart and dizziness (Craske et al., 2010). While the first or second panic attack is totally unexpected, with the repeated experience of panic attacks the person begins to fear them and seeks to find ways to control both the onset and consequences; this results in maladaptive safety behaviours such as those that occur in agoraphobia. Indeed, the majority of people report that their first panic attack occurred in a public place and almost 40 per cent of people with panic attacks resulting in agoraphobia report that their first panic attack happened on a bus, plane, or subway.

Specific Phobia

Fears commonly develop and then diminish throughout childhood. Typically, fear of separation from the caregiver develops between six and 22 months and goes away by 30 months. Fear of unfamiliar adults begins between six and nine months and subsides at 20–24 months. Fears of animals, darkness, and monsters appear between two and six years of age. Fear of school occurs at the beginning of school and often reappears when a child transitions from elementary school to high school. Children between the ages of eight and 16 often fear physical harm to either themselves or their parents (Cox and Taylor, 1999). Most adults can also identify some things that cause them fear, such

Box 9.2 Characteristics of a Panic Attack

- Palpitations
- Sweating
- Trembling or shaking
- Sensations of shortness of breath or smothering
- Feeling of choking
- Chest pain or discomfort
- Nausea or abdominal distress
- Dizziness, light-headedness, feeling faint
- Derealization (feelings of unreality) or depersonalization (feeling detached from self)
- Fear of losing control or going crazy
- Fear of dying
- **Paraesthesias**
- Chills or hot flashes

Source: APA (2013).

as balloons popping or fireworks (loud noises), standing on a chair or ladder (heights), being in a tunnel or elevator (small spaces), or spiders or mice. To others these fears are ridiculous and may seem funny. To those who experience the fears, they may also seem crazy, but they are nevertheless very real. In people with phobias, these fears are felt with such intensity that they result in compensatory behaviours in order to avoid them. For instance, a well-known academic who refuses to travel by airplane when attending conferences or giving talks must factor in several days on either side in order to drive thousands of miles.

Agoraphobia

The word *agoraphobia* is derived from the Greek *agora* or marketplace. We define it as the fear of public and crowded places. In comparison with the general population, people with agoraphobia experience heightened startle reflex, increased heart rate, and emotional arousal in response to feared situations. They then develop anticipatory anxiety, which they manage through avoidance of situations (McTeague et al., 2011). As a result of generalized fears, people with agoraphobia may be unable to leave the house alone, be unable to be in crowded places, or be unable to travel in a car or airplane. Consequently, people with this disorder tend to severely restrict their activities. This has a tremendous impact on the lives of the person suffering from this type of phobia and on the lives of others in the person's family. Compensations often must be made to deal with the fact that this person cannot go out of doors or cannot travel by certain modes of transportation.

Social Phobia (Social Anxiety Disorder)

While most people experience some anxiety in novel situations where they will be evaluated by others, such as job interviews, public speaking, or meeting the parents of a significant other, individuals with social phobia experience incapacitating anxiety in these situations. To reduce the symptoms the person may suddenly leave the social situation or, to avoid the symptoms, the person may simply refuse to attend. However, these approaches serve to reinforce the person's beliefs that he or she is socially incompetent and, consequently, avoidance symptoms increase. Research has established a strong link between behavioural inhibition to unfamiliar and novel situations in children and social phobia in adults (Rotge et al., 2011). Further, experimental design studies have demonstrated that children with high levels of social anxiety symptoms are more attuned to negative affect than positive affect in other people, suggesting that selective attention bias contributes to the disorder (Waters et al., 2012). Social phobia is one of the most common anxiety disorders, particularly in women. At any time about 2 per cent of the population suffer from social anxiety disorder, an additional 3 per cent have subclinical threshold symptoms (that is, where several symptoms exist but not at a level to warrant a diagnosis), and 7.5 per cent have some symptoms of the disorder (Fehm et al., 2008).

Generalized Anxiety Disorder

Generalized anxiety disorder is characterized by persistent anxiety and worry that is out of proportion with actual events or circumstances. This anxiety is often related to minor, everyday occurrences such as work, finances, relationships, and health and safety of loved ones. This pervasive worry is accompanied by a variety of somatic symptoms that together cause significant impairment in social or occupational functioning and marked distress in the sufferer. People with generalized anxiety disorder often experience significantly reduced quality of life in the areas of general health, physical health, bodily pain, vitality, mental health, role functioning due to physical and emotional difficulties, and social functioning compared with those without the disorder (Hoffman et al., 2008). Primary symptoms include trembling, feeling shaky, tension headaches, exaggerated startle reflexes, difficulty sleeping, sweating, diarrhea, and nausea. As a result of the physical symptoms, it is not uncommon that the person will visit his or her family doctor seeking relief for what feels like a biological illness. Paradoxically, the concern over these physical symptoms becomes another cause of stress and worry. For instance, the person may become concerned that the diarrhea is a symptom of colon cancer. Nevertheless, a full medical workup can be in order because the symptoms may be secondary to such factors as excessive caffeine use, alcohol withdrawal, cardiac problems, or hormonal imbalance. By definition this is a chronic condition that may become lifelong, and as it develops as many as 25 per cent of people who suffer from it may also develop panic attacks (Kaplan and Sadock, 1996).

Obsessive-Compulsive Disorder

Obsessive-compulsive disorder (OCD) is a relatively common (affecting 2 per cent of the population), chronic, and disabling disorder that causes significant distress in sufferers and their families. As the name implies, it is characterized by two factors: (1) cognitive obsessions that increase the person's level of anxiety and thus lead to (2) compulsive behaviours aimed at reducing the anxiety. Obsessions are intrusive and persistent thoughts that to others appear inappropriate. Common obsessions include fear of dirt or germs, concerns that the oven or other appliance has been left on and the house will burn down, or concerns that the house or apartment has not been properly secured and someone will break in. These obsessive thoughts cause considerable distress and, consequently, individuals with obsessions usually attempt to ignore, resist, or suppress the thoughts or impulses or to counteract them by other thoughts or actions, resulting in compulsions. Compulsions are repeated behaviours that occur in response to an obsession, usually in a ritualistic way. Compulsions can include behaviours such as handwashing or repeated checking, such as of the oven or the locks, or mental acts such as praying, counting, or repeating words. The person often knows that the compulsion is not rational and thus will attempt to refrain from the behaviour; however, the anxiety then becomes unbearable and he or she must capitulate. In order to qualify for a diagnosis of OCD, these activities must take more than one hour per day to complete. In addition to the ritualistic behaviours, individuals with OCD will engage in avoidance behaviours, such as not shaking hands, so they do not have to engage in the rituals. As indicated in the case example of Nico, the compulsions can begin to interfere with normal functioning and affect all aspects of the individual's life.

OCD occurs at some point in the lives of about 2–3 per cent of people; in young people it is more common in boys than in girls. It is more likely to be found in people who are single, perhaps because of the disruptive nature of the disorder on interpersonal relationships. Epidemiological studies reveal that about half of people with OCD also suffer from another mental health disorder, most often another anxiety disorder or a depressive disorder (Abramowitz et al., 2009).

The Recovery Model and Anxiety

A key aspect of anxiety is that while there is a biological component, several models for understanding and treating anxiety are based on the premise that individuals can learn to control both physiological and emotional responses. Thus, most treatment approaches are highly consistent with the recovery model.

One aspect of this, however, is determining the cause of the anxiety. It is possible that what the person is attributing to a mental health problem (anxiety) is actually a general medical condition that may aggravate or mimic anxiety symptoms. These general medical conditions can include thyroid disorders, respiratory conditions, blood conditions such as anemia, and cardiovascular conditions. Further, as noted earlier in this chapter, it is not unusual for someone with panic disorder to believe that he or she is having a heart attack or suffering from severe asthma. This may indeed be the case, so the social worker should inquire whether a physician has been consulted. Even if the anxiety is exacerbated by or is the manifestation of a medical condition, treatments that help the person assume some mastery over the symptoms can be very helpful. Thus, the recovery process can involve both treating the medical condition and developing strategies to manage or deal with anxiety.

Psychosocial Interventions That Promote Recovery from Anxiety

Psychosocial interventions are a primary method of managing anxiety symptoms. These interventions require a full explanation to clients prior to embarking on them because they can be difficult and increase anxiety for a period of time before they decrease anxiety. Clients thus must decide if this is a reasonable approach to their recovery.

Mindfulness-Based Stress Reduction

A variety of approaches to anxiety management focus on a combination of cognitive, behavioural, and mindfulness-based techniques. Examples of these treatments include stress-inoculation training (Meichenbaum, 1993), cognitive-behavioural stress management (Gaab et al., 2006), mindfulness-based cognitive therapy (Segal et al., 2002), and mindfulness-based stress reduction (Kabat-Zinn, 1982). In general, these approaches incorporate relaxation techniques such as yoga or deep breathining, education regarding sources of stress and common coping techniques, and cognitive awareness and restructuring. A meta-analysis on the use of these techniques with university students concluded that there is compelling evidence as to the effectiveness of these models (Regehr et al., 2013).

The foundations of cognitive-behavioural therapy have been described at length in Chapter 8. Mindfulness has its roots in Buddhism and can be described as detached self-observation (Kabat-Zinn, 1982). Through instruction and practice, individuals learn to consciously direct their focus of attention. When distressing thoughts, emotions, or physical sensations arise, the person observes it as a transient experience, not a permanent state of being. This reduces distress or alarm as the responses or symptoms are seen as passing events that do not require examination or action. At the same time, the mindful person is more sensitive to environmental cues and personal options and thus develops more flexibility in responding to events, which also reduces stress and anxiety (Gardner and Moore, 2007).

Systematic Desensitization and Exposure Therapy

Systematic desensitization and exposure represent another cognitive-behavioural approach in which clients are exposed to anxiety-provoking stimuli in an attempt to develop a habituation response so that the stimulus no longer has power over the individual. As avoidance is prevented, it can no longer be rewarded by negative reinforcement, and anxiety is reduced. The client learns that fear goes away without having to resort to escape (Calhoun and Atkeson, 1991).

The first step in this approach is to develop an anxiety hierarchy in which the person creates a list of things, in order of intensity, that make him or her anxious. Beginning with the lowest level of anxiety-provoking stimuli, the person is exposed to increasingly distressing stimuli until the anxiety decreases. In some models of the treatment, referred to as flooding, the person is exposed to the highest level at the outset (Rothbaum et al., 2000). Exposure can be implemented in a number of different ways. For instance, exposure can be imaginal, in which case the therapist assists the client, who is in a relaxed state, to imagine in vivid detail the feared stimuli. Exposure can also be in vivo, which literally means "in life" or "within a living cell or organism," but in this case means "within the natural environment." Thus, in vivo exposure involves the client being exposed to the actual stimuli. For instance, a person who is fearful of flying may first be encouraged to take the following steps: (1) drive by the airport; (2) go into the airport and look at airplanes; (3) walk down the ramp to the aircraft gate; (4) enter the aircraft while it is on the ground and the door is open; (5) sit in a seat and put the seatbelt on; and (6) take a flight. More recently, virtual reality tools have been used for exposure stimuli. Virtual reality integrates real-time computer graphics, body-tracking devices, visual displays, and other sensory input devices to immerse patients in a computer-generated virtual environment (Powers and Emmelkamp, 2008).

Systematic desensitization combines exposure to a feared stimulus with progressive relaxation techniques. In this model, short exposures to the feared stimuli are interrupted and interspersed with relaxation periods. Clients become skilled in the relaxation techniques and learn to use them whenever in a situation where their anxiety is beginning to be triggered by aversive stimuli. Over time, clients can approach the stimuli with no anxiety response at all (Calhoun and Atkeson, 1991; Rothbaum et al., 2000).

Exposure-based treatments for anxiety have some of the largest effect sizes reported in the literature (Powers and Emmelkamp, 2008), particularly when applied to more severe forms of anxiety such as panic disorders (Sanchez-Meca et al., 2010), although various methods of CBT have also proven to be effective in dealing with anxiety (Norton and Price, 2007; Evans et al., 2008; Regehr et al., 2013). It should be noted, however, that client anxiety will be activated by exposure to treatment, and people need to be aware that the treatment will be acutely uncomfortable in order to be able to consent with full information. Virtual reality methods of exposure have been found in meta-analyses to be equally effective to in vivo exposure. As this model may provide the client with increased control, it may be that this should be the preferred method.

Family Cognitive-Behavioural Therapy

When anxiety problems occur in children, there is often a reciprocal relationship between the parent and the child. That is, children with anxiety disorders are more likely to have parents with anxiety problems (as discussed above, this may be due to both genetic and environmental factors). Parents may facilitate anxiety by reinforcing or modelling avoidance or safety behaviours (Kendall et al., 2008). In adults as well, the family adjusts to the affected person's behaviour and may similarly begin inadvertently to contribute to the problem. Thus, involving the family in CBT treatment has the potential to improve success rates. Family CBT provides education to parents on anxiety and cognitive-behavioural strategies for addressing it. This model aims to modify maladaptive parental beliefs and expectations, teach parents constructive responses to their child's anxious distress, encourage parents to support the child's mastery, and teach parents and children effective communication skills. Further, parents are taught to use the skills themselves when they are feeling acutely anxious or distressed. This model has been found to be highly effective in working with children with anxiety disorders (Ishikawa et al., 2007).

Pharmacological Interventions That Promote Recovery from Anxiety

Due to the distressing nature of anxiety symptoms it is standard practice for medications and psychosocial interventions to be used together (APA, 2000; Antai-Otong, 2007). Medications can reduce acute symptoms while other methods such as CBT can assist the person to control the onset of symptoms and reduce the intensity of symptoms. A risk-benefit analysis of the use of medication should be performed in conjunction with the wishes and preferences of the client.

Anxiety disturbances tend to last for prolonged periods of time and clients often can have a relapse of symptoms. When medication is stopped, the relapse rate is somewhere between 30 and 50 per cent (APA, 2000). Generally, medication is initiated at low dosages and increased at weekly intervals until symptom relief is experienced. After 12 to 18 months a slow and careful withdrawal with frequent consultation is often attempted. Medications used for anxiety disorders are generally the same as used for depression; a more complete description can be found in Chapter 8.

Generally speaking, the first-line medications in anxiety are the SSRIs. This is supported by a significant body of RCT research that demonstrates their efficacy (Antai-Otong, 2007). The older tricyclic antidepressants (TCAs) have also been shown to be effective in the treatment of anxiety, although they tend to have more side effects and are more lethal in overdose (Stahl, 2000; Abramowitz, 2006). It is thought that clients with anxiety, particularly OCD, have more tolerance to the side effects of TCAs than those with depression, thus they are often put on higher doses that are likely required for the treatment of anxiety disorders. The monoamine oxidase inhibitors (MAOIs) have also been proven to be effective, especially in the treatment of panic disorder and social phobia. As discussed in the treatment of depression, however, they have significant drawbacks regarding the possibility of serious **hypertensive** crisis.

The benzodiazapines, which include such drugs as diazepam (Valium), lorazepam (Ativan), and alprzaloam (Xanax), are perhaps the most commonly used medications for all types of anxiety disorders. This is not necessarily because they are the best treatments; in fact, many experts in the field warn against their use, particularly in panic disorders (National Institute for Health and Clinical Excellence, 2007). Extreme care should be taken when using these medications because of the risk of dependency and abuse. Even after only eight weeks of treatment, 35 per cent of clients demonstrate symptoms of dependency and withdrawal. For this reason, many authors suggest that they are absolutely contraindicated in the presence of substance abuse. In addition, sedation and cognitive impairment including memory loss, particularly in the elderly, are common. Clients should not operate motor vehicles or heavy machinery when starting these agents. If they are used at all, they are best used as adjunctive therapy for the first two to four weeks in clients who do not have substance abuse problems or family history of substance use disorder, and only until longer-term treatments such as SSRI medications or CBT can take effect. In those who have used these agents for a period of time it has been demonstrated that CBT is helpful for withdrawing from these medications.

Possible Social Work Interventions in the Case Examples

Case Example 1: Nico

Nico suffers from an obsessive-compulsive disorder that significantly impacts his academic and social functioning.

- Should Nico wish to develop a recovery plan, he should be informed of treatment options, including the various types of cognitive-behavioural and mindfulness-based therapies available. The university may offer these on a group basis, but given the severity of Nico's concerns, individual treatment is most likely also necessary, perhaps combined with a consultation for medication.
- Nico's parents are also affected by his OCD, and with Nico's consent they may wish to be involved or seek social work advice independently. Psychoeducational approaches can be very useful in helping families understand the nature of OCD and possible helpful approaches that they may take.

Case Example 2: Josi

Josi suffers from a panic disorder that has increasingly restricted her activities and has now led to agoraphobia. This form of anxiety is generally highly disruptive and very concerning for those who suffer from it and their families.

- Josi may seek assistance in dealing with her anxiety and panic. Depending on the severity of her problems, she may need considerable assistance in attending appointments with a social worker and may need to begin with home visits if such an option exists.
- The social worker should begin by trying to understand if there are factors in Josi's environment, such as interpersonal stresses, that are contributing to her anxiety and then work with her to resolve some of these issues.
- Josi should be provided with information about various forms of intervention—including cognitive-behavioural approaches, mindfulness training, and possibly medication to control severe symptoms—that may be of assistance to her in managing symptoms while she is attempting to increase her range of activities. She can then decide whether she wishes to participate in any of these interventions in her process of recovery.
- If her family members are significantly affected by her anxiety problems, psychoeducational approaches may be of use to ensure that their approaches are helpful and do not increase anxiety.

Summary

At times, all people are exposed to situations that cause some degree of anxiety and fear. To an extent, anxiety and fear are adaptive. Individuals can prepare for challenging situations as a result of anticipatory anxiety; arousal caused by anxiety can heighten senses and assist people to manage in emergency situations; and fear can provoke people to avoid danger. For many people, however, anxiety can move from being an adaptive response to a maladaptive response that impairs ability and restricts activities and options. In these situations, a variety of intervention approaches can be employed to assist people to move from the state where they feel out of control and, hence, anxious, to regain control over their emotions, their physical reactions, and ultimately their lives.

Discussion Questions

1. How may a social worker assist a student who is feeling significant anxiety related to tests and who feels that this anxiety is severely affecting his/her performance?
2. How may family members assist someone with anxiety problems or exacerbate anxiety problems?
3. In what ways may the structure of mental health services impede work with individuals suffering from anxiety?

Suggested Readings and Websites

AnxietyBC. *Resources, Results, Relief. Complete Home Tool Kit.* At: www.anxietybc.com/resources/selfhelp_home_toolkit.php. This website provides step-by-step instructions on how to manage anxiety as well as information and resources for those suffering from anxiety and their families.

Stahl, B., and E. Goldstein. 2010. *A Mindfulness-Based Stress Reduction Workbook*. Oakland, Calif.: New Harbinger Publications. An easy-to-use workbook and audio CD takes people through the process of MBSR.

10 Neurocognitive Disorders

Learning Objectives

- To identify different types of neurocognitive disorders.
- To discuss the causes of neurocognitive disorders.
- To identify symptoms and challenges associated with neurocognitive disorders.
- To present models for assessing memory loss.
- To discuss special issues for family members.
- To discuss elder abuse in the context of neurocognitive impairment.
- To present evidence-based approaches to recovery.

Case Example 1

Justin is a 22-year-old man who has just been released from a rehabilitation hospital following treatment for traumatic brain injury. Justin was a member of a highly competitive bicycle racing team. One rainy day, during high-altitude training, he lost control of his bike on a downhill stretch and skidded into the path of an oncoming vehicle. Justin underwent neurosurgery and has had a prolonged course of inpatient rehabilitation. As a result of the rehabilitation, Justin has regained many of his functional abilities. However, he remains considerably impaired with respect to some aspects of his thinking, including decision-making and judgement. Justin has returned to the home of his parents; his mother has taken a leave of absence from work to address his needs. Justin is depressed and angry about the limitations his injury imposes on him. When unable to complete tasks that were previously almost automatic for him, he becomes enraged at those trying to help him.

Case Example 2

John is a 53-year-old man who underwent major cardiac surgery secondary to complications caused by Graves' disease, a disorder of the thyroid gland that can result in cardiac, mood, and ocular problems. In the intensive care unit (ICU), John had various tubes and monitors attached to his body, including an IV feeding and medication tube, a catheter, and heart rate and respiration monitors. During the first few days in ICU, John spent most of his time sleeping, coming into consciousness for only brief periods of time. When conscious, he was not sure where he was or why he was there. He recognized his family members but was unable to recall others, such as his doctor. He seemed confused by others and repeatedly asked questions about where he was and why he was being held against his will. Within a few days, John returned to his normal cognitive functioning. Sometime later, however, he revealed to a family member that when in the ICU he believed that he was being held against his will by terrorists. Further, he believed that helicopters were hovering outside his window and armed men in black suits were hanging from these helicopters and attempting to enter his room by breaking through the window. He subsequently realized that as the hospital was a regional trauma centre, and that the helicopters were going to the hospital's heli-pad, carrying critically ill patients.

The Nature of Neurocognitive Disorders

Cognition, or thinking, encompasses all the domains for which our brains are responsible, including memory, language, judgement, problem-solving, and praxis (performing tasks). Neurocognitive disorders are conditions in which there is a significant deficit in cognitive functioning that is considerably different from a previous level of functioning. DSM-5 (APA, 2013) differentiates between more transient neurocognitive disorders, specifically **delirium**, and more enduring forms of neurocognitive disorders (such as Alzheimer's disease and traumatic brain injury). Within the enduring forms of disorders, DSM-5 further differentiates between mild neurocognitive disorders and major neurocognitive disorders. Mild disorders are characterized by cognitive deficits that do not interfere with independence while major disorders do result in the need for assistance with instrumental activities of daily living. This chapter will focus on three major types of neurocognitive impairment: (1) delirium or transient neurocognitive impairment; (2) traumatic brain injury; and (3) progressive neurocognitive impairments such as Alzheimer's disease.

Delirium

Delirium is a disturbance in consciousness and a change in cognition that develops over a short period time, generally secondary to a medical condition or substance abuse. The case of John earlier in this chapter is an example of delirium related to physical trauma. **Delirium tremens** is a particular form of delirium associated with acute alcohol withdrawal. The term, originating in 1813, was described as brain fever secondary to frequent and excessive intoxication (Stern et al., 2010).

The defining characteristic of delirium is a fluctuating capacity to focus and sustain attention. Clients are often disoriented, not knowing who they are or where they are, or more commonly they are unaware of the date or the passage of time. Their mood may change suddenly, often resulting in states of anxiety or fear. At other times they may be euphoric, intrusive, or inappropriate. Characteristically, people suffering from delirium are frightened, often due to visual hallucinations or delusions. Sometimes they act on these delusions and attempt to leave the room or escape from a situation that they see as threatening. The defining characteristic of delirium is that these psychotic symptoms occur when the person is disoriented in time, place, or person. Some people with delirium are hyperactive; others, who are withdrawn and quiet, may be underdiagnosed as they do not come to the attention of others.

Traumatic Brain Injury

As the name implies, traumatic brain injury (TBI) refers to brain damage caused by an external force. In order for a trauma to the head to result in TBI, the person must experience loss of consciousness, altered mental status (feeling confused or disoriented), or retrograde amnesia (Hoge et al., 2008; Maas et al., 2008). Characteristic cognitive symptoms of TBI are: distractability and impaired attention; impaired recent and remote memory; and visual perceptual impairment. Further, people suffering from TBI often lack the flexibility of reasoning and problem-solving abilities necessary to manage a complex environment. Thus, social and adaptive functioning (or emotional intelligence) is impaired (Granacher, 2003). Behavioural issues include impulsivity, disinhibition, anger dyscontrol, inappropriate sexual behaviours, and lack of initiative (Silver et al., 2011). People with TBI frequently also suffer from other concurrent mental health problems. For instance, approximately 25 per cent people experience depression subsequent to a TBI (Granacher, 2003). Among soldiers with TBI, 43.9 per cent report suffering from symptoms of post-traumatic stress disorder compared to 9.1 per cent of soldiers without TBI (Hoge et al., 2008).

Progressive Neurocognitive Disorders

Progressive neurocognitive disorders, also known as **dementias**, are characterized by multiple deficits, including impairment in memory. These disorders are generally associated with advancing age, but they also might be associated with substance abuse. One hundred years ago, Alois Alzheimer first described the clinical presentation and the characteristic changes we now associate with Alzheimer's disease. In earlier times dementia associated with old age was observed relatively infrequently, but advances in medicine and public health have resulted in longer life expectancies and thus increased rates of illness associated with aging.

The costs of progressive neurocognitive disorders are considerable. The primary cost, of course, is a human one; that is, the inestimable anguish caused by seeing a loved and respected family member gradually declining before our eyes. In addition, there are considerable costs to both health care and social services. The annual societal cost of care per patient with dementia in Canada is estimated to be $32,865 (Alzheimer Society, 2010). There are also indirect economic costs related to loss of productivity and increased financial burden on the families of those suffering from this illness. For instance, US figures estimate the cost of caring for people with dementia is $96 billion in direct medical care, $255 billion in long-term residential care, and $253 billion in the unpaid labour of family members who provide care (Alzheimer Society, 2010).

Incidence and Prevalence

Delirium

Delirium is a constellation of signs and symptoms caused by a malfunction of the brain, often secondary to another medical issue. Therefore, delirium is most commonly found in hospital inpatient wards and emergency departments. The incidence in emergency departments is approaching 10 per cent when strict operational criteria for diagnosis are used, and the incidence may be as high as 50 per cent using the criteria of the "presence of altered mental state" alone (Davis, 2005). Sixty–80 per cent of mechanically ventilated patients in hospital intensive care units experience delirium, lasting on average two days. While the acute symptoms of delirium are transient, over 70 per cent of those recovering from critical illnesses continue to experience cognitive impairments one year later and one-third experience severe impairments (Girard et al., 2010). Delirium tremens occurs in 4–15 per cent of people who are withdrawing from substance abuse (Eyer et al., 2011).

Traumatic Brain Injury

Traumatic brain injury is the leading cause of mortality and disability in young people living in high-income countries. Seventy-five per cent of young adults with TBI are male (Maas et al., 2008). This has profound social and economic effects. In 2005, an estimated 1.1 per cent of civilians in the United States, or 3.7 million people, were living on disability due to TBI (Zaloshnja et al., 2008). When military populations are considered, the rates of TBI are staggering. A large US study revealed that 15 per cent of returning soldiers reported injuries consistent with TBI. As a result, Hoge and colleagues (2008: 454) report that "Traumatic brain injury has been labelled a signature injury of the wars in Iraq and Afghanistan." The total financial burden of TBI in the US has been estimated at over $60 billion per year (Maas et al., 2008).

Progressive Neurocognitive Disorders

By the year 2038 an estimated 1.1 million Canadians will suffer from some form of progressive neurocognitive disorder (dementia), up from 500,000 in 2010 (Alzheimer Society, 2010). Approximately two-thirds of these people will have Alzheimer's disease. While estimates vary, a conservative estimate is that 13.9 per cent of those over the age of 71 suffer from dementia; for those over 85 this goes up to 19.6 per cent; and in the over 90 age group, 37.4 per cent have this devastating disease (Plassman et al., 2007). While dementia is universal, there are some differences based on demographic characteristics. Most studies suggest that females are over-represented in the population of those suffering from dementia. There is an inverse relationship between years of education and the risk of dementia; that is, those with higher levels of education are more likely to develop the disease (Ott et al., 1995; Plassman et al., 2007). There are suggestions that urban populations have higher prevalence rates than rural populations. Notable anomalies in the literature suggest that the Cree have a lower prevalence than other groups in North America and there is a lower prevalence in Nigeria than in other parts of the world (Alzheimer's Disease International, 1999). While the reasons for this are not fully understood, one possibility is that different forms of classification result in differences in reported prevalence (Riedel-Heller et al., 2001).

Factors Contributing to Delirium

While there are many causes of delirium, as shown in Table 10.1, substance abuse, intoxication, and withdrawal are common causes. Delirium is common following surgery, particularly cardiac surgery. Clients who have pre-existing risk factors, including high blood pressure, smoking, or a history of

Table 10.1 Causes of Delirium

Category	Specific Causes
Infections	Pneumonia Brain abscess
Traumatic	Head trauma Subdural hematoma
Metabolic	**Endocrine** (adrenal, thyroid, diabetes) Electrolyte abnormalities Drug abuse/withdrawal Toxins/medications Cardiac failure Liver failure Kidney failure
Carcinogenic	Brain tumour
Vascular	Cerebrovascular accident (CVA), i.e., stroke Transient ischemic attack
Miscellaneous	Burns Post-op Seizure-related

pre-existing cognitive impairment, are likely to have a higher prevalence, as are older people. Clients with a history of alcohol and drug abuse are particularly at risk.

Delirium Due to a General Medical Condition

Delirium caused by a medical condition is a disturbance in consciousness that develops over a short period of time (usually hours or days) and tends to fluctuate during the day. It can be associated with central nervous system assaults such as head trauma, cerebrovascular accidents (e.g., stroke), infection, or a brain tumour; metabolic disorders such as **renal failure**, dehydration, or **hypoglycemia**; cardiopulmonary disorders, such as heart failure or respiratory failure; systemic illnesses or infections such as pneumonia; systemic assaults such as trauma or sensory deprivation.

Substance-Related Delirium

Substance intoxication delirium can occur within minutes or hours of taking a particular substance such as cannabis, cocaine, or hallucinogens. It can occur over time with repeated use of some substances such as diazepam (Valium). Usually this resolves within a few hours or days as the substance leaves the body. Substance withdrawal delirium can last for a few hours or up to two to four weeks, depending on the nature of the drug.

Factors Contributing to Traumatic Brain Injury

The extent of the damage caused by assaults on the brain is dependent on the nature, intensity, and duration of the assault and occurs at both the macroscopic and microscopic levels. Macroscopic-level injuries include intracranial contusions, hematomas, swelling, and hypoxia (oxygen deprivation). Microscopic injuries include hemorrhages from torn blood vessels (Maas et al., 2008).

Factors Contributing to Progressive Neurocognitive Disorders

While progressive neurocognitive disorders can be caused by a number of different conditions, such as hypothyroidism or vitamin B12 deficiency (Davis, 2005), they are generally related to one of two forms of deterioration: (1) that affecting the cerebral cortex and (2) that affecting subcortical areas. The cortical dementias include Alzheimer's disease and Pick's disease. Subcortical dementias include Huntington's dementia, Parkinson's dementia, and Lewy body dementia (see Figure 9.1).

Alois Alzheimer's groundbreaking work in 1906 described two types of microscopic findings in the brains of people suffering from Alzheimer's, namely, the amyloid plaque and characteristic tangles in filaments of the brain known as neurofibrillary tangles. Later research has determined that the development of amyloid plaque contributes to the formation of the neurofibrillary tangles, which in turn leads to damage of nerve cells and subsequently their loss or **atrophy**. It has been established that the pathology associated with Alzheimer's results in significant neuronal loss such that the brain is lighter when weighed on post-mortem examination than those of people without this disease (Barcia, 2000; Stahl, 2000). More recently, studies of Alzheimer's have shown that the disease can be inherited through autosomal dominant transmission, and one particular mutated gene has been identified.

Alzheimer's Disease

Alzheimer's disease (AD) is the most common form of cognitive disorder and thus the area where we will focus much of the attention for the remainder of this chapter. In general, AD is diagnosed by ruling out all other causes of neurocognitive impairment. AD can be divided into early onset (before the age of 65) and late onset (after the age of 65). It can also be differentiated based on whether or not there are clinically significant behavioural issues that cause difficulties for family members and caregivers.

Vascular Neurocognitive Disorder

This neurocognitive disorder develops secondarily to vascular disease such as strokes or multiple infarcts. It can occur with or without delirium, delusions, or depressed mood. Generally, symptoms include aphasia (language disturbances), apraxia (difficulty performing tasks), agnosia (failure to recognize objects), and disturbances in executive functioning (planning, organizing, etc.).

Specific Medical Neurocognitive Disorders

A number of neurocognitive disorders are caused by specific medical conditions. These include dementia due to: Parkinson's disease; HIV; Huntington's disease; Pick's disease; and Creutzfeldt-Jakob disease (also known as "mad cow disease").

Substance-Induced Neurocognitive Disorder

This type of disorder is the result of chronic substance use. Korsakoff's syndrome, which is often equated with substance-induced dementia, is a specific condition stemming from a vitamin B1 (thiamine) deficiency caused by chronic alcoholism or severe malnutrition. Alcoholism often results in poor nutrition, which, in addition to inflammation of the stomach lining, leads to thiamine deficiency. Other causes can include dietary deficiencies, prolonged vomiting, eating disorders, or the effects of chemotherapy.

The Course of Progressive Neurocognitive Disorders

The course of Alzheimer's disease is typically characterized by a gradual and subtle onset, followed by a slow progression. The initial symptoms, usually only diagnosable by psychological testing, are referred to as mild cognitive impairment (MCI). MCI progresses to dementia at the rate of approximately 3 to 15 per cent per year, and within 10 years 70 to 80 per cent of cases with MCI will have developed Alzheimer's (Backman, 2008; Craik, 2008). A person with mild cognitive impairment generally experiences isolated memory loss that gradually progresses to more generalized neurocognitive impairment over a period of two to five years. After a further two to three years, assisted living is often necessary due to significant deterioration in functioning. As the disease progresses a number of physical changes occur including appetite disturbance and weight loss, difficulty walking, tremors, and incontinence. Later in the disease, clients have difficulty eating and swallowing and become bedridden, leading to further complications such as bedsores and bronchial infections. Eventually, patients tend to die from pneumonia or blood poisoning, often 9–10 years after the initial diagnosis is made.

Vascular neurocognitive disorder is differentiated by a stepwise intellectual deterioration. This is thought to be caused by small progressive cerebrovascular accidents (CVAs) or strokes. These micro-strokes gradually cause deterioration. Generally, at least one significant stroke has occurred, although this is not always the case. In vascular dementia the clinical history, neurological examination, and brain-imaging studies can be used to confirm the diagnosis. There is generally a family history of vascular disease and the client may have other risk factors such as hypertension, smoking, or obesity. Symptomatology varies significantly due to the fact that different areas of the brain may be targeted. Neuroimaging may demonstrate the exact lesions. Lewy body disease is a progressive neurocognitive disorder with features of Parkinson's disease. People with this disorder not uncommonly suffer delusions and visual hallucinations. The differential diagnosis is complicated by the fact that Lewy body disease may appear in clients with AD. In the frontotemporal dementias such as Pick's disease, there is a marked change in personality and language. This is also characterized by gradual onset and a progressively deteriorating course. In some cases this occurs at a younger age than AD. There is often a family history of frontotemporal dementia.

Symptoms

Memory Loss

All people experience some cognitive differences as they age, and sometimes this leads to dementia. Those who go on to develop dementia have demonstrated memory impairments many years before the clinical diagnosis is made in both AD and vascular neurocognitive disorder (Backman, 2008). The earliest changes tend to be in recent or working memory where encoding and retrieval of information is required (Craik, 2008; Luo and Craik, 2008). This presents as a difficulty noting and remembering names, losing simple objects such as car keys, or forgetting specific events such as appointments or dinner dates. Other types of memory, for instance, general knowledge and biographical information, are generally only affected much later. Moderate cognitive impairment (MCI) can be diagnosable by specific cognitive testing.

Personality Change

It is not unusual to find personality changes in those suffering from progressive neurocognitive diseases, often causing great distress to the family members and friends (Neugroschl et al., 2005). Characteristically occurring are apathy and listlessness, with a narrowing of emotions, especially the loss of warmth and humour. The client seems to lose interest in everything and may sit all day apparently doing very little. Some display embarrassing and disinhibited behaviours, although this is most common in the frontotemporal dementias.

Aggression is not uncommon and may be related to psychotic symptoms, such as delusions and hallucinations, as well as the perplexity of not knowing where they are, or of not recognizing caregivers.

Functional Impairment

The first signs of functional impairment may be related to financial transactions or use of transportation. Later, the client may become easily lost and be unable to discern the function of commonly used appliances such as a PVR or, as things progress, a kettle or a toaster. These initial changes may at first be subtle but as the illness progresses they become more marked. Activities of daily living, including dressing and attention to hygiene, may be impaired, leading to the necessity of providing increased support services.

Language

Generally speaking, the first facet of language to deteriorate is word-finding, that is, remembering the right word to describe something. This may lead to unusual or idiosyncratic speech, such as frequent repetitions or use of **malapropisms**. Later, comprehension and all aspects of language may be affected.

Agnosis

This may initially present itself as a difficulty in recognizing and naming objects. As the dementia progresses there may be significant impairment and lack of recognition of people's faces, even of close friends and family, a symptom that is particularly distressing. Perhaps the only **pathognomonic** sign of AD is the inability to recognize one's own face in the mirror (Lovestone, 2000), which can be very frightening. Pathognomonic refers to a sign or symptom that is so characteristic of a disease that it makes the diagnosis.

Psychosis

Of those suffering from AD, 10 to 50 per cent have delusions. These are characteristically persecutory delusions but may also include delusions of misidentification (Capgras syndrome) or delusions of jealousy. Hallucinations are not quite as common but may include the more usual visual hallucinations as well as auditory hallucinations.

Assessment of Progressive Neurocognitive Disorder

Progressive neurocognitive disorders are usually identified through a careful assessment, sometimes over a period of time in repeated visits. Home visits are often helpful in order to see the client in the context of her or his daily life and to perform functional assessments. These can be surprising. In some cases clients who seemed quite impaired in the unfamiliar surroundings of a hospital can cope quite well at home. In other cases a client who appeared quite coherent at a single interview may appear dysfunctional in the complex atmosphere of home. Since the client is often unable to give a history, collateral information is absolutely vital. Thus, the role of the social worker can be of great assistance to the team in determining the extent of the illness and the consequences for the client and family.

Other members of the interdisciplinary team should be paying attention to possibly treatable causes of dementia such as diabetes, thyroid abnormalities, or vitamin B12 deficiency. Routine laboratory tests such as a full blood count, thyroid test, blood calcium level, a serum B12 level, and fasting glucose should be performed in all cases. A CT scan, to search for other causes such as **subdural hematoma** (a brain injury in which there is bleeding into the lining of the brain) or **hydrocephalus** (abnormal accumulation of bodily fluid in the brain), is helpful and may reveal the typical atrophy (neuronal loss) found in AD (Greenberg and Muraca, 2007).

Brief cognitive screening can be very helpful in identifying dementia, and such screening can be performed by the social worker in any setting (Feldman et al., 2008). These tests are targeted towards the client's needs and abilities and can assist the social worker in determining whether a referral for additional assessment should be made and what types of social work interventions might be most useful. The mini-mental status examination (MMSE) can be performed in 10 minutes and requires little training (see Table 10.2). A maximum score is 30; a score of between 18 and 26 demonstrates mild dementia; a score

Box 10.1 The Clock-Drawing Test

Method:
The person undergoing testing is asked to:

- Draw a clock
- Put in all the numbers
- Set the hands at 10 past 11

Scoring:
There are a number of scoring systems for this test.
The Alzheimer's disease cooperative scoring system is based on a score of five points.

- 1 point for the clock circle
- 1 point for all the numbers being in the correct order
- 1 point for the numbers being in the proper special order
- 1 point for the two hands of the clock
- 1 point for the correct time

A normal score is four or five points.

Table 10.2 The Mini-Mental Satus Exam

Maximum score	Score	
		Orientation
5	( )	What is the: (year) (season) (date) (day) (month)
5	( )	Where are we: (city, province, country) (facility/address) (floor/room)
		Registration
3	( )	Name three objects and have person repeat them back. Give one point for each correct answer on the first trial. 1. ___________ 2. ___________ 3. ___________ Then repeat them (up to 6 times) until all three are learned. [Number of trials ______]
		Attention and calculation
5	( )	Serial 7s. Count backwards from 100 by serial 7s. One point for each correct answer. Stop after 5 answers. [93, 86, 79, 72, 65] Alternatively spell "world" forward and then backward. [D - L - R - O - W]
		Recall
3	( )	Ask for the names of the three objects learned above. Give one point for each correct answer.
		Language
9	( )	Name: a pen (1 point) and a watch (1 point) Repeat the following: "No ifs, ands, or buts" (1 point) Follow a three-stage command: "Take this paper in your [non-dominant] hand, fold it in half, and put it on the floor." (3 points) [1 point for each part correctly performed] Read to self and then do: "Close your eyes" (1 point) Write a sentence [subject, verb, and makes sense] (1 point) Copy design [5-sided geometric figure; 2 points must intersect] (1 point)
Score: /30		

of 10 to 18 indicates moderate dementia; and less than 10 indicates severe dementia. A standardized version of the MMSE based on the work of Molloy and colleagues (1991) can be found online from the British Columbia Ministry of Health (www.health.gov.bc.ca/pharmacare/adti/clinician/pdf/ADTI%20SMMSE-GDS%20Reference%20Card.pdf).

The clock-drawing test (Box 10.1) is a quick and simple test that again requires only a few minutes and little training. The individual is simply asked to draw a clock and write in the numbers and show the time at 10 minutes past 11. The test is surprisingly sensitive and specific.

Special Issues for Family Members Caring for Relatives with Neurocognitive Disorders

Caregiver burden is defined as the negative impact on one's social, occupational, and personal well-being as a result of caring for an infirm person, usually a relative. The burden experienced by caregivers of those with neurocognitive disorders results from the functional deficits of the ill person, the degree to which he or she depends on family members for personal care, for instance, with hygiene, disorientation, and disruptive behaviours such as wandering and aggression (Sussman, 2006). As a result of this burden, family members often experience depression and a variety of physical health problems related to stress (Gonzalez-Salvador et al., 1999). In one study of family caregivers for individuals with Alzheimer's disease, 65 per cent exhibited symptoms of depression (Papastavrou et al., 2007). Clearly, this is an issue of great concern to social workers as the well-being of the client with dementia is highly contingent on the well-being of those family members who participate in that person's care.

Caregiver burden can be experienced by anyone caring for a person with a neurocognitive disorder. In Alzheimer's disease it is most commonly associated with care provided by offspring, primarily adult daughters who become caught between the needs of their impaired parents or parents-in-law and the needs of their own spouses and children. It has recently been suggested that spousal caregivers often experience the highest burden of care. First, spousal caregivers are grieving the loss of their partner, as a result of a long and devastating illness. Although the person with progressive neurocognitive disorder is physically alive, his or her psychological presence in the relationship dissipates as the disease progresses. In addition to facing the loss of their lifelong partner, spousal caregivers of persons with dementia are more likely to struggle with their own health problems, spend more hours per week caregiving, and care for relatives with more severe behavioural problems than other familial caregivers (Sussman and Regehr, 2009).

As indicated earlier, individuals who have traumatic brain injuries are frequently younger people who sustained the injury as a result of an accident or military service. Consequently, caregivers are suddenly tasked with caring for a person who may no longer achieve the goals, hopes, and dreams they have mutually held. Caregiver stress is associated with depression, motor dysfunction, substance misuse, and personality change in the person suffering from a TBI (Davis et al., 2009; Kreutzer et al., 2009; Livingston et al., 2010). As a result of the losses and burdens experienced, caregivers commonly report depression, anxiety, and somatic symptoms (Kreutzer et al., 2009).

A significant degree of caregiver stress has emerged as a result of government policies that focus on deinstitutionalization, which is the movement of the care of the elderly and infirm from institutions to the community. Part of this shift has been ideological; that is, the quality of life is thought to be better for individuals moved to the community. It also has been ideological in that conservative political leaders in North America have been determined in recent years to do away with "big government" and the direct involvement of government in people's lives. Another reason for this move has been financially driven, in that community-based care is far less expensive than institutional care. The lower cost is in large part due to limited resources flowing to community care and a reliance on family members to take over care responsibilities that might otherwise be provided by members of the health-care team (Sussman and Regehr, 2009). For instance, family members may become responsible for medication management, for ensuring the person gets to medical appointments, for assisting with activities of daily living such as showering and dressing, and even for some medical treatments, such as dressing of wounds. Social workers need to become familiar with the nature of tasks required of any family member and advocate for community-based services as required.

Abuse of Older People with Neurocognitive Disorders

In 2002, the World Health Organization (WHO) published the *Toronto Declaration on the Global Prevention of Elder Abuse* that included the following definition: "Elder abuse is a single or repeated act, or lack of appropriate action, occurring within any relationship where there is an expectation of trust, which causes harm or distress to an older person. It can be of various forms: physical, psychological/emotional, sexual, financial, or simply reflect intentional or unintentional neglect." Further, the declaration states: "Elder abuse is the violation of human rights and a significant cause of injury, illness, lost productivity, isolation, and despair. Confronting and reducing elder abuse requires a multi-disciplinary approach." WHO estimates that the rate of elder abuse across Canada, the Netherlands, the United States, Finland, and Great Britain is between 4 and 6 per cent. In Canada, approximately 7 per cent of 4,000 adults aged 65 and older who responded to the 1999 General Social Survey on Victimization (GSS) reported that they had experienced some form of emotional abuse by an adult child, spouse, or caregiver in the past five years, 1 per cent reported physical abuse, and 1 per cent reported financial abuse (Statistics Canada, 2002).

While health-care practitioners are most likely to be in a position to identify abuse of an elderly person, everyone has an obligation to ensure that vulnerable individuals in our society are safe from harm. Several tools exist for screening for abuse; some require training and others are simple to administer without training. One of the most user-friendly tools can be distilled into six short screening questions, as shown in Box 10.2 (Fulmer et al., 2004; Bomba, 2006). The use of these questions not only identifies abuse but also demonstrates an openness to discussing issues of abuse and the desire to offer assistance.

If elder abuse is suspected, there are three issues to consider (Bomba, 2006): (1) Is the person safe? (2) Will the person accept intervention? (3) Does the person have the capacity to refuse intervention? Not all abuse situations constitute an emergency and thus if the person is safe, it is possible to develop a longer-term relationship and move towards a plan to end the abuse if the person agrees to intervention. If the person does not agree to allow assistance, intervention can be forced only if the individual does not have the capacity to consent to or refuse intervention. That is, people are allowed the self-determination to remain in abusive situations if they fully understand the nature and consequences of their decision. If they are not competent to consent or refuse, other options such as Adult Protective Services can be called in to assist (Donovan and Regehr, 2010).

When the assessment reveals that an elderly person has been abused and he or she agrees to the intervention, safety plans and alternative living arrangements can be initiated. The problem arises when the person is unwilling to agree to the intervention. In such a case a determination must be made whether the individual is competent to consent. In order for a person to have this capacity he or she must be able to understand information provided and how that information applies to her or his specific situation. The Ontario Health Care Consent Act (1996), for instance, states that a person is capable of consenting to treatment if "the person is able to understand the information that is relevant to making a decision about the treatment . . . and able to appreciate the reasonably foreseeable consequences of a decision or lack of decision" (section 4[1]). As discussed in Chapter 3, capacity is multi-faceted and fluctuating. For instance, a person may be capable of consenting to a particular procedure at one time but incapable of consenting to the same procedure at another time

Box 10.2 Elder Abuse Screening

1. Are you afraid of anyone in your family?
2. Has anyone close to you tried to hurt or harm you recently?
3. Has anyone close to you called you names or put you down or made you feel bad recently?
4. Does someone in your family make you stay in bed or tell you you're sick when you aren't?
5. Has anyone forced you to do things you did not want to do?
6. Has anyone taken things that belong to you without your agreement?

(Regehr and Kanani, 2010). As a result of the complexities around the issue of consent and the risk of undermining the civil rights and self-determination of elderly individuals, Adult Protective Services as an approach to elder abuse remains highly controversial (Anderson and Mangels, 2006).

Recovery-Oriented Approaches to the Treatment of Delirium

The treatment of delirium can be effectively divided into three separate phases, although inevitably a lot of overlap exists among these phases: investigation of the underlying causes; instituting management of the acute phase; and stabilization and recovery.

Investigation of the Underlying Cause

The first stage of intervention is a thorough evaluation and risk assessment to establish the diagnosis in the context of any underlying conditions that may have predisposed the individual to delirium (Foreman et al., 2003). This will often include collateral information obtained from relatives and caregivers, as the client will be unlikely to give a coherent history. The history should include illnesses and injuries, medications, and, most importantly, premorbid functioning. The client will often be in a hospital setting, thus allowing for a thorough physical examination and workup, including toxicology. Once etiological factors are determined, the underlying cause can be treated or corrected. For example, if the cause is a lack of oxygen (hypoxia), this could indicate that the administration of oxygen may cure the problem.

Management of the Acute Situation

It is sometimes necessary to administer medications on an emergency basis to treat the psychotic symptoms and to prevent the client from harming him/herself or others (Barcia, 2000). Generally speaking, low doses of conventional antipsychotic medication remain the standard intervention (see Table 7.1). In higher doses these medications have side effects that may be troublesome. More recently, the second-generation antipsychotics have been increasingly used and are at least as effective, with fewer side effects (see Table 7.2). In an acutely agitated client a small dose of a short-acting benzodiazepine (Lorazepam) is commonly used, often in conjunction with an antipsychotic.

Stabilization and Recovery

It is essential to provide a therapeutic environment, monitoring the right amount of stimulation, along with calm and consistent reassurance. Both patients and family members should be provided with information about the disorder and the course of recovery. Exposure to familiar people and belongings can help restore calm in somebody who is perplexed about the current situation. Family members can assist by talking about familiar people and events and by reminding the person where they are and what date, time, and season it is. Early mobilization is essential and as the client progresses, cognitively stimulating activities, such as providing conversation, games, and reading matter, as well as constant reality orientation, may be helpful (Foreman et al., 2003). Delirium can be a particularly upsetting experience for clients and their families, and mental health workers should provide follow-up discussions and possibly debriefing or brief therapy if this is considered likely.

Recovery-Oriented Psychosocial Interventions for Traumatic Brain Injury

The recovery model may not immediately seem applicable to working with people with traumatic brain injury. Within the recovery model, however, recovery is not understood to be synonymous with sustained remission or cure. Rather, recovery can be defined as living a satisfying, hopeful, and contributing life even with the limitations caused by the illness (Anthony, 1993). From this perspective, social workers must have an optimistic and hope-inducing view of the ability of people to find meaning in their experiences and to generate narratives about themselves that do not include the disease and subsequent disability (Slade and Hayward, 2007).

Comprehensive-Holistic Rehabilitation Programs

As a consequence of the large number of behavioural and emotional issues associated with TBI, behavioural and psychosocial interventions are an important adjunct to neuropsychological and physical rehabilitation programs (Cattelani et al., 2010). Some models of intervention involve traditional behaviour therapies (BT) aimed at managing and altering specific behavioural problems. Other interventions use cognitive-behavioural therapy (CBT) to address the emotional consequents of TBI. Comprehensive-holistic rehabilitation programs (CHRPs) focus on the development of compensatory behaviours and adaptive skills in light of limitations faced due to TBI. Key elements of this model include: elements of CBT and BT to address emotional and behavioural challenges; active involvement of both clients and their families; vocational and independent living trials; and group activities focusing on peer support, problem-solving, and feedback (Cattelani et al., 2010; Bertisch et al., 2011). The CHRP model requires multi-disciplinary team involvement and individualized recovery planning with clients and the families. A recent systematic review concluded that the CHRP approach is associated with the greatest overall improvement in functioning for people with TBI (Cattelani et al., 2010).

Recovery-Oriented Interventions for Progressive Neurocognitive Disorders

In cases of progressive neurocognitive disorders, early identification and treatment are essential. Various research studies have demonstrated that interventions focused on increased cognitive activity appear to be preventative of dementia and perhaps slow its progress, although this is yet to be well established (Stahl, 2000; Herrmann and Lanctot, 2007; Seow and Gauthier, 2007). These cognitive activities include discussions and any type of intellectual stimulation, such as working on crossword puzzles. It has also been suggested that regular exercise and physical activity also play a preventative role. These activities at least can produce meaning, involve enjoyment, and engender hope.

Caregiver Support and Relief

One form of prevention attempts to address family stress caused by caregiving. In this approach, increased services are offered in the community, such as community nursing and day treatment programs for elderly individuals with physical disabilities (for instance, caused by stroke) or dementia. The notion is that increased services will result in reduced stress and burden. A recent study of spousal caregivers of people with dementia, however, suggests that services alone do not provide a simple solution to caregiver stress. Using interviews and surveys, the study found that in-home services, such as homemakers, nurses, occupational therapists, and case managers, did little to reduce burden of spouses caring for their partners with dementia. In fact, the stress of dealing with multiple service delivery people in the home created additional stress for some. Rather, the only effective service in reducing caregiver stress in this study was the provision of adult day treatment programs (sometimes referred to as daycare) that provided not only respite for the family caregiver, but also opportunities for social interaction for the individual suffering from a neurocognitive disorder (Sussman and Regehr, 2009).

Reminiscence Therapy and Reality Orientation for Progressive Neurocognitive Disorders

Reminiscence therapy involves the recall of life events or the telling of one's life story either to an individual or within a group context. The main objectives of reminiscence therapy are to facilitate the recall of past experiences, strengthen the sense of personal identity, and promote interpersonal functioning, thus improving well-being. In addition, however, reminiscence therapy, particularly in a group context, provides cognitively impaired individuals with opportunities for social interaction and enjoyment. Reminiscence therapy is sometimes combined with other forms of treatment such as art therapy or music therapy. In these cases, the clients with dementia engage in some activity and then engage in discussions about topics that emerge from previous life experiences (Moos and Bjorn, 2006). Controlled studies have demonstrated that this type of intervention both improves cognitive abilities and reduces depression in individuals suffering from dementia (Woods et al., 2005; Moos and Bjorn, 2006; Wang, 2007). In addition, caregiver strain showed a significant decrease for caregivers participating in groups with their relative with dementia in reminiscence therapy, and staff knowledge of group members' backgrounds improved significantly, thereby enhancing interactions between clients and staff. No harmful effects were identified on the outcome measures reported.

Reality orientation (RO) is a model of therapy intended to address disorientation caused by lack of sensory stimuli in people with severe neurocognitive disorders. It is based on the belief that continually and repeatedly telling or showing certain reminders to people with mild to moderate memory loss will result in an increase in interaction with others and improved orientation. In people in the early stages of dementia, RO can involve looking at newspapers and reviewing important issues (Spector et al., 2000). During the process, the person is reminded of the date and of upcoming important events, such as elections. Depending on the progress of the illness, flashcards, games, or puzzles can be used to stimulate mental activity. In very confused individuals, the focus may be on the person's name, family members identified in pictures, or familiar objects. A *Cochrane Review* (Spector et al., 2000) and other meta-analyses (Bates et al., 2004) conclude that RO has a significant short-term effect on cognition and behaviour.

Pharmacology as Part of a Recovery-Oriented Approach to Progressive Neurocognitive Disorders

Medications Targeting Cognitive Functioning

The primary theory that relates to psychopharmacological therapy in dementia is the acetylcholine theory. According to this theory, a substance called acetyl COA combines with choline to produce acetylcholine. This is facilitated by an enzyme called choline acetyl transferase. Acetylcholine, in turn, is broken down into two substances, acetylcholinesterase (AChE) and butyryl cholinesterase (BuChE). It has been established that a deficit of acetylcholine in certain parts of the brain leads to a decrease in memory. Conversely, restoring this deficit by increasing acetylcholine enhances memory. The medications most commonly used are called cholinesterase inhibitors. They work by delaying the breakdown of acetylcholine released into the synaptic cleft, thereby leaving more acetylcholine available.

As a result of these findings, substances that boost acetylcholine levels have been devised and tested experimentally and clinically on clients suffering from dementia. However, despite early excitement about this approach, the results have been somewhat disappointing. While the response to these medications tends to be detectable on psychological testing and perhaps on rating scales done by caregivers, unfortunately, the response is not detectable by the client. Generally speaking, the effects last for six months and, for reasons that are unclear, the client then reverts to her or his previous level of functioning. This may mean that the deterioration is delayed for six months, meaning in some cases six precious months at home as opposed to the nursing home (Birks, 2006; Seow and Gauthier, 2007).

It is postulated that amyloid plaque formation causes inflammation in the brain that may be partly responsible for the symptoms of dementia. For this reason Aspirin and other anti-inflammatory drugs have been used in the treatment of dementia. At this stage there is little evidence to support their use. Research is underway in an attempt to find vaccines to prevent beta amyloid formation. This is a very exciting possibility, although it is unlikely that such vaccines will be available in the near future.

A growing body of evidence from observational and anecdotal sources suggests that omega-3 fatty acid supplements may have a protective effect against dementia. The few clinical trials available have shown that at best there was an arrested decline in patients with mild forms of AD. Various other agents have been used in the treatment of dementia, with varying degrees of success. Folic acid is one of the vitamins that has shown some promise in general use. It is known that decreased folic acid can be one of the reversible causes of dementia and it is thought that this deficit may play a more general role in cognitive disorders. However, the routine use of folic acid has not been proven to have a positive effect. Ginkgo biloba demonstrated some early promise but the more exacting *Cochrane Review* demonstrated that although early trials showed some promise, these trials were small and unsatisfactory. Larger and more rigorous trials found no difference between placebo and ginkgo biloba. It is postulated that **circadian rhythms** are disturbed in dementia and this may result in some of the symptoms. Therefore, if the timing systems are synchronized by bright-light therapy (see Chapter 8) and melatonin is taken at night, this regime may moderately improve sleep, attenuate cognitive function, and decrease aggression (Riemersma-van der Lek et al., 2008).

Medications Targeting Neuropsychiatric Symptoms

The prevalence of agitation and aggression is alarmingly high in dementia and results in substantial anguish to clients and their caregivers. The first line of treatment is thought to be the SSRI antidepressants, which are discussed in Chapter 8. Generally speaking, doses are significantly lower than those used in younger clients with mood disorders. A number of other agents have proved to be successful, including some of the anticonvulsant mood stabilizers, such as carbamazepine as well as trazodone and buspirone (Glancy and Knott, 2003). Often, agitation and aggression are secondary to delusions and hallucinations and, therefore, antipsychotics have been widely used for these disorders. Although conventional antipsychotics were used for many years, recently the second-generation agents have been used (Ballard et al., 2006). The effects have been modestly successful, with a response rate of over 60 per cent. A recent comprehensive study, the CATIE-AD, however, has demonstrated disappointing results in the risk-benefit balance in the use of antipsychotics in dementia (Herrmann and Lanctot, 2007). Nevertheless, short-term administration can be useful, although consideration should be given to weaning the client off these medications if possible.

Possible Social Work Interventions in the Case Examples

Case Example 1: Justin

Justin is suffering from traumatic brain injury that has resulted in significant impairments in cognitive and physical functioning, personality change, and violence that results from frustration with his limitations and lack of cognitive capacity to cope with frustration. This is a disturbing and frightening situation for both Justin and his family.

- The social worker will be part of a multi-disciplinary team assisting Justin and his family through a comprehensive-holistic rehabilitation program. It is thus vital that the team is clear on the goals for Justin's recovery and the role of each member of the team in achieving these goals.
- Psychoeducational approaches will be critical for Justin and his family so they can understand opportunities and challenges that are commonly experienced after traumatic brain injury and do not blame Justin for issues outside his control or excuse him from behaviours that are within his control.
- Justin may benefit from cognitive-behavioural therapy to address his emotional and behavioural responses to his situation.
- The social worker may further run group treatments that provide Justin with peer feedback, support, and social opportunities to assist him with reintegration into his community.

Case Example 2: John

John was suffering from delirium subsequent to major cardiac surgery. This delirium was relatively short-lived and cleared before he was discharged from hospital. A social worker involved in this case is most likely a medical social worker who regularly works in an ICU or on a surgical unit.

- Social work interventions in this case would focus on the family. In large part this will involve psychoeducation about the nature of post-operative delirium and reassurance that this is a normal and transient reaction. In addition, the social worker may discuss plans for John's return home and adjustments that will have to be made based on his medical condition.

Summary

Three types of illnesses are generally grouped together as neurocognitive disorders. The first, delirium, is usually a transient state of confusion secondary to either substance abuse or a major medical problem, often one that results in surgery. The second is traumatic brain injury, in which neurocognitive damage is inflicted by an external assault. The third type consists of progressive neurocognitive disorders or dementias, which are characterized by progressive deterioration in cognitive functioning that increasingly affects social interactions, emotional responses, and behaviour, and eventually is related to physical decline. In all types of neurocognitive disorders, work with family focuses on support, psychoeducation, and advocacy for resources. In cases of TBI, intensive work can involve addressing the emotional impact of the losses experienced and developing compensatory strategies for social and vocational reintegration. In dementia, work with clients can involve collaborating to restore and preserve memory and cognitive functioning through active use of cognitive strategies (such as reality orientation and reminiscence) and active engagement in satisfying activities.

Discussion Questions

1. What differentiates delirium from progressive neurocognitive disorders?
2. How might social work interventions differ when working with clients and families suffering from delirium, traumatic brain injury, and progressive neurocognitive disorders?

3. How may the recovery model be applied to work with clients with progressive neurocognitive disorders?
4. In what ways can social workers use advocacy skills with respect to work with clients with traumatic brain injuries?

Suggested Readings and Websites

Alzheimer's Society. "Living with Dementia." At: www.alzheimer.ca/en/Living-with-dementia. This site is an invaluable resource for families and clients that contains information, resources, and "brain-boosting" activities.

World Health Organization. 2002. *Toronto Declaration on the Global Prevention of Elder Abuse*. At: www.who.int/ageing/projects/elder_abuse/alc_toronto_declaration_en.pdf. The Toronto Declaration specifies the international commitment to address elder abuse.

11 Substance-Related Disorders

Learning Objectives

- To identify factors contributing to substance-related disorders.
- To identify and describe substances of abuse.
- To present models for assessing substance-related disorders.
- To present a spectrum of interventions for substance use.

Case Example 1

Lily is a happily married 34-year-old woman who stays at home caring for her six-year-old son. She was an accomplished ice dancer and met her husband, a stockbroker who works long hours, while travelling to an international competition. Lily's father struggled with alcoholism, and her parents separated when she was in her teens. Lily suffers from repetitive migraines. She worked with her family practitioner to find a suitable medication, but the only one that worked well was OxyContin, an opiate that is addictive and subject to abuse. The doctor prescribed 30 tablets at a time for her migraines, to be taken up to three times a day when the need arose. As time went by, Lily began using more and more medication and frequently phoned her family practitioner's office for a repeat prescription. Her doctor tried to limit the prescriptions as best she could. However, Lily then went to see another doctor and began obtaining repeat prescriptions for the same medication. In time, even this became insufficient and on one occasion she slipped the doctor's prescription pad into her pocket and wrote a prescription for herself (for 30 tablets). The pharmacist became suspicious and called the police, who charged Lily with fraud.

Case Example 2

Salvatore is a 27-year-old who dropped out of high school at 15 and began working in his father's contracting business. As a teenager he smoked marijuana daily and occasionally used crack cocaine, which he did not like because he said "it made me paranoid." At age 18 Sal was admitted to hospital after using crack and was diagnosed with substance-induced psychosis. He returned to his parent's home but continued to use drugs and was readmitted to hospital on two occasions in a psychotic state. He was subsequently diagnosed as suffering from schizophrenia. His doctor prescribes risperidone (Risperdal) injections for his psychotic symptoms and benztropine (Cogentin) to reduce the side effects of the other medication. Sal indicates that he smokes marijuana every day because it reduces intolerable feelings of anxiety. He also has discovered that benztropine "gives him a buzz" and therefore he purchases additional amounts from other patients. Salvatore hangs around a coffee shop near the hospital, he is unable to work, and when he is at home he isolates himself in his room.

Case Example 3

David is a 70-year-old who was admitted to hospital after a minor accident that resulted in a complicated fracture of his leg. The reparative surgery was uneventful, but two to three days after surgery David became disoriented, somewhat frightened, and appeared to be reacting to visual hallucinations. He was diagnosed as having delirium tremens and was treated by the hospital staff. The abnormalities in his mental state resolved within 24 hours. Further history revealed that David had been in the habit of consuming a bottle of whisky a day for the past 20 years. Although his wife frequently suggested he cut down on his drinking and seek help, he had never admitted to having a problem. David is a retired family practitioner who has been married for 40 years. He has three sons, all of whom are accomplished professionals. He is somewhat shy and retiring, eschewing crowds, parties, and social events. However, when the family has a barbecue or other event he is often the life and soul of the party.

The Nature of Substance-Related Disorders

It is impossible to avoid issues of substance abuse in any branch of mental health work. Given the extraordinarily high prevalence of use and misuse of prescription, illicit, and over-the-counter substances and their pernicious effect on other disorders, the impact on our clients, their families, and society is staggering. Substance abuse is central to social work practice, with one estimate suggesting that 61 per cent of social workers see people with substance-related disorders in some capacity, including assessment and referral; 19 per cent are involved in the treatment of substance abuse (Rapp et al., 2003). Substance-related disorders contribute to a number of psychosocial and physical problems (Minozzi et al., 2008). These problems are diverse and multiple. Fifty per cent of traffic deaths are attributed to alcohol. Substance use significantly contributes to interpersonal aggression (such as intimate partner violence and child abuse), crime, and homicide. Mood and anxiety disorders and suicide are significantly related to substance abuse. Other social problems include unemployment and subsequent debt and homelessness.

The World Health Organization published a report entitled the *Global Status Report on Alcohol and Health* (2011) in which it is suggested that 2.5 million deaths per year are attributable to harmful use of alcohol. This represents 6.2 per cent of all male deaths and 1.1 per cent of female deaths. Forty-two per cent of all alcohol-attributable deaths are due to intentional and unintentional injuries incurred during intoxication. WHO estimates that 9.2 per cent of disease worldwide can be attributed to alcohol use. Such alcohol-related diseases include cancer, hypertension, cardiovascular disease, liver cirrhosis, fetal alcohol syndrome, and psychiatric disorders. In addition, alcohol contributes to motor vehicle accidents, interpersonal violence, and suicide (Witkiewitz and Marlatt, 2006).

Alcohol-related costs account for 1 to 5 per cent of the gross domestic product (GDP) of countries across the world. These costs include treatment, prevention, law enforcement, and lost productivity. The United States spends 2.7 per cent of its GDP on the direct costs of alcohol abuse (Rehm et al., 2009) and has 0.9 per cent GDP in productivity losses related to drug abuse (UN, 2012). Canada spends 1.4 per cent of its GDP on direct costs of alcohol abuse (Rehm et al., 2009). In 2010 the abuse of illegal drugs and alcohol cost the Canadian economy an estimated $23 billion, including $4.4 billion in health care and $5.4 billion in crime (Canadian Centre on Substance Abuse, 2011). In England, alcohol misuse alone results in 17 million workdays lost per year; alcohol-related crime and disorder cost the country £7.3 billion annually and lost productivity due to alcohol costs £6.4 billion (Luty and Carnwath, 2008).

Substance-related disorders, as defined by DSM-5, can involve the abuse of prescription medications that were originally intended to treat another medical issue, street or illegal drugs, and/or alcohol. DSM-5 identifies two main types of substance-related disorders: (1) *substance use disorders* and (2) *substance-induced disorders*. Substance use disorder refers to the "cluster of cognitive, behavioural, and physiological symptoms indicating that the individual continues using the substance despite significant substance-related problems" (APA, 2013: 483). For instance, alcohol use disorder includes a problematic pattern of use characterized by unsuccessful efforts to reduce use, excessive time spent in activities necessary to obtain alcohol, craving, failure to fulfill major role obligations, tolerance (the need for increased amount to become intoxicated), and/or withdrawal. Substance-induced disorders include intoxication, withdrawal, substance-induced psychosis, and substance-induced depressive disorder.

Incidence and Prevalence

According to the 2011 Canadian Alcohol and Drug Use Monitoring Survey, 9.1 per cent of Canadians over the age of 15 have used cannabis in the past year. This rate is twice as high for males (12.2 per cent) than for females (6.2 per cent). Approximately 39 per cent of Canadians report using cannabis at some point in their lives. Reported lifetime usage for other illicit drugs is as follows: hallucinogens (11.4 per cent), cocaine (10.6 per cent), speed (6.4 per cent), and ecstasy (4.1 per cent). Among people 15–24 years of age, 4.8 per cent used cocaine or crack, speed, hallucinogens, ecstasy, or heroin in the past year. Interestingly, this is a significant decrease from the 2004 survey, which reported rates of illicit drug use of 11.3 per cent in that population (Health Canada, 2011). Fischer et al. (2006) indicate that the patterns of illicit drug use have changed in Canada, such that heroin use has become more marginalized, particularly outside of Vancouver and Montreal, giving way to the use of prescription opioids. The United Nations *World Drug Report* (2012) indicates that the worldwide prevalence of any illicit drug (including cannabis) is 3.4–6.6 per cent. Globally, cannabis is the mostly commonly used illicit drug, with the highest prevalence being report in Oceania (New Zealand and Australia) at 9.1–14.6 per cent, followed by North America at 10.8 per cent.

Canada's "Low-Risk Alcohol Drinking Guidelines" suggest that women should drink no more than 10 drinks per week and two per day; men should drink no more than 15 drinks per week and three per day (Canadian Centre on Substance Abuse, 2011). Fourteen per cent of Canadian adults surveyed in Health Canada's 2011 Alcohol and Drug Use Monitoring Survey consumed alcohol at a level considered to be a chronic risk for such illnesses as liver disease. Ten per cent consumed alcohol at a level consistent with acute risk of injury and overdose (Health Canada, 2011). Young people between the ages of 15 and 24 were more likely to exceed the acute risk, although consumption of alcohol among youth has decreased from 82.9 per cent in 2004 to 70.8 per cent in 2011.

Factors Contributing to Substance Use Disorders

When discussing the causes of substance use disorders it should always be borne in mind that multiple factors are at play, one or more of which may have salience in a particular individual. Substance use disorders therefore involve a complex interaction of the particular drug on a particular host. Factors inherent to the drug itself are both social/environmental (for instance, availability, legal status, and social norms) and biochemical. The drug must have the ability to easily cross the blood–brain barrier, and drugs with a short half-life (that is, those metabolized by the body more quickly) tend to be more addictive than those with a long half-life. Related to this, drugs with a rapid onset, such as crack, are likely more addictive than those with a slower mode of onset such as MDMA (methylenedioxymethamphetamine/ecstasy). From a social/environmental perspective, longitudinal analysis has revealed that during adolescence and early adulthood factors such as availability and acceptability of substance use within a particular social group are primary determinants, but with increased age, genetic predeterminants begin to take precedence (Gillespie et al., 2007).

The literature is not clear if the drug of choice is determined by a fit between the individual and his or her intrapsychic needs and the actions of the particular drug. If this is indeed the case, then it supports the hypothesis that at least a proportion of drug abuse relates to self-medication, although the relationship may be complex (Lev-Ran et al., 2012), such as illustrated in Case Example 1. For instance, women with anxiety disorders may be prescribed benzodiazepines (e.g., Valium), and because of the inherent addictive potential, some become abusers of this drug. Similarly, some individuals with attention deficit hyperactivity disorder (ADHD) may find that illegal psychostimulants are helpful in treating their symptoms.

Psychosocial Factors

Alcohol and cannabis use have been demonstrated to begin in adolescence. Those who use cannabis heavily in both adolescence and young adulthood tend to continue daily cannabis use and graduate to greater overall illicit substance use. They also demonstrate poorer social outcomes (Patton et al., 2007). In early adulthood there may be experimentation with a number of different substances. Some people appear to settle into a drug of choice. These choices are seemingly determined by current trends, availability, peer groups, and gender (Pihl, 1999). The presence of behavioural problems with impulsivity in adolescence, and the adult equivalent, anti-social personality, is a powerful determinant of substance use disorder (Wall and Kohl, 2007; Leyton and Cox, 2009). A childhood history of neglect and/or physical and sexual abuse is another risk factor (Min et al., 2007).

Biological Factors

As with other mental health challenges, biological factors play a central role in the development of substance use disorders. For instance, daily alcohol consumption during pregnancy is strongly associated with neurobehavioural **disinhibition** in offspring during childhood and adolescence, which can be followed by a substance use disorder that continues into adulthood (Chapman et al., 2007). Further, it is likely that at least a part of the vulnerability for developing substance use disorders is genetically mediated. Family, twin, and adoption studies have all pointed to a strong genetic contribution to substance abuse that is likely as high as 50 to 60 per cent of the predictability (True et al., 1999; Kendler et al., 2003). To date, research has not revealed a single gene for substance abuse, but rather it appears that a number of genes acting through a variety of mechanisms make an individual particularly vulnerable to substance use disorders (Vanyukov et al., 2007).

One hypothesis suggests there is a neurochemical pathway for drug-seeking behaviour. This is supported by a number of diverse findings. For instance, abnormalities in dopamine transmission have been found to be associated with substance abuse (Haberstick et al., 2007). Recently, the role of norepinephrine has been explored as a second neurotransmitter that interacts with dopamine in this reward system (Weinshenker and Schroeder, 2007). Also, the speed at which alcohol is metabolized by the liver enzymes has been found to be directly proportional to the risk of dependency. In other words, those who quickly develop tolerance to alcohol because it is metabolized more quickly, and who therefore presumably do not experience negative effects so quickly early on, tend to develop an alcohol use disorder. From a neuroanatomical perspective, the **mesolimbic dopamine pathway** is hypothesized to be the part of the brain that appreciates thrills or pleasure (see Figure 9.1). These thrills can be natural highs mediated by the body's own equivalent of drugs (endorphins) or synthetic highs derived from a variety of drugs. The process promotes the motivation and behavioural drive to seek rewards. When drugs are used repeatedly, this system is conditioned to trigger drug-seeking behaviour from stimuli that we know as craving or withdrawal, or even from cues such as associating with people in places where drugs are normally used.

The Association between Substance Use Disorders and Other Mental Health Problems

Substance use problems frequently co-occur with other mental health problems and are referred to as **concurrent disorders**. The Canadian Centre on Substance Abuse (2009) suggests that over 50 per cent of people seeking treatment for an addiction also suffer from a mental disorder and that 15–20 per cent of people with mental disorders have substance use problems. The presence of any mental health problem increases the probability of having an addictive disorder by 2.7 times (Goldstein et al., 2007). In one study of inhalant users, 70 per cent met the criteria for at least one lifetime mood, anxiety, or personality disorder (Wu and Howard, 2006). Concurrent disorders therefore affect large numbers of people. For instance, it is estimated that 130,000 people in British Columbia alone suffer from concurrent disorders (Krausz, 2009).

Some disorders are associated with higher rates of substance abuse than others. For instance, the odds ratio for having a substance use disorder in an individual diagnosed with schizophrenia is 4.5:1 as compared with the general population (Regier et al., 1990). Among those with drug use disorders, the prevalence of anti-social personality disorder is 18 per cent (Nathan, Skinstad, and Langenbucher, 1999). This is generally considered to be associated with a poor outcome and greater severity of the disorder.

The risk of having a substance use disorder is at least double for people suffering from mood disorders than for the general population. Van Laar et al. (2007) note that any use of cannabis increases the risk of depression and bipolar disorder, and this was particularly so in more frequent users. They conclude that the association of cannabis use and the first incidence of these disorders is significant, but the underlying mechanism has yet to be delineated.

Anxiety disturbances are highly associated with alcohol and drug use problems (Brady et al., 2007; Levander et al., 2007). In 75 per cent of these cases, the anxiety disorder predated the substance use disorder (Stewart, 2009). This relationship has led to the "tension-reduction hypothesis" of alcohol use and abuse; that is, the view that people use substances in order to obtain relief from their anxiety, although other authorities suggest a "common factor" model (Lev-Ran et al., 2012). However, similar to many drugs, the ability of alcohol to reduce anxiety is inconsistent. Alcohol withdrawal is most clearly associated with increased anxiety, and therefore, in this situation ingestion of alcohol decreases anxiety, promoting the addiction cycle. In this way, the interactions of alcohol and anxiety tend to become a vicious cycle, increasing difficulties in the assessment and treatment of both problems.

A strong base of research literature supports the association between ADHD and substance use disorders (Wilens, 2004). Studies suggest that between 20 and 40 per cent of people treated for substance use have childhood histories of ADHD. Further, among adults who are treated for ADHD, approximately one-third have substance use problems and one-fifth to one-third are abusers of other substances (Klein and Mannuzza, 2010). The relationship is not unidirectional in that it could well be mediated by family history of antisocial behaviour, sensation-seeking, and impulsivity, as well as abuse and neglect. It has also been postulated that a common genetic risk factor for ADHD and substance use disorders exists, perhaps mediated through impulsivity and risk-taking. It is also possible that some people with ADHD choose psychostimulants in an attempt to self-medicate. However, the effects of cocaine and its derivatives are generally unpredictable on these individuals.

Concurrent disorders present a particular challenge in terms of treatment, given the fragmentation and compartmentalization that characterize mental health care and substance-related treatment in Canada. Funding sources, philosophies, and types of treatment differ to such a degree that programs for one type of disorders may specifically exclude those with other types of disorders (Krausz, 2009). Clearly, this presents a considerable challenge for social workers and their clients. Leyton and Cox (2009) present a comprehensive model for understanding the factors contributing to concurrent substance use disorders and mental health disorders. Their model (Figure 11.1) further outlines interventions that can facilitate the path to recovery.

Drugs of Abuse

Opiates

Opium is derived from opium poppies and has been used for some 6,000 years (Winstock and Strang, 2000). Opium over the years has been used by many cultures, most famously epitomized by the Opium Wars of the 1800s, occasioned when the British, having colonized India and its almost inexhaustible supply of opium, were able to trade this for tea in China, resulting in widespread abuse of opium. In 1805, morphine was synthesized and its use by the medical establishment was cemented. Any medication with such a powerful action was likely to be abused, but it was not until the mid-nineteenth century that Britain enacted legislation controlling its use. It was 50 years later before the United States enacted legislation.

Heroin (diamorphine) has long been considered the most commonly abused opiate. It can be injected, smoked, or taken intranasally. Recently, a variety of opiates have been commonly abused, including OxyContin and Oxycocet. These are prescribed for pain management and their use increased dramatically with the medical profession's acceptance that they can be used for non-cancer pain management. As a result, large amounts have been diverted to the streets and sold illegally on the black market, becoming widely abused by polydrug abusers (Ahmadi et al., 2007).

The brain has **endogenous** opiate receptors that affect the norepinephrine neurons located in the locus coeruleus (see Figure 9.1). There is a fairly rapid onset of dependency and tolerance. The effects of opiates include pain reduction, drowsiness, and euphoria. Withdrawal symptoms are characterized by a massive surge in norepinephrine activity. The classic withdrawal symptom involves a severe flu-like illness with rapid pulse and high blood pressure and goose bumps, hence the term "going cold turkey."

One of the more modern sequelae of opiate use has been the risk of transmission of viruses among injecting drug users, including HIV and hepatitis B and C. The United Nations *World Drug Report* suggests that, among injecting

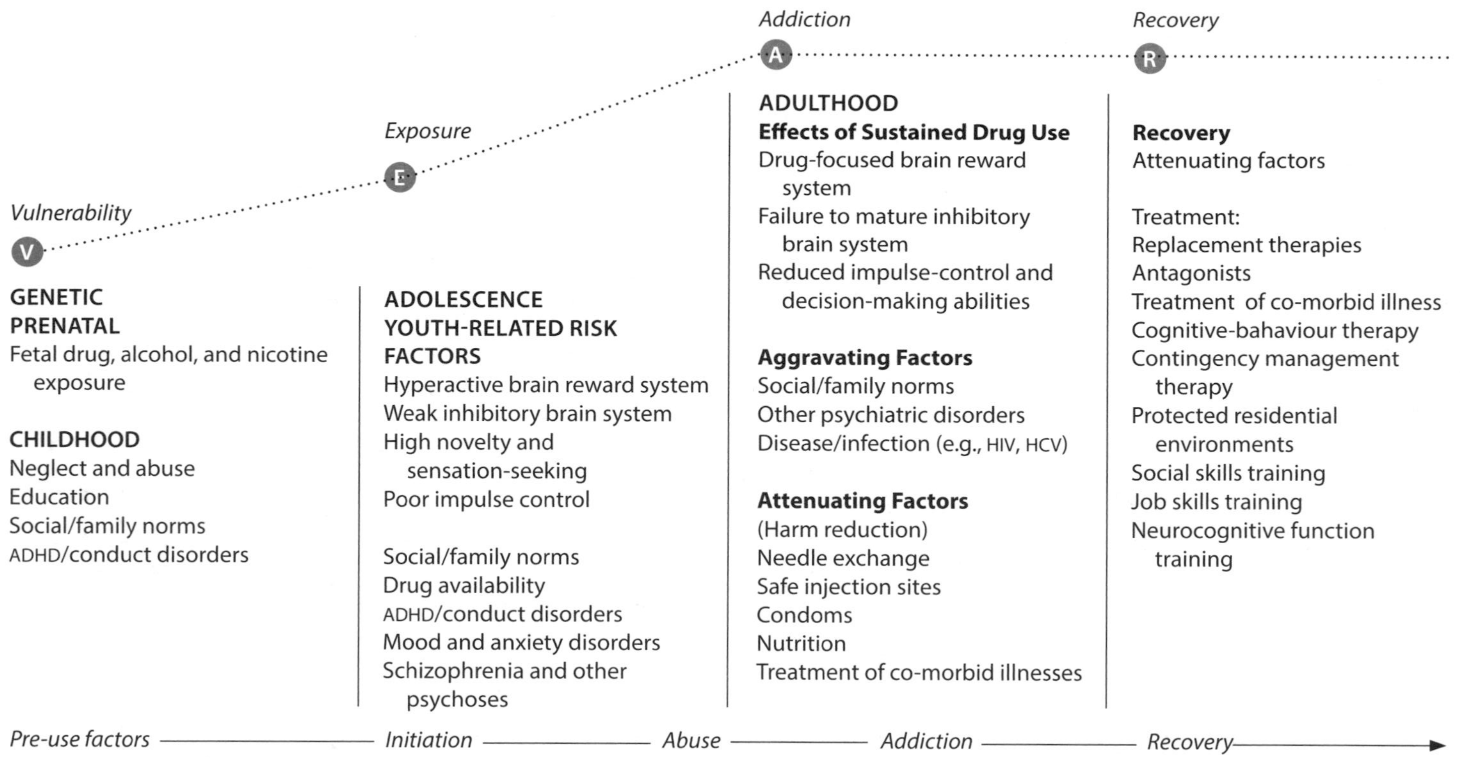

Vulnerability (V) · · · *Exposure* (E) · · · *Addiction* (A) · · · *Recovery* (R)

GENETIC
PRENATAL
Fetal drug, alcohol, and nicotine exposure

CHILDHOOD
Neglect and abuse
Education
Social/family norms
ADHD/conduct disorders

ADOLESCENCE
YOUTH-RELATED RISK FACTORS
Hyperactive brain reward system
Weak inhibitory brain system
High novelty and sensation-seeking
Poor impulse control

Social/family norms
Drug availability
ADHD/conduct disorders
Mood and anxiety disorders
Schizophrenia and other psychoses

ADULTHOOD
Effects of Sustained Drug Use
Drug-focused brain reward system
Failure to mature inhibitory brain system
Reduced impulse-control and decision-making abilities

Aggravating Factors
Social/family norms
Other psychiatric disorders
Disease/infection (e.g., HIV, HCV)

Attenuating Factors
(Harm reduction)
Needle exchange
Safe injection sites
Condoms
Nutrition
Treatment of co-morbid illnesses

Recovery
Attenuating factors

Treatment:
Replacement therapies
Antagonists
Treatment of co-morbid illness
Cognitive-bahaviour therapy
Contingency management therapy
Protected residential environments
Social skills training
Job skills training
Neurocognitive function training

Pre-use factors —— *Initiation* —— *Abuse* —— *Addiction* —— *Recovery* →

Figure 11.1 Transition Points and Treatment Targets for Co-morbid Disorders: The Vear Model of Addiction

Source: Canadian Centre on Substance Abuse (2009).

drug users, the worldwide prevalence of HIV is 20 per cent, that for hepatitis C it is 46.7 per cent, and that for hepatitis B it is 14.4 per cent. This has been at the heart of harm-reduction strategies, utilizing such services as needle exchanges and methadone substitution, which aim to decrease some of the harmful sequelae.

Psychostimulants

The first use of psychostimulants is believed to have been among South American Indians, who used coca leaves in religious rituals. Later, these leaves were reduced to powdered cocaine that was used for medicinal purposes. A small amount of cocaine was included in the original recipe for Coca-Cola, perhaps leading to its success. Early in the twentieth century, abuse of cocaine began to be noticed, and in the 1970s it became a popular recreational drug (Seivewright, 2000). In the 1990s it was discovered that a more potent type of cocaine could be produced by simply converting it to its hydrochloride form, which could either be smoked or used intravenously, leading to a very rapid onset of action. This form is known as crack and some have suggested that it can produce tolerance or withdrawal after its first ingestion, making it a prime drug of dependency.

Amphetamines were used as early antidepressants and also as appetite suppressants (Seivewright, 2000). However, since the 1970s they have been the subject of increasing recreational drug use. More recently, amphetamines have been converted to a more potent preparation known as methylamphetamine, which can be taken orally, intranasally, or intravenously.

The characteristic effects of stimulants include increased energy, euphoria, and decreased appetite. This is sometimes accompanied by **insomnia** and, in some cases, a paranoid psychosis and confusion. Not infrequently, other drugs such as alcohol, benzodiazepines, cannabis, or even heroin are used to counter the stimulant effects at the end of a long session of use. The **deleterious** effects are legion, including weight loss, dental problems, and infections resulting from injection. In addition, stimulants can adversely affect the heart, causing heart attacks or strokes. When taken in pregnancy they can cause premature labour and placental abruption. They are associated with anxiety, depression, and psychosis, which can be indistinguishable from schizophrenia. They are also particularly associated with interpersonal aggression. As noted earlier, the most recent Alcohol and Drug Use Monitoring Survey reports a reduction in use of psychostimulants between 2004 and 2011. In particular the use of cocaine or crack decreased from 1.9 per cent in 2004 to 0.9 per cent in 2011 (Health Canada, 2011).

Hallucinogens

Drugs that alter the sense of perception and mood are referred to as hallucinogens, which cause visual, aural, and sense-of-touch hallucinations. These, too, have been used for thousands of years, often in the form of various types of mushrooms. In 1938 Albert Hoffman synthesized lysergic acid diethylamide (LSD) in an effort to find a synthetic medication to induce childbirth. It is recorded that he ingested a small amount on his fingertips and experienced the first LSD trip. He returned to the lab and ingested a small amount for experimental purposes and recorded his experiences. However, he was able to record little and was accompanied home on his bicycle by a student soon thereafter (Abraham, 2000). LSD was later used experimentally in psychiatry and provided the basis for a theory of the neuropharmacology of schizophrenia. By the 1960s the abuse of LSD became increasingly common. LSD is active in minute quantities that can be placed on sugar cubes or blotting paper. LSD users tend to start in adolescence and since the drug is not known to produce physical dependency most users abstain by their mid-twenties.

Various plants and fungi have hallucinogenic properties, including psilocybin mushrooms, which are common in many parts of Europe and North America and are used recreationally (Hyde et al., 1978). As has been suggested, the primary effects of these plants are changes in sensory imagery, resulting in visual illusions and sometimes hallucinations. The loss of control sometimes leads to panic, known as a bad trip. In vulnerable individuals a psychosis may be generated similar to that seen in schizophrenia.

PCP (phencyclidine), also known as "angel dust," was originally used as an anesthetic. It is often mixed with a variety of drugs and sold on the street under idiosyncratic names such as "dust" or "mist" (Abraham, 2000). It can be taken orally or smoked, the latter route causing an almost immediate effect. It has a complicated neuropharmacological profile mediated by a number of different types of receptors. The resultant high or intoxication includes agitation, impaired judgement, and a particular type of eye movement (**nystagmus**). It is said to be particularly conducive to violence. Delirium and a psychotic disorder can be produced. There is some evidence that it can produce physiological **dependence**.

Club Drugs

A number of drugs have more recently been popularized in raves and dance clubs, both in North America and Europe. The mode of action of these drugs is heterogeneous; the only characteristics they share are the popular venues for their use.

Ketamine has similar actions to PCP, acting at the glutamate synapses. Like PCP, it was originally developed some time ago as an anesthetic and was used in some early psychiatric experiments. Sometimes called "K" or "Special K," its actions include **analgesia** and amnesia, with some stimulant as well as depressant effects. Ketamine has a somewhat less hallucinogenic action than

PCP. Higher degrees of intoxication can cause hallucinations, delusions, paranoia, and in very high doses it can cause coma, extremely high body temperatures, and muscle breakdown.

Gamma hydroxybutyrite (GHB) was originally developed as an agent for the treatment of various sleep disorders but quickly became a drug of abuse. It has become known, along with rohypnol, as a "date rape drug" because of its ability to cause disorientation and rapid-onset sedation as well as some retrograde amnesia.

Ecstasy is one of the substituted amphetamines, whose action is very similar to the other amphetamines although it may be weaker in its effects (Jacobs and Fehr, 1987). This was first synthesized in the 1980s as one of the new designer drugs. It is said to elevate mood, increase self-confidence, and increase libido. In higher doses, it may cause increased blood pressure and pulse with profuse sweating. Some people have paradoxical effects of increased anxiety and panic, and hallucinations and delusions have been reported. Cases of dependence have been reported. Chronic users appear to have altered serotonin transport mechanisms resulting in mood disorders and contributing to dependency.

Another amphetamine on the market is crystal meth. Although relatively new to the drug scene, it is estimated to have been used by 25 million people worldwide during 2013. This makes it the most widely used illicit drug after cannabis. It can be ingested in tablet form, but if smoked or injected it causes an immediate "rush." It has a longer duration of action than cocaine and users often stay awake for more than 10 days. The short-term feelings of increased confidence, energy, and sexual performance often wear off to a period of anxiety, depression, and fatigue. Long-term consequences include a characteristic dental decay, weight loss, psychosis and paranoia, picking at skin, and irritability (Bramness and Kornor, 2007; Schreiber et al., 2008). Animal studies suggest that high-dose methylamphetamine damages dopamine nerve terminals in the corpus striatum, the same area that is damaged in Parkinson's disease (Buxton and Dove, 2008; Kish, 2008) (see Figure 9.1). Preliminary data suggest that chronic use may cause brain damage in humans. Crystal meth is highly addictive and the social, physical, and occupational sequelae can be devastating.

A newcomer to this market is the group of drugs referred to as "bath salts." These are sometimes available from the Internet or drug paraphernalia shops. They include the active chemicals from Khat, a herb commonly used in the region of the horn of Africa. The effects of these chemicals (methyldioxypyrovalerone, methedrone) are amphetamine-like, although extreme violence and even cannibalism have been reported anecdotally (Canadian Centre on Substance Abuse, 2012).

Screening for Substance Use

The first issue in the treatment of substances is identifying whether the person has substance use disorder. While a large number of screening tools exist and can be found both in the literature and from helpful sources such as the Centre for Addiction and Mental Health, some very simple tools are available for routine screening. One example of such a tool that is widely used is the CAGE (Mayfield et al., 1974). The CAGE consists of four simple questions, as shown in Table 11.1.

Canada's Anti-Drug Strategy

Canada began a concerted effort to address substance abuse beginning in 1987 with the original publication of *Canada's Drug Strategy (CDS)*. In October 2007, the government of Canada released a new plan entitled the *National Anti-Drug Strategy (NADS)*. Unlike the original *Drug Strategy*, which had the overall stated aim of reducing the harm associated with alcohol and other drugs to individuals, families, and communities, *NADS* "focuses on prevention and access to treatment for those with drug dependencies, while at the same time getting tough on drug dealers and producers who threaten the safety of our youth and communities" (Government of Canada, 2012). The current strategy has three pillars: prevention, treatment, and enforcement. Critics suggest, however, that despite the stated emphasis on prevention and treatment, 70 per cent of the $64 million allocated to the initiative is focused on law enforcement, leaving only 4 per cent to prevention, 17 per cent to treatment, and 2 per cent to harm reduction (DeBeck et al., 2009). Correspondingly, a fourth pillar in the original *CDS* plan, harm reduction, is no longer part of the current *NADS* strategy. The *CDS* endorsed needle exchange and methadone maintenance therapy (MMT), as well as abstinence-oriented treatments. A 2010 review of the *NADS* concluded that "the provinces and territories have different objectives and priorities

Table 11.1 The CAGE Screening Tool

C	Cut down	Have you ever felt you should cut down on your drinking?
A	Annoyed	Have people annoyed you by criticizing your drinking?
G	Guilty	Have you felt guilty about your drinking?
E	Eye-opener	Have you ever had a drink first thing in the morning to steady your nerves or get rid of a hangover?

Scoring

Each yes response equals a score of 1. A total score of 1 may indicate the need for further discussion. A total score of 2 or greater is clinically significant, suggesting a current or past alcohol problem and, therefore, warranting a more in-depth assessment.

[than the national strategy]: they focus on substance abuse in general rather than the use of illicit drugs, support harm reduction, and take a more holistic approach to substance use issues" (Department of Justice, 2010: 11). British Columbia has been a leader in responding to injection drug use at a provincial level, and the program in Vancouver has long been cited as an example for the rest of the country.

Harm-Reduction Interventions to Assist with Recovery

The recovery model originated in the area of substance abuse and then moved to other areas of mental health. From this perspective, clients must take ownership over their problem of substance use and work to manage or eliminate its consequences. Part of using this model is to acknowledge that many people with substance use disorders will not choose to move towards total abstinence. Therefore, although the social worker, members of the health-care team, and others in the client's life may believe that total abstinence is the best option, they must recognize that the client has control over his or her recovery process.

Harm reduction is a policy framework and model of intervention that seeks to eliminate the negative consequences of substance use for those who choose not to engage in abstinence. Harm reduction is based on five assumptions:

1. Substance use is a reality of our world and thus it is more realistic to focus on reducing harm than eliminating substance use.
2. Although abstinence is the most effective means for reducing harm, it is not necessarily an objective of substance users.
3. Substance use inherently causes harm; however, some of the most serious harms (HIV/AIDS, hepatitis C, overdoses, etc.) can be eliminated without complete abstinence.
4. Services to the client must be user-friendly and relevant if they are to be effective.
5. Substance use must be understood from a broader societal perspective and not just at an individual level (MacMaster, 2004).

MacMaster argues that such an approach is highly consistent with social work values because it is based on client self-determination and engages the client as a partner in determining goals and strategies for change.

Needle Exchange

Needle exchange in large part stems from the desire to reduce risk of transmission of HIV, hepatitis C, and other diseases that are spread through needle-sharing. Canada has had needle exchange programs since 1987; however, Canada's first official exchange did not open until 1989 in Vancouver. By 1993 the federal government was cost-sharing outreach programs in four provinces. Kits including needles, bleach, and condoms were originally distributed from fixed sites and through street outreach; this program was then expanded to mobile vans to increase the geographical area in which outreach can occur. In addition, some pharmacies now provide syringe exchange services. Although there are obvious concerns about needle exchange programs in prisons, related in part to security issues, self-report prevalence of HIV among male inmates is 4.6 per cent and self-report prevalence of hepatitis C is 31 per cent (Correctional Services Canada, 2010). As a result, there is support for needle exchange programs at the policy level, although there is administrative resistance. Early research using US Centers for Disease Control data and comparing cities with and without needle exchange programs suggested that such programs are effective in reducing HIV rates (Hurley et al., 1997). Nevertheless, an outbreak of HIV among injection drug users in Vancouver in the late 1990s and early 2000s called this conclusion into question. A recent analysis pointed to the high risk of this population and policy concerns that failed to prevent the outbreak of HIV in Vancouver (Hyshka et al., 2012), but public perception of the failure of these programs remains an issue.

Needle exchange is rarely provided in isolation. Other components include education regarding safer methods of drug ingestion; provision of safe space where staff can monitor client's health status; behaviour therapy with goals of reduction; and medication treatments (Rosenberg and Phillips, 2003).

Methadone Maintenance Programs

Methadone maintenance treatment (MMT) is a long-term opioid replacement therapy that is used to manage dependence, reduce illicit opioid use, and increase treatment adherence. Methadone is a liquid medication, taken orally, that removes the euphoric effects of heroin and reduces withdrawal symptoms. Effects last for 24 to 36 hours. The aim is to allow the individual to return to normal functioning at work or school. MMT programs have been supported by the federal government for several years. In fact, the sale and control of methadone are managed by the Office of Controlled Substances within Health Canada. In order to prescribe methadone, physicians must be licensed through the Controlled Drugs and Substances Act, and 699 physicians in Canada had these prescribing privileges in 2001 (Public Health Agency of Canada, 2001). MMT programs are also available in federal and some provincial correctional facilities where inmates were enrolled in programs prior to incarceration.

Over the last 15 years another opiod, buprenorphine, has been widely used in substitution therapy (Connock et al., 2007). It has the advantage of alternate-day administration, and in one available form it has a substance built in that prevents its use intravenously should it be diverted to street trafficking. Some data suggest that it is as effective as MMT in every treatment goal.

A *Cochrane Review* of methadone maintenance programs suggests that at higher doses methadone can be effective in reducing use of heroin and cocaine. However, the reviewers do note the important fact that methadone causes dependence and higher doses are more likely to promote this (Faggiano et al., 2003).

Controlled Drinking

Controlled drinking as a form of harm reduction has a much longer history than other approaches. In the 1970s a great international debate occurred in the research literature and popular press about the viability of controlled drinking that focused on the work of Sobell and Sobell at the Addiction Research Foundation (ARF) in Toronto. The debate centred on a treatment method for severely dependent alcoholics and the nature and validity of research outcomes from studies conducted at ARF. The results from these studies suggested that moderate drinking may be a viable and preferred treatment goal for some individuals dealing with excessive drinking (Marlatt and Witkiewitz, 2002). Although some considered the findings to be exaggerated claims of success, the researchers suggested the debate occurred solely because the findings undermined the philosophy and beliefs of Alcoholic Anonymous (Sobell and Sobell, 1995). More recent reviews of many programs on controlled drinking suggest that moderate drinking is an achievable goal for some people with alcoholism problems (Carey et al., 2007).

Controlled drinking models come in a number of different forms that have been reviewed by Witkiewitz and Marlatt (2006). *Behavioural self-control training* (BSCT) is a multi-component therapy that includes self-monitoring of quantity, frequency, and urges to drink, establishment of goals and rewards, and drink refusal skills. This model has been found in meta-analyses to be effective in reducing drinking and superior to both abstinence approaches and other controlled-drinking approaches. *Moderation-oriented cue exposure* (MOCE) is based on classical conditioning and the extinguishing of the relationship between drink-related cues and drinking. Again, this model has established effectiveness. *Guided self-change* (GSC), the original model developed by the Sobells, is a strengths-based psychoeducational model that has empirical support. *Behavioural couples therapy* (BCT) is a more recent model that engages both the person who has the substance use disorder and his/her partner, and has been shown to reduce drinking and improve the couple's relationship. Finally, *mindfulness-based relapse prevention* (MBRP) incorporates both cognitive-behavioural therapy strategies and meditation. Although this model has not been extensively tested, early studies are suggesting that it may be effective in reducing substance use in former inmates.

A self-help group using this particular model is Moderation Management (MM), which has the aim of reducing drinking to non-harmful levels. The program is offered in both traditional face-to-face groups and over the Internet. When compared to AA programs, MM attracts a higher percentage of women (66 per cent versus 33 per cent) with higher levels of education (94 per cent had at least one year of college versus an average 11 years of school for AA). MM emphasizes balance in all areas of life and encourages discussions about other life problems and emotional issues (Kosok, 2006). Recent meta-analyses support the use of Internet-based MM interventions as an effective means of reducing drinking in the general population and in college students (Carey et al., 2009; White et al., 2010).

Other Recovery-Oriented Psychosocial Interventions

Abstinence Programs

Alcoholics Anonymous (AA) is the most widely used self-help intervention in the world, with more than 2 million members. It is described as "a fellowship of men and women who share their experience, strength and hope with each other that they may solve their common problem and help others to recover from alcoholism" (Alcoholics Anonymous, 1972). AA views alcoholism as a disease that controls the minds and bodies of those who suffer from it. From this perspective, abstinence from alcohol use is necessary for healing and control. AA is founded on the 12-Step Model of Recovery (Box 11.1).

AA as a self-help model is highly attractive to some people suffering from substance use disorders and provides a great deal of support and comfort. As a result, the 12-Step model has been expanded to other forms of addiction such as narcotics. For other people this model is not consistent with their world view or their means of seeking support. Social workers should be well aware of this model of intervention and assist clients to make their own decisions about its usefulness for them.

Motivational Interviewing

Motivation has characteristically been seen as a central issue in the treatment of substance use disorders, leading to the belief that only when the client "hits rock bottom" and the consequences of substance use are too severe will he or she be motivated to change. Studies of motivation for treatment do suggest that there is some truth to this old belief. Rapp, Siegal, and DeLiberty (2003), in a study on motivation in substance abusers, determined that motivation was associated with severity of substance abuse, whereas, surprisingly perhaps, legal coercion or self-referral for treatment was not. This is an important finding, as practitioners are frequently suspicious of the motivation of those individuals who are forced to attend treatment by the courts. Also of note, motivation on

Box 11.1 The 12-Step Model of Recovery

1. We admitted we were powerless over alcohol—that our lives had become unmanageable.
2. Came to believe that a Power greater than ourselves could restore us to sanity.
3. Made a decision to turn our will and our lives over to the care of God as we understood Him.
4. Made a searching and fearless moral inventory of ourselves.
5. Admitted to God, to ourselves and to another human being the exact nature of our wrongs.
6. Were entirely ready to have God remove all these defects of character.
7. Humbly asked Him to remove our shortcomings.
8. Made a list of all persons we had harmed, and became willing to make amends to them all.
9. Made direct amends to such people wherever possible, except when to do so would injure them or others.
10. Continued to take personal inventory and when we were wrong promptly admitted it.
11. Sought through prayer and meditation to improve our conscious contact with God, as we understood Him, praying only for knowledge of His will for us and the power to carry that out.
12. Having had a spiritual awakening as the result of these steps, we tried to carry this message to alcoholics, and to practice these principles in all our affairs.

entry into the program was not related to severity of substance use at the six-month follow-up. Thus, those who do not appear to be motivated at the outset have a more or less equal chance of recovery six months later. How, then, do social workers enhance and sustain motivation in clients for whom substance abuse is causing deleterious effects on their lives?

Motivational interviewing is derived from the Stages of Change Model (also referred to as the transtheoretical model of change) proposed by Prochaska and DiClemente (1982) and shown in Table 11.2. The model asserts that people will pass through five stages on their way to resolving problem behaviour: pre-contemplation, contemplation, preparation, action, and maintenance. It is acknowledged, however, that people will not go through the stages in an orderly or linear fashion; rather, people may cycle through stages many times before change is maintained. An additional stage—relapse—has been suggested. The Stages of Change Model implies that change is rarely sudden. Each stage requires a certain task in order to facilitate the change.

Motivational interviewing is a cognitive-behavioural technique first proposed by Miller and Rollnick in 1991 (see Box 11.2). The key in this approach is to not tell people that they may have a problem or what steps they should take. The approach underlines the importance of people describing or discussing their own perceptions of their own problems. Motivational interviewing has five basic principles: (1) express empathy; (2) avoid argument; (3) develop

Table 11.2 Stages of Change

Stage	Person's Experience	Social Worker's Task
Pre-contemplation	The person is not aware of or does not acknowledge the problem that others identify.	To heighten doubt or ambivalence about the problem behaviour
Contemplation	The person begins to be ambivalent about the possibility of making a change but has not made any plans to effect change as yet. There may be some discomfort or self-doubt as the person begins to weigh the pros and cons of making a change.	To support resolution of the ambivalence in the direction of a healthy behavioural change To review with the client the consequences of changing and not changing
Preparation	The person expresses the intention to make a change and begins to consider steps that would lead to change. Change is imminent.	To help the person consider the available change options and their relative advantages and to ultimately select an appropriate course of action
Action	Deliberate strategies are used by the person to change or modify behaviour or the environment to achieve the goal.	To provide support carrying out the change plans
Maintenance	Change is maintained by the person for at least six months; the challenge is to hold on to the gains that have been made.	To provide positive feedback about the change and cotinuously develop strategies to overcome obstacles in maintaining the change
Relapse	The person returns to the former pattern of problem behaviour. He or she may again deny it is a problem or feel remorse for having relapsed.	To accept setbacks and encourage return to an earlier stage of change

Source: Adapted from Prochaska and DiClemente (1982).

discrepancy; (4) roll with resistance; and (5) support self-efficacy (Miller and Rollnick, 2002). The process begins, as do all forms of treatment, with establishing rapport, setting an agenda, and assessing readiness for change. In large part, the success of this model depends on the social worker's willingness to follow the client at his or her own pace and not impose change from the outside.

Motivational interviewing is a brief, low-cost approach to intervention that has established effectiveness with a variety of populations suffering substance use disorders (Burke et al., 2003; Vasilaki et al., 2006; Carey et al., 2007). It has not been shown to be more effective than other models of intervention for smoking or HIV risk-taking. Further, a *Cochrane Review* found no evidence

Box 11.2 Motivational Interviewing

Express empathy	• Convey acceptance for a person as he/she is; historical factors led to the current state of affairs. • Listen, reflect, and seek to understand the history of this person or place; few people can move to change unless they believe that the person encouraging change understands how they got here in the first place and the ongoing challenges that they face (Regehr and Bober, 2005).
Avoid argument	• Active challenging of a person's position or beliefs will result in a defensive position and arguments for not changing. • Question, ask for clarification, encourage the client to hear himself or herself.
Develop discrepancy	• Assist the person to see how the current behaviour places him/her on a trajectory away from important goals or values. • Provide information and, when appropriate, brief advice.
Roll with resistance	• Reframe resistance as ambivalence (a less judgemental or pejorative term); change implies unpredictability and uncertainty in one's life. • Understand that there's a difference between people who may not want to change and those who may not know how to change.
Support self-efficacy	• Identify strengths. • Celebrate successes.

Source: Adapted from Miller and Rollnick (1991).

that motivational interviewing is any more effective than any other psychosocial intervention in treating individuals who suffer from both severe mental illness and substance use (Cleary et al., 2008). Thus, social workers should be cautious not to assume that it will be helpful in addressing all presenting problems.

Pharmacological and Medical Approaches to Support Recovery from Substance Use Disorders

From the perspective of health-care professionals, the primary goal of treatment for substance use disorders is to successfully withdraw the person from the substance to reduce the acute harms he or she is suffering. The secondary goal is to decrease use and possibly achieve abstinence. Because substance use generally involves relapse, a third goal is increasing the time between relapses and decreasing the number of relapses (Pihl, 1999). Finally, a goal that has been adopted recently is to reduce the psychological and physical harm that is secondary to a substance use disorder.

The primary thrust of treatment of these disorders has been in the realm of psychosocial therapies. Psychopharmacologists have only sparingly contributed to the field of substance use disorders. It is unclear whether this is because they have not been hopeful about any possible success of pharmacological approaches or if they feared that they would never be accepted. There are, however, some new treatments that may be of significant value (Vocci and Appel, 2007). In particular, the UK NICE guidelines recommend the early use of two medications, acamprosate and naltrexone, based on good evidence of their efficacy in preventing relapse when combined with psychosocial therapies (National Institute for Health and Clinical Excellence, 2011).

Management of Withdrawal

Withdrawal from substances is a complex process that often requires medical intervention. For example, if withdrawal from alcohol has previously been complicated by seizures or delirium tremens, or the individual has severe cardiac disease, then a hospital setting may be the appropriate place to attempt withdrawal. This may also be the case where people are suffering from other mental health problems that can be exacerbated during the process of withdrawal.

The pharmacological management of withdrawal from a particular substance is generally achieved by taking advantage of cross-tolerance with other agents (Pihl, 1999; Budney et al., 2007; Lanier et al., 2007; Nava et al., 2007). Therefore, a drug in the same or similar class is usually given for withdrawal. Usually, for instance, long-acting benzodiazepines are given for alcohol withdrawal because they have similar actions. B vitamins or multivitamins are often also given adjunctively for prevention of neurological complications. Some experts suggest reducing the amount of benzodiazepines by 20 per cent each day and finally stopping medication after three to five days. Other medications include beta-adrenergic blockers such as propanolol, or alpha-adrenergic receptor agonists such as clonidine, as well as gabapentin (an **anticonvulsant**). As noted above, early use of acamprosate not only treats withdrawal symptoms but helps prevent relapse.

For opiate withdrawal, a number of agents have been used, including clonidine, methadone, and bupenorphine. They are often accompanied by medications for nausea and vomiting (Amato et al., 2004). Cocaine and amphetamine withdrawal can generally be managed without any acute treatment other than supportive and symptomatic care. Contrary to popular opinion, withdrawal symptoms from cannabis dependence are more severe than many people are aware of. Common symptoms include irritability, anxiety, decreased appetite, weight loss, restlessness, and sleep difficulty (Budney et al., 2007). Usually these symptoms can be managed without medication, although one trial effectively used oral THC (the chemical found in cannabis) to suppress withdrawal symptoms.

Longer-Term Psychopharmacology for Alcohol Use Disorders

Several medications are used to help people break the cycle of long-term alcohol use disorders. These medications can reduce cravings for alcohol. For instance, the medication Naltrexone has been used with some success (Ciraulo et al., 1997; Anton, 2008). The problem with this type of treatment is it demands sustained motivation, so that if the client does not take it one day he or she may experience craving and relapse. Consequently, an extended-release, injectable form of Naltrexone increases success in some clients (Ciraulo et al., 2008).

The most commonly known medication to control alcohol use disorders, however, is disulfiram or **Antabuse**. Alcohol is converted to acetaldehyde in the body and then broken down for elimination. Antabuse blocks the elimination of acetaldehyde in the body, which causes unpleasant adverse effects. It is taken on a daily basis, usually in the morning; should the client drink in the day he or she would experience the unpleasant effects of flushing, choking, nausea, vomiting, and high blood pressure. Although Antabuse was widely used in the 1980s, it is used less frequently today. One of the major problems is that it requires the patient to take the drug on a regular basis.

Pharmacology for Opiate Use Disorders

As noted earlier in the chapter, the combination of psychosocial treatment and pharmacological treatment can reduce some of the harms with drug abuse, including the risk of infectious diseases, criminal activity, suicide, and accidental overdoses. Methadone is a synthetic oral opiate with a long half-life that can be given orally on a daily basis. The evidence over a period of 40 years has established that it is helpful in decreasing harm when used for maintenance therapy in association with psychosocial therapies. A number of studies suggest that it decreases criminal behaviour and promotes employment in certain groups of patients. A Cochrane meta-analysis suggested that higher doses are more successful than lower doses in preventing the client from supplementing with illegally obtained opiates. Many clinics administer methadone on a daily basis either by a nurse in the clinic or by a pharmacist. Eventually, clients may earn the privilege of "carry-outs" that they can take home and self-administer (Amato et al., 2004).

Benzodiazepines (for instance, Xanax or Valium) should be avoided in the treatment of opioids, despite the wishes of the client. As discussed previously, these drugs are associated with disinhibition that may lead to relapse and in fact appear to worsen depression (Schreiber et al., 2008). They are also associated with negative outcomes such as risk of overdose and death, and also contribute to poorer retention in substitution programs. Surprisingly, despite these contraindications, in one study it was noted that 40 per cent of patients in a substitution program received at least one benzodiazepine drug (Bramness and Kornor, 2007).

Pharmacological Treatment of Cocaine Dependence

The most researched medications for use in the pharmacological treatment of cocaine dependence are antidepressants (Silva de Lima et al., 2003). The use of SSRIs has become widespread to alleviate the dysphoria with associated cravings (Moeller et al., 2007). Anticonvulsants are a second group of medications used with some success; however, a *Cochrane Review* suggested that there was no evidence to support their use at this time (Minozzi et al., 2008). Other drugs have been tried in the long-term treatment of cocaine abuse, including disulfiram (Antabuse). Antabuse is used on the basis of two supportive theories. First of all, 60 to 90 per cent of cocaine-dependent individuals abuse alcohol. As well, Antabuse diminishes the pleasurable experiences of cocaine. Regular administration, therefore, may reduce the reward effects of cocaine and thereby prevent relapse.

Possible Social Work Interventions in the Case Examples

Case Example 1: Lily

Lily began to use and then abuse prescription medication as an attempt to eliminate the pain caused by her migraine headaches. As she became increasingly dependent, she eluded the attempts of her family doctor to limit her use by first double-doctoring and then by forging prescriptions. This has now resulted in criminal charges.

- Lily's motivation for recovery will need to be assessed. Presumably, she will now have external factors that contribute to motivation related to legal charges and family pressure.
- Motivational interviewing may be useful as a means for supporting Lily to attain whatever goals she has set for herself.
- Groups and treatment programs focused on the specific needs of women or on the needs of professionals with substance use problems may also be useful for Lily because she may distance herself from programs that serve a population with a wider range of social issues related to substance use.

- The social worker should seek Lily's permission to work directly with her family physician to develop a co-ordinated plan for managing her pain while dealing with her substance use disorder.

Case Example 2: Salvatore

Salvatore concurrently suffers from schizophrenia and substance use disorder. Treatment will thus need to focus on both these disorders.

- As Salvatore identifies that he uses marijuana to cope with anxiety, a consultation with his prescribing physician would be a good starting point to determine if his medication regime is optimal, given his feelings of anxiety.
- Salvatore may be willing to consider other forms of treatment aimed at reducing anxiety, such as cognitive-behavioural approaches.
- It will be important to explore whether changes in his social environment may reduce Salvatore's perceived need for substances and increase his ability to engage in other meaningful activities.

Case Example 3: David

David has a long-standing history of alcohol abuse that for the most part he has managed to hide from others. However, as his health status becomes compromised, the effects of alcohol use become more pronounced.

- The social worker should engage David and his wife in a discussion about the substance use and the effects. At this time the social worker can determine which stage of change David may be in.
- The health-related issues associated with David's drinking will require collaboration of the health-care team.
- If David agrees, motivational interviewing, perhaps combined with controlled drinking or abstinence, may be appropriate.

Summary

Substance-related disorders are a pervasive problem in most societies and certainly in Western society. Although these disorders affect people from all walks of life, they are commonly experienced by individuals who may also seek social work assistance for other problems such as mental health problems, impulse control issues, or histories of abuse and neglect. Therefore, social workers need to develop the skills to assess and intervene appropriately in these cases.

Discussion Questions

1. What legal, moral, and ethical issues could a social worker confront when working with clients with substance-related disorders?
2. How may harm-reduction programs coincide or conflict with social work values and ethics?
3. How may self-help groups, such as AA, intersect with social work interventions?
4. How can social workers assist family members of individuals with substance-related disorders?

Suggested Readings and Websites

Canadian Centre on Substance Abuse. 2009. *Substance Abuse in Canada: Concurrent Disorders*. Ottawa: Canadian Centre on Substance Abuse. This is a very accessible guide that provides a wealth of information regarding the understanding and treatment of concurrent disorders.

———. 2011. "Canada's Low Risk Drinking Guidelines." At: www.ccsa.ca/Eng/Priorities/Alcohol/Canada-Low-Risk-Alcohol-Drinking-Guidelines/Pages/default.aspx. All social workers should be familiar with the low risk drinking guidelines and be prepared to share them with clients.

Prochaska, J., and C. DiClemente. 1982. "Transtheoretical Therapy: Towards a More Integrated Model of Change," Psychotherapy Research and Practice 19, 3: 276–88.

12 Personality Disturbance

Learning Objectives

- To identify factors contributing to the development of personality disturbance.
- To identify types of personality disturbance.
- To present evidence-based psychosocial interventions that promote recovery.

Case Example 1

The Wilsons were a pleasant couple who consulted your agency years ago regarding the adoption of David. David's biological mother was a 16-year-old who had substance abuse problems. His biological father was a member of a biker gang who was violent, controlling, and abusive, eventually culminating in a jail sentence. David was made a ward of the Children's Aid Society at age five and went into foster care. John and Nancy Wilson adopted David at age seven, believing that with the support of social workers and their community, they could provide a stable home, which indeed appeared to be the case. David was bright and intelligent, but nevertheless was always in trouble at school, where he was often reported to be fighting and stealing other children's lunches. Later he truanted from school, was caught vandalizing property in the park, shoplifting, and subsequently setting fire to a building. The Wilsons were always there for him, but at the age of 16 he decided he wanted to go out west and seek adventure. He lived on the streets of Vancouver for a while and became involved in drug dealing and minor gang activity. He had various minor skirmishes with the law, often ending up in youth facilities. This pattern continued when he became an adult and he was in and out of jail for the next three years. The Wilsons are at a loss as to how to help him and contact you to see if you can offer some therapy.

Case Example 2

When the ambulance pulled up in front of the large corner house, neighbours gathered to try to determine who was injured or ill. It turned out to be a tenant in the basement apartment of some well-known people in the neighbourhood. Terry Barnes died of cardiac arrest at the age of 58. Very few people recalled even seeing him on the street. No one had spoken to him. The homeowners commented that he had lived there for more than 10 years, since before they purchased the house. He was pleasant but a little strange when they spoke to him; he was never forthcoming with personal information. They believed that he worked for a large insurance company in the area of data processing. Although he did not discuss it, they were aware he was interested in the occult. It was only after his death that they discovered that the room in the basement was set up to practise witchcraft rituals. He had mentioned to them on a number of occasions that he believed somebody was entering his apartment while he was at work, and he had devised his own complicated security network. The landlords did not know his next of kin and were not sure who to notify that he had died. A few days later the police indicated that they had contacted a sister who lived in the same city. When she came to pick up the possessions of her brother, she said that Terry had always been quiet and had few friends even in high school. He did attend family gatherings at holiday times but she did not know much about his life as he was "a very private guy."

The Nature of Personality Disturbance

Personality is comprised of emotional and behavioural traits that characterize an individual's interactions with the daily world. Personality traits result in patterns of perceiving and relating to the environment and others. These traits are relatively stable and are evident in a wide range of interpersonal and social contexts. When personality traits become inflexible and maladaptive and cause significant functional impairment or subjective distress, they may be considered to be personality disorders (Kaplan and Sadock, 1996). Personality disorders are perhaps the most controversial of diagnostic categories because they are somewhat arbitrary. In addition, the term *personality disorder* is often used pejoratively. Everyone has some maladaptive personality traits, perhaps a bit of narcissism, hysteria, or obsessive behaviour. These traits fall on a continuum from being mildly annoying or amusing to highly problematic. So at what point does a person move from having traits that sometimes interfere with relationships with others to having a personality disorder? This question has been hotly debated in the literature for decades. In an attempt to address the problem, in the development of DSM-5 a new approach to the diagnosis of

Box 12.1 Characteristics of a Personality Disturbance

- An enduring pattern of perception, emotional response, interpersonal functioning, and/or impulse control that deviates markedly from the expectations of an individual's culture.
- The enduring pattern is inflexible and pervasive across a broad range of situations.
- The enduring pattern leads to significant distress or impairment in social, occupational, and other domains.
- The enduring pattern is stable and can be traced back to adolescence or early adulthood.
- The enduring pattern is not due to a mental disorder, substance abuse, or a medical condition.

Source: Adapted from APA (2013).

personality disorders was proposed. In this approach personality disorders are no longer viewed to have a threshold for diagnosis. Rather, it was proposed that clinicians would rate the degree to which a client matches the description of a personality disorder type on a scale of 1 (no match) to 5 (very good match) (Skodol et al., 2011). In the end, however, DSM-5 retained a "categorical perspective that personality disorders are qualitatively distinct clinical syndromes" (APA, 2013: 646). Nevertheless, an alternative model for personality disorders is presented in the third section of DSM-5. This model focuses on the dimensions of impairment in personality functioning and pathological personality traits. It remains to be seen whether this alternative model gains popularity and eventually replaces the categorical model of diagnosis.

For the purposes of this chapter, *personality disturbance* will be used to describe individuals who come into contact with social workers and other mental health professionals and who, by the nature of their personality traits, are blocked from achieving certain life goals (see Box 12.1). For instance, they are unable to sustain meaningful relationships with significant others, family, or friends; they are unable to sustain employment or complete a desired course of education as a result of maladaptive patterns; or they are frequently in contact with the law because of anti-social behaviour towards others. In order to be considered a personality disorder or disturbance, these traits are not **transient** but endure for many years and can be traced back to adolescence and early adulthood.

Incidence and Prevalence

The prevalence of personality disturbance has been reported to be 4.4 to 15 per cent in general population studies conducted in Canada, the United States, and Scandinavia (Ekselius et al., 2001; Paris, 2010). Prevalence rates in the general population vary according to type of personality disturbance: anti-social (0.6–4.1 per cent), avoidant (1.9–2.4 per cent), obsessive-compulsive (0.9–7.9 per cent), paranoid, (0.7–4.4 per cent), schizotypal (0.6 per cent), borderline (0.5–5.9 per cent) (Samuels et al., 2002; Grant et al., 2004; Paris, 2010). Differences in reported incidence rates are related to study design, including the training of the evaluators, the instruments used to measure disturbances, and population studied. In large part, however, the rates depend on where researchers draw the line between personality traits and personality disorder (Paris, 2010).

Older individuals are less likely to be diagnosed with personality disturbances than younger persons. This may be because the intensity of problematic personality traits tends to diminish over the life course, in part perhaps because neurochemistry changes with aging, resulting in diminished impulsive and aggressive behaviour. It may also be in part due to the high suicide rate of individuals with certain types of personality disturbances.

Factors Contributing to Personality Disturbance

The causes of personality disturbance vary to some degree with the specific type of personality problem. In general, however, as with all other mental health challenges, the etiology is best understood as the combined effect of biology, individual intrapsychic factors, and environment. Paris (1994), for instance, suggested that biological factors may be reflected in underlying temperament, which in turn is a major influence on the development of personality traits and ultimately personality disturbances. In discussing causation, it is important to note that not all personality disturbances have received equal attention in terms of research and the clinical and academic literature; consequently, more is known about some types of personality disturbance, such as anti-social personality and borderline personality, and less about others, such as schizotypal. This is in part due to general population incidence and in part due to the relative burden on society and the mental health system of the various types of personality disturbance.

Social Environmental Factors

Various psychosocial theories address the development of personality disturbances. For instance, anti-social behaviour in children has been described as the direct outcome of a breakdown in parental family management. Anti-social children often come from disadvantaged families characterized by financial difficulties, inadequate parenting, absent parents, and parental substance abuse. These families may further be living in dangerous and disorganized neighbourhoods (Martens, 2000).

In borderline personality, risk factors are related to a variety of childhood experiences and fall into three categories: trauma, early separation or loss, and abnormal parenting (Paris, 1994). Of these, trauma has received the greatest focus and has been repeatedly proposed as an explanation for the development of borderline personality (Herman and van der Kolk, 1987). That is, intense trauma, particularly if it is repressed, can produce a chronic form of post-traumatic disorder that affects the personality (see Chapter 6). Supporting this hypothesis are studies that point to long-term effects of childhood sexual abuse—including depression, suicidality, substance abuse, problems in intimate relationships, and revictimization, all of which resemble borderline pathology. It should be noted, however, that we are becoming increasingly aware of the heritability components of borderline personality, with some research suggesting that genetic factors may account for 42–68 per cent of the variance (Gunderson, 2011).

Intrapsychic Factors

One formulation is that personality disturbances emanate from disordered attachments. As described earlier, these can be of a highly destructive form such as seen in abusive childhood experiences. Even in less extreme situations, however, early attachment patterns are seen to be reflected in adult attachment behaviour (Bowlby, 1979). Attachment experiences, especially in childhood, become incorporated into perceptions of self and other. When early relationships with caregivers are marked with hostility, victimization, and blaming, later relationships are bound to be seen through the filter of these past experiences. That is, individuals who have experienced negative relationships with others are more likely to be suspicious of the motives of others and are less likely to trust that others are truly interested in their welfare. Individuals who have had abusive or neglectful parents are likely to have developed self-protective mechanisms to reduce the possibility that they will be hurt. These same individuals will find it more difficult to open themselves up to warm and loving relationships with others for fear they will again be emotionally harmed. The nature of individual expectations and relationship skills play a large part in determining both the types of people with whom one will associate and how they will be accepted.

Attachment patterns fall into four categories:

- *Secure attachment* is the most common and is found in 55 to 65 per cent of adults and children. People with secure attachment are likely to have had warm and responsive caregivers who met their needs. As a result, they have the ability to form and sustain relationships with others, have a positive view of self and others, and are able to cope with life crises.
- *Avoidant and dismissive attachment* is found in 15 to 23 per cent of people. Caregivers for people in this category were likely to be punishing and dismissive. In adulthood these individuals downplay affect, are

suspicious of close relationships, and are overly self-reliant. In the extreme, this may contribute to avoidant personality disorder or obsessive-compulsive personality disorder.

- *Ambivalent, dependent, and preoccupied attachment* occurs in 8 to 12 per cent of children and adults. Caregivers were likely to be emotionally erratic and intermittently available. This results in people who are preoccupied with relationships and a need for security; who are very concerned with the opinions of others; who develop coercive strategies to maintain relationships; and who exhaust others and drive them away. This may contribute to personality disorders with histrionic or dependent features.
- *Disorganized, controlling, and unresolved attachment* occurs in approximately 15 per cent of people, resulting from caregivers who were unpredictable and scary. As a result, individuals can have unresolved losses and traumas, and relationships that are difficult and hazardous, even volatile and violent. This may contribute to the development of antisocial or borderline personality disorder.

Self-schema theory builds on the concepts of attachment and suggests that as a result of early-life experiences, people develop cognitive structures or schemas regarding themselves and others. From this perspective, each person has a personality characterized in part by elements of his or her schematic repertoire. Schemas are cognitive maps of the world that organize information in a given sphere. Each person has schemas related to him/herself, such as: I am lovable or unlovable; I am competent or incompetent; I am worthy or unworthy. Each person also has schemas related to others, such as: people are essentially trustworthy or untrustworthy; people are likely to help or not help me. These schemas help a person to predict the likely outcome of any given interaction or relationship. Schemas can be viewed as pervasive in that they influence the present, colour memories of the past, and promise to extend to the future. Schemas are also tenacious and do not easily adapt to new information (Horowitz, 1991). Personality disturbances can be understood to be constellations of maladaptive beliefs or schemas that influence perceptions, emotions, and behaviours. Schemas determine the understanding of a given situation, the emotional response, and consequently the behaviour of the person. As a result, although schemas are formed through early life experiences, they are self-reinforcing through subsequent encounters with the world and other people. Thus, a person with a dependent personality may believe that he or she is helpless; that he or she must rely on others in order to manage in life; and that others may abandon him or her and therefore must be held very close. In the end, this behaviour may drive others away.

Neurobiological Factors

Researchers are increasingly finding neurobiological underpinnings of certain personality disturbances. In anti-social personality, for instance, brain injuries and **cerebrovascular disorders** have been found to cause anti-social and psychopathic personality changes. Some brain **lesions**, such as frontal lobe lesions, are related to specific core features of anti-social personality and borderline personality such as impulsivity and disinhibition (Martens, 2000). Magnetic resonance imaging (MRI) studies of people with borderline personality have also demonstrated reduced volume in the frontal lobe, hippocampus, and amygdala (Lis et al., 2007) and hyper-responsiveness in the amygdala during exposure to emotional stimuli (Gunderson, 2011). In addition, there is evidence of a link between monoamine oxidase (MAO) activity and sensation-seeking and impulsivity. Specifically, associations have been found between low serotonin function and aggressive behaviour and higher levels of 5-hydroxy indoleacetic acid and impulsivity, irritability, hostility, and aggression (Martens, 2000). Abnormal electroencephalograms (EEGs) are also reported in people with impulse disorders and aggression.

Perhaps the most persuasive evidence of the role of neurobiology in the development of personality disturbances is that of anti-social personality. A number of studies have demonstrated EEG abnormalities and brain-imaging abnormalities suggesting low perfusion, that is, blood flow, in the frontal lobes of the brain. The frontal lobes are involved in executive decision-making and functioning as well as inhibition of inappropriate behaviours. These findings, therefore, are consistent with the idea that minor abnormalities in this region could produce callous, poorly planned, and disinhibited behaviour, which are characteristically seen in the anti-social personality (Carrasco and Lecic-Tosevski, 2000). There have even been some studies that suggest a neurobiological basis for moral behaviour (Moll et al., 2002). This finding is a topic of great discussion in the field of forensic mental health where the focus is on the nature of the cause of the crime, the rationality of the perpetrator, and his or her responsibility (Silva, 2009).

Genetic Factors

Increasingly, research is supporting the notion that personality disturbances are genetically transmitted. For instance, a review of 51 studies suggested that 41 per cent of the risk for developing anti-social personality disorder can be attributed to genetic factors (Slutske, 2001). Twin studies with respect to anti-social personality in adults have found concordance rates of 51.5 per cent for male monozygotic twins versus 23.1 per cent concordance with male–male dizygotic twins. Interestingly, however, twin studies with juveniles find delinquency concordance rates at 87 per cent for monozygotic twins versus 72 per cent for dizygotic, perhaps suggesting stronger environmental influences at a younger age. Lyons and colleagues (1995), in teasing this out with a cohort of 3,226 pairs of male twins, discovered that five of 10 symptoms of juvenile delinquency could be attributed to genetics and the other five to environmental factors, whereas eight of nine symptoms of adult anti-social personality disorder could be attributed to genetics. Similarly, family proband studies, that is, studies that examine the development of traits or illnesses across generations of a family, demonstrate inheritance factors related to impulsivity and aggression in borderline personality (Paris, 1994; Gunderson, 2011). Other researchers have looked at the heritability of traits that contribute to overall personality. It is estimated that the heritability of traits is between 34 and 56 per cent. Specific traits are emotional **dysregulation** (38 per cent), novelty-seeking (34 per cent), harm avoidance (41 per cent), reward dependence (44 per cent), persistence (37 per cent), self-directedness (49 per cent), and co-operativeness (47 per cent) (Livesley, 2005a).

Types of Personality Disturbance

The fifth edition of the *Diagnostic and Statistical Manual for Mental Disorders* (DSM-5) identifies 10 different types of personality disorders: paranoid, schizoid, schizotypal, anti-social, narcissistic, avoidant, borderline, histrionic, dependent, and obsessive-compulsive. These disorders fall into three clusters: (1) disturbances characterized by odd or unusual behaviour (schizoid); (2) disturbances characterized by externalizing behaviours such as aggression towards others and dramatic, erratic behaviour; and (3) disturbances characterized by internalizing behaviours such as fear and anxiety (see Table 12.1).

Paranoid

Paranoid personality occurs in people who display a pervasive distrust and suspiciousness of others such that their motives are interpreted as malevolent. This begins by early adulthood and is present in a variety of contexts. These people tend to suspect that others are exploiting, harming, or deceiving them, and perceive attacks on their character or reputation that are not apparent to

Table 12.1 Types of Personality Disturbances

Schizoid Cluster (odd/eccentric/unusual)	Exerrnalizing Cluster (dramatic/aggressive/erratic)	Internalizing Cluster (anxious/fearful)
• Paranoid • Schizoid • Schizotypal	• Anti-social • Borderline • Histrionic • Narcissistic	• Avoidant • Dependent • Obsessive-compulsive

others. Remarks of others or events are interpreted as having demeaning or threatening messages. Individuals are preoccupied with doubts about loyalty or trustworthiness and are reluctant to confide in others. This frequently presents as recurrent suspicions (without justification) regarding fidelity of spouse or partner. This diagnosis is differentiated from paranoid schizophrenia and delusional disorder by the absence of psychotic features.

Paranoid symptoms can also occur as a result of a variety of medical conditions. For instance, paranoid ideation is associated with illicit drug use and solvent abuse. Diseases of aging such as Alzheimer's disease may also produce paranoid thinking. Evidence also reveals that paranoid symptoms may be related to sensory deprivation caused by such disabilities as deafness or blindness. Finally, environmental factors, such as social factors related to immigration and threatening social situations that result in experiences of powerlessness, may produce paranoid thinking. These possibilities should be ruled out before entering into a treatment plan with a person experiencing paranoia (Regehr and Glancy, 1999).

Schizoid

Schizoid personality most resembles a person suffering from the negative symptoms of schizophrenia but without the acute psychotic symptoms. Schizoid individuals neither desire nor enjoy close relationships and rather are detached, solitary loners. These individuals will seek out activities and employment that do not require them to interact with others, such as computer programming. Affect is restricted and the person does not appear to react to criticism or positive life experiences. Expression is often hard to read and interactions are often bland. These behaviours appear to begin early in life and those later diagnosed as having schizoid personality disorder are frequently described as solitary and underachieving in childhood (Wolff et al., 1991).

Schizoid personality may have unique etiological factors. One study looking at the after-effects of famine in Holland from 1944 to 1946 noted that those individuals who were in utero during the famine had higher levels of schizoid personality disorder, particularly if they were male (Hoek et al., 1996). Further, schizoid personality disorder is associated with low body weight in male children and adolescents (Hebebrand et al., 1997).

Schizotypal

Schizotypal individuals are usually described by others as odd, eccentric, or peculiar. They frequently have unusual beliefs that are not held with the same delusional conviction of individuals who suffer from schizophrenia but are rather characterized as superstitious. People with schizotypal personality may believe that they have supernatural powers or extraordinary perceptual abilities that are not understood in their cultural context. This is sometimes described as magical thinking. Their behaviour is considered unusual by others and their dress tends to be **idiosyncratic**. Individuals with schizotypal personality have impaired ability to relate to others and acute discomfort in interpersonal relationships. While schizotypal personality is one of the less commonly found personality disturbances, it is most strongly associated with lower quality of life and lower integration into the community (Skodol et al., 2011).

There is considerable overlap between schizotypal personality and Asperger's syndrome, which is on the autism spectrum in childhood (Wolff et al., 1991; Hurst et al., 2007). Asperger's is characterized by social difficulties, communication impairments, and repetitive-restricted activities. Schizotypal personality is associated with cognitive-perceptual difficulties, deficits in emotional awareness, and difficulties with emotional processing, all of which result in difficulties in reading social cues and differentiating between idiosyncratic beliefs and the beliefs of others in their environment (Berenbaum et al., 2006).

Anti-Social

Anti-social personality disorder (which is sometimes referred to as sociopathic, psychopathic, or ASPD) is perhaps the disturbance that has the largest impact on others in society. Indeed, for this reason it has been suggested that it was the first personality disturbance identified in the field of mental health. Pinel in 1809 described *manie sans delire* (mania without delirium), which involved emotional instability and social drift and was seen to be caused by inadequate education or a perverse, unreserved constitution (Sass, 2007). Sometime later, American psychiatrist Cleckley in his 1941 classic *The Mask of Sanity* described the psychopath as a person with anti-social behaviour that was not be derived from "psychosis, neurosis or mental handicap." Elements of psychopathic personality in this description included: superficial charm; unreliability and insincerity; inability to accept blame or shame; failure to learn from experience; incapacity for love; lacking emotion; poor interpersonal relationships; and inability to follow one's aim in life (Ogloff, 2006). This description is remarkably similar to present-day descriptions of anti-social personality, which is characterized by criminal, aggressive, and impulsive behaviour, conscience impairment, and substance abuse.

Although almost impossible to evaluate, it has been estimated that approximately 3 to 4 per cent of people in the general population would meet the criteria for anti-social personality, or using stricter criteria of psychopathy, less than 1 per cent of people. By contrast, 15 per cent of male prisoners, 10 per cent of forensic patients, and 7 per cent of female prisoners meet the criteria of psychopathy (Ogloff, 2006). Common biological, genetic, and environmental bases have been suggested for substance abuse and anti-social personality. For instance, disturbances in prefrontal functioning may be a common biological ground that links anti-social personality and substance abuse (Martens, 2000). Individuals with anti-social personality have a prevalence rate of substance use disorder of 83.6 per cent, a rate almost 30 times higher than the general population (Regier et al., 1990).

Borderline

While anti-social personality may provide the biggest challenges to society, borderline personality perhaps provides the biggest challenges to the mental health system. Indeed, it is estimated that 15–20 per cent of patients in inpatient mental health facilities and outpatient mental health clinics suffer from the disorder (Gunderson, 2011). Borderline personality is defined as a pervasive pattern of instability in interpersonal relationships, self-image, and affect, and marked impulsivity that frequently results in episodes of self-harm and suicide attempts (see Chapter 5). This disturbance is characterized by frantic efforts of an individual to avoid real or imagined abandonment. Relationships are initially viewed in an idealized form but the needs of the individual with borderline personality often overwhelm others, and in the end they leave or fail to live up to expectations and are rejected. Personal identity tends to be unstable and there are frequent and dramatic shifts, including changes in goals, values, friends, and sexual identity. Affective instability, ranging from elation to despair and fury are commonly experienced. Underlying this is a chronic sense of emptiness. People with borderline personality frequently present at mental health services desperate for assistance; however, they often drop out of treatment when a crisis is averted or because therapists are unable to meet their expectations and needs.

As noted earlier, one of the central formulations regarding the development of borderline personality is childhood abuse, particularly sexual abuse (Herman and van der Kolk, 1987). This formulation was first proposed by Stern in 1938 in his ground breaking paper on borderline pathology where he noted that cruelty, neglect, and brutality of parents of many years' duration are factors found in these patients. This is seen to affect identity formation, that is, views of self, and regulation, that is, the ability to modulate emotion and manage stress. Herman (1992) described the manner in which chronic childhood abuse creates a climate of terror that results in profoundly disrupted relationships, pathological attachments, constant alertness, distrust of others, self-hatred and self-blame, and disassociation. Herman suggests that this leads to a complex form of post-traumatic stress disorder (see Chapter 6), and in extreme cases, personality disturbance in the form of borderline personality. More recently high rates of heritability, in terms of both the disorder itself and various characteristics of the disorder (such as impulsivity and emotional dysregulation), have been identified. These factors undoubtedly intersect with childhood neglect and abuse in the development of the disorder (Gunderson, 2011).

Histrionic

An individual with histrionic personality is uncomfortable with situations where he or she is not the centre of attention. He or she can be described as seductive, provocative, and dramatic. Emotions are close to the surface and readily shared with all others. Histrionic personality disturbance is characterized by: (1) discomfort in situations wherein he or she is not the centre of attention; (2) sexually seductive or provocative behaviour; (3) rapidly shifting and shallow expression of emotions; (4) use of physical appearance to draw attention to him/herself; (5) an overly impressionistic style of speech; (6) self-dramatization, theatricality, and exaggerated emotional expression; (7) suggestibility; and (8) perception of greater intimacy in relationships than actually exists (APA, 2013). If personality is viewed on a continuum, these characteristics can be found in many people, famous and not famous; however, the prevalence of the disturbance at a clinical level is said to be 2 to 3 per cent and it is equally diagnosed in men and women (Nestadt et al., 1990). Among those with histrionic personality disorder, males are more likely to have coexisting anti-social personality and women are more likely to have co-existing somatization disorder (Lilienfeld et al., 1986).

Narcissistic

Narcissistic personality disturbance is characterized by a grandiose sense of self-importance, superficiality, shallowness, and a lack of empathy for others. Specifically, narcissistic personality is indicated by: (1) a grandiose sense of importance; (2) preoccupation with fantasies of success; (3) a belief in one's special or unique status; (4) a need for excessive admiration; (5) a sense of entitlement; (6) exploitation of others; (7) a lack of empathy; (8) envy of others; (9) arrogance (APA, 2013). Narcissistic personality is of particular interest because it provokes less distress in those suffering from it than in those in interpersonal relationships with narcissistic individuals. For instance, in a study that measured counter-transference in psychiatrists and psychologists working with narcissistic individuals, clinicians reported feeling anger, resentment, and dread in working with them; devalued and criticized by the client; and avoidant to the point of wanting to discontinue treatment (Miller et al., 2007). Similarly, these characteristics are likely to cause failures in intimate and other social relationships. As a result, treatment approaches to narcissistic personality often focus on the individual's partner, the one who suffers in the relationship, not the affected person.

Avoidant

An individual with avoidant personality avoids social contact for fear of criticism, disapproval, and rejection. He or she experiences feelings of inadequacy and longs for closeness, but is thwarted by an intense fear of intimacy. An area of considerable controversy in the literature is the overlap between social phobia (an anxiety disturbance—see Chapter 9) and avoidant personality disorder and whether the resulting anxiety and behaviour are the result of a mental health problem or reflect a constellation of personality traits.

Avoidant personality is characterized by social inhibition that is manifested by: (1) impairments in self-functioning related to low self-esteem and unrealistic personal standards; (2) impairments in interpersonal functioning related to preoccupation with criticism and rejection; (3) detachment, withdrawal, intimacy avoidance, and lack of enjoyment; (4) negative affect, including fearfulness and anxiety (APA, 2013). Social phobia, by contrast, is described as intense fear and anxiety in social or performance situations, which frequently has an onset in the mid-teens. Such situations can include parties where one is expected to meet new people, public speaking, and presentations in class if the person is a student. The distinction, therefore, is the pervasive nature of the pattern of behaviour and beliefs that span a wide range of contexts. Regardless of the theoretical distinction, however, researchers have found a moderate overlap of about 30 per cent between these two types of social distress. Twin studies have suggested that the genetic factors in social phobia and avoidant personality are identical (Reichborn-Kjennerud et al., 2007). These authors suggest that different life events may determine whether a person develops a personality disturbance that also impacts intimate personal relationships or whether the anxiety is more limited to social and performance situations. Regardless of the distinction, however, these individuals find themselves significantly impacted by their fears and, as a result, often lead quite isolated lives.

Dependent

An individual with dependent personality has a pervasive and excessive need for others to assume responsibility for most areas of life. This frequently leads to passivity, submission, and clinging behaviour resulting from a fear of separation or abandonment. In considering this formulation, however, environmental factors must be considered. For instance, elderly persons who suddenly find themselves in nursing homes or other institutional settings that thwart customary habits and activities and undermine sense of competence may appear to be dependent and unable to make decisions; however, this may not be part of a lifetime pattern of behaviour but merely a reaction to the current situation. Although concerns have been raised that diagnosis of dependent personality disorder may be gender-biased, at least one study found no gender differences in diagnosis (Reich, 1990).

Obsessive-Compulsive

Obsessive-compulsive personality falls on the continuum with obsessive-compulsive disorder (see Chapter 9). In this disturbance, perfectionism interferes with task completion. The personality is characterized by rigidity, perfectionism, isolation of affect, interpersonal control, and harsh conscience. The individual is: (1) preoccupied with details, rules, and lists; (2) perfectionist to the point that it interferes with task completion; (3) excessively devoted to work; (4) overly conscientious; (5) unable to discard worthless objects; (6) reluctant to delegate tasks; (7) miserly in spending style; and (8) rigid and stubborn (APA, 2013). From a developmental perspective, obsessive-compulsive personality can be seen to be overly conforming and suggests an overly strong identification with rigid parental expectations.

Recovery-Oriented Psychosocial Approaches to Intervention

The personality disturbances are highly divergent and thus a wide range of interventions can be considered. Some approaches can be understood to be more general and address common features. For instance, cognitive therapy is frequently recommended for addressing dysfunctional beliefs that result in problematic behaviours and attitudes (Beck and Freeman, 1990). Various forms of psychotherapy are also frequently used to address underlying causes and consequences of personality disruption. This discussion of psychosocial interventions begins with considering common challenges and helpful approaches to addressing personality disturbance. Other approaches are more specific to particular types of problems. Borderline personality, in particular, has received a great deal of attention both in the development of treatment models and in the testing of these models. In this chapter we will focus on two specific forms of treatment that have been empirically tested: dialectical behaviour therapy and interpersonal therapy. We will also focus our discussion on interventions with individuals with impulse control problems because these individuals are at greatest risk of harm to both self and others and consume the most mental health resources when compared to other forms of personality disturbance.

General Issues and Approaches

People with personality disturbances present with a range of issues that make intervention challenging for mental health practitioners, and change is difficult for those who suffer the consequences of their own personality challenges. One issue is the pervasive nature of personality problems that begin early in life and affect all aspects of the person's interpersonal world.

Personality and the ingrained behaviours and beliefs associated with it are slow to change, regardless of the negative consequences to a person's life. A second issue is the degree to which we all defend our own personality structures, even if we know they are at times problematic. These structures evolved for a reason and are integral to who we know we are as a person. Thus, the suggestion that certain aspects of our own personality should change is highly threatening. This, then, leads to an additional challenge: individuals with personality disturbances who present to mental health practitioners and programs have a great deal of difficulty committing to a change process and thus frequently drop out of treatment. If they do not drop out of treatment, the personality traits that cause problems in other interpersonal relationships also cause problems in the treatment relationship. Therapeutic alliance can be difficult to establish and sustain. Mental health practitioners must also work hard to manage their own reactions to the individual's personality style, such as the example of therapists reacting with anger to feelings of being belittled by narcissistic clients. As a result of these challenges, some common principles can be useful in working with individuals with personality problems (Livesley, 2005b, 2007):

- *Provide multiple interventions delivered in an integrated and co-ordinated manner.* Individuals with personality disturbances who present to treatment frequently are dealing with a range of issues that affect many aspects of their lives. Thus, treatment approaches must address these varied issues. For instance, couple or family intervention may be required to address problems in close relationships; cognitive-behavioural approaches may be useful in targeting particular problematic patterns and behaviours; crisis intervention approaches may be needed during periods of acute risk and stress; and medication may be needed to target certain issues such as obsessive behaviours or impulsivity and aggression. Frequently, these varied interventions will be offered by different members of the interdisciplinary team. As a result, communication and integration of approaches are vital to ensure that professionals are not working at cross-purposes.
- *Provide support, empathy, and validation.* Because individuals with personality problems often encounter conflicts with others in their lives and simultaneously experience a great deal of anxiety about their own worthiness, empathy, support, and reinforcement for positive gains are important. Acknowledgement of the challenges and difficulty associated with change is also helpful.
- *Provide stability and set limits.* Individuals with personality challenges that include impulse control frequently have chaotic lives and chaotic relationships. Individuals with other types of personality challenges seek to

control their own environments through limiting new contacts or repetitive behaviours. Although the social worker should be available for support and empathy, it is also important to set reasonable limits on access (such as specified meeting times and appropriate number of telephone contacts) and to set expectations for behaviour (for instance, threatening the receptionist does not mean that you receive additional time with the social worker).

- *Work to contain distress.* While the social worker must validate experiences of distress experienced by the client, encouragement of the expression of feelings of distress often leads to escalation of emotion and a decreased ability of the client to manage. The focus should remain on the here and now and not on an exploration of previous life issues that will lead to emotional and behavioural disorganization. Work with the client to identify triggering situations and find ways to avoid these triggers, reframe the understanding of the situation, or deal with issues before emotional dysregulation occurs.
- *Be prepared for crises.* Individuals with impulse control issues related to their personality disturbance will have periods of crisis that may need changes in treatment approaches for a period of time. The task of the social worker is to ensure safety and assist the person to return to the previous level of functioning as soon as possible. Hospitalization may be required at times of acute crisis when there is no other way to ensure safety, but in general there is little evidence that hospitalization is of lasting assistance. A general rule, therefore, is to avoid hospitalization whenever possible by mobilizing community-based supports (Biskin and Paris, 2012).
- *Understand that change is slow.* As noted earlier, the nature of personality disturbance is pervasive and enduring and any change will occur slowly. If short-term treatment is all that is available, goals should be very modest and it should be understood that the person is likely to need other forms of intervention at other times.
- *Understand that motivation to change behaviour and attitudes, regardless of the consequences to the person's life, will fluctuate.* Consider the Stages of Change Model and techniques of motivational interviewing described in Chapter 11 as possible approaches for understanding and encouraging willingness to change.
- *Maintain a recovery model orientation.* Regardless of the views of either the social worker or others in the client's life about the need to change behaviours or attitudes, the client must be in control of her/his treatment and recovery process. Reviewing the consequences of the current problems and identifying possible courses of action will empower the client to make decisions.

Dialectical Behaviour Therapy

Dialectical behaviour therapy (DBT) is a comprehensive treatment that blends cognitive-behavioural approaches with acceptance-based practices adopted from Zen Buddhism. This model was first proposed by Marsha Linehan and colleagues (1991) as a result of the shortcomings of traditional CBT, which focused on changing client thoughts and behaviours but did not simultaneously attend to issues of acceptance and validation, resulting in treatment dropout. A dialectical philosophy blends and balances acceptance and motivation for change. From this perspective, mindfulness is incorporated into CBT in order to: (1) increase clients' control over their attentional processes; (2) assist clients to integrate emotional and rational thinking; and (3) experience a sense of unity with themselves, others, and the universe (Lynch et al., 2006). The manualized treatment approach includes four basic modes of intervention, including individual therapy (one hour per week for one year), a skills training group (2.5 hours per week), telephone consultation with clients, and weekly consultative team meetings to support therapists. The approach focuses on reducing life-threatening and suicidal behaviours. Specific aspects of DBT can be found in Box 12.2.

DBT has a considerable base of evidence to support its use in the treatment of borderline personality disorder. According to a *Cochrane Review*, evidence from randomized controlled trials (RCTs) demonstrates that DBT is helpful on a wide range of outcomes, such as admission to hospital or incarceration in prison, but the small size of included studies limits confidence in their results (Binks et al., 2006). Across studies, DBT results in reductions of self-injurious

Box 12.2 Aspects of Dialectic Behaviour Therapy

Mindfulness	• Focusing on the moment, becoming one with the current experience • Awareness of own emotions without judgement
Distress tolerance	• Crisis survival strategies • Acceptance of reality
Emotional regulation	• Observe and identify emotional states • Reduce automatic responses to situations • Decrease vulnerability to negative emotions (reducing arousal) • Increase experience of positive emotions (focus on positives)
Interpersonal effectiveness	• Assertiveness training • Cognitive restructuring • Balancing personal objectives with retaining relationships and maintaining self-esteem

behaviour, suicide attempts and ideation, hopelessness and depression (Robins and Chapman, 2004; Kliem, Kroger & Kosfelder, 2010). Nevertheless, one of the major problems with DBT is that it is resource-intensive and expensive, and thus it has not been instituted in many areas. Because the initial treatment phase lasts one year, there are often long waiting lists for treatment in places where the treatment is available (Paris, 2005).

Interpersonal Therapy

Interpersonal therapy (IPT) is based on the premise that distress occurs within an interpersonal context. Originally based on attachment theory, the model assumes that upsetting events trigger negative moods and that these moods, in turn, impair interpersonal functioning, thereby leading to further negative events (Markowitz et al., 2007; Ravitz et al., 2008). The model was developed in the early 1970s for the treatment of depression, and more recently it has been adapted for use with individuals with personality disorders, specifically borderline personality. Interpersonal therapy in the area of personality disturbance emphasizes understanding the meaning of interpersonal relationships in explaining maladaptive behaviour. The model focuses on the development of cognitive schemas based on early-life experiences with important attachment figures (Marziali and Munroe-Blum, 1994). IPT sessions are structured to focus on the individual's interpersonal successes and setbacks. Interpersonal successes are reinforced by the therapist. Interpersonal setbacks are met first with empathy for the client, followed by strategies for dealing with such situations in the future.

A common model of delivery of the IPT model is through group intervention. The IPT model of group therapy was designed to create a therapeutic context in which the person suffering from a personality disorder is able to replicate problematic interpersonal behaviours without having to resort to fight-or-flight strategies. The group therapists avoid "fighting" by affirming the client's world view and helping him or her expand the range of choices of behaviour and response. In particular, the therapists value the client's past attempts to manage life stresses (Marziali and Munroe-Blum, 1994). The group therapy model offers multiple and varied opportunities to interact with others and observe the consequences of both the client's own response to situations and the consequences of other people's responses. In addition, the intensity of the relationship with the therapist is reduced in the group setting and more responsibility and control are experienced by the client.

Interpersonal therapy has a broad base of empirical support. Randomized controlled trials have demonstrated efficacy with depression, eating disorders, substance abuse disorders, anxiety disorders, and personality disorder (Markowitz et al., 2007; Ravitz et al., 2008). An RCT that compared IPT groups to individual psychotherapy demonstrated significant improvements in both types of treatment in areas of psychosocial adjustment and self-reported depression (Marziali and Munroe-Blum, 1994). A further RCT has demonstrated that combined IPT and drug therapy is more effective than drug treatment (fluoxetine) alone in working with individuals with borderline personality disorder (Bellino, Rinaldi & Bogetto, 2010). Group treatment has the benefit of being more cost-effective than individual work.

Pharmacological Interventions

As noted earlier in this chapter, personality disturbances tend to be very difficult to treat because of their pervasive and ingrained nature. As we have discussed, the very problems such as splitting (viewing people as all good or all bad and often pitting people against one another) or distrust, characteristic of some individuals with personality challenges, render it quite difficult to form a good therapeutic alliance and to sustain this alliance over the long period of time necessary for change. Pharmacotherapy in personality disturbances is generally used to modify certain neurotransmitter systems that are responsible for specific symptoms inherent in personality variables (Soloff, 2005). In administering pharmacotherapy, all the general principles of treatment noted earlier apply. Most particularly, the goals of treatment should be agreed upon jointly with the client. Communication between members of the treatment team is essential (Schlesinger and Silk, 2005). Pharmacotherapy administered alone can never be considered the singular effective treatment in the complex problems associated with personality disturbance.

Pharmacological treatments with people suffering from personality challenges tend to focus on specific symptoms or manifestations of the disturbance. For instance, one of the most commonly used types of medication in borderline personality and anti-social personality is the antipsychotic group of drugs. Generally speaking, antipsychotics decrease implusivity, decrease anxiety, and produce a calming effect. They can also be used to reduce psychotic symptoms such as delusions of persecution, delusions of reference, and hallucinations that may accompany micropsychotic episodes. In schizotypal personality and paranoid personality disturbances, antipsychotics can address the symptoms that resemble those of schizophrenia..

Antidepressants are also commonly used in clients suffering from personality disturbances, for depressive symptoms as well as anger and impulsivity (Glancy and Knott, 2002). Mood stabilizers can target instability of mood, particularly in clients with borderline personality distrubance. While lithium is sometimes prescribed in these cases, its efficacy is uncertain and caution should be taken because it is lethal in overdose (Links et al., 1990).

Perhaps the most commonly used medications in personality disturbances are the benzodiazepines, such as Valium. Peteet and Gutheil (1979) talk about the "Catch-22" wherein clients request and crave benzodiazepines but benzodiazepines tend to worsen their condition. These medications tend to produce disinhibition, increased anger, and increased deliberate self-harm, and should be considered as **contraindicated** in borderline personality disorder (Carrasco and Lecic-Tosevski, 2000).

Possible Social Work Interventions in the Case Examples

Case Example 1: David

David is likely to be diagnosed with anti-social personality disorder. He has an extended history of conflicts with others and illegal behaviour. He has little concern about the impact of his behaviour on others.

- As David's parents are approaching the social worker for assistance, the first intervention is to provide supportive counselling to them and provide them with information about possible resources for David.
- If David is willing to enter treatment, there are a number of options. These include: admission to a treatment centre for substance abuse; enrolment in an anger management group; connection with the John Howard Society for job-readiness training; and individual therapy for problem-solving, support, and motivational interviewing

Case Example 2: Terry

Terry had characteristics of schizotypal personality. People like Terry will rarely come to the attention of social workers or other members of the health-care team. They function relatively independently and have few contacts with others. Those around them view them as odd or idiosyncratic, but in general know little about them.

- If Terry had approached a social worker as a result of his distress, interpersonal therapy to address his concerns about social interactions may have been useful.
- Cognitive therapy may have been helpful in addressing Terry's idiosyncratic beliefs.

Summary

Personality disorders represent a wide range of problems in interpersonal functioning that can cause considerable distress to the individual suffering from the disorder and to those in the individual's family and social circle. Personality disorders are insidious in their etiology, are often caused by many factors, and begin early in life. As a result of the pervasive and persistent nature of these disorders, treatment is challenging and no clear approaches have high rates of success in a short time frame. Change relies on long-term approaches to alter interactional patterns and self-perceptions. While this is occurring, crisis intervention at the time when life stresses interfere with functioning is frequently necessary.

Discussion Questions

1. How can social workers engage in discussions about personality disturbances without becoming blaming or pejorative?
2. How can social workers intervene in the interdisciplinary team if other members are stigmatizing or rejecting of clients with personality disturbances?
3. What challenges might a social worker encounter in her or his individual work with a client who has a personality disturbance?

Suggested Readings and Websites

Beck, A., and A. Freeman. 1990. *Cognitive Therapy of Personality Disorders*. New York: Guilford. This classic book outlines the application of cognitive therapy for people suffering from personality disturbance.

Bowlby, J. 1979. *The Making and Breaking of Affectional Bonds*. London: Tavistock Publications. This is a foundational text for social workers and provides a basis for understanding many of the challenges our clients face.

Skodol, A., D. Bender, L. Morey, L. Clark, J. Oldham, R. Alarcon, et al. 2011. "Personality disorder types proposed for DSM-5," *Journal of Personality Disorders* 25, 2: 136–69. This article gives an excellent overview of the types of personality disturbance and the changes between DSM-IV and DSM-5.

Glossary

Advanced directive: Instructions about health-care decisions made prior to when the individual is no longer able to make those decisions due to medical or other incapacitation.

Affidavit: A written statement where the writer/signer swears to the truth of the document before a notary or other judicial officer.

Akathisia: A syndrome characterized by extreme restlessness and inability to remain still; a subjective feeling of muscular agitation often accompanied by pacing.

Amphetamines: Stimulant drugs that increase levels of norepinephrine, serotonin, and dopamine in the brain.

Analgesia: The inability to feel pain while still conscious.

Anomie: Defined by Emile Durkheim as a state of normlessness or social disintegration.

Antabuse: A drug used in the treatment of alcoholism to limit the metabolism of alcohol, thereby making the client extremely nauseous if he or she consumes alcohol.

Anticonvulsant: A drug to help with seizures, it prevents the rapid firing of neurons that precipitate a seizure.

Anxiolytic: A drug prescribed for the treatment of anxiety.

Arousal symptoms: One of the three clusters of acute stress and post-traumatic stress symptoms, which include difficulty falling or staying asleep, emotional outbursts, difficulty concentrating, hypervigilance, and exaggerated startle response.

Atrophy: The partial or complete wasting away of a part of the body or organ.

Autosomal dominant: A pattern of trait transmission (or inheritance) in which an individual has one gene containing the illness and one gene not containing the illness on a pair of chromosomes; as a result, the person has a 50–50 chance of passing on the mutant gene and therefore the disorder to each of his or her children.

Avoidance symptoms: One of the three clusters of acute stress and post-traumatic stress symptoms, which include efforts to avoid thoughts or stimuli reminiscent of the event that caused the stress.

Benztropine: A drug used to treat Parkinson's disease, akathisia, and dystonia.

Cerebrospinal fluid: A bodily fluid that collects in and around the brain.

Cerebrovascular disorders: Dysfunctions in the brain related to the blood vessels that supply blood to the brain.

Chronicity: Persistent or chronic, as of a long-lasting medical or mental health condition.

Circadian rhythms: The 24-hour cycle of the day for all living beings on earth.

Civil liberties: Limits set by the government on its power, meant to protect people from the government and its potential misuses of power.

Coercion: The practice of manipulating a person to behave in an involuntary way, sometimes by use of fear, threats, or intimidation.

Co-morbid: The presence of more than one disease or disorder occurring at the same time.

Computerized axial tomography (CAT): A technology using a computer to take pictures of the body through "slices" that can be then put together to gain an accurate three-dimensional picture of what is going on in the body.

Concordance: The presence of the same trait in two individuals.

Concurrent disorders: The co-occurrence of mental illness and substance abuse.

Confabulation: The filling in of memory gaps with false descriptions of events, often linked with suggestibility in severe amnesic syndromes.

Consent and Capacity Board: An independent board legislated by government that conducts hearings by its members, including lawyers, psychiatrists, and other members of the public, to review the application of restrictions under mental health legislation.

Contraindicated: A situation where certain drugs, procedures, or activities would be deemed inadvisable.

Cortisol: The primary stress hormone.

Criminal Code: The full statutory listing and explanation of criminal offences and procedures in Canada.

Crisis: A period of psychological disequilibrium experienced as a result of a hazardous event or situation that constitutes a significant problem that cannot be remedied by using familiar coping strategies.

Cyclothymia: A chronic, fluctuating mood disturbance that involves numerous periods of depressive symptoms and some periods of manic symptoms.

Deleterious: Harmful in an unexpected or subtle way.

Delirium: A sudden state of severe confusion and rapid changes in brain function, sometimes associated with hallucinations and hyperactivity.

Delirium tremens: An acute, sometimes fatal, episode of delirium usually caused by withdrawal or abstinence from alcohol following habitual use.

Dementia: A progressive disease of the brain that results in declining cognitive function beyond that of normal aging.

Dependence: A maladaptive pattern of substance use leading to clinically significant impairment or distress that further includes withdrawal; tolerance; ingestion of larger amounts than intended; unsuccessful efforts to cut down; excessive time spent in activities related to substances; narrowing of interests; and continued use despite knowledge of physical or psychological problems likely attributable to the substance.

Depersonalization: An alteration in the perception of the self in which someone feels detached from self and sees him/herself as if from outside the body.

Derealization: The change of perception of the external world in which events appear unreal or strange.

Detainment: A procedure whereby a person is detained in hospital pursuant to the applicable Mental Health Act or other legal means.

Dipsomania: An old term for an uncontrollable craving for alcohol.

Disinhibition: The reduction or loss of inhibition.

Dissociation: An altered state in which thoughts, emotions, perceptions, and/or memories are disrupted and split off from the reality of what is happening in the present.

Dissociative symptoms: A fourth cluster of symptoms of acute stress disorder that includes persistent inability to experience positive emotions, an altered sense of reality, and an inability to remember important aspects of the event that was the source of the stress.

Dizygotic twins: Non-identical twins; also known as fraternal twins.

Double bind: A situation where a person is faced with two conflicting demands by someone who has a close and powerful relationship with the individual.

Dysmetabolic syndrome: A condition characterized by weight gain, accompanied by elevated cholesterol, lipids, and triglycerides, as well as by insulin resistance, which may lead to diabetes.

Dysphoria: An uncomfortable, unpleasant mood characterized by sadness, anxiety, irritability, or restlessness.

Dysregulation: An emotional response not found under the normal accepted range of emotional reactions to a specific situation.

Dystonia: A neurological disorder that induces muscle contractions in the body that can result in abnormal postures.

Electroencephalograms (EEGs): Measurements of electrical activity in the brain made by an instrument called an electroencephalograph, which involves attaching electrodes to the scalp.

Endocrine: A system of glands (e.g., thyroid, pituitary, adrenal) that release hormones and help regulate metabolism, growth, development, and mood.

Endogenous: Something that arises from an organism, tissue, or cell.

Epigenetics: Chemical changes to gene expression based on environmental influences.

Epistemology: The theory of knowledge; a philosophy concerned with the conceptions of knowledge.

Equilibrium: A stable or balanced state.

Etiology: The study of causation, most often used in describing the origins of disease.

Euphoria: A state of intense happiness or well-being.

Euthanasia: Originally meaning "good death"; today, better understood as the active acceleration of death by someone (often a health-care professional) in a situation where the individual is suffering from a painful or incapacitating illness that will result in imminent death.

Evidence-based practice: The use of interventions for which there is sufficiently persuasive evidence to support their effectiveness in attaining the desired outcomes.

Existential anxiety: Anxiety caused by a belief in the meaninglessness of life.

Fetal alcohol syndrome (FAS): A disorder first manifesting at birth associated with women who drink alcohol during pregnancy; the offspring have certain characteristic features.

G8: An international forum of governments, including Canada, France, Germany, Italy, Japan, Russia, the United Kingdom, and the United States.

Global assessment of functioning (GAF): A numeric scale from 0 to 100 used by mental health professionals to rate the social, occupational, and psychological functioning of adult patients.

Gliosis: An abnormality of brain neurons that is generally considered a sign of past inflammation caused by infection or other types of brain injury.

Hallucinations: Abnormal perceptions without a real stimulus.

Holistic: The ideology that a system cannot be understood by looking at its parts, only by looking at it as a whole.

Hydrocephalus: Abnormal accumulation of bodily fluid in the brain.

Hypertensive: A condition of chronic high blood pressure.

Hypoglycemia: A disorder characterized by low blood sugar.

Hypomania: A less severe form of mania; although the symptoms are similar to mania, hypomanic episodes differ in that they do not cause significant distress or impair one's work, family, or social life.

Hypothyroidism: A condition in which the body has low levels of the thyroid hormone thyroxin.

Iatrogenic: An adverse effect or complication caused by medical treatment or advice.

Idiosyncratic: Unusual temperament or personality trait.

Inefficacious: Not producing a desired objective.

Informed consent: A legal term in which a person can be said to have given consent to treatment based on a reasonable understanding and appreciation of the risks, benefits, and alternatives to that treatment.

Insidious: A condition appearing so slowly that it seems harmless at first, even though it is potentially very harmful.

Insomnia: A condition in which a person either cannot sleep or has extreme difficulty in falling or staying asleep.

Insulin shock therapy: A treatment of some mental illnesses that involved injecting a patient with large amounts of insulin, thereby inducing a coma in which doctors believed the brain metabolism would slow and return to normal healthy levels.

Interprofessional: A working environment in which several professions that collaborate.

Intrapsychic: Internal psychological processes.

Intrusion symptoms: One of the three clusters of acute stress and post-traumatic stress symptoms that include intrusive thoughts, nightmares, and feelings as if the event were recurring, and intense psychological and/or physiological distress at exposure to cues that retrigger the event.

Irritable heart: The reactions of soldiers, first referenced in the US Civil War and continuing to World War I, which are now understood to be the arousal symptoms of post-traumatic stress.

Jurisdiction: The authority granted to a legal body or political leader to make decisions on legal matters and hold responsibility.

Labile: Instability, for example, of moods, wherein the expression of laughter, smiling, or crying uncontrollably is suddenly expressed and may last for several minutes.

Lesions: Abnormal tissues found on the body, usually resulting from disease or trauma.

Lunatic: Historically, a common term for a person who was mentally ill, a condition formerly called lunacy.

Magnetic resonance imaging (MRI): A technique that produces a three-dimensional image of the structure of the body.

Malapropisms: Substitution of incorrect words that sound similar to the words intended, usually with a comedic effect.

Mania: Excitement manifested by physical or mental hyperactivity, disorganized behaviour, and elevation of mood.

Melancholia: A type of severe depression characterized by biological symptoms such as a lack of energy, poor appetite and sleep, and a slowing down of bodily processes.

Mesolimbic dopamine pathway: A neural pathway in the brain and a part of the limbic system.

Meta-analyses: A combination of results from several studies, added together and subject to statistical analysis.

Monomania An obsolete term for a delusional disorder in which the person focuses on only one false belief.

Monozygotic twins: Twins who share the same genetic structure; also known as identical twins.

Neuraesthenia: A psychological disorder characterized by chronic fatigue and weakness, loss of memory, and generalized aches and pains, formerly thought to result from exhaustion of the nervous system.

Neurodevelopmental: The development of the brain and nervous system.

Neuroleptic: A form of antipsychotic medication.

Neuroleptic malignant syndrome (NMS): A serious neurological and metabolic disorder caused by a reaction to neuroleptic or antipsychotic drugs.

Neuropsychiatry: A focus within psychiatry on neurological contributions to mental disorder.

Neuron: A nerve cell that sends and receives electrical signals over long distances within the body.

Neurotransmitters: Chemicals that relay information between neurons or between a neuron and another cell.

Nigrostriatal pathway: One of the four main dopamine pathways in the brain.

Nystagmus: A type of eye movement in which movement in one direction is smooth and fast and movement in the other direction is jerky.

Orbitofrontal: The area of the brain associated with decision-making.

Panic attacks: Sudden, discrete episodes of very intense anxiety accompanied by feelings of impending doom and the bodily manifestations of anxiety.

Paraesthesia: Tingling, numbness, or prickling of a person's skin.

Parasuicide: An action in which someone mimics the act of suicide but does not intend suicide (usually involving self-harm, such as cutting).

Paresis: A condition of loss of or impaired movement of body parts.

Pathognomonic: A symptom that is so indicative of a disease that it virtually diagnoses the disease by its presence.

Pejorative: Aimed at discrediting or downplaying the merit of something.

Phenothiazines: A group of antipsychotic drugs.

Pluralistic society: The idea that many different beliefs, values, and ideas operate in society, which may all be correct and also in conflict with each other.

Positron emission tomography (PET): A nuclear medicine technique that provides a three-dimensional image of the chemical processes in the body.

Post-traumatic stress disorder (PTSD): A set of avoidance, arousal, and intrusion symptoms that follow exposure to a life-threatening event.

Power of attorney: A system of authorizing someone to make decisions on another person's behalf regarding legal or medical matters.

Prefrontal lobotomies: A surgical procedure formerly used to treat severe mental illnesses, which involves cutting the connections to and from the prefrontal cortex.

Prodromal: An early non-specific symptom (or set of symptoms) indicating the start of an illness before specific symptoms occur.

Prognosis: A prediction as to how a disease will progress and the severity of the effects of a condition on a patient.

Psychoanalysis: A theoretical orientation and therapeutic method developed by Sigmund Freud that studies and treats psychological functioning and behaviour.

Psychoeducation: Education to clients about their own medical illness or psychological disturbances.

Psychologization: The focus on psychological causes for a person's feeling of distress.

Psychotropic medications: Medications capable of affecting the mind, emotions, and behaviour; they act primarily on the central nervous system where they alter brain function, resulting in temporary changes in perception, mood, consciousness, and behaviour.

Public trustee: An office that operates under legislation and works on behalf of a charitable or public group or individual to guide or make financial decisions.

Readmission: Being readmitted to hospital after successfully concluding treatment but later relapsing.

Recidivism: To relapse or fall back; generally applied to repeat criminal offenders.

Recourse: An action of turning to someone for help or assistance.

Recovery model: An approach to mental disorder or substance dependence that emphasizes and supports an individual's potential for recovery.

Relapse: When a person is affected by a condition in which he/she was previously affected and thought to have under control (for example, depression).

Renal failure: A condition in which the kidneys do not function properly.

Resilience: The innate ability to withstand stress and adverse events.

Retrograde amnesia: The inability to recall events or information that was encoded into memory before a specific event (for example, surgery or an accident).

Schizophrenogenic: The belief that certain factors, for example, parental behaviour, can have a negative impact on a child's mental health, specifically causing schizophrenia.

Secondary loss: The loss of something, for example, a job, after already having suffered a loss, such as a home destroyed in a tornado or a loved one killed in an accident.

Separation anxiety: Where a child (or adult) fears or experiences separation from his or her main attachment figure.

Shell shock: A World War I term for what is now known as post-traumatic stress.

Social determinants of health: The economic and social conditions that can determine an individual's health.

Somatization: The focus on physical symptoms when a person is feeling distress.

Stigma: Social disapproval of actions, beliefs, a condition, or a way of being that is against cultural norms or expectations.

Subdural hematoma: A brain injury in which there is bleeding into the lining of the brain.

Subpoena: A written demand for someone to appear before the court or face punishment if he or she refuses.

Substitute decision-making: The situation where a person is found incapable or unable to make her or his own decisions whereby specific legal criteria exist for another person to make decisions about that person's treatment on her/his behalf.

SWOT analysis: A strategic plan that evaluates Strengths, Weaknesses, Opportunities, and Threats involved in a project or intervention.

Tardive dyskinesia: A neurological condition caused by the long-term use of neuroleptics, resulting in involuntary and repetitive actions.

Transinstitutionalization: The movement of people with mental health problems from psychiatric hospitals to prisons as a consequence of reducing the number of available psychiatric beds.

Tourette's syndrome: A neurological disorder characterized by tics (sudden and repetitive motor movements or vocalizations).

Transient: Passing through quickly.

Ulysses Contract: A freely made decision about one's own future that sets out the person's preference in case of medical or other incapacitation.

World Health Organization: An agency of the United Nations that monitors outbreaks of infectious diseases such as SARS, malaria, and AIDS and sponsors international efforts to prevent and treat diseases and illness.

References

Chapter 1

American Psychiatric Association (APA). 2013. *Diagnostic and Statistical Manual of Mental Disorders*, 5th edn. Washington: APA Press.

Bateson, G., D.D. Jackson, J. Haley, and J.H. Weakland. 1956. "Toward a Theory of Schizophrenia," *Behavioral Science* 1: 251–64.

Bellamy, J.L., S.E. Bledsoe, L. Fang, J. Manuel, and E.J. Mullen. 2011. "Addressing the Barriers to EBP Implementation in Social Work: Reflections from the BEST Project," in T. Rzepnicki, S. McCracken, and H. Briggs, eds, *From Task-centered Social Work to Evidence-based and Integrative Practice: Reflections on History and Implementation*. Chicago: Lyceum Books Inc, 136–55.

Bentley, K., and J. Walsh. 2006. *The Social Worker and Psychotropic Medication: Toward Effective Collaboration with Mental Health Clients, Families, and Providers*. Belmont, Calif.: Thomson.

———, ———, and R. Farmer. 2005. "Social Work Roles and Activities Regarding Psychiatric Medication: Results of a National Survey," *Social Work* 50, 4: 295–303.

Blackstock, C., I. Brown, and M. Bennett. 2007. "Reconciliation: Rebuilding the Canadian Child Welfare System to Better Serve Aboriginal Children and Youth," in I. Brown, F. Chaze, D. Fuchs, J. Lafrance, S. McKay, and S. Thomas-Prokop, eds, *Putting a Human Face on Child Welfare: Voices from the Prairies*. Toronto: Centre of Excellence for Child Welfare.

Bradley, S. 2003. "The Psychology of the Psychopharmacology Triangle: The Client, Clinicians, the Medications," *Social Work in Mental Health* 1, 4: 29–50.

Canadian Alliance on Mental Illness and Mental Health. 2006. *Framework for Action on Mental Illness and Mental Health: Recommendations to Health and Social Policy Leaders of Canada for a National Action Plan on Mental Illness and Mental Health*, www.camimh.ca/frameworkforaction.htm.

Canadian Association of Social Workers (CASW). 2001. *The Role of Social Work in Mental Health*. Ottawa: CASW.

———. 2005. *Code of Ethics*. Ottawa: CASW.

———. 2013. *The Role of Social Work in Mental Health*, www.casw-acts.ca/en/role-social-work-mental-health.

Canadian Mental Health Association (CMHA). 2008. *Back to Basics: Enhancing Our Capacity to Promote Consumer Participation and Inclusion: Discussion Guide on Recovery*, www.cmha.ca/data/2/rec_docs/692_Discussion%20Guide%20on%20Recovery.pdf.

Canterbury v. Spence. 1972. 464 F.2d 772 (D.C.Cir.).

Carpenter, L. 2002. "Mental Health Recovery Paradigm: Implications for Social Work," *Health and Social Work* 27, 2: 86–94.

Cohen, C., C. Abdallah, and S. Diwan. 2010. "Suicide Attempts and Associated Factors in Older Adults with Schizophrenia," *Schizophrenia Research* 119, 1–3: 253–7.

Daubert v. Merrell Dow Pharmaceuticals. 1993. 509 U.S. 579.

Deegan, P. 1996. "Recovery and the Conspiracy of Hope," presented at the Sixth Annual Mental Health Services Conference of Australia and New Zealand.

Farkas, M., C. Gagne, W. Anthony, and J. Chamberlin. 2005. "Implementing Recovery-oriented Evidence-based Programs: Identifying the Critical Dimensions," *Community Mental Health Journal* 41, 2: 141–58.

Faulkner Schofield, R., and M. Amodeo. 1999. "Interdisciplinary Teams in Health Care and Human Service Settings: Are They Effective?" *Health and Social Work* 24, 3: 210–19.

Floersch, J. 2003. "The Subjective Experience of Youth Psychotropic Treatment," *Social Work in Mental Health* 1, 4: 51–69.

Frye v. United States. 1923. 293 F. 1013 (D.C. Cir.).

Gibbs, L.E., and E. Gambrill. 2002. "Evidence-based Practice: Counterarguments to Objections," *Research on Social Work Practice* 12, 3: 452–76.

Gilbert, J. 2008. "Interprofessional Primary Care Teams: Observations on Realism," Plenary Presentation, Accelerating Primary Care, Edmonton, 13 Feb.

Haley, J. 1976. *Problem-Solving Therapy*. San Francisco: Jossey-Bass.

Health Canada. 2002. *A Report on Mental Illnesses in Canada*, www.cmha.ca/bins/content_page.asp?cid=4-42-215.

Hopp v Lepp. 1980. 112 D.L.R. (3d) 67 (S.C.C.).

Horne, R., L. Graupner, S. Frost, J. Weinman, S. Wright, and M. Hankins. 2004. "Medicine in a Multi-cultural Society: The Effect of Cultural Background on Beliefs about Medication," *Social Science & Medicine* 59: 1307–13.

Institute of Health Economics. 2010. *The Cost of Mental Health and Substance Abuse Services in Canada*, www.ihe.ca/documents/Cost%20of%20Mental%20Health%20Services%20in%20Canada%20Report%20June%202010.pdf.

Lim, K.-L., P. Jacobs, A. Ohinmaa, D. Schopflocher, and C. Dewa. 2008. "A New Population-based Measure of the Burden of Mental Illness in Canada," *Chronic Diseases in Canada* 28, 3: 92–8.

Longhofer, J., J. Floersch, and J. Jenkins. 2003. "Medication Effect Interpretation and the Social Grid of Management," *Social Work in Mental Health* 1, 4: 71–89.

Mental Health Commission of Canada (MHCC). 2009. *Toward Recovery and Well-Being: A Framework for a Mental Health Strategy for Canada*, www.mentalhealthcommission.ca/English/Pages/Reports.aspx.

———. 2012. *Changing Directions, Changing Lives: A Mental Health Strategy for Canada*, strategy.mentalhealthcommission.ca/download/.

Mintz, D. 2005. "Teaching the Prescriber's Role: The Psychology of Psychopharmacology," *Academic Psychiatry* 29, 2: 187–94.

Myers, L., and B. Thyer. 1997. "Should Social Work Clients Have the Right to Effective Treatment?" *Social Work* 42, 3: 288–98.

National Association of Social Workers (NASW). 2009. "Mental Health," www.socialworkers.org/pressroom/features/issue/mental.asp.

Navaneelan, T. 2012. *Suicide Rates: An Overview*. Ottawa: Statistics Canada.

O'Brien, A., and K. Calderwood. 2010. "Living in the Shadows: A Canadian Experience of Mental Health Social Work," *Social Work in Mental Health* 8, 4: 319–35.

Ontario Association of Social Workers (OASW). 2006. *Role of Social Work in Mental Health*. Toronto: OASW.

President's New Freedom Commission on Mental Health. 2003. *Achieving the Promise: Transforming Mental Health in America, Final Report*, www.mentalhealthcommission.gov/reports/FinalReport/downloads/FinalReport.pdf.

Porta, M. 2004. "Is There Life after Evidence-based Medicine?" *Journal of Evaluation in Clinical Practice* 10, 2: 147–52.

Proctor, E.K., and A. Rosen. 2004. "Concise Standards for Developing Evidence-based Practice Guidelines," in A. Roberts and K. Yeager, eds, *Evidence-Based Practice Manual: Research and Outcome Measures in Health and Human Services*. New York: Oxford University Press.

R. v. J. (J.-L.). 1999. 130 C.C.C. (3d) 541 (Que. C.A.).

Reese, D., and M. Sontag. 2001. "Successful Interprofessional Collaboration on the Hospice Team," *Health and Social Work* 26, 3: 167–75.

Regehr, C., and B. Antle. 1997. "Coercive Influences: Informed Consent in Court Mandated Social Work Practice," *Social Work* 42, 3: 300–6.

———, S. Stern, and A. Shlonsky. 2007. "Operationalizing Evidence Based Practice: The Development of a Research Institute in Evidence Based Social Work," *Research on Social Work Practice* 17, 3: 408–16.

Rief, W., Y. Nestoriuc, S. Weiss, E. Welzel, A.J. Barsky, and S.G. Hofmann. 2009. "Meta-analysis of the Placebo Response in Antidepressant Trials," *Journal of Affective Disorders* 118, 1–3: 1–8.

Rosen, A., and E. Proctor. 2002. "Standards for Evidence-Based Social Work Practice," in A. Roberts and G. Greene, eds, *Social Worker's Desk Reference*. New York: Oxford University Press.

Saarni, S., and H. Gylling. 2004. "Evidence-based Medicine Guidelines: A Solution to Rationing or Politics Disguised as Science?" *Journal of Medical Ethics* 30, 2: 171–5.

Sackett, D., W. Rosenberg, J. Gray, R. Haynes, and W. Richardson. 1996. "Evidence-based Medicine: What It Is and What It Isn't," *British Medical Journal* 312, 7023: 71–2.

Salyers, M., and S. Tsemberis. 2007. "ACT and Recovery: Integrating Evidence-based Practice and Recovery Orientation on Assertive Community Treatment Teams," *Community Mental Health* 43, 6: 619–41.

Skelton, M. 1996. "Social Work," in E. Shorter, ed., *TPH: History and Memories of the*

Toronto Psychiatric Hospital, 1925–1966. Toronto: Wall & Emerson.

Sluzki, C.E., J. Beavin, A. Tarnopolsky, and E. Veron. 1967. "Transactional Disqualification: Research on the Double Bind," *Archives of General Psychiatry* 4: 494–504.

Sowers, W. 2005. "Transforming Systems of Care: The American Association of Community Psychiatrists Guidelines for Recovery Oriented Services," *Community Mental Health Journal* 41, 6: 757–74.

Statistics Canada. 2003. "Canadian Community Health Survey: Mental Health and Well-being," www.camh.net/news_events/key_camh_facts_for_media/addictionmentalhealthstatistics.html.

Teicher, M. 1952a. "The Role of the Psychiatric Social Worker," *Canadian Welfare* 27, 8: 14–20.

———. 1952b. "Let's Abolish Social Service Exchange," *Social Work Journal* 33, 1: 28–31.

Toseland, R., J. Zaneles-Palmer, and D. Chapman. 1986. "Teamwork in Psychiatric Settings," *Social Work* 31: 46–52.

Towns, A., and K. Schwartz. 2012. "Social Workers' Role in the Canadian Mental Health Care System," *Research on Social Work Practice* 22, 2: 214–18.

US Department of Labor. 2012. *Occupational Outlook Handbook, 2012–2013 Edition, Social Workers*, www.bls.gov/ooh/Community-and-Social-Service/Social-workers.htm.

Warner, R. 2009. "Recovery from Schizophrenia and the Recovery Model," *Current Opinion in Psychiatry* 22: 374–80.

Webb, S. 2001. "Some Considerations on the Validity of Evidence-based Practice in Social Work," *British Journal of Social Work* 31, 1: 57–79.

Williams, C., and A. Collins. 1999. "Defining New Frameworks for Psychosocial Intervention," *Psychiatry* 62: 61–78.

Wilson, M., R. Hayward, S. Tunis, E. Bass, and G. Guyatt. 1995. "Users' Guides to the Medical Literature: VIII. How to Use Clinical Practice Guidelines: B. What Are the Recommendations and Will They Help You in Caring for Your Patients?" *Journal of the American Medical Association (JAMA)* 274, 20: 1630–2.

Witkin, S.L. 1998. "The Right to Effective Treatment and the Effective Treatment of Rights: Rhetorical Empiricism and the Politics of Research," *Social Work* 43, 1: 75–80.

——— and W.D. Harrison. 2001. "Whose Evidence and for What Purpose?" *Social Work* 46, 4: 293–6.

World Health Organization (WHO). 2007. "What Is Mental Health?" www.who.int/features/qa/62/en/index.html.

Chapter 2

Alberta Health. 2012. "Health Funding Allocations for 2012–2013," www.health.alberta.ca/about/health-funding.html.

Andreae, D. 2002. "Canadian Values and Ideologies and Social Work Practice," in F.J. Turner, ed., *Social Work Practice: A Canadian Perspective*. Toronto: Prentice-Hall.

Auton (Guardian ad litem of) v. British Columbia (Attorney General). 2004. S.C.C. 78, 3 S.C.R. 657.

BC Mental Health and Addiction Services. 2008. "BC Mental Health Timeline," www.bcmhas.ca/AboutUs/History.htm.

Canada Health Act, R.S.C. 1985. c. C-6, www.canlii.org/ca/sta/c-6/.

Canadian Alliance on Mental Illness and Mental Health. 2006. *Framework for Action on Mental Illness and Mental Health: Recommendations to Health and Social Policy Leaders of Canada for a National Action Plan on Mental Illness and Mental Health*, www.cmha.ca/data/1/rec_docs/601_CAMIMH%20English%20Lowres.pdf.

Canadian Institute for Health Information (CIHI). 2010. "Health Care Spending to Reach $192 Billion This Year," www.cihi.ca/CIHI-ext-portal/internet/en/Document/spending+and+health+workforce/spending/RELEASE_28OCT10.

Canadian Journal of Public Health. 2004. "A Needs Assessment of Federal Inmates: Mental Health," 95 (supplement 1): S36–S48.

Corrigan, P., K. Sokol, and N. Rüsch. 2011. "The Impact of Self-Stigma and Mutual Help Programs on the Quality of Life of People with Serious Mental Illnesses," *Community Mental Health Journal* 10.1007/s10597-011-9445-2.

Edginton, B. 2002. "Early Treatment of the Insane in Ontario," presented at the meetings of the Canadian Society for the History of Medicine, Toronto.

Delaney, R. 2009. "The Philosophical and Value Base of Canadian Social Welfare," in J. Turner and F. Turner, eds, *Canadian Social Welfare*, 6th edn. Toronto: Pearson Education Canada.

Duffin, J. 2000. *History of Medicine: A Scandalously Short Introduction*. Toronto: University of Toronto Press.

First Nations Child and Family Caring Society of Canada. 2008. "Joint Declaration of Support for Jordan's Principle," www.fncaringsociety.com/jordans-principle.

Goering, P., D. Wasylenki, W. Lancee, and S.J. Freeman. 1984. "From Hospital to Community: Six-Month and Two-Year Outcomes for 505 Patients," *Journal of Nervous and Mental Disease* 172, 11: 667–73.

Government of Canada. 2002. "Romanow Report Promises Sweeping Changes to Medicare," www.hc-sc.gc.ca/english/care/romanow/hcc0403.html.

———. 2008. "1957—Advent of Medicare in Canada: Establishing Public Medical Care Access," www.canadianeconomy.gc.ca/English/economy/1957medicare.html.

Government of Ontario. 2012. *Ontario's Action Plan for Health Care*, www.health.gov.on.ca/en/ms/ecfa/healthy_change/docs/rep_healthychange.pdf.

Harcourt, B. 2000. "From the Asylum to the Prison: Rethinking the Incarceration Revolution," *Texas Law Review* 84: 1751–86.

Hartford, K., T. Schrecker, M. Wiktorowicz, J. Hoch, and C. Sharp. 2003. "Four Decades of Mental Health Policy in Ontario, Canada," *Administration and Policy in Mental Health* 31, 1: 65–73.

Health Canada. 1999. *Toward a Healthy Future: Second Report on the Health of Canadians*, www.phac-aspc.gc.ca/ph-sp/phdd/report/subin.html.

———. 2002. "Canada Health Act Overview," www.hc-sc.gc.ca/hcs-sss/medi-assur/cha-lcs/overview-apercu-eng.php.

———. 2006. "Fetal Alcohol Spectrum Disorder," www.hc-sc.gc.ca/iyh-vsv/diseases-maladies/fasd-etcaf_e.html#he.

Hick, S. 2006. *Social Work in Canada: An Introduction*. Toronto: Thompson Educational Publishing.

Kirby, M. 2008. "Mental Health in Canada: Out of the Shadows Forever," *Canadian Medical Association Journal* 178, 10: 1320–2.

Lamb, H.R. 1998. "Deinstitutionalization at the Beginning of the New Millennium," *Harvard Review of Psychiatry* 6: 1–10.

——— and L.E. Weinberger. 1998. "Persons with Severe Mental Illness in Jails and Prisons: A Review," *Psychiatric Services* 49: 483–92.

Link, B., J. Phelan, M. Bresnahan, A. Stueve, and B. Pescosolido. 1999. "Public Conceptions of Mental Illness: Labels, Causes, Dangerousness, and Social Distance," *American Journal of Public Health* 89, 9: 1328–33.

Lurie, S. 2005. "Comparative Mental Health Policy: Are There Lessons to Be Learned?" *International Review of Psychiatry* 17, 2: 97–101.

———. 2012. "Walkom: The Downside of Ontario's Health-Care Reforms," Letter to the Editor, *Toronto Star*, 1 Feb.

McNeill, T., and D. Nicholas. 2009. "Our System of Health Care," in J. Turner and F. Turner, eds, *Canadian Social Welfare*, 6th edn. Toronto: Pearson Education Canada.

Mental Health Commission of Canada. 2012. *Changing Directions, Changing Lives: A Mental Health Strategy for Canada*, http://strategy.mentalhealthcommission.ca/download/.

Menzies, R. 1995. "The Making of Criminal Insanity in British Columbia: Granby Farrant and the Provincial Mental Home, Colquitz, 1919–1933," in H. Foster and J. McLaren, eds, *Essays in the History of Canadian Law: British Columbia and the Yukon*. Toronto: University of Toronto Press, 274–313.

Ministry of Health and Long Term Care. 2002. *The Time Is Now: Themes and Recommendations for Mental Health Reform in Ontario*, www.health.gov.on.ca/english/providers/pub/mhitf/provincial_forum/provincial_forum.html.

Nelson, G. 2006. "Mental Health Policy in Canada," in A. Westhues, ed., *Canadian Social Policy: Issues and Perspectives*. Waterloo, Ontario: Wilfrid Laurier University Press.

Offord, D., M. Boyle, D. Campbell, J. Cochrane, P. Goering, et al. 1994. *Mental Health in Ontario: Selected Findings from the Mental Health Supplement of the Ontario Health Survey*. Toronto: Ministry of Health.

Ontario Ministry of Health. 1991. *The Road to Reform: Final Report of the Implementation Strategy Sub-Committee*. Toronto: Ontario Ministry of Health.

Public Health Agency Canada. 2008. "What Determines Health?" www.phac-aspc.gc.ca.

Regehr, C., and K. Kanani. 2010. *Essential Law for Social Work Practice in Canada*, 2nd edn. Toronto: Oxford University Press.

Regier, D.A., W.E. Narrow, D.S. Rae, R.W. Manderscheid, B.Z. Locke, and F.K. Goodwin. 1993. "The De Facto US Mental and Addictive Disorders Service System: Epidemiologic Catchment Area Prospective 1-year Prevalence Rates of Disorders and Services," *Archives of General Psychiatry* 50, 2: 85–94.

Sapers, H. 2011. *Annual Report of the Office of the Correctional Investigator 2010–2011*, www.oci-bec.gc.ca/rpt/annrpt/annrpt20102011-eng.aspx#ss1a.

Shera, W., U. Aviram, B. Healy, and S. Ramon. 2002. "Mental Health Systems Reform: A Multi Country Comparison," *Social Work in Health Care* 35, 1–2: 547–75.

Skelton, M. 1996. "Social Work," in E. Shorter, ed., *TPH: History and Memories of the Toronto Psychiatric Hospital, 1925–1966*. Toronto: Wall & Emerson.

Steele, L.S., C.S. Dewa, E. Lin, and K.L. Lee. 2007. "Education Level, Income Level and Mental Health Services Use in Canada: Associations and Policy Implications," *Healthcare Policy/Politiques de Santé* 3, 1: 96–106.

Standing Senate Committee on Social Affairs, Science and Technology. 2002. *The Health of Canadians—The Federal Role*. Ottawa: Senate Canada, www.parl.gc.ca/37/2/parlbus/commbus/senate/Com-e/soci-e/rep-e/repoct02vol6-e.htm.

Standing Senate Committee on Social Affairs, Science and Technology. 2006. *Out of the Shadows at Last: Transforming Mental Health, Mental Illness and Addiction Services in Canada*. Ottawa: Senate Canada, www.parl.gc.ca/39/1/parlbus/commbus/senate/com-e/soci-e/rep-e/rep02may06-e.htm.

Thomlison, R., and C. Bradshaw. 2002. "Canadian Political Processes and Social Work Practice," in F. Turner, ed., *Social Work Practice: A Canadian Perspective*. Toronto: Prentice-Hall.

Yearwood-Lee, E. 2008. *Mental Health Policies: Historical Overview*. Victoria: Legislative Library of British Columbia.

Chapter 3

Ahmed v. Stefaniu. 2006. O.J. No. 4185.

Alberta Health. 2012. "Community Treatment Orders," www.health.alberta.ca/newsroom/community-treatment-orders-MHA.html.

Alberta Mental Health Act, S.A. 2000, c. M-13.1, www.canlii.org/ab/laws/sta/m-13/.

Ambrosini, D., and A. Crocker. 2007. "Psychiatric Advance Directives and the Right to Refuse Treatment in Canada," *Canadian Journal of Psychiatry* 52, 6: 397–402.

Antle, B., and C. Regehr. 2003. "Meta-Ethics in Social Work Research: Beyond Individual Rights and Freedoms," *Social Work* 48, 1: 135–44.

Appelbaum, P. 1985. "Tarasoff and the Clinician: Problems in Fulfilling the Duty to Protect," *American Journal of Psychiatry* 142: 425–9.

———. 1991. "Advance Directives for Psychiatric Treatment," *Hospital and Community Psychiatry* 42: 983–4.

———. 1994. *Almost a Revolution*. New York: Oxford University Press.

Badding, N. 1989. "Client Involvement in Case Recording," *Social Casework* 70, 9: 539–48.

Bagby, M. 1987. "The Effects of Legislative Reform on Admission Rates to Psychiatric Units of General Hospitals," *International Journal of Law and Psychiatry* 10: 383–94.

———, J. Thompson, S. Dickens, and M. Nohara. 1991. "Decision-making in Psychiatric Commitment: An Experimental Analysis," *American Journal of Psychiatry* 48: 28–33.

Bay, M. 2004. "1933–2003: Lessons from 70 Years of Experience with Mental Health, Capacity and Consent Legislation in Ontario," *Health Law in Canada* 24, 3: 36–43.

———, S. Fram, M. Silberfeld, C. Shushelski, and H. Bloom. 1996. "Capacity and Substitute Decision Making for Personal Care," in H. Bloom and M. Bay, eds, *A Practical Guide to Mental Health, Capacity and Consent Law of Ontario*. Toronto: Carswell.

B.H. v. Alberta (Director of Child Welfare). 2002. 329 A.R. 395 (Alta. Q.B.).

Burlington Post. 2001. "Brian's Law Broadens Criteria for Treatment of Mentally Ill," 17 Oct.

Canadian Association of Social Workers (CASW). 2005. *Code of Ethics*. Ottawa: CASW.

———. 2007. *Informed Consent and Confidentiality: CASW Guidelines*. Ottawa: CASW.

Canadian Charter of Rights and Freedoms. 1982. Part 1 of the Constitution Act, 1982, Being Schedule B to the Canada Act (U.K.), 1982, s. 11.

Capponi, P. 2003. *Beyond the Crazy House*. Toronto: Penguin.

Carlisle, J. 1996. "Duty to Warn: Report from Council," Members' Dialogue, *Canadian Medical Association* (July–Aug.): 21.

Chaimowitz, G., and G. Glancy. 2002. "The Duty to Protect," *Canadian Journal of Psychiatry* 47: 1–4.

———, G. Glancy, and J. Blackburn. 2000. "The Duty to Warn and Protect: Impact on Practice," *Canadian Journal of Psychiatry* 45: 899–904.

Ciarlariello v. Schacter. 1993. 2 S.C.R. 119.

College of Physicians and Surgeons of Nova Scotia. 2006. *Guidelines for Medical Record Keeping*, www.cpsns.ns.ca/guidetomedrec.html#31.

Consent to Treatment and Health Care Directives Act, S.P.E.I. 1996. c. 10, www.canlii.org/pe/laws/sta/c-17.2/20041117/whole.html.

Dickens, B. 2002. "Informed Consent," in J. Downie, T. Caulfield, and C. Flood, eds, *Canadian Health Law and Policy*. Toronto: Butterworths.

Downie, J., T. Caulfield, and C. Flood, eds. 2002. *Canadian Health Law and Policy*. Toronto: Butterworths.

Dykeman, M.J. 2000. *Canadian Health Law Practice Manual*. Toronto: Butterworths.

Etchells, E., G. Sharpe, P. Walsh, J. Williams, and P. Singer. 1996. "BioEthics for Clinicians: Consent," *Canadian Medical Association Journal* 155: 177–80.

Fowler, L. 2004. *Powers of Attorney*. Toronto: Law Society of Upper Canada.

Gelman, S. 1992. "Risk Management through Client Access to Case Records," *Social Work* 37, 1: 73–9.

Gibbs v. Gibbs. 1985. 1 W.D.C.P. 6 (Ont. S.C.).

Glancy, D., and G. Glancy. 2008. "The Case That Has Psychiatrists Running Scared: *Ahmed v. Stefaniu*," *Journal of the American Academy of Psychiatry and the Law* 37, 2: 250–256.

Glancy, G., C. Regehr, and A. Bryant. 1998. "Confidentiality in Crisis: Part II—Confidentiality of Treatment Records," *Canadian Journal of Psychiatry* 43, 12: 1006–11.

Goffman, I. 1961. *Asylums: Essays on the Social Situation of Mentally Ill and Other Inmates*. Chicago: Aldine.

Gordon, R., and S. Verdun-Jones. 1983. "The Right to Refuse Treatment: Commonwealth Developments and Issues," *International Journal of Law and Psychiatry* 6: 57–73.

Government of Saskatchewan. 2002. *Adult Guardianship Manual*, www.justice.gov.sk.ca/adx/aspx/adxGetMedia.aspx?DocID=128,117,113,81,1,Documents&MediaID=83&Filename=Applicationpkg.pdf.

Gray, J., M. Shone, and P. Liddle. 2000. *Canadian Mental Health Law and Policy*. Toronto: Butterworths.

Gutheil, T. 1980. "In Search of True Freedom: Drug Refusal, Involuntary Medication, and 'Rotting with Your Rights On'," *American Journal of Psychiatry* 137: 327–8.

———. 1986. "The Right to Refuse Treatment: Paradox, Pendulum and the Quality of Care," *Behavioral Sciences and the Law* 4: 265–77.

Hardin, H. 1993. "Uncivil Liberties: Far from Respecting Civil Liberties, Legal Obstacles to Treating the Mentally Ill Limit or Destroy the Liberty of the Person," *Vancouver Sun*, 2 July, www.psychlaws.org/JoinUs/CatalystArchive/CatWinter02.htm.

Hawkes, E. 2012. "Forced Medication Saved My Life," *National Post*, 18 June, A16.

Health Care Consent Act, S.O. 1996, c. 2, www.e-laws.gov.on.ca/html/statutes/english/elaws_statutes_96h02_e.htm.

Hiltz, D., and A. Szigeti. 2004. *A Guide to Consent and Capacity Law in Ontario*. Toronto: LexisNexis Canada.

Hoffman, R., and L. Putnam. 2004. *Not Just Another Call: Police Response to People with Mental Illnesses in Ontario*. Toronto: Centre for Addiction and Mental Health.

Incompetent Persons Act. 1989. R.S., c. 218, s. 1, www.gov.ns.ca/legislature/legc/statutes/incompet.htm.

Involuntary Psychiatric Treatment Act. 2005. R.S.N.S., c. 42, www.gov.ns.ca/legislature/legc/bills/59th_1st/3rd_read/b203.htm.

Jankovic, J., K. Yeeles, C. Katsakou, T. Amos, R. Morriss, D. Rose, P. Nichol, R. McCabe, and S. Priebe. 2011. "Family Caregivers' Experiences of Involuntary Psychiatric Hospital Admissions of Their Relatives—a Qualitative Study," *PLoS ONE* 6, 10: 1–7.

Kakhost, A., J. Perry, and D. Frank. 2012. "Assessing the Outcome of Compulsory Treatment Orders on Management of Psychiatric Patients at 2 McGill University Associated Teaching Hospitals," *Canadian Journal of Psychiatry* 57, 6: 359–65.

Katsakou, C., D. Rose, T. Amos, L. Bowers, R.

McCabe, D. Oliver, T. Wykes, and S. Priebe. 2011. "Psychiatric Patients' Views on Why Their Involuntary Admission Was Right or Wrong: A Qualitative Study," *Social Psychiatry and Psychiatric Epidemiology*. DOI: 10.1007/s00127-011-0427-z.

Ketchum v. Hislop. 1984. 54 B.C.L.R. 327 B.C.S.C.

Kress, K. 2006. "Rotting with Their Rights On: Why the Criteria for Ending Commitment or Restraint of Liberty Need Not Be the Same as the Criteria for Initiating Commitment or Restraint of Liberty, and How the Restraint May Sometimes Justifiably Continue after Its Prerequisites Are No Longer Satisfied," *Behavioral Sciences and the Law* 24, 4: 573–98.

Lieff, S., and A. Fish. 1996. "Financial Capacity, Contracts and Property," in H. Bloom and M. Bay, eds, *A Practical Guide to Mental Health, Capacity and Consent Law of Ontario*. Toronto: Carswell.

Marshall v. Curry. 1933. 3 D.L.R. 260 (N.S.S.C.).

Martin, B. and K. Cheung. 1985. "Civil Commitment in Ontario: The Effect of Legislation on Clinical Practices," *Canadian Journal of Psychiatry* 30, 4: 259–64.

McInerney v. MacDonald. 1992. 2 S.C.R. 138.

Mela, M. 2012. "Legal Leverage," *British Journal of Psychiatry* 200: 81–2.

Mental Health Act, C.C.S.M. c. M110, www.canlii.org/mb/laws/sta/m-110/index.html.

Ministry of Health and Long-Term Care. 2000. "Brian's Law: Mental Health Legislative Reform," www.health.gov.on.ca/english/public/program/mentalhealth/mental_reform/brians_law.html.

Monahan, J., R. Bonnie, P. Appelbaum, P. Hyde, H. Steadman, and M. Swartz. 2001. "Mandated Community Treatment: Beyond Outpatient Commitment," *Psychiatric Services* 52, 9: 1198–1205.

Morris, J., M. Ferguson, and M. Dykeman. 1999. *Canadian Nurses and the Law*, 2nd edn. Toronto: LexisNexis Canada.

Nakhost, A., J.C. Perry, and D. Frank. 2012. "Assessing the Outcome of Compulsory Treatment Orders on Management of Psychiatric Patients at 2 McGill University-Associated Hospitals," *Canadian Journal of Psychiatry* 57, 6: 359–65.

Nelson, E. 2002. "The Fundamentals of Consent," in J. Downie, T. Caulfield, and C. Flood, eds, *Canadian Health Law and Policy*. Toronto: Butterworths.

O'Brien, A., and S. Farrell. 2005. "Community Treatment Orders: Profile of a Canadian Experience," *Canadian Journal of Psychiatry* 50: 27–30.

———, ———, and S. Faulkner. 2009. "Community Treatment Orders: Beyond Hospital Utilization Rates. Examining the Association of Community Treatment Orders with Community Engagement and Supportive Housing," *Community Mental Health Journal* 45: 415–19.

O'Donoghue, B., J. Lyne, M. Hill, L. O'Rourke, S. Daly, C. Larkin, L. Feeney, and E. O'Callaghan. 2011. "Perceptions of Involuntary Admission and Risk of Subsequent Readmission at One-Year Follow-up: The Influence of Insight and Recovery Style," *Journal of Mental Health* 20, 3: 249–59.

O'Reilly, R., D. Keegan, and J. Elias. 2000. "A Survey of the Use of Community Treatment Orders by Psychiatrists in Saskatchewan," *Canadian Journal of Psychiatry* 45: 79–81.

Ontario College of Social Workers and Social Service Workers (OCSWSSW). 2005. *Privacy Toolkit for Social Workers and Social Service Workers: Guide to the Personal Health Information Protection Act, 2004 (PHIPA)*. Toronto: OCSWSSW, www.ocswssw.org/sections/pdf/PHIPA_Toolkit_Final_Web.pdf.

P. (L.M.) v. F. (D.). 1994. 22 C.C.L.T. (2d) 312 (Ont. Gen. Div.).

Page, S. 1980. "New Civil Commitment Legislation: The Relevance of Commitment Criteria," *Canadian Journal of Psychiatry* 25: 646–50.

Paul, M., D. Foreman, and L. Kent. 2000. "Outpatient Clinical Attendance Consent from Children and Young People: Ethical and Practical Considerations," *Clinical Child Psychology and Psychiatry* 5, 2: 203–11.

R. v. Mills. 1997. A.J. 891 (Alta. Ct. Q.B.).

R. v. O'Connor. 1995. 4 S.C.R. 411.

Re T.D.D. 1999. 171 Dominion Law Reports (4th) 761 (Sask. Q.B.).

Regehr, C., and B. Antle. 1997. "Coercive Influences: Informed Consent in Court Mandated Social Work Practice," *Social Work* 42, 3: 300–6.

———, A. Bryant, and G. Glancy. 1997. "Confidentiality of Treatment for Victims of Sexual Violence," *The Social Worker* 65, 3: 137–45.

——— and K. Kanani. 2010. *Essential Law for Social Work Practice in Canada*, 2nd edn. Toronto: Oxford University Press.

Reibl v. Hughes. 1980. 2 S.C.R. 880.

Ritchie, J., R. Sklar, and W. Steiner. 1998. "Advance Directives in Psychiatry: Resolving Issues of Autonomy and Competence," *International Journal of Law and Psychiatry* 21, 3: 245–60.

Rozovsky, L. 2003. *The Canadian Law of Consent to Treatment*. Toronto: Butterworths.

Schneider, R. 1988. *Ontario Mental Health Statutes*. Toronto: Carswell.

Schnurr, B. 2004. *Court Appointment of Guardians for Mentally Incapable Persons*. Toronto: Law Society of Upper Canada.

Schwartz K., A.M. O'Brian, V. Morel, M. Armstrong, C. Fleming, and P. Moore. 2010. "Community Treatment Orders: The Service User Speaks. Exploring the Lived Experience of Community Treatment Orders," *International Journal of Psychosocial Rehabilitation* 15, 1: 39–50.

Sevels v. Cameron. 1995. O.J. No. 381 (Ontario Court of Justice, General Division).

Sheehan, K., and T. Burns. 2011. "Perceived Coercion and the Therapeutic Relationship: A Neglected Association," *Psychiatric Services* 62: 471–6.

Sklar, R. 2007. "Starson v. Swayze: The Supreme Court Speaks Out (Not All That Clearly) on the Question of 'Capacity'," *Canadian Journal of Psychiatry* 52, 6: 390–5.

Smith v. Jones. Can. 1999. 1 S.C.R. 455.

Sneiderman, R., J. Irvine, and P. Osborne. 2003. *Canadian Medical Law*, 3rd edn. Toronto: Thompson.

Solomon, R., and L. Visser. 2005. *A Legal Guide for Social Workers*. Toronto: Ontario Association of Social Workers.

Starson v Swayze. 2003. 1 S.C.R. 722.

Statutes of Canada. 1997. c. 30 (Bill C-46, 1996), An Act to Amend the Criminal Code (production of records in sexual offence proceedings).

Swartz, M.S., and J.W. Swanson. 2004. "Involuntary Outpatient Commitment, Community Treatment Orders, and Assisted Outpatient Treatment: What's in the Data?" *Canadian Journal of Psychiatry* 49, 9: 585–91.

Szasz, T. 1963. *Law, Liberty and Psychiatry*. New York: Macmillan.

Tarasoff v. Regents of University of California. 1976. 17 Cal.3d 425.

The Vulnerable Persons Living with a Mental Disability Act, S.M. 1993. c. 29, www.gov.mb.ca/fs/pwd/vpact.html.

Torrey, E., and R. Kaplan. 1995. "A National Survey of the Use of Outpatient Commitment," *Psychiatric Services* 46: 778–84.

Trueman, S. 2003. "Community Treatment Orders in Nova Scotia—The Least Restrictive Alternative?" *Health Law Journal* 11, 1.

United Nations (UN). 1948. *Universal Declaration of Human Rights*, www.un.org/Overview/rights.html.

———. 1990. *Convention on the Rights of the Child*, www.unhchr.ch/html/menu3/b/k2crc.htm.

Vayda, E., and M. Satterfield. 1997. *Law for Social Workers*. Toronto: Carswell.

Chapter 4

Abdullah, T., and T. Brown. 2011. "Mental Illness Stigma and Ethnocultural Beliefs, Values, and Norms: An Integrative Review," *Clinical Psychology Review* 31: 934–48.

Aboriginal Justice Implementation Commission. 2004. *The Justice System and Aboriginal People*, www.ajic.mb.ca/volumel/toc.html.

Alarcón, R., A. Becker, R. Lewis-Fernández, R. Like, P. Desai, E. Foulks, et al. 2009. "Issues for DSM-V: The Role of Culture in Psychiatric Diagnosis," *Journal of Nervous and Mental Disease* 197, 8: 559–60.

American Psychiatric Association (APA). 2000. *Diagnostic and Statistical Manual of Mental Disorders*, 4th edn. Washington: APA Press.

———. 2013. *Diagnostic and Statistical Manual of Mental Disorders*, 5th edn. Washington: APA Press.

Barrera, I., and C. Jordan. 2011. "Potentially Harmful Practices: Using the DSM with People of Color," *Social Work in Mental Health* 9: 272–86.

Baydala, L., J. Sherman, C. Rasmussen, E. Wikman, and H. Janzen. 2006. "ADHD Characteristics in Canadian Aboriginal Children," *Journal of Attention Disorders* 9, 4: 642–7.

Bhugra, D., and K. Bhui. 2001. *Cross-Cultural Psychiatry: A Practical Guide*. London: Arnold.

Bierman, A., A. Johns, B. Hyndman, C. Mitchell, N. Degani, A. Shack, et al. 2012. *Social Determinants of Health and Populations at*

Risk. POWER: Project for Ontario Women's Health Evidence-Based Report, www.powerstudy.ca/.

Blackstock, C. 2009a. "When Everything Matters: Comparing the Experiences of First Nations and Non-Aboriginal Children Removed from Their Families in Nova Scotia from 2003 to 2005," Ph.D. thesis, University of Toronto.

———. 2009b. "Why Addressing the Over-Representation of First Nations Children in Care Requires New Theoretical Approaches Based on First Nations Ontology," *Journal of Social Work Values and Ethics* 6, 3: 1–18.

Bohn, D. 2003. "Lifetime Physical and Sexual Abuse, Substance Abuse, Depression and Suicide Attempts among Native American Women," *Issues in Mental Health Nursing* 24: 333–52.

Canadian Centre for Justice Statistics. 2005. *Family Violence in Canada: A Statistical Profile*. Ottawa: Statistics Canada.

Canadian Institutes of Health Research (CIHR). 2013. "Institute of Gender and Health," www.cihr-irsc.gc.ca/e/8673.html.

Chan, B. 2010. "Negative Caregiving Experience: A Predictor of High Expressed Emotion among Caregivers of Relatives with Schizophrenia," *Social Work in Mental Health* 8: 375–97.

Corcoran, J., and J. Walsh. 2010. *Clinical Assessment and Diagnosis in Social Work Practice*. New York: Oxford University Press.

Department of Health. 2003. *Delivering Race Equality: A Framework for Action*. London: Department of Health, www.dh.gov.uk/en/Consultations/Closedconsultations/DH_4067441.

Dilling, H. 2000. "Classification," in M. Gelder, J. Lopez-Ibor, and N. Andreasen, eds, *New Oxford Textbook of Psychiatry*. Oxford: Oxford University Press.

Drolet, D. 2007. "Minding the Gender Gap," *University Affairs* (10 Sept.).

Dura-Vila, G., and M. Hodes. 2012. "Cross-cultural Study of Idioms of Distress among Spanish Nationals and Hispanic American Migrants: Susto, Nervios and Ataque de Nervios," *Social Psychiatry and Psychiatric Epidemiology* 47, 10: 1627–37.

Fearon, P., J. Kirkbride, C. Morgan, P. Dazzan, K. Morgan, T. Lloyd, et al. 2006. "Incidence of Schizophrenia and Other Psychoses in Ethnic Minority Groups: Results from the MRC AESOP Study," *Psychological Medicine* 36: 1541–50.

Gara, M., W. Vega, S. Arndt, M. Escamilla, D. Fleck, W. Lawson, I. Lesser, et al. 2012. "Influence of Patient Race and Ethnicity on Clinical Assessment in Patients with Affective Disorders," *Archives of General Psychiatry*. DOI: 10.1001/archgenpsychiatry.2011.2040.

Goel, R. 2000. "No Women at the Center: The Use of the Canadian Sentencing Circle in Domestic Violence Cases," *Wisconsin Women's Law Journal* 15: 293–334.

Gold, N. 2002. "The Nature and Function of Social Work Assessment," in F. Turner, ed., *Social Work Practice: A Canadian Perspective*. Toronto: Prentice-Hall.

Goldberg, D. and R. Murray. 2006. *The Maudsley Handbook of Practical Psychiatry*. New York: Oxford University Press.

Gong-Guy, E., R. Cravens, and T. Patterson. 1991. "Clinical Issues in Mental Health Service Delivery to Refugees," *American Psychologist* 46, 6: 642–8.

Gourdine, R., T. Baffour, and M. Teasley. 2011. "Autism and the African American Community," *Social Work in Public Health* 26, 4: 454–70.

Hacking, I. 1998. *Mad Travelers: Reflections on the Reality of Transient Mental Illnesses*. Cambridge, Mass.: Harvard University Press.

Harkness, D. 2011. "The Diagnosis of Mental Disorders in Clinical Social Work: A Review of Standards of Care," *Clinical Social Work Journal* 39: 223–31.

Health Canada. 2011. *A Statistical Profile on the Health of First Nations in Canada*, www.hc-sc.gc.ca/fniah-spnia/pubs/aborig-autoch/stats-profil-atlant/index-eng.php.

Hwang, W., H. Myers, J. Abe-Kim, and J. Ting. 2008. "A Conceptual Paradigm for Understanding Culture's Impact on Mental Health: The Cultural Influences on Mental Health Model," *Clinical Psychology Review* 28: 211–27.

International Federation of Social Work. 2013. "Definition of Social Work," ifsw.org/policies/.

Johnson, J., and D. Stewart. 2010. "DSM-V: Toward a Gender-Sensitive Approach to Psychiatric Diagnosis," *Archives of Women's Mental Health* 13: 17–19.

Kaplan, H., and B. Sadock. 1996. *Concise*

Textbook of Clinical Psychiatry. Baltimore: Williams & Wilkins.

Kendell, R., and A. Zealley. 1983. *Companion to Psychiatric Studies*. New York: Churchill Livingstone.

Kraemer, H., D. Kupfer, W. Narrow, D. Clarke, and D. Regier. 2010. "Moving Toward DSM-5: The Field Trials," *American Journal of Psychiatry* 167: 1158–9.

———, ———, ———, ———, and ———. 2012. "DSM-5: How Reliable Is Reliable Enough?" *American Journal of Psychiatry* 169: 13–15.

Kuhl, E., D. Kupfer, and D. Regier. 2011. "Patient-Centered Revisions to the DSM-5," *Virtual Mentor* 13: 873–9.

Kutchins, H., and S. Kirk. 1997. *Making Us Crazy: DSM—the Psychiatric Bible and the Creation of Mental Disorders*. New York: Free Press.

Lai, D. 2004. "The Impact of Culture on Depressive Symptoms of Elderly Chinese Immigrants," *Canadian Journal of Psychiatry* 49, 12: 820–7.

Luhrmann, T. 2007. "Social Defeat and the Culture of Chronicity: Or, Why Schizophrenia Does So Well Over There and So Badly Here," *Culture, Medicine and Psychiatry* 31: 135–72.

Mandell, D., R. Ittenbach, S. Levy, and J. Pinto-Martin. 2007. "Disparities in Diagnosis Received Prior to Autism Spectrum Disorder," *Journal of Autism Developmental Disorder* 37: 1795–1802.

Mitchell, R. 2003. "Ideological Reflections on the DSM-IV-R (or pay no attention to that man behind the curtain, Dorothy)," *Child and Youth Care Forum* 32, 5: 281–98.

Morgan, C., J. Kirkbride, J. Leff, T. Craig, G. Hutchinson, et al. 2007. "Parental Separation, Loss and Psychosis in Different Ethnic Groups: A Case Control Study," *Psychological Medicine* 37: 495–503.

Native Women's Association of Canada (NWAC). 2004. *Background Paper, Aboriginal Health Canada: Aboriginal People's Roundtable, Health Sectoral Session*. Ottawa: Native Women's Association.

Newman, B., V. Clemmons, and P. Dannenfelser. 2007. "The Diagnostic and Statistical Manual of Mental Disorders in Graduate Social Work Education: Then and Now," *Journal of Social Work Education* 43, 2: 297–307.

Office of the Correctional Investigator. 2012. *Spirit Matters: Aboriginal People and the Corrections and Conditional Release Act*, www.oci-bec.gc.ca/cnt/rpt/pdf/oth-aut20121022-eng.pdf.

Ponniah, K., M. Weissman, S. Bledsoe, H. Verdeli, M. Gameroff, L. Mufson, H. Fitterling, and P. Wickramaratne. 2011. "Training in Structured Diagnostic Assessment Using DSM-IV Criteria," *Research on Social Work Practice* 21: 452–8.

Probst, B. 2012. "'Walking the Tightrope': Clinical Social Workers' Use of Diagnostic and Environmental Perspectives," *Clinical Social Work Journal*. DOI: 10.1007/s10615-012-0394-1.

Royal Commission on Aboriginal Peoples. 1996a. *Breaking the Silence*. Ottawa: Supply and Services Canada.

Royal Commission on Aboriginal Peoples. 1996b. *Bridging the Cultural Divide: A Report on Aboriginal People and the Criminal Justice System in Canada*. Ottawa: Supply and Services Canada.

Ryder, A., J. Yang, X. Zhu, S. Yao, J. Yi, S. Heine, and M. Bagby. 2008. "The Cultural Shaping of Depression: Somatic Symptoms in China, Psychological Symptoms in North America?" *Journal of Abnormal Psychology* 117, 2: 300–13.

Selten, J., E. Cantor-Graae, and R. Kahn. 2007. "Migration and Schizophrenia," *Current Opinions in Psychiatry* 20: 111–15.

Setia, M., A. Quesnel-Vallee, M. Abrahamowicz, P. Tousignant, and J. Lynch. 2011. "Access to Health Care in Canadian Immigrants: A Longitudinal Study of the National Population Health Survey," *Health and Social Care in the Community* 19, 1: 70–9.

Statistics Canada. 2001a. "The People: Equity Groups," www43.statcan.ca/02/02e/02e_008d_e.htm.

———. 2001b. "2001 Census Aboriginal Profile," www12.statcan.ca/english/profil01/AP01/Index.cfm?Lang=E.

Usalcas, J. 2011. *Aboriginal People and the Labour Market: Estimates from the Labour Force Survey, 2008–2010*. Statistics Canada Catalogue no. 71-588-X, no. 3, www.statcan.gc.ca/pub/71-588-x/71-588-x2011003-eng.pdf.

Veling, W., E. Susser, J. van Os, J. Mackenbach, J. Selten, and H. Hoek. 2008. "Ethnic Density of Neighbourhoods and Incidence of Psychotic Disorders among Immigrants," *American Journal of Psychiatry* 165: 66–73.

Weerasekera, P. 1993. "Formulation: A Multiperspective Model," *Canadian Journal of Psychiatry* 38: 351–8.

Widiger, T., and L. Clark. 2000. "Toward DSM-V and the Classification of Psychopathology," *Psychological Bulletin* 126, 6: 946–63.

Wilson, D., and D. MacDonald. 2010. *The Income Gap between Aboriginal Peoples and the Rest of Canada.* Ottawa: Canadian Centre for Policy Alternatives, www.policyalternatives.ca/sites/default/files/uploads/publications/reports/docs/Aboriginal%20Income%20Gap.pdf.

Chapter 5

Agerbo, E., D. Gunnell, J.P. Bonde, P.B. Mortensen, and M. Nordentoft. 2007. "Suicide and Occupation: The Impact of Socio-economic, Demographic and Psychiatric Differences," *Psychological Medicine* 37, 8: 1131–40.

American Psychiatric Association (APA). 2013. *Diagnostic and Statistical Manual of Mental Disorders*, 5th edn. Washington: APA Press.

Bocchetta, A., D. Fadda, G. Satta, M. Del Zompo, G.J. Gessa, and P. Cocco. 2007. "Long-Term Lithium Treatment and Survival from External Causes Including Suicide," *Journal of Clinical Psychopharmacology* 27, 5: 544–6.

Brent, D., and J. Mann. 2005. "Family Genetic Studies, Suicide and Suicidal Behaviour," *Journal of Medical Genetics, Part C (Semin. Med. Genet.)* 133C: 13–24.

Canadian Association of Social Workers (CASW). 2005. *Code of Ethics.* Ottawa: CASW.

———. 2005. *Guidelines for Ethical Practice.* Ottawa: CASW.

Caplan, G. 1964. *Principles of Preventive Psychiatry.* New York: Basic Books.

Carballo, J., J. Harkavy-Friedman, A. Burke, L. Sher, E. Baca-Garcia, G. Sullivan, M. Grunenbaum, R. Parsey, J. Mann, and M. Oquendo. 2008. "Family History of Suicidal Behaviour and Early Traumatic Experiences: Additive Effect on Suicidality and Course of Bipolar Illness?" *Journal of Affective Disorders* 109: 57–63.

Cardish, R. 2007. "Psychopharmacologic Management of Suicidality in Personality Disorders," *Canadian Journal of Psychiatry* 52, S1: S115–S127.

CBC. 2002. "Suicide Stalks Manitoba Reserve," www.cbc.ca/canada/story/2002/07/25/shamattawa020725.html.

———. 2010. "RCMP to Build Rink in Troubled Reserve," www.cbc.ca/news/canada/manitoba/story/2010/02/19/mb-shamattawa-rink-rcmp-manitoba.html.

Chang, S., D. Gunnell, J. Sterne, T. Lu, and A. Cheng. 2009. "Was the Economic Crisis 1997–1998 Responsible for Rising Suicide Rates in East/Southeast Asia? A Time-Trend Analysis for Japan, Hong Kong, South Korea, Taiwan, Singapore and Thailand," *Social Science and Medicine* 66, 7: 1322–31.

Cheng, A., K. Hawton, C. Lee, and T. Chen. 2007. "The Influence of Media Reporting of Suicide of a Celebrity on Suicide Rates in a Population-based Study," *International Journal of Epidemiology* 36: 1229–34.

Chudley, A., J. Cornry, J. Cokk, C. Loock, T. Rosales, and N. LeBlanc. 2005. "Fetal Alcohol Spectrum Disorder: Canadian Guidelines for Diagnosis," *Canadian Medical Association Journal* 172, 5: S1–S21.

Clark, S., and R. Goldney. 1995. "Grief Reactions and Recovery in a Support Group for People Bereaved by Suicide," *Crisis* 16, 1: 27–33.

Cochrane-Brink, K., J. Lofchy, and I. Sakinofsky. 2000. "Clinical Rating Scales in Suicide Risk Assessment," *General Hospital Psychiatry* 22: 445–51.

Cohen, C., C. Abdallah, and S. Diwan. 2010. "Suicide Attempts and Associated Factors in Older Adults with Schizophrenia," *Schizophrenia Research* 119, 1–3: 253–7.

Corey, G., M. Corey, and P. Callanan. 1998. *Issues and Ethics in the Helping Professions*, 5th edn. Pacific Grove, Calif.: Brooks/Cole.

Courtet, P., F. Jollant, D. Castelnau, C. Buresi, and A. Malafosse. 2005. "Suicidal Behavior: Relationship between Phenotype and Serotonergic Genotype," *American Journal of Medical Genetics* 133: 25–33.

Courtet, P., I. Gottesman, and T. Gould. 2011. "The Neuroscience of Suicidal Behaviours: What Can We Expect from Endophenotype Strategies? *Translational Psychiatry* 1: 1–7.

Cumming, S., T. Covic, and E. Murrell. 2006. "Deliberate Self-Harm: Have We Scratched the Surface?" *Behaviour Change* 23, 3: 186–99.

Dhillon, S. 2012. "Landmark Assisted Suicide Case Raises 'Arguable Grounds for Appeal,'" *Globe and Mail*, 17 June.

Draper, B., J. Snowdon, and M. Wyder. 2008. "A Pilot Study of the Suicide Victim's Last

Contact with a Health Professional," *Crisis* 29, 2: 96–101.

Durkheim, E. 1951 [1897]. *Suicide*. New York: Free Press.

Ernst, C., N. Mechawar, and G. Turecki. 2009. "Suicide Neurobiology," *Progress in Neurobiology* 89: 315–33.

Ferry, J. 2000. "No Easy Answer to High Native Suicide Rates," *Lancet* 355, 9207: 906–7.

Forde, S., and C. Devaney. 2006. "Postvention: A Community-based Family Support Initiative and Model of Responding to Tragic Events Including Suicide," *Child Care in Practice* 12, 1: 53–61.

Gibbons, R.D., K. Hur, D.K. Bhaumik, and J. Mann. 2005. "The Relationship between Antidepressant Medication Use and Rate of Suicide," *Journal of the American Medication Association* 62: 165–72.

Golan, N. 1978. *Treatment in Crisis Situations*. New York: Free Press.

Harris, E., and B. Barraclough. 1997. "Suicide as an Outcome for Mental Disorders: A Meta-analysis," *British Journal of Psychiatry* 170: 205–28.

Harriss, L., and K. Hawton. 2005. "Suicide Intent in Deliberate Self-Harm and Risk of Suicide: The Predictive Power of the Suicide Intent Scale," *Journal of Affective Disorders* 86: 225–33.

Hawton, K., D. Zahl, and R. Weatherall. 2003. "Suicide Following Deliberate Self-Harm: Long-term Follow-up of Patients Who Presented to a General Hospital," *British Journal of Psychiatry* 182: 537–42.

Health Canada. 2005. "Intentional and Unintentional Injury Profile for Aboriginal Peoples in Canada," www.hc-sc.gc.ca/fniah-spnia/pubs/promotion/_injury-bless/2001_trauma/5c_suicide-eng.php.

———. 2006. "Suicide Prevention," www.hc-sc.gc.ca/fniah-spnia/promotion/suicide/index-eng.php.

Herman, J. 1992. *Trauma and Recovery*. New York: Basic Books.

Hopmeyer, E., and A. Werk. 1994. "A Comparative Study of Family Bereavement Groups," *Death Studies* 18: 243–56.

Hor, K., and M. Taylor. 2010. "Suicide and Schizophrenia: A Systematic Review of Rates and Risk Factors," *Journal of Psychopharmacology* 24, 11 (supplement 4): 81–90.

Kaplan, H., and B. Sadock. 1996. *Concise Textbook of Clinical Psychiatry*. Baltimore: Williams and Wilkins.

Kaslow, N., and S. Aronson. 2004. "Recommendations for Family Interventions Following a Suicide," *Professional Psychology: Research and Practice* 35, 3: 240–7.

Kirmayer, L., G. Brass, T. Holton, K. Paul, C. Simpson, and C. Tait. 2007. *Suicide among Aboriginal People in Canada*. Ottawa: Aboriginal Healing Foundation.

———, C. Simpson, and M. Cargo. 2003. "Healing Traditions: Culture, Community and Mental Health Promotion with Canadian Aboriginal Peoples," *Australian Psychiatry* 11 (supplement): S15–S23.

Leenaars, A. 2000. "Suicide Prevention in Canada: A History of a Community Approach," *Canadian Journal of Mental Health* 19, 2: 57–73.

Luoma, J., C. Martin, and J. Pearson. 2002. "Contact with Mental Health and Primary Care Providers before Suicide: A Review of the Evidence," *American Journal of Psychiatry* 159, 6: 909–16.

MacNeil, M.S. 2008. "An Epidemiologic Study of Aboriginal Adolescent Risk in Canada: The Meaning of Suicide," *Journal of Child and Adolescent Psychiatric Nursing* 21, 1: 3–12.

Mamo, D. 2007. "Managing Suicidality in Schizophrenia," *Canadian Journal of Psychiatry* 52 (supplement 1): S59–S70.

Mann, J., C. Waternaux, G. Haas, and K. Malone. 1999. "Toward a Clinical Model of Suicidal Behavior in Psychiatric Patients," *American Journal of Psychiatry* 156, 2: 181–9.

Maple, M. 2005. "Parental Bereavement and Youth Suicide: An Assessment of the Literature," *Australian Social Work* 58, 2: 179–87.

McGirr, A., J. Paris, A. Lesage, J. Renaud, and G. Turecki. 2009. "An Examination of DSM-IV Borderline Personality Disorder Symptoms and Risk for Death by Suicide: A Psychological Autopsy Study," *Canadian Journal of Psychiatry* 54, 2: 87–92.

Miller, A., and J. Glinski. 2000. "Youth Suicidal Behaviour: Assessment and Intervention," *Journal of Clinical Psychology* 56, 9: 1131–52.

Mishna, F., B. Antle, and C. Regehr. 2002. "Social Work with Clients Contemplating Suicide: Complexity and Ambiguity in the Clinical, Ethical and Legal Considerations," *Clinical Social Work Journal* 30, 3: 265–80.

——, C. Regehr, and B. Antle. 2003. "Canadian Legal and Ethical Parameters for Working with Suicidal Clients," *Canadian Social Work* 5, 1: 17–28.

Mustard, C., A. Bielecky, J. Etches, R. Wilkins, M. Tjepkema, B. Amick, P. Smith, W. Gnam, and K. Aronson. 2010. "Suicide Mortality by Occupation in Canada, 1991–2001," *Canadian Journal of Psychiatry* 55, 6: 369–76.

Narveson, J. 1986. "Moral Philosophy and Suicide," *Canadian Journal of Psychiatry* 31: 104–7.

Nelson, F.L. 1984. "Suicide: Issues of Prevention, Intervention, and Facilitation," *Journal of Clinical Psychology* 40, 6: 1328–33.

Nierenberg, A., J. Alpert, B. Gaynes, D. Warden, S. Wisniewski, M. Biggs, M. Trivedi, J. Barkin, and J. Rush. 2008. "Family History of Completed Suicide and Characteristics of Major Depressive Disorder: A STARD (sequenced treatment of alternatives to relieve depression) Study," *Journal of Affective Disorders* 108: 129–34.

Office of the Chief Coroner. 2011. *Death Review of Youth Suicides at the Pikangikum First Nation*, www.mcscs.jus.gov.on.ca/stellent/groups/public/@mcscs/@www/@com/documents/webasset/ec093490.pdf.

Olfson, M., D. Shaffer, S.C. Marcus, and T. Greenberg. 2003. "Relationship Between Antidepressant Medication Treatment and Suicide in Adolescents," *American Medical Association* 60: 978–82.

Parrish, M., and J. Tunkle. 2005. "Clinical Challenges Following an Adolescent's Death by Suicide: Bereavement Issues Faced by Family, Friends, Schools and Clinicians," *Clinical Social Work Journal* 33, 1: 81–102.

Posner, K., G. Brown, B. Stanley, D. Brent, K. Yershova, M. Oquendo, G. Currier, G. Melvin, L. Greenhill, S. Shen, and J. Mann. 2011. "The Columbia Suicide Severity Rating Scale: Initial Validity and Internal Consistency Findings from Three Multisite Studies with Adolescents and Adults," *American Journal of Psychiatry* 168: 1266–77.

Regehr, C., and K. Kanani. 2010. *Essential Law for Social Work Practice in Canada*, 2nd edn. Toronto: Oxford University Press.

Reinecke, M. 2000. "Suicide and Depression," in F. Dattlilio and A. Freeman, eds, *Cognitive-Behavioral Strategies in Crisis Intervention*. New York: Guilford Press, 84–125.

Reynolds, L. 2008. "Wave of Suicides Hits Troubled First Nation," *Winnipeg Free Press*, 9 May, www.canada.com/topics/news/national/story.html?id=98e9d38e-6a6e-4ef7-a7d3-fe149eb35381.

Roberts, A., and G. Everly. 2006. "A Meta-analysis of 36 Crisis Intervention Studies," *Brief Treatments and Crisis Intervention* 6, 1: 10–21.

Roberts, A.R., ed. 2000. *Crisis Intervention Handbook: Assessment, Treatment, and Research*. New York: Oxford University Press.

Special Senate Committee on Euthanasia and Assisted Suicide. 1995. *On Life and Death: Final Report*, www.parl.gc.ca/content/sen/committee/351/euth/rep/lad-tc-e.htm.

Statistics Canada. 2010. "Suicides and Suicide Rates," www40.statcan.ca/l01/cst01/hlth66a-eng.htm.

Swanson, S., and I. Colman. 2013. "Association between Exposure to Suicide Risk and Suicidality Outcomes in Youth," *Canadian Medical Association Journal*. DOI: 10.1503/cmja.121377.

Tiedemann, M., and D. Valiquet. 2008. *Euthanasia and Assisted Suicide in Canada*. Ottawa: Parliament of Canada, www.parl.gc.ca/Content/LOP/researchpublications/919-e.htm.

von Borczyskowski, A., F. Lindblad, B. Vinnerljung, R. Reintjes, and A. Hjern. 2011. "Familial Factors and Suicide: An Adoption Study in a Swedish National Cohort," *Psychological Medicine* 41: 749–58.

While, D., H. Bickley, A. Roscoe, K. Windfuhr, S. Rahman, J. Shaw, L. Appleby, and N. Kapur. 2012. "Implementation of Mental Health Service Recommendations in England and Wales and Suicide Rates, 1997–2006: A Cross-sectional and Before-and-After Observational Study," *Lancet*, 2 Feb. DOI: 10.1016/S0140-6736(11)61712-1.

World Health Organization (WHO). 2011. "Suicide Prevention," www.who.int/mental_health/prevention/suicide_rates/en/.

Zhang, P., R.E. Roberts, Z. Liu, X. Meng, J. Tang, et al. 2012. "Hostility, Physical Aggression and Trait Anger as Predictors for Suicidal Behavior in Chinese Adolescents: A School-Based Study," *PLoS ONE* 7, 2: e31044. DOI: 10.1371/journal.pone.0031044.

Chapter 6

Agorastos, A., C. Marmar, and C. Otte. 2011. "Immediate and Early Behavioral Interventions for the Prevention of Acute and Posttraumatic Stress Disorder," *Current Opinion in Psychiatry* 24: 526–32.

American Psychiatric Association (APA). 1980. *Diagnostic and Statistical Manual of Mental Disorders*, 3rd edn. Washington: APA Press.

———. 2013. *Diagnostic and Statistical Manual of Mental Disorders*, 5th edn. Washington: APA Press.

Antai-Otong, D. 2007. "The Art of Prescribing: Pharmacologic Management of Posttraumatic Stress Disorder," *Perspectives in Psychiatric Care* 43, 1: 55–9.

Armour, M.P. 2002. "Experiences of Covictims of Homicide: Implications for Research and Practice," *Trauma, Violence, & Abuse* 3, 2: 109–24.

Bernardy, N., B. Lund, B. Alexander, and M. Friedman. 2012. "Prescribing Trends in Veterans with Posttraumatic Stress Disorder," *Journal of Clinical Psychiatry* 73, 3: 297–303.

Bisson, J., A. Ehlers, R. Matthews, S. Pilling, D. Richards, and S. Turner. 2007. "Psychological Treatments for Chronic Post-traumatic Stress Disorder: Systematic Review and Meta-analysis," *British Journal of Psychiatry* 190: 97–104.

Bisson, J.I., P.L. Jenkins, J. Alexander, and C. Bannister. 1997. "Randomized Controlled Trial of Psychological Debriefing for Victims of Acute Burn Trauma," *British Journal of Psychiatry* 171: 78–81.

Blanchard, E.B., E.J. Hickling, N. Mitnick, A.E. Taylor, W.R. Loos, and T.C. Buckley. 1995. "The Impact of Severity of Physical Injury and Perception of Life Threat in the Development of Post-traumatic Stress Disorder in Motor Vehicle Accident Victims," *Behaviour Research and Therapy* 33, 5: 529–34.

Bleich, A., M. Gelkopf, and Z. Solomon. 2003. "Exposure to Terrorism, Stress-related Mental Health Symptoms, and Coping Behaviors among a Nationally Representative Sample in Israel," *JAMA* 290, 5: 612–20.

Boelen, P., J. van den Bout, and J. Keijser. 2003. "Traumatic Grief as a Disorder Distinct from Bereavement-Related Depression and Anxiety: A Replication Study with Bereaved Mental Health Care Patients," *American Journal of Psychiatry* 160, 7: 1339–41.

———, J. Keijser, M. van den Hout, and J. van den Bout. 2007. "Treatment of Complicated Grief: A Comparison between Cognitive-Behavioral Therapy and Supportive Counseling," *Journal of Consulting and Clinical Psychology* 75, 2: 277–84.

Bonanno, G.A., S. Galea, A. Bucciarelli, and D. Vlahov. 2007. "What Predicts Psychological Resilience after Disaster? The Role of Demographics, Resources and Life Stress," *Journal of Consulting and Clinical Psychology* 75, 5: 671–82.

Bowlby, J. 1980. *Attachment and Loss*, vol. 3. New York: Basic Books.

Bowman, M.L. 1999. "Individual Differences in Posttraumatic Distress: Problems with the DSM-IV Model," *Canadian Journal of Psychiatry* 44, 1: 21–33.

Bradley, R., J. Greene, E. Russ, L. Dutra, and D. Weston. 2005. "A Multi-dimensional Meta-analysis of Psychotherapy for PTSD," *American Journal of Psychiatry* 162, 2: 214–27.

Brewin, C.R., B. Andrews, and J.D. Valentine. 2000. "Meta-analysis of Risk Factors for Posttraumatic Stress Disorder in Trauma-exposed Adults," *Journal of Consulting and Clinical Psychology* 68, 5: 748–66.

Briere, J. 2000. "Treating Adult Survivors of Severe Childhood Abuse and Neglect: Further Development of an Integrative Model," in J.E.B. Myers et al., eds, *The APSAC Handbook on Child Maltreatment*, 2nd edn. Thousand Oaks, Calif.: Sage, 175–203.

Bryant, R. 2012. "Grief as a Psychiatric Disorder," *British Journal of Psychiatry* 201, 1: 9–10.

Bryant, R.A., and A.G. Harvey. 1996. "Posttraumatic Stress Reactions in Volunteer Firefighters," *Journal of Traumatic Stress* 9, 1: 51–62.

Burgess, A., and L. Holstrum. 1974. "Rape Trauma Syndrome," *American Journal of Psychiatry* 131: 981–6.

Burton, Robert. 1651. *The Anatomy of Melancholia*. Reprint: New York: John Wiley and Sons, 1850.

Calhoun, K.S., and B.M. Atkeson. 1991. *Treatment of Rape Victims: Facilitating Psychosocial Adjustment*. Toronto: Pergamon Press.

Calohan, J., K. Peterson, E. Perskind, and M. Raskind. 2010. "Prazosin Treatment of Trauma Nightmares and Sleep Disturbance in Soldiers Deployed in Iraq," *Journal of Traumatic Stress* 23, 5: 645–8.

Caplan, G. 1964. *Principles of Preventive Psychiatry*. New York: Basic Books.

CBC. 2011. "Grande Prairie Teens Laid to Rest," 28 Oct., www.cbc.ca/news/canada/edmonton/story/2011/10/28/edmonton-funerals-grande-prairie-teens.html.

Cooper, J., J. Carty, and M. Creamer. 2005. "Pharmacotherapy for Posttraumatic Stress Disorder: Empirical Review and Clinical Recommendations," *Australian and New Zealand Journal of Psychiatry* 39, 8: 674–82.

Ehlers, A., and D. Clark. 2003. "Early Psychological Interventions for Adult Survivors of Trauma: A Review," *Biological Psychiatry* 53, 9: 817–26.

Eisenman, D.P., L. Gelberg, H. Liu, and M.F. Shapiro. 2003. "Mental Health and Health-related Quality of Life among Adult Latino Primary Care Patients Living in the United States with Previous Exposure to Political Violence," *JAMA* 290, 5: 627–34.

Follette, V.M., J.I. Ruzek, and F.R. Abueg, eds. 1998. *Cognitive-Behavioral Therapies for Trauma*. New York: Guilford Press.

Foy, D., S. Glynn, P. Schnurr, M. Jankowski, M. Wattenberg, D. Weiss, et al. 2000. "Group Therapy," in E.B. Foa, T.M. Keane, and M.J. Friedman, eds, *Effective Treatments for PTSD: Practice Guidelines for the International Society for Traumatic Stress Studies*. New York: Guilford Press.

Freedy, J.R., H.S. Resnick, D.G. Kilpatrick, B.S. Dansky, and R.P. Tidwell. 1994. "The Psychological Adjustment of Recent Crime Victims in the Criminal Justice System," *Journal of Interpersonal Violence* 9, 4: 450–68.

Freud, S. 1957 [1917]. "Mourning and Melancholia," in J. Strachey, ed. and trans., *Standard Edition of the Complete Psychological Works of Sigmund Freud*, vol. 14. London: Hogarth Press, 152–70.

Glancy, G.D., and T.F. Knott. 2003. "Part III: The Psychopharmacology of Long-Term Aggression—Toward an Evidence-based Algorithm," *Bulletin of the Canadian Psychiatric Association* 35: 13–18.

Green, B.L., J.L. Krupnick, P. Stockton, L. Goodman, C. Corcoran, and R. Petty. 2001. "Psychological Outcome Associated with Traumatic Loss in a Sample of Young Women," *American Behavior Scientist* 44, 5: 817–37.

Harvey, A.G., R.A. Bryant, and N. Tarrier. 2003. "Cognitive Behaviour Therapy for Posttraumatic Stress Disorder," *Clinical Psychology Review* 23, 3: 501–22.

Hembree, E.A., and F.B. Foa. 2003. "Interventions for Trauma-related Emotional Disturbances in Adult Victims of Crime," *Journal of Traumatic Stress* 16, 2: 187–99.

Herman, J. 1992. *Trauma and Recovery*. New York: Basic Books.

Hobfoll, S.E. 2001. "The Influence of Culture, Community, and the Nested-Self in the Stress Process: Advancing Conservation of Resources Theory," *Applied Psychology: An International Review* 50, 3: 337–421.

Humphrey, G.M., and D.G. Zimpfer. 1996. *Counselling for Grief and Bereavement*. London: Sage.

Jones, E. 2006. "Historical Approaches to Post-combat Disorders," *Philosophical Transactions of the Royal Society of Britain* 361: 533–42.

Kaltman, S., and G.A. Bonanno. 2003. "Trauma and Bereavement: Examining the Impact of Sudden and Violent Deaths," *Anxiety Disorders* 17, 2: 131–47.

Kardiner, A. 1941. *Traumatic Neuroses of War*. New York: Hoeber.

Kessler, R.C., P. Berglund, O. Delmer, R. Jin, K.R. Merikangas, and E.E. Walters. 2005. "Lifetime Prevalence and Age-of-Onset Distributions of DSM-IV Disorders in the National Comorbidity Survey Replication," *Archives of General Psychiatry* 62, 6: 593–602.

Koenen, K.C. 2006. "Developmental Epidemiology of PTSD: Self-regulation as a Central Mechanism," *Annals New York Academy of Science* 1071: 255–66.

Kübler-Ross, E. 1969. *On Death and Dying*. New York: Macmillan.

LeBlanc, V., C. Regehr, B. Jelley, and I. Barath. 2008. "The Relationship between Coping Styles, Performance and Responses to Stressful Scenarios in Police Recruits," *International Journal of Stress Management* 15, 1: 76–93.

Lindauer, R.J., M. Olff, E.P. van Meijel, I.V. Carlier, and B.P. Gersons. 2006. "Cortisol, Learning, Memory and Attention in Relation to Smaller Hippocampal Volume in Police

Officers with Posttraumatic Stress Disorder," *Biological Psychiatry* 59, 2: 171–7.

Lindemann, E. 1944. "Symptomatology and Management of Acute Grief," *American Journal of Psychiatry* 101: 141–8.

MacKenzie, J. 1920. "The Soldier's Heart and War Neurosis: A Study in Symptomology," *British Medical Journal* 1, 3093: 491–4.

Mancini, A., P. Griffin, and G. Bonanno. 2012. "Recent Trends in the Treatment of Prolonged Grief," *Current Opinions in Psychiatry* 25, 1: 46–51.

Marmar, C.R., D.S. Weiss, T.J. Metzler, K.L. Delucchi, S.R. Best, and K.A. Wentworth. 1999. "Longitudinal Course and Predictors of Continuing Distress Following Critical Incident Exposure in Emergency Services Personnel," *Journal of Nervous and Mental Disorders* 187, 1: 15–22.

Mayou, R., A. Ehlers, and M. Hobbs. 2000. "Psychological Debriefing for Road Traffic Accident Victims," *British Journal of Psychiatry* 176: 589–93.

McFarlane, A., and R. Yehuda. 1996. "Resilience, Vulnerability and the Course of Posttraumatic Reactions," in B. van der Kolk, A. McFarlane, and L. Weisaeth, eds, *Traumatic Stress: The Effects of Overwhelming Experience on Mind, Body, and Society*. New York: Guilford Press.

McLaughlin, K., P. Berglund, M. Gruber, R. Kessler, N. Sampson, and A. Zaslavsky. 2011. "Recovery from PTSD following Hurricane Katrina," *Depression and Anxiety* 28, 6: 439–46.

Mollica, R.F., K. McInnes, C. Poole, and S. Tor. 1998. "Dose-effect Relationships of Trauma to Symptoms of Depression and Post-traumatic Stress Disorder among Cambodian Survivors of Mass Violence," *British Journal of Psychiatry* 173: 482–8.

Morgan, C.A., S. Wang, A. Rasmusson, G. Hazlett, G. Anderson, and D.S. Charney. 2001. "Relationship among Plasma Cortisol, Catecholamines, Neuropeptide Y, and Human Performance during Exposure to Uncontrollable Stress," *Psychosomatic Medicine* 63: 412–22.

Mott, F.W. 1918. "War Psychoneurosis. Neurasthenia: The Disorders and Disabilities of Fear," *Lancet* 1: 127–9.

Najarian, L.M, A.K. Goenjian, D. Pelcovitz, F. Mandel, and B. Najarian. 2001. "The Effect of Relocation after a Natural Disaster," *Journal of Traumatic Stress* 14, 3: 511–26.

Norris, F.H., M.J. Friedman, and P.J. Watson. 2002. "60,000 Disaster Victims Speak: Part II. Summary and Implications of the Disaster Mental Health Research," *Psychiatry* 65, 3: 240–60.

Oppenheimer, B.S., and M.A. Rothschild. 1918. "The Psychoneurotic Factor in the 'Irritable Heart of Soldiers,'" *British Medical Journal* 2, 3002: 29–31.

Orcutt, H.K., D.J. Erickson, and J. Wolfe. 2002. "A Prospective Analysis of Trauma Exposure: The Mediating Role of PTSD Symptomatology," *Journal of Traumatic Stress* 15, 3: 259–66.

Ozer, E.J., S.R. Best, T.L. Lipsey, and D.S. Weiss. 2003. "Predictors of Posttraumatic Stress Disorder and Symptoms in Adults: A Meta-analysis," *Psychological Bulletin* 129, 1: 52–73.

——— and D.S. Weiss. 2004. "Who Develops Posttraumatic Stress Disorder?" *Current Directions in Psychological Science* 13, 4: 169–72.

Page, H.W. 1883. *Injuries of the Spine and Spinal Cord, without Apparent Mechanical Lesion and Nervous Shock, in their Surgical and Medico-legal Aspects*. London: J. & A. Church.

Pole, N. 2007. "The Psychophysiology of Posttraumatic Stress Disorder: A Meta-analysis," *Psychological Bulletin* 133, 5: 725–46.

Prigerson, H.G., M.K. Shear, S.C. Jacobs, C.F. Reynolds, P.K. Maciejewski, J.R. Davidson, et al. 1999. "Consensus Criteria for Traumatic Grief: A Preliminary Empirical Test," *British Journal of Psychiatry* 174: 67–73.

Regehr, C. 2001. "Crisis Debriefing Groups for Emergency Responders: Reviewing the Evidence," *Brief Treatment and Crisis Intervention* 1: 87–100.

———. 2009. "Social Support as a Mediator of Psychological Distress in Firefighters," *Irish Journal of Psychology* 30, 1: 85–96.

———, R. Alaggia, J. Dennis, A. Pitts, and M. Saini. 2012. "Interventions to Reduce Distress in Adult Victims of Sexual Violence and Rape," *Campbell Systematic Reviews*.

———, ———, L. Lambert, and M. Saini. 2008. "Victims of Sexual Violence in the Canada Criminal Courts," *Victims & Offenders* 3, 1: 99–113.

——— and T. Bober. 2005. *In the Line of Fire:*

Trauma in the Emergency Services. New York: Oxford University Press.

——— and E. Marziali. 1999. "Response to Sexual Assault: A Relational Perspective," *Journal of Nervous and Mental Disease* 187, 10: 618–23.

———, ———, and K. Jansen. 1999. "A Qualitative Analysis of Strengths and Vulnerabilities in Sexually Assaulted Women," *Clinical Social Work Journal* 27, 2: 171–84.

——— and T. Sussman. 2004. "Intersections between Grief and Trauma: Towards an Empirically Based Model for Treating Traumatic Grief," *Brief Treatment and Crisis Intervention* 4, 3: 289–309.

Regehr, K., and C. Regehr. 2012. "Let Them Satisfy Their Lust on Thee: Titus Andronicus as a Window into Societal Understanding of PTSD," *Traumatology* 18, 2: 27–34.

Resnick, H.S., D.G. Kilpatrick, C.L. Best, and T.L. Kramer. 1992. "Vulnerability-Stress Factors in Development of Posttraumatic Stress Disorder," *Journal of Nervous and Mental Disease* 180, 7: 424–30.

Roberts, A.R., ed. 2000. *Crisis Intervention Handbook: Assessment, Treatment, and Research*. New York: Oxford University Press.

Rock, P. 1998. *After Homicide: Practical and Political Responses to Bereavement*. Oxford: Oxford University Press.

Rothbaum, B., and E. Foa. 1996. "Cognitive-Behavioral Therapy for Posttraumatic Stress Disorder," in B.A. van der Kolk, A.C. McFarlane, and L. Weisaeth, eds, *Traumatic Stress: The Effects of Overwhelming Experience on Mind, Body, and Society*. New York: Guilford Press.

———, E.B. Foa, D.S. Riggs, T. Murdock, and W. Walsh. 1992. "A Prospective Examination of Posttraumatic Stress Disorder in Rape Victims," *Journal of Traumatic Stress* 5, 3: 455–75.

Rutter, M. 1993. "Resilience: Some Conceptual Considerations," *Journal of Adolescent Health* 14, 8: 626–31.

Schoenfeld, F.B., C.R. Marmar, and T.C. Neylan. 2004. "Current Concepts in Pharmacotherapy for Posttraumatic Stress Disorder," *Psychiatric Services* 55, 5: 519–31.

Schuter, S.R., and S. Zisook. 1993. "The Course of Normal Grief," in M.S. Stroebe, W. Stroebe, and R.O. Hansson, eds, *Handbook of Bereavement: Theory, Research and Intervention*. New York: Cambridge University Press.

Shalev, A. 2002. "Acute Stress Reactions in Adults," *Biological Psychiatry* 51, 7: 532–43.

Shay, J. 1994. *Achilles in Vietnam: Combat Trauma and the Undoing of Character*. New York: Scribner.

Shea, A., C. Walsh, H. MacMillan, and M. Steiner. 2004. "Child Maltreatment and HPA Axis Dysregulation: Relationship to Major Depressive Disorder and Post-Traumatic Stress Disorder in Females," *Psychoneuroendocrinology* 30, 2: 162–78.

Shear, M.K. 2010. "Exploring the Role of Experiential Avoidance from the Perspective of Attachment Theory and Dual Process Model," *Omega* 61, 4: 357–69.

———, E.F. Frank, E. Foa, C. Cherry, C.F. Reynolds, J. Vander Bilt, et al. 2001. "Traumatic Grief: A Pilot Study," *American Journal of Psychiatry* 158: 1506–8.

———, T. Monk, P. Houck, et al. 2007. "An Attachment-based Model of Complicated Grief Including the Role of Avoidance," *European Archives of Psychiatry and Clinical Neuroscience* 257: 453–61.

Sherin, J., and C. Nemeroff. 2011. "State of the Art: Post-traumatic Stress Disorder: The Neurobiological Impact of Psychological Trauma," *Dialogues in Clinical Neuroscience* 13, 3: 263–78.

Solomon, S.D., and D.M. Johnson. 2002. "Psychosocial Treatment of Posttraumatic Stress Disorder: A Practice Friendly Review of Outcome Research," *Journal of Clinical Psychology* 58, 8: 947–59.

Stein, D.J., J.C. Ipser, and S. Seedat. 2005. "Pharmacotherapy for Post-Traumatic Stress Disorder (PTSD)," *Cochrane Database of Systematic Reviews*, Issue 4, Art. No.: CD002795. DOI: 10.1002/14651858.CD002795.pub2.

Stroebe, M., H. Schut, and C. Finkenauer. 2001. "The Traumatization of Grief? A Conceptual Framework for Understanding the Trauma-Bereavement Interface," *Israel Journal of Psychiatry and Related Sciences* 38, 3–4: 185–201.

Tarrier, N., H. Pilgrim, C. Sommerfield, B. Faragher, M. Reynolds, E. Graham, et al. 1999. "A Randomized Trial of Cognitive Therapy and Imaginal Exposure in the Treatment of Chronic Posttraumatic Stress Disorder," *Journal of Consulting and Clinical Psychology* 67, 1: 13–18.

Tedeschi, R., C. Park, and L. Calhoun. 1998.

Post-Traumatic Growth: Positive Change in the Aftermath of Crisis. Mahwah, NJ: Lawrence Erlbaum and Associates.

Thomas, E., D. Saumier, and A. Brunet. 2012. "Peritraumatic Distress and the Course of Posttraumatic Stress Disorder Symptoms: A Meta-Analysis," *Canadian Journal of Psychiatry* 57, 2: 122–9.

Thompson, M.P., F.H. Norris, and R.B. Ruback. 1998. "Comparative Distress Levels of Inner-City Family Members of Homicide Victims," *Journal of Traumatic Stress* 11, 2: 223–2.

Trickey, D., A. Siddaway, R. Meiser-Stedman, L. Serpell, and A. Field. 2012. "A Meta-analysis of Risk Factors for Post-traumatic Stress Disorder in Children and Adolescents," *Clinical Psychology Review* 32: 122–38.

Vaiva, G., F. Ducrocq, K. Jezequel, B. Averland, P. Lestaval, A. Brunet, and C. Marmar. 2003. "Immediate Treatment with Propranolol Decreases Posttraumatic Stress Disorder Two Months after Trauma," *Biological Psychiatry* 54: 947–9.

Van Ameringen, M., C. Mancini, B. Patterson, and M.H. Boyle. 2008. "Post-Traumatic Stress Disorder in Canada," *CNS Neuroscience & Therapeutics* 14: 171–81.

van der Kolk, B.A. 1997. "The Psychobiology of Posttraumatic Stress Disorder," *Journal of Clinical Psychiatry* 58 (supplement 9): 16–24.

——— and O. van der Hart. 1989. "Pierre Janet and the Breakdown of Adaptation in Psychological Trauma," *American Journal of Psychiatry* 146, 12: 1530–40.

Wittmeier, B. 2011. "Four Teens Killed in Alberta Car Crash," *National Post*, 23 Oct., news.nationalpost.com/2011/10/23/four-teens-killed-in-alberta-car-crash/.

Worden, J.W. 1991. *Grief Counseling and Grief Therapy: A Handbook for the Mental Health Practitioners*. New York: Springer.

Yehuda, R. 1999. "Biological Factors Associated with Susceptibility to Posttraumatic Stress Disorder," *Canadian Journal of Psychiatry* 44, 1: 34–9.

———. 2002. "Clinical Relevance of Biologic Findings in PTSD," *Psychiatric Quarterly* 73, 2: 123–33.

———, K. Koenen, S. Galea, and J. Flory. 2011. "The Role of Genes in Defining a Molecular Biology of PTSD," *Disease Markers* 30: 67–76.

——— and A.C. McFarlane. 1995. "Conflict between Current Knowledge of Post-traumatic Stress Disorder and Its Original Conceptual Basis," *American Journal of Psychiatry* 152: 1705–13.

Chapter 7

Abel, K., R. Drake, and J. Goldstein. 2010. "Sex Differences in Schizophrenia," *International Review of Psychiatry* 22, 5: 417–28.

American Psychiatric Association (APA). 2013. *Diagnostic and Statistical Manual of Mental Disorders*, 5th edn. Washington: APA Press.

Andresen, R., L. Oades, and P. Caputi. 2003. "The Experience of Recovery from Schizophrenia: Towards an Empirically Validated Stage Model," *Australian and New Zealand Journal of Psychiatry* 37: 586–94.

Arseneault, L., M. Cannon, J. Witton, and R.M. Murray. 2004. "Causal Association between Cannabis and Psychosis: Examination of the Evidence," *British Journal of Psychiatry* 184: 110–17.

Bachrach, L. 1993. "Continuity of Care and Approaches to Case Management for Long-Term Mentally Ill Patients," *Hospital and Community Psychiatry* 44, 5: 465–8.

Bateson, G., D.D. Jackson, J. Haley, and J.H. Weakland. 1956. "Toward a Theory of Schizophrenia," *Behavioral Science* 1: 251–64.

Berglund, N., J. Vahlne, and A. Edman. 2003. "Family Intervention in Schizophrenia: Impact on Family Burden and Attitude," *Social Psychiatry and Psychiatric Epidemiology* 38: 116–21.

Bezchlibnyk-Butler, K.Z., and J.J. Jeffries. 2005. *Clinical Handbook of Psychotropic Drugs*, 15th edn. Ashland: Hogrete and Huber.

Bradshaw, W. 2003. "Use of Single System Research to Evaluate the Effectiveness of Cognitive-Behavioural Treatment of Schizophrenia," *British Journal of Social Work* 33, 7: 885–9.

Brown, A.S. 2006. "Prenatal Infection as a Risk Factor for Schizophrenia," *Schizophrenia Bulletin* 32, 2: 200–2.

Canadian Mental Health Association (CMHA). 2008. *Back to Basics: Enhancing Our Capacity to Promote Consumer Participation and Inclusion: Discussion Guide on Recovery*, www.cmha.ca.

Cardno, A., E. Marshall, B. Coid, A. Macdonald, T. Ribchester, N. Davies, et al. 1999. "Relationships, Symptom Dimensions and Genetic Liability to Psychotic Disorders:

Maudsley Twin Psychosis Series," *Archives of General Psychiatry* 56: 162–8.

Carpenter, L. 2002. "Mental Health Recovery Paradigm: Implications for Social Work," *Health and Social Work* 27, 2: 86–94.

Chadwick, P., and P. Trower. 1996. "Cognitive Therapy for Punishment Paranoia: A Single Case Experiment," *Behavioural Research and Therapy* 34, 4: 351–6.

Chan, B. 2010. "Negative Caregiving Experience: A Predictor of High Expressed Emotion among Caregivers of Relatives with Schizophrenia," *Social Work in Mental Health*, 8: 375–397.

Chan, B., and A. O'Brien. 2011. "The Right of Caregivers to Access Health Information of Relatives with Mental Illness," *International Journal of Law and Psychiatry* 34: 386–92.

Chen, W., and E. Lukens. 2011. "Well Being, Depressive Symptoms, and Burden among Parent and Sibling Caregivers of Persons with Severe and Persistent Mental Illness," *Social Work and Mental Health* 9: 397–416.

Chien, W., W. Chan, and D. Thompson. 2006. "Effects of a Mutual Support Group for Families of Chinese People with Schizophrenia: 18 Month Follow-up," *British Journal of Psychiatry* 189: 41–9.

Cohen, D. 2002. "Research on the Drug Treatment of Schizophrenia: A Critical Appraisal and Implications for Social Work Education," *Journal of Social Work Education* 38, 2: 217–39.

Compton, M., P. Weiss, J. West, and N. Kaslow. 2005. "The Associations between Substance Use Disorders, Schizophrenia-spectrum Disorders, and Axis IV Psychosocial Problems," *Social Psychiatry and Psychiatric Epidemiology* 40: 939–46.

Consensus Panel. 2004. "Consensus Development Conference and Antipsychotic Drugs and Obesity and Diabetes," *Diabetes Care* 27: 596–601.

Coodin, S., D. Staley, B. Cortens, R. Derochers, and S. McLandress. 2004. "Patient Factors Associated with Missed Appointments in Persons with Schizophrenia," *Canadian Journal of Psychiatry* 49, 2: 145–8.

Deegan, P. 1996. "Recovery and the Conspiracy of Hope," paper presented at the Sixth Annual Mental Health Services Conference of Australia and New Zealand.

Dickerson, F. 2000. "Cognitive-Behavioural Psychotherapy for Schizophrenia: A Review of Recent Empirical Studies," *Schizophrenia Research* 43: 71–90.

Dixon, L. 1999. "Dual Diagnosis of Substance Abuse in Schizophrenia: Prevalence and Impact on Outcomes," *Schizophrenia Research* 35 (supplement): s93–s100.

Faris, R.B.L., and H.W. Dunham. 1939. *Mental Disorders in Urban Areas: An Ecological Study of Schizophrenia and Other Psychoses.* New York: Hafner Publishing.

Farkas, M., C. Gagne, W. Anthony, and J. Chamberlin. 2005. "Implementing Recovery-oriented Evidence-based Programs: Identifying the Critical Dimensions," *Community Mental Health Journal* 41, 2: 141–58.

Goar, C. 2012. "Micro-loans Unlock the Trap of Mental Illness," *Toronto Star*, 10 Jan.

Gogtay, N., N. Vyas, R. Testa, S. Wood, and C. Pantelis. 2011. "Age of Onset of Schizophrenia: Perspectives from Structural Neuroimaging Studies," *Schizophrenia Bulletin* 37, 3: 504–13.

Goldner, E., L. Hsu, P. Waraich, and J. Somers. 2002. "Prevalence and Incidence Studies of Schizophrenic Disorders: A Systematic Review of the Literature," *Canadian Journal of Psychiatry* 47: 833–43.

Gong-Guy, E., R. Cravens, and T. Patterson. 1991. "Clinical Issues in Mental Health Service Delivery to Refugees," *American Psychologist* 46, 6: 642–8.

Gruber, E., M. Kajevic, M. Aguis, and S. Martic-Biocina. 2006. "Group Psychotherapy for Parents of Patients with Schizophrenia," *International Journal of Social Psychiatry* 52, 6: 487–500.

Haley, J. 1976. *Problem-Solving Therapy*. San Francisco: Jossey-Bass.

Hegelstadt, W.T.V., T.K. Larsen, B. Auestad, J. Evensen, U. Haahr, I. Joa, et al. 2012. "Long-term Follow-up of the TIPS Early Detection in Psychosis Study: Effects on 10-year Outcome," *American Journal of Psychiatry* 169: 374–80.

Hogarty, G. 1997. "Three Year Trials of Personal Therapy among Schizophrenic Patients Living Independent of Family," *American Journal of Psychiatry* 154: 1504–13.

Hollingshead, A.B., and F.C. Redlich. 1954. "Schizophrenia and Social Structure," *American Journal of Psychiatry* 110: 695–701.

Horowitz, M. 1991. *Person Schemas and*

Maladaptive Interpersonal Problems. Chicago: University of Chicago Press.

Hwang, W., H. Myers, J. Abe-Kim, and J. Ting. 2008. "A Conceptual Paradigm for Understanding Culture's Impact on Mental Health: The Cultural Influences on Mental Health Model," *Clinical Psychology Review* 28: 211–27.

Jablensky, A. 2000. "Epidemiology of Schizophrenia: The Global Burden of Disease and Disability," *European Archives of Psychiatry and Clinical Neuroscience* 250: 274–85.

———, R. Schwartz, and T. Tomov. 1980. "WHO Collaborative Study of Impairments and Disabilities Associated with Schizophrenic Disorders," *Acta Psychiatrica Scandinavica Supplementum* 285: 152–63.

Jobe, T.H., and M. Harrow. 2005. "Long-term Outcome of Patients with Schizophrenia: A Review," *Canadian Journal of Psychiatry* 50: 892–900.

Kendler, K.S., M. McGuire, A.M. Gruesberg, A. Ohare, M. Spellman, and D. Walsh. 1993. "The Roscommon Family Study 1: Methods, Diagnosis of Probands, and Risk of Schizophrenia in Relatives," *Archives of General Psychiatry* 50: 527–40.

Kinderman, P., and R. Bentall. 1996. "Self-Discrepancies and Persecutory Delusions: Evidence for a Model of Paranoid Ideation," *Journal of Abnormal Psychology* 105, 1: 106–13.

Krabbendam, L., and J. van Os. 2005. "Schizophrenia and Urbanicity: A Major Environmental Influence—Conditional on Genetic Risk," *Schizophrenia Bulletin* 31, 4: 795–9.

Kraepelin, E. 1904. "Vergleichende Psychiatric," *Zentralblatt für Nervenheilkunde und Psychiatrie* 27: 433–7 [English translation: Wright, J. 1974. "Comparative Psychiatry," in S.R. Hirsch and M. Shepherd, eds, *Themes and Variations in European Psychiatry* (Bristol: John Wright & Sons)].

Kuipers, E. 2006. "Family Interventions in Schizophrenia: Evidence for Efficacy and Proposed Mechanisms of Change," *Journal of Family Therapy* 28, 1: 73–80.

———, P. Garety, D. Fowler, G. Dunn, P. Bebbington, D. Freeman, et al. 1997. "London–East Anglia Randomized Controlled Trial of Cognitive-Behavioural Therapy for Psychosis. I: Effects of the Treatment Phase," *British Journal of Psychiatry* 171, 10: 319–27.

LaFave, H., H. de Sousa, and G. Gerber. 1996. "Assertive Community Treatment of Severe Mental Illness: A Canadian Experience," *Psychiatric Services* 47, 7: 757–9.

Leucht, S., C. Corves, D. Arbter, R. Engel, C. Li, and J. Davis. 2009. "Second-Generation versus First-Generation Antipsychotic Drugs for Schizophrenia: A Meta-analysis," *Lancet*: 31–41.

Levy, E., N. Pawliuk, R. Joober, S. Abadi, and A. Malla. 2012. "Medication-Adherent First-Episode Psychosis Patients Also Relapse: Why?" *Canadian Journal of Psychiatry* 57, 2: 78–84.

Magliano, L., A. Fiorillo, C. De Rosa, C. Malangone, and M. Maj. 2005. "Family Burden in Long-term Disease: A Comparative Study in Schizophrenia vs. Physical Disorders," *Social Science and Medicine* 61, 2: 313–22.

Malla, A.K., R.M.G. Norman, and R. Joober. 2005. "First Episode Psychosis, Early Intervention and Outcome: What Have We Learned?" *Canadian Journal of Psychiatry* 50, 14: 881–91.

——— and A.J. Pelosi. 2010. "Is Treating Patients with First-Episode Psychosis Cost-Effective? Ample Evidence Supports Specialized Early Intervention," *Canadian Journal of Psychiatry* 55, 1: 3–8.

Morrison, A., P. French, S. Stewart, M. Birchwood, D. Fowler, et al. 2012. "Early Detection and Intervention Evaluation for People at Risk of Psychosis: Multisite Randomised Controlled Trial," *British Medical Journal* 344: e2233. DOI: 10.1136/bmj.e2233.

Muhlbauer, S. 2002. "Navigating the Storm of Mental Illness: Phases in the Family Journey," *Qualitative Health Research* 12, 8: 1076–92.

Murray, A.M., and D.J. Castle. 2000. "Genetic and Environmental Aetiological Factors," in M.G. Gelder, J.J. Lopez-Iber, and N. Andreasen, eds, *New Oxford Textbook of Psychiatry*. Oxford: Oxford University Press.

National Institute of Mental Health. 1991. *Caring for People with Severe Mental Disorders: A National Plan of Research to Improve Services*, DHHS Publication No. ADM 91 1762. Washington: US Government Printing Office.

Neill, R. 1994. "Social Work, Helping the Family to Cope with Schizophrenia: Psychoeducational Programs in the Community," *The Social Worker* 62, 2: 89–92.
Nelson, G., T. Aubry, and A. Lafrance. 2007. "A Review of the Literature on the Effectiveness of Housing and Support, Assertive Community Treatment, and Intensive Case Management Interventions for Persons with Mental Illness Who Have Been Homeless," *American Journal of Orthopsychiatry* 77, 3: 350–61.
Nordt, C., B. Muller, W. Rossler, and C. Lauber. 2007. "Predictors and Course of Vocational Status, Income and Quality of Life in People with Severe Mental Illness: A Naturalistic Inquiry," *Social Science and Medicine* 65, 7: 1420–9.
Owen, F., and M.D.C. Simpson. 1995. "The Neurochemistry of Schizophrenia," in S.R. Hirsch and D.R. Weinberger, eds, *Schizophrenia*. Oxford: Blackwell Science.
Owens, D., and E. Johnstone. 2006. "Precursors and Prodromata of Schizophrenia: Findings from the Edinburgh High Risk Study and Their Literature Context," *Psychological Medicine* 36, 11: 1501–14.
Perlick, D., R. Rosenheck, R. Kaczynski, M. Swartz, J. Canive, and J. Lieberman. 2006. "Components and Correlates of Family Burden in Schizophrenia," *Psychiatric Services* 57, 8: 1117–25.
Picchioni, M., and R. Murray. 2007. "Schizophrenia," *British Medical Journal* 335, 7610: 91–5.
Public Health Agency of Canada. 2002. *A Report on Mental Illnesses in Canada*. Ottawa: Health Canada, www.phac-aspc.gc.ca.
Raging Spoon. 2008. "About Us: History," www.ragingspoon.com/history.htm.
Salyers, M., and S. Tsemberis. 2007. "ACT and Recovery: Integrating Evidence-based Practice and Recovery Orientation on Assertive Community Treatment Teams," *Community Mental Health Journal* 43, 6: 619–41.
Sluzki, C.E., J. Beavin, A. Tarnopolsky, and E. Veron. 1967. "Transactional Disqualification: Research on the Double Bind," *Archives of General Psychiatry* 16, 4: 494–504.
Snowdon, L. 2007. "Explaining Mental Health Treatment Disparities: Ethnic and Cultural Differences in Family Involvement," *Cultural and Medical Psychiatry* 31, 3: 389–402.
Sowers, W. 2005. "Transforming Systems of Care: The American Association of Community Psychiatrists Guidelines for Recovery-oriented Services," *Community Mental Health Journal* 41, 6: 757–74.
Stein, L., and M. Test. 1980. "Alternative to Mental Hospital Treatment. I. Conceptual Model, Treatment Program, and Clinical Evaluation," *Archives of General Psychiatry* 37, 4: 392–7.
Test, M. 2002. "Guidelines for Assertive Community Treatment Teams," in A. Roberts and G. Greene, eds, *Social Worker's Desk Reference*. New York: Oxford University Press.
Thara, R. 2004. "Twenty-Year Course of Schizophrenia: The Madras Longitudinal Study," *Canadian Journal of Psychiatry* 49, 8: 564–9.
Walker, E.F., T. Savoie, and D. Davis. 1994. "Neuromotor Precursors of Schizophrenia," *Schizophrenia Bulletin* 20, 3: 441–51.
Williams, C., and A. Collins. 2002. "The Social Construction of Disability in Schizophrenia," *Qualitative Healthy Research* 12, 3: 297–309.
World Health Organization (WHO). 2012. "Schizophrenia," www.who.int/mental_health/management/schizophrenia/en/.
Yang, J., S. Law, W. Chow, L. Andermann, R. Steinberg, and J. Sadavoy. 2005. "Assertive Community Treatment for Persons with Severe and Persistent Mental Illness in Ethnic Minority Groups," *Psychiatric Services* 56, 9: 1053–5.

Chapter 8

Abrams, L., and L. Curran. 2007. "Not Just a Middle Class Affliction: Crafting a Social Work Research Agenda on Postpartum Depression," *Health and Social Work* 32, 4: 289–96.
Akiskal, H. 2004. "Mood Disorders: Historical Introduction and Conceptual Overview," in B.J. Sadock and V.A. Sadock, eds, *Comprehensive Text Book of Psychiatry*, 8th edn. Philadelphia: Lippincott Williams & Wilkins.
Albert, J. 1994. "Rethinking Difference: A Cognitive Therapy Group for Chronic Mental Patients," *Social Work with Groups* 17, 1–2: 105–21.
Allan, C., U. Kalu, C. Sexton, and K. Ebmeier. 2012. "Transcranial Stimulation in

Depression," *British Journal of Psychiatry* 200, 1: 10–11.

American Psychiatric Association (APA). 2000. *Diagnostic and Statistical Manual of Mental Disorders*, 4th edn. Washington: APA Press.

———. 2002. *Practice Guidelines for the Treatment of Psychiatric Disorders Compendium*. Washington: APA Press.

———. 2013. *Diagnostic and Statistical Manual of Mental Disorders*, 5th edn. Washington: APA Press.

Bearden, C., P. Thompson, M. Dalwani, K. Hayashi, A. Lee, M. Nicoletti, et al. 2007. "Greater Cortical Gray Matter Density in Lithium-treated Patients with Bipolar Disorder," *Biological Psychiatry* 62, 1: 7–16.

Beck, A. 1967. *Depression: Clinical, Experimental, and Theoretical Aspects*. New York: Hoeber Press.

———, J. Rush, B. Shaw, and G. Emery. 1979. *Cognitive Therapy of Depression*. New York: Guilford Press.

Belmaker, R., and G. Agam. 2008. "Major Depressive Disorder Mechanisms of Disease," *New England Journal of Medicine* 358, 1: 55–67.

Birmaher, B., D. Axelson, K. Monk, C. Kalas, B. Goldstein, M. Hickey, et al. 2009. "Lifetime Psychiatric Disorders in School-aged Offspring of Parents with Bipolar Disorder: The Pittsburgh Bipolar Offspring Study," *Archives of General Psychiatry* 66, 3: 287–96.

Bledsoe, S., and N. Grote. 2006. "Treating Depression during Pregnancy and the Postpartum: A Preliminary Meta-analysis," *Research on Social Work Practice* 16, 2: 109–20.

Blier, P. 2008. "Do Antidepressants Really Work?" *Journal of Psychiatry and Neuroscience* 33, 2: 89–90.

Blisker, D., E. Goldner, and E. Anderson. 2012. "Supported Self-Management: A Simple, Effective Way to Improve Depression Care," *Canadian Journal of Psychiatry* 57, 4: 203–9.

Bocking, C., P. Spinhoven, A. Schene, M. Koeter, L. Wouters, J. Huyser, et al. 2005. "Preventing Relapse/Recurrence in Recurrent Depression with Cognitive Therapy: A Randomized Controlled Trial," *Journal of Consulting and Clinical Psychology* 73, 4: 647–57.

Brown, G.W., and T. Harris. 1978. *Social Origin of Depression*. London: B Press.

Capponi, P. 2003. *Beyond the Crazy House*. Toronto: Penguin.

Carpenter, L., S. Yasmin, and L. Price. 2002. "A Double-Blind, Placebo-Controlled Study of Antidepressant Augmentation with Mirtazapine," *Biological Psychiatry* 51, 2: 183–8.

Casey, P., and B. Kelly. 2007. *Fish's Clinical Psychopathology: Signs and Symptoms in Psychiatry*, 3rd edn. London: Royal College of Psychiatrists.

Coelho, H., P. Canter, and E. Ernst. 2007. "Mindfulness-based Cognitive Therapy: Evaluating Current Evidence and Informing Future Research," *Journal of Consulting and Clinical Psychology* 75, 6: 1000–5.

Danilenko, K., and R. Levitan. 2012. "Seasonal Affective Disorder," in T. Schlaepfer and C. Nemeroff, eds, *Neurobiology of Psychiatric Disorders: Handbook of Clinical Neurology*, vol. 106. Philadelphia: Elsevier, 279–88.

de Mello, M.F., M.J. de Jesus, J. Bacaltchuk, H. Verdeli, and R. Neugebauer. 2005. "A Systematic Review of Research Findings on the Efficacy of Interpersonal Therapy for Depressive Disorders," *European Archives of Psychiatry and Clinical Neuroscience* 255, 2: 75–82.

Deshauer, D., D. Moher, D. Fergusson, E. Moher, M. Sampson, and J. Grimshaw. 2008. "Selective Serotonin Reuptake Inhibitors for Unipolar Depression: A Systematic Review of Classic Long-term Randomized Controlled Trials," *Canadian Medical Association Journal* 178, 10: 1293–301.

Detera-Wadleigh, S.D., C.-Y. Liu, M. Maheshwari, I. Cardona, W. Corona, and N. Akula. 2007. "Sequence Variation in DOCK9 and Heterogeneity in Bipolar Disorder," *Psychiatric Genetics* 17, 5: 274–86.

Dilsaver, S. 2011. "An Estimate of the Minimum Economic Burden of Bipolar I and II Disorders in the United States: 2009," *Journal of Affective Disorders* 129: 79–83.

Eaton, W., A. Kalaydjian, D. Scharfstein, B. Mezuk, and Y. Ding. 2007. "Prevalence and Incidence of Depressive Disorder: The Baltimore ECA Follow-up, 1981–2004," *Acta Psychiatrica Scandanavica* 116, 3: 182–8.

Elkin, I., M.T. Shea, J.T. Watkins, S.D. Imber, S.M. Sotsky, J.F. Collins, et al. 1989. "National Institute of Mental Health Treatment of Depression Collaborative Research Program: General Effectiveness of Treatments," *Archives of General Psychiatry* 46, 11: 971–82.

Eschweiler, G., R. Vonthein, R. Bode, M. Huell, A. Conca, O. Peters, et al. 2007. "Clinical Efficacy and Cognitive Side Effects of Bifrontal versus Right Unilateral Electroconvulsive Therapy (ECT): A Short-term Randomized Controlled Trial in Pharmaco-resistant Major Depression," *Journal of Affective Disorders* 101, 1–3: 149–57.

Fanous, A.H., M.C. Neale, S.H. Aggen, and K.S. Kendler. 2007. "A Longitudinal Study of Personality and Major Depression in a Population-based Sample of Male Twins," *Psychological Medicine* 37, 8: 1163–72.

Farb, N., A. Anderson, and Z. Segal. 2012. "The Mindful Brain and Emotion Regulation in Mood Disorders," *Canadian Journal of Psychiatry* 57, 2: 70–7.

Fergusson, D., J. Boden, and J. Horwood. 2007. "Recurrence of Major Depression in Adolescence and Early Adulthood, and Later Mental Health, Educational and Economic Outcomes," *British Journal of Psychiatry* 191: 335–42.

Fisher, M. 1995. "Group Therapy Protocols for Persons with Personality Disorders Who Abuse Substances: Effective Treatment Alternatives," *Social Work with Groups* 18, 4: 71–89.

Fitzgerald, P., T. Oxley, A. Laird, J. Kulkarni, G. Egan, and Z. Daskalakis. 2006. "An Analysis of Functional Neuroimaging Studies of Dorsolateral Prefrontal Cortical Activity in Depression," *Psychiatry Research: Neuroimaging* 148, 1: 33–45.

Fournier, J., R. DeRubeis, R. Shelton, R. Gallop, J. Amsterdam, and S. Hollon. 2008. "Antidepressant Medication v. Cognitive Therapy in People with Depression with and without Personality Disorder," *British Journal of Psychiatry* 192: 124–9.

Furukawa, T.A., A. Cipriani, B. Corrado, and J.R. Geddes. 2007. "Long-term Treatment of Depression with Antidepressants: A Systematic Narrative Review," *Canadian Journal of Psychiatry* 52, 9: 545–52.

———, H. McGuire, and C. Barbui. 2003. "Low Dosage Tricyclic Antidepressants for Depression," *Cochrane Database of Systematic Reviews* Issue 3, Art. No.: CD003197. DOI: 10.1002/14651858.CD003197.

Garlow, S., J. Rosenberg, D. Moore, A. Haas, B. Koestner, H. Hendin, and C. Nemeroff. 2008. "Depression, Desperation, and Suicidal Ideation in College Students: Results from the American Foundation for Suicide Prevention College Screening Project and Emory University," *Depression and Anxiety* 25: 482–8.

Geddes, J., and UK ECT Review Group. 2003. "Efficacy and Safety of Electroconvulsive Therapy in Depressive Disorders: A Systematic Review and Meta-analysis," *Lancet* 361, 9360: 799–808.

George, M., S. Lisanby, D. Avery, W. McDonald, V. Durkalski, et al. 2010. "Daily Left Prefrontal Transcranial Magnetic Stimulation Therapy for Major Depressive Disorder," *Archives of General Psychiatry* 67, 3: 507–16.

Golden, R., B. Gaynes, D. Ekstrom, R. Hamer, F. Jacobsen, T. Suppes, K. Wisner, and C. Nermeroff. 2005. "The Efficacy of Light Therapy in Treatment of Mood Disorders: A Review and Meta-analysis of the Evidence," *American Journal of Psychiatry* 162: 656–62.

Gregory, V. 2010. "Cognitive-Behavioral Therapy for Mania: A Meta-analysis of Randomized Controlled Trials," *Social Work in Mental Health* 8: 483–94.

Grote, N., and S. Bledsoe. 2007. "Predicting Postpartum Depressive Symptoms in New Mothers: The Role of Optimism and Stress Frequency during Pregnancy," *Health and Social Work* 32, 2: 107–18.

Hajek, T., J. Kozeny, M. Kopecek, M. Alda, and C. Hoschl. 2007. "Reduced Subgenual Cingulated Volumes in Mood Disorders: A Meta-analysis," *Journal of Psychiatry: Neuroscience* 33, 2: 91–9.

Heller, N., and R. Northcut. 1996. "Utilizing Cognitive-Behavioural Techniques in Psychodynamic Practice with Clients Diagnosed as Borderline," *Clinical Social Work Journal* 24: 203–15.

Howland, R.H., and M.E. Thase. 1999. "Affective Disorders: Biological Aspects," in T. Millon, P.H. Blaney, and R.D. Davis, eds, *Oxford Textbook of Psychopathology*. New York: Oxford University Press.

Ingram, R.E., W. Scott, and G. Siegle. 1999. "Depression: Social and Cognitive Aspects," in T. Millon, P.H. Blaney, and R.D. Davis, eds, *Oxford Textbook of Psychopathology*. New York: Oxford University Press.

Jacka, F., J. Pasco, A. Mykleturn, L. Williams, A. Hodge, S. O'Reilly, and G. Nicholson. 2010. "Association of Western and Traditional Diets with Depression and Anxiety in

Women," *American Journal of Psychiatry* 167: 305–311.

Janicak, P., J. Davis, R. Gibbons, S. Ericksen, S. Chang, and P. Gallagher. 1985. "Efficacy of ECT: A Meta-analysis," *American Journal of Psychiatry* 142, 3: 297–302.

Jensen, C. 1994. "Psychosocial Treatment of Depression in Women: Nine Single-Subject Evaluations," *Research on Social Work Practice* 4, 3: 267–82.

Jones, S. 2004. "Psychotherapy of Bipolar Disorder: A Review," *Journal of Affective Disorders* 80, 2–3: 101–14.

Kasper, S., T.A. Wehr, J.J. Bartko, P.A. Gaist, and N.E. Rosenthal. 1989. "Epidemiological Findings of Seasonal Changes in Mood and Behavior: A Telephone Survey of Montgomery County, Maryland," *Archives of General Psychiatry* 46, 9: 823–33.

Kelsoe, J.R. 2005. "Mood Disorders: Genetics," in B.J. Sadock and V.A. Sadock, eds, *Comprehensive Textbook of Psychiatry*, 8th edn. Philadelphia: Lippincott Williams & Wilkins.

Kho, K.H., A.H. Zwinderman, and B.A. Blansjaar. 2005. "Predictors for the Efficacy of Electroconvulsive Therapy: Chart Review and Naturalistic Study," *Journal of Clinical Psychiatry* 66, 7: 894–9.

Lam, R., P. Chan, M. Wilkins-Ho, and L. Yatham. 2008. "Repetitive Transcranial Magnetic Stimulation for Treatment-Resistant Depression: A Systematic Review and Analysis," *Canadian Journal of Psychiatry* 53, 9: 621–31.

Lara-Cinisomo, S., and B. Griffin. 2007. "Factors Associated with Major Depression in Mothers in Los Angeles," *Women's Health Issues* 17, 5: 316–24.

Lima, M.S., J. Moncrieff, and B. Soares. 2005. "Drugs versus Placebo for Dysthymia," *Cochrane Database of Systematic Reviews* Issue 2, Art. No.: CD001130. DOI: 10.1002/14651858.CD001130.

Lisanby, S.H. 2007. "Electroconvulsive Therapy for Depression," *New England Journal of Medicine* 357, 19: 1939–45.

Loo, C., P. Sheehan, M. Pigot, and W. Lyndon. 2007. "A Report on Mood and Cognitive Outcomes with Right Unilateral Ultrabrief Pulsewidth (0.3 ms) ECT and Retrospective Comparison with Standard Pulsewidth Right Unilateral ECT," *Journal of Affective Disorders* 103, 1–3: 277–81.

Lurie, S. 2012. "And Now for Something Completely Different . . . Self-Management," *Canadian Journal of Psychiatry* 57, 4: 201–2.

McDowell, D., and R. Clodfelter. 2001. "Depression and Substance Abuse: Considerations of Etiology, Comorbidity, Evaluation and Treatment," *Psychiatric Annuals* 31: 244–51.

Mur, M., M.J. Portella, A. Martinez-Aran, J. Pifarre, and E. Vieta. 2007. "Persistent Neuropsychological Deficit in Euthymic Bipolar Patients: Execute Function as a Core Deficit," *Journal of Clinical Psychiatry* 68: 1078–86.

Nakagawa, A., N. Watanabe, I.M. Omori, C. Barbui, A. Cipriani, H. McGuire, R. Churchill, and T.A. Furukawa. 2009. "Milnacipran versus Other Antidepressive Agents for Depression," *Cochrane Database of Systematic Reviews* Issue 3. Art. No.: CD006529. DOI: 10.1002/14651858. CD006529.pub2.

Nanri, A., T. Mizoue, Y. Matsushita, et al. 2009. "Association between Serum 25-Hydroxyvitamin D and Depressive Symptoms in Japanese: Analysis by Survey Season," *European Journal of Clinical Nutrition* 63, 12: 1444–7.

Nierenberg, A.A., M. Fava, M.H. Trivedi, and S.R. Wisniewski. 2006. "A Comparison of Lithium and T(3) Augmentation Following Two Failed Medication Treatments for Depression: StarD Report," *American Journal of Psychiatry* 163, 9: 1519–30.

Nivoli, A., F. Colom, A. Murru, I. Pacchiarotti, P. Castro-Loli, A. González-Pinto, K. Fountoulakis, and E. Vieta. 2011. "New Treatment Guidelines for Acute Bipolar Depression: A Systematic Review," *Journal of Affective Disorders* 129: 14–26.

Nwulia, E.A., M.K. Zandi, D.F. MacKinnon, J.R. DePaulo Jr, and M.G. McInnis. 2007. "Genome-wide Scan of Bipolar II Disorder," *Bipolar Disorders* 9, 6: 580–8.

O'Reardon, J.P. 2007. "Efficacy and Safety of Transcranial Magnetic Stimulation in the Acute Treatment of Major Depression: A Multisite Randomized Controlled Trial," *Biological Psychiatry* 62, 11: 1208–16.

Oswald, P., D. Souery, S. Kasper, Y. Lecrubier, S. Montgomery, and S. Wyckaert. 2007. "Current Issues in Bipolar Disorder: A Critical Review," *European Neuropsychopharmacology* 17, 11: 687–95.

Oyane, N.M., I. Bjelland, S. Pallesen, F. Holsten, and B. Bjorvatn. 2007. "Seasonality Is Associated with Anxiety and Depression: The Hordaland Health Study," *Journal of Affective Disorders* 105, 1–3: 147–55.

Parker, G. 2000. "Diagnosis, Classification, and Differential Diagnosis of the Mood Disorders," in M.G. Gelder, J. Lopez-Ibor Jr, and N.C. Andreasen, eds, *New Oxford Textbook of Psychiatry*. Oxford: Oxford University Press.

Perrin, J., S. Merz, D. Bennett, J. Currie, D. Steele, I. Reid, and C. Schwazbauer. 2012. "Electroconvulsive Therapy Reduces Frontal Cortical Connectivity in Severe Depressive Disorder," *Proceedings, National Academy of Science* 109, 14: 5464–8.

Phillips, N., C. Hammen, P. Brennan, J. Najman, and W. Bor. 2005. "Early Adversity and the Prospective Prediction of Depressive and Anxiety Disorders in Adolescents," *Journal of Abnormal Child Psychology* 33, 1: 13–24.

Prudich, J. 2005. "Electroconvulsive Therapy," in B.J. Sadock and V. Sadock, eds, *Kaplan & Sadock's Comprehensive Textbook of Psychiatry*, 8th edn. Philadelphia: Lippincott Williams & Wilkins.

Public Health Agency of Canada. 2002. *A Report on Mental Illnesses in Canada*. Ottawa: Health Canada, www.phac-aspc.gc.ca.

Ravitz, P., R. Maunder, and C. McBride. 2008. "Attachment, Contemporary Interpersonal Theory and IPT: An Integration of Theoretical, Clinical and Empirical Perspectives," *Journal of Contemporary Psychotherapy* 38, 1: 11–21.

Regehr, C. 2000. "Cognitive-Behavioural Therapy," in P. Lehmann and N. Coady, eds, *Theoretical Perspectives in Direct Social Work Practice: An Eclectic-Generalist Approach*. New York: Springer.

———, G. Glancy, and A. Pitts. 2013. "Interventions to Reduce Stress in University Students: A Review and Meta-Analysis," *Journal of Affective Disorders* 148, 1: 1–11.

Rihmer, Z., and J. Angst. 2005. "Mood Disorders: Epidemiology," in B.J. Sadock and V. Sadock, eds, *Kaplan & Sadock's Comprehensive Textbook of Psychiatry*, 8th edn. Philadelphia: Lippincott Williams & Wilkins.

Romans, S., M. Cohen, and T. Forte. 2011. "Rates of Depression and Anxiety in Urban and Rural Canada," *Social Psychiatry and Psychiatric Epidemiology* 46, 7: 567–75.

Rosenthal, N., D. Sack, J. Gillin, A. Lewy, F. Goodwin, Y. Davenport, et al. 1984. "Seasonal Affective Disorder: A Description of the Syndrome and Preliminary Findings with Light Therapy," *Archives of General Psychiatry* 41, 1: 72–80.

Rouget, B., and J. Aubry. 2007. "Efficacy of Psychoeducational Approaches on Bipolar Disorders: A Review of the Literature," *Journal of Affective Disorders* 98, 1–2: 11–12.

Sanchez-Villegas, A., M. Delgado-Rodriguez, A. Alonso, L. Schlatter, F. Lahortiga, L. Majern, and M. Martinez-Gonzales. 2009. "Association of the Mediterranean Dietary Pattern with the Incidence of Depression," *Archives of General Psychiatry* 66: 1090–8.

Schaefer, H.S., K.M. Putnam, R.M. Benca, and R.J. Davidson. 2006. "Event-related Functional Magnetic Resonance Imaging Measures of Neural Activity to Positive Social Stimuli in Pre-and Post-Treatment Depression," *Journal of Biopsychology* 60, 9: 974–86.

Scott, J., Y. McNeill, J. Cavanagh, M. Cannon, and R. Murray. 2006. "Exposure to Obstetric Complications and Subsequent Development of Bipolar Disorder: Systematic Review," *British Journal of Psychiatry* 189: 3–11.

Segal, Z., J. Teasdale, and M. Williams. 2002. *Mindfulness-Based Cognitive Therapy for Depression*. New York: Guilford Press.

Shaffer, A., J. Cairney, A. Cheung, S. Veldhuizen, and A. Levitt. 2006. "Community Survey of Bipolar Disorder in Canada: Lifetime Prevalence and Illness Characteristics," *Canadian Journal of Psychiatry* 51, 1: 9–16.

Shiloh, R., D. Nutt, and A. Wizeman. 2005. *Clinical Handbook of Psychotropic Drugs*, 15th edn. Ashland: Hogrefe and Huber.

Smith, L.A., V. Cornelius, A. Warnock, A. Bell, and A.H. Young. 2007. "Effectiveness of Mood Stabilizers and Antipsychotics in the Maintenance Phase of Bipolar Disorder: A Systematic Review of Randomized Controlled Trials," *Bipolar Disorders* 9, 4: 394–412.

Stahl, S. 2008. *Essential Psychopharmocology*. New York: Cambridge University Press.

Subramanian, K. 1991. "Structured Group Work for the Management of Chronic Pain: An Experimental Investigation," *Research on Social Work Practice* 1, 1: 32–45.

Talbot, N., and S. Gamble. 2007. "IPT for

Women with Trauma Histories in Community Mental Health Care," *Journal of Contemporary Psychotherapy* 38, 1: 35–44.

Turner, E., A. Matthews, E. Linardatos, R.A. Tell, and R. Rosenthal. 2008. "Selective Publication of Antidepressant Trials and Its Influence on Apparent Efficacy," *New England Journal of Medicine* 358, 3: 252–60.

Vieta, E., J.R. Calabrese, J.M. Goikolea, S. Raines, and W. Macfadden. 2007. "Quetiapine Monotherapy in the Treatment of Patients with Bipolar I or II Depression and a Rapid-Cycling Disease Course: A Randomized, Double-blind, Placebo-controlled Study," *Bipolar Disorders* 9, 4: 413–25.

Vittengl, J., L. Clark, T. Dunn, and R. Jarrett. 2007. "Reducing Relapse and Recurrence in Unipolar Depression: A Comparative Meta-analysis of Cognitive-Behavioral Therapy's Effects," *Journal of Clinical and Counselling Psychology* 25, 3: 475–88.

Vonk, R., A.C. van der Schot, R.S. Kahn, W.A. Nolen, and H.A. Drexhage. 2007. "Is Autoimmune Thyroiditis Part of the Genetic Vulnerability (or an Endophenotype) for Bipolar Disorder?" *Biological Psychiatry* 62, 2: 135–40.

Widiger, T., and L.A. Clark. 2000. "Toward DSM-V and the Classification of Psychopathology," *Psychological Bulletin* 126, 6: 946–63.

Wild, T., N. el-Guebaly, B. Fischer, S. Brissette, S. Brochu, J. Bruneau, L. Noel, J. Rehm, M. Tyndall, and P. Mun. 2005. "Comorbid Depression among Untreated Illicit Opiate Users: Results from a Multisite Canadian Study," *Canadian Journal of Psychiatry* 50, 9: 512–18.

Williams, J., Y. Alatiq, C. Barnhofer, M. Fennell, D. Duggan, S. Hepburn, et al. 2008. "Mindfulness-based Cognitive Therapy in Bipolar Disorder: Preliminary Evaluation of Immediate Effects on Between Episode Functioning," *Journal of Affective Disorders* 107, 1–3: 275–9.

Yatham, L., S. Kennedy, S. Parikh, S. Beaulieu, C. O'Donovan, G. MacQueen, R.S. McIntyre, et al. 2009. "Canadian Network for Mood and Anxiety Treatments (CANMAT) and International Society for Bipolar Disorders (ISBD) Collaborative Update on CANMAT Guidelines for the Management of Patients with Bipolar Disorder: Update 2009," *Bipolar Disorders* 11: 225–55.

Chapter 9

Abramowitz, J.S. 2006. "The Psychological Treatment of Obsessive-Compulsive Disorder," *Canadian Journal of Psychiatry* 51, 7: 407–30.

———, S. Taylor, and D. McKay. 2009. "Obsessive-Compulsive Disorder," *Lancet* 374: 491–9.

American Psychiatric Association (APA). 2000. *Diagnostic and Statistical Manual of Mental Disorders*, 4th edn. Washington: APA Press.

Antai-Otong, D. 2007. "The Art of Prescribing. Pharmacotherapy of Obsession-Compulsive Disorder: An Evidence-based Approach," *Perspectives in Psychiatric Care* 43, 4: 219–22.

Bandura, A. 1977. "Self-Efficacy: Toward a Unifying Theory of Behavioral Change," *Psychological Review* 84, 2: 191–215.

Bewick, B., G. Koutsopoulou, J. Miles, E. Slaa, and M. Barkham. 2010. "Changes in Undergraduate Students' Psychological Well-being as They Progress through University," *Studies in Higher Education* 35, 6: 633–45.

Calhoun, K., and B. Atkeson. 1991. *Treatment of Rape Victims: Facilitating Psychosocial Adjustment*. New York: Pergamon Press.

Cox, B., and S. Taylor. 1999. "Anxiety Disorders: Panic and Phobias," in T. Millon, P. Blaney, and R. Davis, eds, *Oxford Textbook of Psychopathology*. New York: Oxford University Press, 81–113.

Craggs, S. 2012. "One-third of McMaster Students Battle Depression: Survey," CBC News, www.cbc.ca/hamilton/news/story/2012/10/02/hamilton-mental-illness-awareness-week.html.

Craske, M., K. Kircanski, A. Epstein, H. Wittchen, D. Pine, R. Lewis-Fernández, and D. Hinton. 2010. "Panic Disorder: A Review of DSM-IV Panic Disorder and Proposals for DSM-V," *Depression & Anxiety* 27, 2: 93–112.

Dubovsky, S. 2008. "The Neuroanatomy of Obsessive-Compulsive Disorder Directs Its Treatment," *Biology Psychiatry* 63: 557.

Evans, S., S. Ferrando, M. Findler, C. Stowell, C. Smart, and D. Haglin. 2008. "Mindfulness-based Cognitive Therapy for Generalized Anxiety Disorder," *Journal of Anxiety Disorders* 22, 4: 716–21.

Fehm, L., K. Beesdo, F. Jacobi, and A. Fiedler. 2008. "Social Anxiety Disorder above and below the Diagnostic Threshold: Prevalence, Comorbidity and Impairment in the General

Population," *Social Psychiatry and Psychiatric Epidemiology* 43, 4: 257–65.

Gaab, J., L. Sonderegger, S. Scherrer, and U. Ehlert. 2006. "Psychoneuroendocrine Effects of Cognitive-Behavioral Stress Management in a Naturalistic Setting—a Randomized Controlled Trial," *Psychoneuroendocrinology* 31: 428–38.

Gardner, F., and Z. Moore. 2007. *The Psychology of Enhancing Human Performance*. New York: Springer.

Gwynn, R., H. McQuistion, K. McVeigh, R. Garg, T. Frieden, and L. Thorpe. 2008. "Prevalence, Diagnosis, and Treatment of Depression and Generalized Anxiety Disorder in a Diverse Urban Community," *Psychiatric Services* 59, 6: 641–7.

Hettema, J., C. Prescott, and K. Kendler. 2004. "Genetic and Environmental Sources of Covariation between Generalized Anxiety Disorder and Neuroticism," *American Journal of Psychiatry* 161, 9: 1581–7.

Hoffman, D.L., E.M. Dukes, and H. Wittchen. 2008. "Human and Economic Burden of Generalized Anxiety Disorder," *Depression and Anxiety* 25, 1: 72–90.

Ishikawa, S., I. Okajima, H. Matsuoka, and Y. Sakano. 2007. "Cognitive Behavioural Therapy for Anxiety Disorders in Children and Adolescents: A Meta-Analysis," *Child and Adolescent Mental Health* 12, 4: 164–72.

Kabat-Zinn, J. 1982. "An Outpatient Program in Behavioral Medicine for Chronic Pain Patients Based on Practice of Mindfulness Meditation: Theoretical Considerations and Preliminary Results," *General Hospital Psychiatry* 4: 33–47.

Kaplan, H., and B. Sadock. 1996. *Concise Textbook of Clinical Psychiatry*. Baltimore: Williams and Wilkins.

Kendall, P.C., J.L. Hudson, E. Gosch, E. Flannery-Schroeder, and C. Suveg. 2008. "Cognitive-Behavioral Therapy for Anxiety Disordered Youth: A Randomized Clinical Trial Evaluating Child and Family Modalities," *Journal of Consulting and Clinical Psychology* 76, 2: 282–97.

Kessler, R., P. Berglund, O. Demler, R. Jin, K. Merikangas, and E. Walters. 2005. "Lifetime Prevalence and Age of Onset Distributions of DSM-IV Disorders in the National Comorbidity Survey Replication," *Archives of General Psychiatry* 62: 593–602.

Lunau, K. 2012. "Mental Health Crisis on Campus: Canadian Students Feel Hopeless, Depressed, Even Suicidal," *Maclean's*, 5 Sept.

Mathew S., R. Price, and D. Charney. 2008. "Recent Advances in the Neurobiology of Anxiety Disorders: Implications for Novel Therapeutics," *American Journal of Medical Genetics* 148C: 89–98.

May, R. 1950. *The Meaning of Anxiety*. New York: The Ronald Press Company.

McTeague, L., P. Lang, M. Laplante, and M. Bradley. 2011. "Aversive Imagery in Panic Disorder: Agoraphobia Severity, Comorbidity and Defensive Physiology," *Biological Psychiatry* 70, 5: 415–24.

Meichenbaum, D. 1993. "Stress Inoculation Training: A Twenty-Year Update," in L. Woolfolk and P. Lehrer, eds, *Principles and Practice of Stress Management*, 2nd edn. New York: Guilford, 373–406.

Mojtabai, R. 2005. "Culture-Bound Syndromes with Psychotic Features," in B.J. Sadock and V. Sadock, eds, *Kaplan and Sadock's Comprehensive Textbook of Psychiatry*, 8th edn. Philadelphia: Lippincott Williams and Wilkins, 1536–8.

National Institute for Health and Clinical Excellence. 2007. "Anxiety (amended): Management of Anxiety (Panic Disorder, with or without Agoraphobia, and Generalized Anxiety Disorder) in Adults in Primary, Secondary and Community Care," 4–46.

Nivoli, A., F. Colum, A. Murru, I. Pacchiatrotti, P. Castro-Loli, K. Fountoulakis, and E. Vieta. 2011. "New Treatment Guidelines for Acute Bipolar Depression: A Systematic Review," *Journal of Affective Disorders* 129: 14–26.

Norton, P.J. and E.P. Price. 2007. "A Meta-analytic Review of Cognitive-behavioral Treatment Outcome across the Anxiety Disorders," *Journal of Nervous and Mental Disease*, 195: 521–31.

Pinard, G. 2006. "The Pharmacologic and Psychological Treatment of Obsessive-Compulsive Disorder," *Canadian Journal of Psychiatry* 51, 7: 405–6.

Powers, M.B., and P. Emmelkamp. 2008. "Virtual Reality Therapy for Anxiety Disorders: A Meta-analysis," *Journal of Anxiety Disorders* 22: 561–9.

Public Health Agency of Canada. 2002. *A Report on Mental Illnesses in Canada*. Ottawa: Health Canada, ch. 4, Anxiety, www.phac-aspc.gc.ca/publicat/miic-mmac/chap_4_e.html.

Regehr, C., D. Glancy, and A. Pitts. 2013. "Interventions to Reduce Stress in University Students: A Review and Meta-Analysis," *Journal of Affective Disorders* 148, 1: 1–11.

Rotge, J., D. Grabot, B. Aouizerate, A. Pelissolo, J. Lepine, and J. Tignol. 2011. "Childhood History of Behavioural Inhibition and Comorbidity Status in 256 Adults with Social Phobia," *Journal of Affective Disorders* 129, 1: 338–41.

Rothbaum, B., E. Meadows, P. Resick, and D. Foy. 2000. "Cognitive Behavioural Therapy," in W. Foa, T. Keane, and M. Friedman, eds, *Effective Treatments for PTSD: Practice Guidelines from the International Society for Traumatic Stress Studies*. New York: Guilford Press.

Sanchez-Meca, J., A. Rosa-Alcazar, F. Marin-Martinez, and A. Gomez-Conesa. 2010. Psychological Treatment of Panic Disorder with or without Agoraphobia: A Meta-analysis," *Clinical Psychology Review* 30, 1: 37–50.

Segal, Z., J. Teasdale, and M. Williams. 2002. *Mindfulness-Based Cognitive Therapy for Depression*. New York: Guilford Press.

Seligman, M., and J. Garber. 1980. *Human Helplessness*. Toronto: Academic Press.

Selye, H. 1936. "A Syndrome Produced by Diverse Nocuous Agents," *Nature* 138: 32.

Smoller J., E. Gardner-Schuster, and J. Covino. 2008. "The Genetic Basis of Panic and Phobic Anxiety Disorders," *American Journal of Medical Genetics* 148C: 118–26.

——— and S. Faraone. 2008. "Genetics of Anxiety Disorders: Complexities and Opportunities," *American Journal of Medical Genetics* 148C: 85–8.

Spiegel, D.A., and D.H. Barlow. 2000. "Generalized Anxiety Disorders," in M.G. Gelder, J. Lopez-Ibor Jr, and N.C. Andreasen, eds, *New Oxford Textbook of Psychiatry*. Oxford: Oxford University Press.

Stahl, S.M. 2000. "Anxiety Disorders and Anxiolytics," in Stahl, *Essential Psychopharmacology: Neuroscientific Basis and Practical Applications*, 3rd edn. Cambridge: Cambridge University Press, 721–71.

Walker, L. 1979. *The Battered Woman*. New York: Harper and Row.

Waters, A.M., K. Mogg, B.P. Bradley, and D.S. Pine. 2012. "Attention Bias for Angry Faces in Children with Social Phobia," *Journal of Experimental Psychopathology* 2: 475–89.

Chapter 10

Alzheimer Society of Canada. 2010. *Rising Tide: The Impact of Dementia on Canadian Society*. Toronto: Alzheimer Society of Canada.

Alzheimer's Disease International. 1999. *Factsheet: The Prevalence of Dementia*, Apr. London: Alzheimer's Disease International, 1–2.

American Psychiatric Association (APA). 2013. *Diagnostic and Statistical Manual of Mental Disorders*, 5th edn. Washington: APA Press.

Anderson, J., and N. Mangels. 2006. "Helping Victims: Social Services, Health Care Interventions in Elder Abuse," in R. Summers and A. Hoffman, eds, *Elder Abuse: A Public Health Perspective*. Washington: American Public Health Association, 139–66.

Anthony, W. 1993. "Recovery from Mental Illness: The Guiding Vision of Mental Health Services in the 1990s," *Psychosocial Rehabiliation* 16: 11–23.

Arai, M. 2006. "Elder Abuse in Japan," *Educational Gerontology* 32, 1: 13–23.

Backman, L. 2008. "Memory and Cognition in Preclinical Dementia: What We Know and What We Do Not Know," *Canadian Journal of Psychiatry* 53, 6: 354–60.

Ballard, C., J. Waite, and J. Birks. 2006. "Atypical Antipsychotics for Aggression and Psychosis in Alzheimer's Disease," *Cochrane Database of Systematic Reviews* Issue 1, Art. No.: CD003475. DOI: 10.1002/14651858. CD003476.pub2.

Barcia, D. 2000. "Delirium, Dementia, and Amnesic and Other Cognitive Disorders," in M.G. Gelder, J.J. Lopez-Ibor Jr, and N.C. Andreasen, eds, *New Oxford Textbook of Psychiatry*. Oxford: Oxford University Press, 377–81.

Bates, J., J. Boote, and C. Beverley. 2004. "Psychosocial Interventions for People with Milder Dementing Illness: A Systematic Review," *Journal of Advanced Nursing* 45, 6: 644–58.

Bertisch, H., J. Rath, D. Langenbahn, R. Sherr, and L. Diller. 2011. "Group Treatment in Acquired Brain Injury Rehabilitation," *Journal for Specialists in Group Work* 46, 4: 264–77.

Birks, J. 2006. "Cholinesterase Inhibitors for Alzheimer's Disease," *Cochrane Database of Systematic Reviews* Issue 1. Art. No.: CD005593. DOI: 10.1002/14651858. CD005593.

Bomba, P. 2006. "Use of a Single Page Elder Abuse Assessment and Management Tool: A Practical Clinician's Approach to Identifying Elder Mistreatment," in J. Mellor and P. Bownell, eds, *Elder Abuse and Mistreatment: Policy, Practice and Research*. Binghamton, NY: Haworth Press, 103–22.

Cattelani, R., M. Zettin, and P. Zoccolotti. 2010. "Rehabilitation Treatments for Adults with Behavioral and Psychosocial Disorders Following Acquired Brain Injury: A Systematic Review," *Neuropsychological Review* 20: 52–85.

Craik, F.I. 2008. "Memory Changes in Normal and Pathological Aging," *Canadian Journal of Psychiatry* 53, 6: 343–5.

Davis, K.L. 2005. "Delirium, Dementia, and Amnestic and Other Cognitive Disorders and Mental Disorders to a General Medical Condition," in B.J. Sadock and V. Sadock, eds, *Comprehensive Textbook of Psychiatry*, 8th edn. Philadelphia: Lippincott Williams & Wilkins, 1053.

Davis, L., A. Sander, M. Struchen, M. Sherer, R. Nakase-Richardson, and J. Malec. 2009. "Medical and Psychosocial Predictors of Caregiver Distress and Perceived Burden Following Traumatic Brain Injury," *Journal of Head Trauma Rehabiliation* 24, 3: 145–54.

Donovan, K. and C. Regehr. 2010. "Elder Abuse: Clinical, Ethical, and Legal Considerations in Social Work Practice," *Clinical Social Work Journal* 38: 174–82.

Eyer, F., T. Schuster, N. Felgenhauer, R. Pfab, T. Strubel, B. Saugel, and T. Zilker. 2011. "Risk Assessment of Moderate to Severe Alcohol Withdrawal—Predictors for Seizures and Delirium Tremens in the Course of Withdrawal," *Alcohol and Alcoholism* 46, 4: 427–33.

Feldman, H.H., C. Jacova, A. Robillard, A. Garcia, T. Chow, and M. Borrie. 2008. "Diagnosis and Treatment of Dementia: 2. Diagnosis," *Canadian Medical Association Journal* 178, 7: 825–36.

Foreman, M.D., L.C. Mion, L. Trygstad, and K. Fletcher. 2003. "Delirium: Strategies for Assessing and Treatment," in M. Mezey, T. Fulmer, I. Abraham, and D.A. Zwicker, eds, *Geriatric Nursing Protocols for Best Practice*, 2nd edn. New York: Springer, 116–40.

Fulmer, T., L. Guadagno, C. Bitondo, and M. Connolly. 2004. "Progress in Elder Abuse Screening and Assessment Instruments," *Journal of the American Geriatrics Society* 52, 2: 297–304.

Granacher, R. 2003. *Traumatic Brain Injury: Methods for Clinical and Forensic Neuropsychiatric Assessment*. Boca Raton, Fla: CRC Press.

Girard, T., J. Jackson, P. Pandharipande, B. Pun, J. Thompson, A. Shintani, et al. 2010. "Delirium as a Predictor of Long-term Cognitive Impairment in Survivors of Critical Illness," *Critical Care Medicine* 38, 7: 1513–20.

Glancy, G.D., and T.F. Knott. 2003. "Psychopharmacology of Violence—Part V," *American Academy of Psychiatry and the Law Newsletter* 28, 3: 8–9.

Gonzalez-Salvador, M., C. Arango, C. Lyketsos, and A. Barba. 1999. "The Stress and Psychological Morbidity of the Alzheimer Patient Caregiver," *International Journal of Geriatric Psychiatry* 14: 701–10.

Greenberg, D.E., and M. Muraca. 2007. "Guideline for Cognitive Impairment: Is This Dementia? Symptoms to Management," in D.E. Greenberg and M. Muraca, eds, *Canadian Clinical Practice Guidelines*. Toronto: Elsevier Canada, 45–50.

Herrmann, N., and K.L. Lanctot. 2007. "Pharmacologic Management of Neuropsychiatric Symptoms of Alzheimer Disease," *La Revue Canadienne de Psychiatrie* 52, 10: 630–46.

Hoge, C., D. McGurk, J. Thomas, A. Cox, C. Engel, and C. Castro. 2008. "Mild Traumatic Brain Injury in US Soldiers Returning from Iraq," *New England Journal of Medicine* 31, 5: 453–63.

Hux, M.J., B.J. O'Brien, M. Iskedjian, R. Goeree, M. Gagnon, and S. Gauthier. 1998. "Relation between Severity of Alzheimer's Disease and Costs of Caring," *Canadian Medical Association Journal* 159, 5: 457–65.

Kreutzer, J., L. Rapport, J. Marwitz, C. Harrison-Felix, T. Hart, M. Glenn, and F. Hammond. 2009. "Caregiver's Well-being after Traumatic Brain Injury: A Multicenter Prospective Investigation," *Archives of General Rehabilitation* 90, 6: 939–46.

Livingston, L., R. Kennedy, J. Marwitz, J. Arango-Lasprilla, L. Rapport, T. Bushnick, and K. Gary. 2010. "Predictors of Family Caregivers' Life Satisfaction after Traumatic Brain Injury at One and Two Years Post-injury: A Longitudinal Multi-Center Investigation," *NeuroRehabilitation* 27: 73–81.

Lovestone, S. 2000. "Dementia: Alzheimer's Disease," in M.G. Gelder, J.J. Lopez-Ibor Jr, and N.C. Andreasen, eds, *New Oxford Textbook of Psychiatry*. Oxford: Oxford University Press, 387–96.

Luo, L., and F.I. Craik. 2008. "Aging and Memory: A Cognitive Approach," *Canadian Journal of Psychiatry* 53, 6: 346–53.

Maas, A., N. Stocchetti, and R. Bullock. 2008. "Moderate and Severe Traumatic Brain Injury in Adults," *Lancet* 7: 728–41.

Massoud, F. 2007. "Maladie d'Alzheimer," *Canadian Family Physician* 53, 1: 50–4.

Molloy, D., E. Alemayehu, and R. Roberts. 1991. "Reliability of a Standardized Mini-Mental State Examination Compared with the Traditional Mini-Mental State Examination," *American Journal of Psychiatry* 148, 1: 102–5.

Moos, I., and A. Bjorn. 2006. "Use of the Life Story in the Institutional Care of People with Dementia: A Review of Intervention Studies," *Ageing and Society* 26, 3: 431–54.

Murman, D.L., Q. Chen, B.S. Powell, S.B. Kuo, C.J. Bradley, and C.C. Colenda. 2002. "The Incremental Direct Costs Associated with Behavioural Symptoms in AD," *Neurology* 59: 1721–9.

Neugroschl, J.A., A. Kolevzon, S.C. Samuels, and D.B. Marin. 2005. "Dementia. In Delirium, Dementia, and Amnestic and Other Cognitive Disorders and Mental Disorders due to a General Medical Condition," in B. Sadock and V. Sadock, eds, *Comprehensive Textbook of Psychiatry*. Philadelphia: Lippincott Williams & Wilkins, 1069–106.

Ontario Health Care Consent Act. 1996. S.O. 1996, c. 2, Sch. A, www.e-laws.gov.on.ca/html/statutes/english/elaws_statutes_96h02_e.htm.

Ott, A., M. Breteler, F. van Harskamp, J. Claus, T. van der Cammen, E. Diederick, et al. 1995. "Prevalence of Alzheimer's Disease and Vascular Dementia: Association with Education. The Rotterdam Study," *British Medical Journal* 30: 970–3.

Papastavrou, E., A. Kalokerinou, S. Papacostas, H. Tsangari, and P. Sourtizi. 2007. "Caring for a Relative with Dementia: Family Caregiver Burden," *Journal of Advanced Nursing* 58, 5: 446–57.

Plassman, B.L., K.M. Langa, G.G. Fisher, S.G. Heeringa, D.R. Weird, M.B. Ofstedal, et al. 2007. "Prevalence of Dementia in the United States: The Aging, Demographics, and Memory Study," *Neuroepidemiology* 29: 125–32.

Regehr, C., and K. Kanani. 2010. *Essential Law for Social Work Practice in Canada*, 2nd edn. Toronto: Oxford University Press.

Riedel-Heller, S.G., A. Busse, C. Aurich, H. Matschinger, and M.C. Angermeyer. 2001. "Prevalence of Dementia According to DSM-III-R and ICD-10," *British Journal of Psychiatry* 179: 250–4.

Riemersma-van der Lek, R.F., D.F. Swaab, J. Twisk, E.M. Hol, W.J. Hoogendijk, and V. Someren. 2008. "Effect of Bright Light and Melatonin on Cognitive and Noncognitive Function in Elderly Residents of Group Care Facilities," *Journal of the American Medical Association* 299, 22: 2642–55.

Seow, D., and S. Gauthier. 2007. "Pharmacotherapy of Alzheimer Disease," *La Revue Canadienne de Psychiatrie* 52, 10: 620–9.

Silver, J., T. McAllister, and S. Yudofsky. 2011. *Textbook of Traumatic Brain Injury*. Arlington, VA: American Psychiatric Association Press.

Slade, M., and M. Hayward. 2007. "Recovery, Psychosis and Psychiatry: Research Is Better Than Rhetoric," *Acta Psychiatrica Scandinavica* 116, 2: 81–3.

Spector, A., M. Orrell, S. Davies, and B. Woods. 2000. "Reality Orientation for Dementia," *Cochrane Database of Systematic Reviews* Issue 3, Art. No.: CD001119. DOI: 10.1002/14651858.CD001119.pub2.

Stahl, S.M. 2000. "Dementia and Its Treatment," in Stahl, *Essential Psychopharmacology: Neuroscientific Basis and Practical Applications*, 3rd edn. Cambridge: Cambridge University Press, 899–942.

Statistics Canada. 2002. *Family Violence in Canada: A Statistical Profile*. Ottawa: Statistics Canada.

Stern, T., A. Gross, T. Stern, S. Nejad, and J. Maldonado. 2010. "Current Approaches to Recognition and Treatment of Alcohol Withdrawal and Delirium Tremens: 'Old Wine in New Bottles' or 'New Wine in

Old Bottles," *Primary Care Companion to the Journal of Clinical Psychiatry* 12, 3: PCC.10r00991.

Sussman, T. 2006. "Negotiating Community Care as a Stress: The Experience of Spousal Caregivers," paper presented at the 4th Annual National Gerontological Social Work Conference, Chicago.

——— and C. Regehr. 2009. "The Influence of Community-Based Services on the Burden of Spouses Caring for Their Partners with Dementia," *Social Work in Health* 34, 1: 29–39.

Tauriac, J., and N. Scruggs. 2006. "Elder Abuse among African Americans," *Educational Gerontology* 32, 1: 37–48.

Wang, J. 2007. "Group Reminiscence Therapy for Cognitive and Affective Function of Demented Elderly in Taiwan," *International Journal of Geriatric Psychiatry* 22: 1235–40.

Woods, B., A. Spector, C. Jones, M. Orrell, and S. Davies. 2005. "Reminiscence Therapy for Dementia," *Cochrane Database of Systematic Reviews* Issue 2, Art. No.: CD001120. DOI: 10.1002/14651858.CD001120.pub2.

World Health Organization (WHO). 2002. *Toronto Declaration on the Global Prevention of Elder Abuse*, www.who.int/ageing/projects/elder_abuse/alc_toronto_declaration_en.pdf.

Zaloshnja, E., T. Miller, J. Langlois, and A. Selassie. 2008. "Prevalence of Long-term Disability from Traumatic Brain Injury in the Civilian Population of the United States, 2005," *Journal of Head Trauma Rehabilitation* 23, 6: 394–400.

Chapter 11

Abraham, H.D. 2000. "Disorders Relating to the Use of Phencyclidine and Hallucinogens," in M.G. Gelder, J.J. Lopez-Ibor Jr, and N.C. Andreasen, eds, *New Oxford Textbook of Psychiatry*. Oxford: Oxford University Press, 535–8.

Ahmadi, J., S. Pridmore, A. Alimi, A. Cheraghi, A. Arad, H. Parsaeyan, et al. 2007. "Epidemiology of Opium Use in the General Population," *American Journal of Drug and Alcohol Abuse* 33, 3: 483–91.

Alcoholics Anonymous. 1972. *A Brief Guide to Alcoholics Anonymous*. New York: Alcoholics Anonymous World Wide Services, www.alcoholics-anonymous.org/en_pdfs/p-42_abriefguidetoaa.pdf.

Amato, L., S. Minozzi, M. Davoli, S. Vecchi, M. Ferri, and S. Mayet. 2004. "Psychosocial and Pharmacological Treatments versus Pharmacological Treatments for Opioid Detoxification," *Cochrane Database of Systematic Reviews* Issue 4, Art. No.: CD005031. DOI: 10.1002/14651858.CD005031.

American Psychiatric Association (APA). 2013. *Diagnostic and Statistical Manual of Mental Disorders*, 5th edn. Washington: APA Press.

Anton, R. 2008. "Naltrexone for the Management of Alcohol Dependence," *New England Journal of Medicine* 359: 715–21.

Bezchlibnyk-Butler, K., J. Jeffries, and A. Virani, eds. 2007. *Clinical Handbook of Psychotropic Drugs*, 17th edn. Seattle: Hogrefe & Huber.

Brady, K.T., B.K. Tolliver, and M.L. Verduin. 2007. "Alcohol Use and Anxiety: Diagnostic and Management Issues," *American Journal of Psychiatry* 164, 2: 217–21.

Bramness, J., and H. Kornor. 2007. "Benzodiazepine Prescription for Patients in Opioid Maintenance Treatment in Norway," *Drug and Alcohol Dependence* 90, 2–3: 203–9.

Budney, A.J., R.G. Vandrey, J.R. Hughes, B.A. Moore, and B. Bahrenburg. 2007. "Oral Delta-9-tetrahydrocannabinol Suppresses Cannabis Withdrawal Symptoms," *Drug and Alcohol Dependence* 86, 1: 22–9.

Burke, B., H. Arkowitz, and M. Menchola. 2003. "The Efficacy of Motivational Interviewing: A Meta-analysis of Controlled Clinical Trials," *Journal of Counselling and Clinical Psychology* 71, 5: 843–61.

Buxton, J.A., and N.A. Dove. 2008. "The Burden and Management of Crystal Meth Use," *Canadian Medical Association Journal* 178, 12: 1537–9.

Canadian Centre on Substance Abuse. 2009. *Substance Abuse in Canada: Concurrent Disorders*. Ottawa: Canadian Centre on Substance Abuse.

———. 2011. "Canada's Low-Risk Drinking Guidelines," www.ccsa.ca/Eng/Priorities/Alcohol/Canada-Low-Risk-Alcohol-Drinking-Guidelines/Pages/default.aspx.

———. 2012. "Bath Salts," www.ccsa.ca/2012%20CCSA%20Documents/CCSA-CCENDU-Drug-Alert-Bath-Salts-2012-en.pdf.

Carey, K., L. Scott-Sheldon, M. Carey, and K. DeMartini. 2007. "Individual Level Interventions to Reduce College Student

Drinking: A Meta-analytic Review," *Addictive Behaviors* 32, 11: 2469–94.

———, ———, J. Eliott, J. Bolles, and M. Carey. 2009. "Computer-driven Interventions to Reduce College Student Drinking: A Meta-analysis," *Addiction* 104, 11: 1807–19.

Chapman, K., R. Tarter, L. Kirisci, and M. Cornelius. 2007. "Childhood Neurobehavior Disinhibition Amplifies the Risk of Substance Use Disorder: Interaction of Parental History and Prenatal Alcohol Exposure," *Journal of Developmental and Behavioral Pediatrics* 28, 3: 219–24.

Ciraulo, A.M., N. Alpert, and K.J. Franko. 1997. "Naltrexone for the Treatment of Alcoholism," *American Family Physician* 56, 3: 803–6.

Ciraulo, D.A., Q. Dong, B. Silverman, D. Gastfriend, and H. Pettinati. 2008. "Early Treatment Response in Alcohol Dependence with Extended-release Naltrexone," *Journal of Clinical Psychiatry* 69, 2: 190–5.

Cleary, M., G. Hunt, S. Matheson, N. Siegfried, and G. Walter. 2008. "Psychosocial Interventions for People with Both Severe Mental Illness and Substance Misuse," *Cochrane Database of Systematic Reviews* Issue 1, Art. No. CD001088. DOI: 10.1002/14651858.

Connock, M., A. Juarez-Garcia, S. Jowett, E. Frew, Z. Liu, R. Taylor, et al. 2007. "Methadone and Buprenorphine for the Management of Opioid Dependence: A Systematic Review and Economic Evaluation," *Health Technology Assessment* 11, 9.

Correctional Services of Canada. 2010. "Prevalence of Injection Drug Use among Male Offenders," www.csc-scc.gc.ca/text/rs-rch/smmrs/rs/rs10-02/rs10-02-eng.shtml.

DeBeck, K., E. Wood, J. Montaner, and T. Kerr. 2009. "Canada's New Federal 'National Drug Strategy': An Informal Audit of Reported Funding Allocation," *International Journal of Drug Policy* 20, 2: 188–91.

Department of Justice. 2010. *National Anti-Drug Strategy Implementation Evaluation: Final Report*. Ottawa.

Faggiano, F., F. Vigna-Taglianti, E. Versino, and P. Lemma. 2003. "Methadone Maintenance at Different Dosages for Opioid Dependence," *Cochrane Database of Systematic Reviews* Issue 3, Art. No. CD002208. DOI: 10.1002/14651858.CD002208.

Fischer, B., J. Rehm, J. Patra, and M. Cruz. 2006. "Changes in Illicit Opioid Use across Canada," *Canadian Medical Association Journal* 175, 11: 1385–7.

Gillespie, N., K. Kendler, C. Prescott, S. Aggen, C. Gardner, K. Jacobson, et al. 2007. "Longitudinal Modeling of Genetic and Environmental Influences on Self-reported Availability of Psychoactive Substances: Alcohol, Cigarettes, Marijuana, Cocaine and Stimulants," *Psychological Medicine* 37: 947–59.

Goldstein, R.B., W.M. Compton, A.J. Pulay, W.J. Ruan, R.P. Pickering, F.S. Simon, et al. 2007. "Antisocial Behavioural Syndromes and DSM-IV Drug Use Disorders in the United States: Results from the National Epidemiologic Survey on Alcohol and Related Conditions," *Drug and Alcohol Dependence* 90, 2–3: 145–58.

Government of Canada. 2012. "National Anti-Drug Strategy," www.nationalantidrugstrategy.gc.ca/.

Haberstick, B., D. Timberlake, A. Smolen, J. Sakai, C. Hopfer, R.P. Corley, et al. 2007. "Between and Within Family Associations of Dopamine Receptor D2 TaqIA Polymorphism and Alcohol Abuse and Dependence in a General Population Sample of Adults," *Journal of Studies of Alcohol and Drugs* 68, 3: 362–70.

Hall, W., and L. Degenhardt. 2007. "Prevalence and Correlates of Cannabis Use in Developed and Developing Countries," *Current Opinion Psychiatry* 20, 4: 393–7.

Health Canada. 1996. *Canada's Drug Strategy*. Ottawa: Health Canada, www.caw.ca/whatwedo/substanceabuse/pdf/CanadasDrugStrategy.pdf.

———. 2005. *Canadian Addiction Survey*. Ottawa: Health Canada.

———. 2011. "Major Findings from the Canadian Alcohol and Drug Use Monitoring Survey (CADUMS)," www.hc-sc.gc.ca/hc-ps/drugs-drogues/stat/index-eng.php.

Hurley, S., D. Jolley, and J. Kaldor. 1997. "Effectiveness of Needle Exchange Programs for Prevention of HIV Infection," *Lancet* 349: 1797–800.

Hyde, C., G. Glancy, P. Omerod, D. Hall, and G. Taylor. 1978. "The Abuse of the Indigenous Mushroom: A New Fashion and Some Psychiatric Complications," *British Journal of Psychiatry* 132: 602–4.

Hyshka, E., S. Strathdee, E. Wood, and R. Kerr. 2012. "Needle Exchange and the HIV Epidemic in Vancouver: Lessons Learned from 15 Years of Research," *International Journal of Drug Policy* 23, 4: 261–70.

Jacobs, M., and K. Fehr. 1987. *Drugs and Drug Abuse: A Reference Text*, 2nd edn. Toronto: Addiction Research Foundation.

Kendler, K., C. Prescott, J. Myers, and M. Neale. 2003. "The Structure of Genetic and Environmental Risk Factors for Common Psychiatric and Substance Use Disorders in Men and Women," *Archives of General Psychiatry* 60, 9: 929–37.

Kirisci, L., R. Tarter, A. Mezzich, and M. Vanyukov. 2007. "Developmental Trajectory Classes in Substance Use Disorder Etiology," *Psychology of Addictive Behaviours* 21, 3: 287–96.

Kish, S. 2008. "Pharmacologic Mechanisms of Crystal Meth," *Canadian Medical Association Journal* 178, 13: 1679–82.

Klein, R., and S. Mannuzza. 2010. "Comorbidity in Adult Attention-Deficit Hyperactivity Disorder," in W. Retz and R.G. Klein, eds, *Attention-Deficit Hyperactivity Disorder (ADHD) in Adults*. Key Issues in Mental Health, vol. 176. Basel: Karger, 126–43.

Kosok, A. 2006. "A Moderation Management Program in 2004: What Type of Drinker Seeks Controlled Drinking," *International Journal of Drug Policy* 17, 4: 295–303.

Krausz, R. 2009. "An Introduction to Concurrent Disorders," in Canadian Centre on Substance Abuse, *Substance Abuse in Canada: Concurrent Disorders*. Ottawa: Canadian Centre on Substance Abuse, 6–11.

Kruger, R.F., K.E. Markon, C.J. Patrick, S.D. Benning, and M.D. Kramer. 2007. "Linking Antisocial Behaviour, Substance Use, and Personality: An Integrative Quantitative Model of the Adult Externalizing Spectrum," *Journal of Abnormal Psychology* 116, 4: 645–66.

Lanier, R.K., A. Umbricht, J.A. Harrison, E.S. Nuwayser, and G.E. Bigelow. 2007. "Evaluation of a Transdermal Buprenorphine Formulation in Opioid Detoxification," *Addiction* 102, 10: 1648–56.

Levander, E., M.A. Frye, S. McElroy, T. Suppes, H. Grunze, W.A. Nolen, et al. 2007. "Alcoholism and Anxiety in Bipolar Illness: Differential Lifetime Anxiety Comorbidity in Bipolar I Women with and without Alcoholism," *Journal of Affective Disorders* 101, 1–3: 211–17.

Lev-Ran, S., S. Imtiaz, B. Taylor, K. Shield, J. Rehm, and B. Le Foll. 2012. "Gender Differences in Health-Related Quality of Life among Cannabis Users: Results from the National Epidemiologic Survey on Alcohol and Related Conditions," *Drug and Alcohol Dependence* 123: 190–200.

Leyton, M., and S. Cox. 2009. "Impulsivity and Substance Use Disorders," in Canadian Centre on Substance Abuse, *Substance Abuse in Canada: Concurrent Disorders*. Ottawa: Canadian Centre on Substance Abuse, 30–7.

Luty, J., and T. Carnwath. 2008. "Specialised Alcohol Treatment Services Area Luxury the NHS Cannot Afford," *British Journal of Psychiatry* 192: 245–7.

MacMaster, S. 2004. "Harm Reduction: A New Perspective on Substance Abuse Services," *Social Work* 49, 3: 356–63.

Marlatt, G., and K. Witkiewitz. 2002. "Harm Reduction Approaches to Alcohol Use: Health Promotion, Prevention and Treatment," *Addictive Behaviors* 27, 6: 867–86.

Marshall, J. 2000. "Alcohol Dependence and Alcohol Problems," in M.G. Gelder, J.J. Lopez-Ibor Jr, and N.C. Andreasen, eds, *New Oxford Textbook of Psychiatry*. Oxford: Oxford University Press, 482–8.

Mayfield, D., G. McLeod, and P. Hall. 1974. "The CAGE Questionnaire: Validation of a New Alcoholism Screening Instrument," *American Journal of Psychiatry* 131, 10: 1121–3.

Miller, W.R., and S. Rollnick. 1991. *Motivational Interviewing*. London: Guilford Press.

——— and ———. 2002. *Motivational Interviewing*, 2nd edn. New York: Guilford Press.

Min, M., K. Farkas, S. Minnes, and L.T. Singer. 2007. "Impact of Childhood Abuse and Neglect on Substance Abuse and Psychological Distress in Adulthood," *Journal of Traumatic Stress* 20, 5: 833–44.

Minozzi, S., L. Amato, M. Davoli, M. Farrell, A.A. Lima Reisser, P.P. Pani, et al. 2008. "Anticonvulsants for Cocaine Dependence," *Cochrane Database of Systematic Reviews* Issue 2, Art. No.: CD006754. DOI: 10.1002/14651858.CD006754.pub2.

Moeller, F.G., J.M. Schmitz, J.L. Steinberg, C.M. Green, C. Reist, L.Y. Lai, et al. 2007. "Citalopram Combined with Behavioral

Therapy Reduces Cocaine Use: A Double-Blind, Placebo-Controlled Trial," *American Journal of Drug and Alcohol Abuse* 33, 3: 367–78.

Moss, H.B., C.M. Chen, and H.Y. Yi. 2007. "Subtypes of Alcohol Dependence in a Nationally Representative Sample," *Drug and Alcohol Dependence* 9, 2–3: 149–58.

Nathan, P.E., A.H. Skinstad, and J.W. Langenbucher. 1999. "Substance Abuse: Diagnosis, Comorbidity, and Psychopathology," in T. Millon, P.H. Blaney, and R.D. Davis, eds, *Oxford Textbook of Psychopathology*. Oxford: Oxford University Press.

Nava, F., S. Premi, E. Manzato, W. Campagnola, A. Lucchini, and G.L. Gessa. 2007. "Gamma-Hydroxybutayrate Reduces Both Withdrawal Syndrome and Hypercortisolism in Severe Abstinent Alcoholics: An Open Study vs. Diazepam," *American Journal of Drug and Alcohol Abuse* 33, 3: 379–92.

National Institute for Health and Clinical Excellence. 2011. *Diagnosis, Assessment and Management of Harmful Drinking and Alcohol Dependence*. London: Royal College of Psychiatrists.

Patton, G.G., C. Coffey, M.T. Lynskey, S. Reid, S. Hemphill, J.B. Carlin, et al. 2007. "Trajectories of Adolescent Alcohol and Cannabis Use into Young Adulthood," *Addiction* 102, 4: 607–15.

Pelc, I., P. Verbanck, O. LeBon, M. Gavrilovic, K. Lion, and P. Lehert. 1997. "Efficacy and Safety of Acamprosate in the Treatment of Detoxified Alcohol-dependent Patients: A 90-day Placebo-controlled Dose-finding Study," *British Journal of Psychiatry* 171: 73–7.

Pihl, R.O. 1999. "Substance Abuse: Etiological Considerations," in T. Millon, P.H. Blaney, and R.D. Davis, eds, *Oxford Textbook of Psychopathology*. Oxford: Oxford University Press, 249–76.

Prochaska, J., and C. DiClemente. 1982. "Transtheoretical Therapy: Towards a More Integrated Model of Change," *Psychotherapy Research and Practice* 19, 3: 276–88.

Public Health Agency of Canada. 2001. *Harm Reduction and Injection Drug Use: An International Comparative Study of Contextual Factors Influencing the Development and Implementation of Relevant Policies and Programs*, www.phac-aspc.gc.ca/hepc/pubs/hridu-rmudi/index-eng.php.

Rapp, R., H. Siegal, and N. DeLiberty. 2003. "Demographic and Clinical Correlates of Client Motivation among Substance Abusers," *Health and Social Work* 28, 2: 107–15.

Regehr, C., and T. Bober. 2005. *In the Line of Fire: Trauma in the Emergency Services*. New York: Oxford University Press.

Regier, D.A., M.E. Farmer, D.S. Rae, B.Z. Locke, B.J. Keith, L.L. Judd, et al. 1990. "Comorbidity of Mental Health Disorders with Alcohol and Other Drug Abuse," *Journal of the American Medical Association* 264, 19: 2511–18.

Rehm, J., C. Mathers, S. Popova, M. Thavorncharoensap, Y. Teerawattananon, and J. Patra. 2009. "Global Burden of Disease and injury and Economic Cost Attributable to Alcohol Use and Alcohol-Use Disorders," *Lancet* 373: 2223–33.

Rohsenow, D., R. Miranda, J. McGeary, and P. Monti. 2007. "Family History and Antisocial Traits Moderate Naltrexone's Effects on Heavy Drinking in Alcoholics," *Experimental and Clinical Psychopharmacology* 15, 3: 272–81.

Rosenberg, H., and K. Phillips. 2003. "Acceptability and Availability of Harm-Reduction Interventions for Drug Abuse in American Substance Abuse Treatment Agencies," *Psychology of Addictive Behavior* 17, 3: 203–10.

Schreiber, S., E. Peles, and M. Adelson. 2008. "Association between Improvement in Depression, Reduced Benzodiazepine (BDZ) Abuse, and Increased Psychotropic Medication Use in Methadone Maintenance Treatment (MMT) Patients," *Drug and Alcohol Dependence* 92, 1–2: 79–85.

Seivewright, N. 2000. "Disorders Relating to the Use of Amphetamine and Cocaine," in M.G. Gelder, J.J. Lopez-Ibor Jr, and N.C. Andreasen, eds, *New Oxford Textbook of Psychiatry*. Oxford: Oxford University Press, 231–4.

Silva de Lima, M., M. Farrell, A.A. Lima Reisser, and B. Soares. 2003. "Antidepressants for Cocaine Dependence," *Cochrane Database of Systematic Reviews* Issue 2, Art. No.: CD002950. DOI: 10.1002/14651858.CD002950.

Sobell, M., and L. Sobell. 1995. "Controlled Drinking after 25 Years: How Important Was the Great Debate?" *Addiction* 90: 1149–53.

Stewart, S. 2009. "Anxiety Disorders and Substance Use Disorders," Canadian Centre on Substance Abuse, *Substance Abuse in Canada: Concurrent Disorders*. Ottawa: Canadian Centre on Substance Abuse, 20–9.

True, W., H. Xian, J. Scherrer, P. Madden, K. Bucholz, A. Heath, et al. 1999. "Common Genetic Vulnerability for Nicotine and Alcohol Dependence in Men," *Archives of General Psychiatry* 56, 7: 655–61.

United Nations (UN). 2012. *World Drug Report*, www.unodc.org/documents/data-and-analysis/WDR2012/WDR_2012_web_small.pdf.

van Laar, M., S. van Dorsselaer, K. Monshouwer, and R. de Graaf. 2007. "Does Cannabis Use Predict the First Incidence of Mood and Anxiety Disorders in the Adult Population," *Addiction* 102, 8: 1251–60.

Vanyukov, M.M., B.S. Maher, B. Devlin, G.P. Kirillova, L. Kirisci, L.M. Yu, et al. 2007. "The MAOA Promoter Polymorphism, Disruptive Behaviour Disorders, and Early Onset Substance Use Disorder: Gene–Environment Interaction," *Psychiatric Genetics* 17, 6: 323–32.

Vasilaki, E., S. Hosier, and M. Cox. 2006. "The Efficacy of Motivational Interviewing as Brief Intervention for Excessive Drinking: A Meta-analytic Review," *Alcohol and Alcoholism* 41, 3: 328–35.

Vocci, F.J., and N.M. Appel. 2007. "Approaches to the Development of Medications for the Treatment of Methamphetamine Dependence," *Addiction* 102 (supplement 1): 96–106.

Wall, A.E., and P.L. Kohl. 2007. "Substance Use in Maltreated Youth: Findings from the National Survey of Child and Adolescent Well-being," *Child Maltreatment* 12, 1: 20–30.

Weinshenker, D., and J. Schroeder. 2007. "There and Back Again: A Tale of Norepinephrine and Drug Addiction," *Neuropsychopharmacology* 32: 1433–51.

White, A., D. Kavanagh, H. Stallman, B. Klein, F. Kay-Lambkin, J. Proudfoot, J. Drennan, et al. 2010. "Online Alcohol Interventions: A Systematic Review," *Journal of Medical Internet Research* 12, 5: e62.

Wilens, T. 2004. "Attention-Deficit/Hyperactivity Disorder and Substance Use Disorders: The Nature of the Relationship, Subtypes at Risk, and Treatment Issues," *Psychiatric Clinics of North America* 27, 2: 283–301.

Winstock, A.R., and J. Strang. 2000. "Opiates: Heroin, Methadone, and Buprenorphine," in M.G. Gelder, J.J. Lopez-Ibor Jr, and N.C. Andreasen, eds, *New Oxford Textbook of Psychiatry*. Oxford: Oxford University Press.

Witkiewitz, K., and G. Marlatt. 2006. "Overview of Harm Reduction Treatments for Alcohol Problems," *International Journal of Drug Policy* 17, 4: 285–94.

World Health Organization (WHO). 2004. *Global Status Report on Alcohol*. Geneva: WHO.

———. 2011. *Global Status Report on Alcohol and Health*. Geneva: WHO, www.who.int/substance_abuse/publications/global_alcohol_report/msbgsruprofiles.pdf.

Wu, L.T. and M.O. Howard. 2006. "Psychiatric Disorders in Inhalant Users: Results from the National Epidemiologic Survey on Alcohol and Related Conditions," *Drug and Alcohol Dependence* 88, 2–3: 146–55.

Chapter 12

American Psychiatric Association (APA). 2000. *Diagnostic and Statistical Manual of Mental Disorders*, 4th edn. Washington: APA Press.

———. 2001. *Practice Guideline for the Treatment of Patients with Borderline Personality Disorder*. Washington: APA Press.

———. 2013. *Diagnostic and Statistical Manual of Mental Disorders*, 5th edn. Washington: APA Press.

Beck, A., and A. Freeman. 1990. *Cognitive Therapy of Personality Disorders*. New York: Guilford.

Bellino, S., C. Rinaldi, and F. Bogetto. 2010. "Adaptation of Interpersonal Psychotherapy to Borderline Personality Disorder: A Comparison of Combined Therapy and Single Pharmacotherapy," *Canadian Journal of Psychiatry* 55, 2: 74–81.

Berenbaum, H., M. Boden, J. Baker, M. Dizen, R. Thompson, and A. Abramowitz. 2006. "Emotional Correlates of the Different Dimensions of Schizotypal Personality Disorder," *Journal of Abnormal Psychology* 115, 2: 359–68.

Binks, C.A., M. Fenton, L. McCarthy, T. Lee, C.E. Adams, and C. Duggan. 2006. "Psychological Therapies for People with Borderline Personality Disorder," *Cochrane Database of Systematic Reviews* Issue 1, Art. No.: CD005652. DOI: 10.1002/14651858.CD005652.

Biskin, R., and J. Paris. 2012. "Management of Borderline Personality Disorder," *Canadian Medical Association Journal* 184, 17: 1897–902.

Bowlby, J. 1979. *The Making and Breaking of Affectional Bonds*. London: Tavistock.

Carrasco, J., and D. Lecic-Tosevski. 2000. "Specific Types of Personality Disorder," in M.G. Gelder, J.J. Lopez-Ibor Jr, and N.C. Andreasen, eds, *New Oxford Textbook of Psychiatry*. Oxford: Oxford University Press, 927–53.

Ekselius, L., M. Tillfors, T. Furmark, and M. Fredrikson. 2001. "Personality Disorders in the General Population: DSM-IV and ICD-10 Defined Prevalence as Related to Sociodemographic Profile," *Personality and Individual Differences* 30: 311–20.

Glancy, G., and T. Knott. 2002. "Part I: The Psychopharmacology of Long-Term Aggression—Toward an Evidence-Based Algorithm," *Bulletin of the Canadian Psychiatric Association* 34, 6: 13–18.

Grant, B., D. Hasin, F. Stinson, D. Dawson, S. Chou, W. Ruan, et al. 2004. "Prevalence, Correlates, and Disability of Personality Disorders in the United States: Results from the National Epidemiologic Survey on Personality Disorder," *Journal of Clinical Psychiatry* 65: 948–58.

Gunderson, J. 2011. "Borderline Personality Disorder," *New England Journal of Medicine* 364, 21: 2037–42.

Health Canada. 2002. *A Report on Mental Illnesses in Canada*. Ottawa: Health Canada, www.cmha.ca/bins/content_page.asp?cid=4-42-215.

Hebebrand, J., K. Hennighausen, S. Nau, G. Himmelmann, E. Schulz, H. Schafer, and H. Remschmidt. 1997. "Low Body Weight in Male Children and Adolescents with Schizoid Personality Disorder or Asperger's Disorder," *Acta Psychiatrica Scandinavica* 96, 1: 64–7.

Herman, J. 1992. *Trauma and Recovery*. New York: Basic Books.

——— and B. van der Kolk. 1987. "Traumatic Antecedents of Borderline Personality Disorder," in B. van der Kolk, ed., *Psychological Trauma*. New York: American Psychiatric Press, 111–26.

Hoek, H., E. Susser, K. Buck, L. Lumey, S. Lin, and J. Gorman. 1996. "Schizoid Personality Disorder after Prenatal Exposure to Famine," *American Journal of Psychiatry* 153: 1637–9.

Horowitz, M. 1991. *Person Schemas and Maladaptive Interpersonal Patterns*. Chicago: University of Chicago Press.

Hurst, R., R. Nelson-Gray, J. Mitchell, and T. Kwapil. 2007. "The Relationship of Asperger's Characteristics and Schizotypal Personality Traits in a Non-Clinical Adult Sample," *Journal of Autism Developmental Disorders* 37: 1711–20.

Kaplan, H., and B. Sadock. 1996. *Concise Textbook of Clinical Psychiatry*. Baltimore: Williams and Wilkins.

Kliem, S., C. Kröger, and J. Kosfelder. 2010. "Dialectical Behavior Therapy for Borderline Personality Disorder: A Meta-analysis Using Mixed-effects Modeling," *Journal of Consulting and Clinical Psychology* 78, 6: 936–51.

Lilienfeld, S., C. Van Valkenburg, K. Larntz, and H. Akiskal. 1986. "The Relationship of Histrionic Personality Disorder to Antisocial Personality and Somatization Disorders," *American Journal of Psychiatry* 143, 6: 718–22.

Linehan, M., H. Armstrong, A. Suarez, D. Allmon, and H. Heard. 1991. "Cognitive-Behavioural Treatment of Chronically Parasuicidal Borderline Patients," *Archives of General Psychiatry* 48: 1060–4.

Links, P.S., M. Steiner, I. Boiago, and D. Irwin. 1990. "Lithium Therapy for Borderline Patients: Preliminary Findings," *Journal of Personality Disorder* 4: 173–81.

Lis, E., B. Greenfield, M. Henry, J.M. Guile, and G. Daugherty. 2007. "Neuroimaging and Genetics of Borderline Personality Disorder: A Review," *Journal of Psychiatry and Neuroscience* 32, 3: 162–73.

Livesley, J. 2005a. "Behavioural and Molecular Genetic Contributions to a Dimensional Classification of Personality Disorder," *Journal of Personality Disorders* 19, 2: 131–55.

———. 2005b. "Principles and Strategies for Treating Personality Disorder," *Canadian Journal of Psychiatry* 50, 8: 442–50.

———. 2007. "An Integrated Approach to the Treatment of Personality Disorder," *Journal of Mental Health* 16, 1: 131–48.

Lynch, T., A. Chapman, Z. Rosenthal, J. Kuo, and M. Linehan. 2006. "Mechanisms of Change in Dialectical Behavior Therapy: Theoretical and Empirical Observations," *Journal of Clinical Psychology* 62, 4: 459–80.

Lyons, M., W. True, S. Eisen, J. Goldberg, J.

Meyer, S. Faraone, L. Eaves, and M. Tsuang. 1995. "Differential Heritability of Adult and Juvenile Antisocial Traits," *Archives of General Psychiatry* 52, 11: 906–15.

Markowitz, J., K. Bleinberg, H. Pessin, and A. Skodol. 2007. "Adapting Interpersonal Psychotherapy for Borderline Personality Disorder," *Journal of Mental Health* 16, 1: 103–16.

Martens, W. 2000. "Antisocial and Psychopathic Personality Disorders: Causes, Course, and Remission—a Review Article," *International Journal of Offender Therapy and Comparative Criminology* 44, 4: 406–30.

Marziali, E., and H. Munroe-Blum. 1994. *Interpersonal Group Psychotherapy for Borderline Personality Disorder*. New York: Basic Books.

Miller, J., K. Campbell, and P. Pilkonis. 2007. "Narcissistic Personality Disorder: Relations with Distress and Functional Impairment," *Comprehensive Psychiatry* 48: 170–7.

Moll, J., R. Oliveira-Souza, P. Eslinger, I. Bramati, J. Mourao-Miranda, P. Andreiuolo, and L. Pessoa. 2002. "The Neural Correlate of Moral Sensitivity: A Functional Magnetic Resonance Imaging Investigation of Basic and Moral Emotions," *Journal of Neuroscience* 22: 2730–6.

Nestadt, G., A. Romanoski, R. Chahal, and A. Merchant. 1990. "An Epidemiological Study of Histrionic Personality Disorder," *Psychological Medicine* 20, 2: 413–22.

Ogloff, J.R.P. 2006. "Psychopathy-Antisocial Personality Disorder Conundrum," *Australian and New Zealand Journal of Psychiatry* 40, 6: 519–28.

Paris, J. 1994. "The Etiology of Borderline Personality Disorder: A Biopsychosocial Approach," *Interpersonal Biological Processes* 57, 4: 316–25.

———. 1999. "Borderline Personality Disorder," in T. Millon, P.H. Blaney, and R.D. Davis, eds, *Oxford Textbook of Psychopathology*. Oxford: Oxford University Press, 628–52.

———. 2005. "Recent Advances in the Treatment of Borderline Personality Disorder," *Canadian Journal of Psychiatry* 50, 8: 435–41.

———. 2010. "Estimating the Prevalence of Personality Disorders in the Community," *Journal of Personality Disorders* 24, 4: 405–11.

Peteet, J.R., and T.G. Gutheil. 1979. "The Hospital and the Borderline Patient: Management Guidelines for the Community Mental Health Center," *Psychiatric Quarterly* 51: 106–18.

Ravitz, P., R. Maunder, and C. McBride. 2008. "Attachment, Contemporary Interpersonal Theory and IPT: An Integration of Theoretical, Clinical and Empirical Perspectives," *Journal of Contemporary Psychotherapy* 38: 11–21.

Regehr, C., and G. Glancy. 1999. "Paranoid Disorders," in F. Turner, ed., *Adult Psychopathology: A Social Work Perspective*, 2nd edn. New York: Free Press.

Regier, D.A., M.E. Farmer, D.S. Rae, B.Z. Locke, B.J. Keith, L.L. Judd, et al. 1990. "Comorbidity of Mental Health Disorders with Alcohol and Other Drug Abuse," *Journal of the American Medical Association* 264, 19: 2511–18.

Reich, J.H. 1990. "Comparisons of Males and Females with DSM-III Dependent Personality Disorder," *Psychiatry Research* 33, 2: 207–14.

Reichborn-Kjennerud, T., N. Czajkowski, S. Torgersen, M. Neale, R. Orstavik, K. Tambs, and K. Kendler. 2007. "The Relationships between Avoidant Personality Disorder and Social Phobia: A Population-based Twin Study," *American Journal of Psychiatry* 164, 11: 1722–8.

Robins, C., and A. Chapman. 2004. "Dialectical Behaviour Therapy: Current Status, Recent Developments, and Future Directions," *Journal of Personality Disorders* 18: 73–9.

Rocca, P., L. Marchiaro, E. Cocuzza, and F. Bogetto. 2000. "Treatment of Borderline Personality Disorder with Risperidone," *Journal of Clinical Psychiatry* 63: 241–4.

Samuels, J., W. Eaton, O. Bienvenu, C. Brown, P. Costa, and G. Nestadt. 2002. "Prevalence and Correlates of Personality Disorders in a Community Sample," *British Journal of Psychiatry* 180: 536–42.

Sass, H. 2007. "Conceptual History of Psychopathology," Address to the American Academy of Psychiatry and the Law annual meeting, 24 Oct.

Schlesinger, A., and K. Silk. 2005. "Collaborative Treatment," in J. Oldham, A. Skodol, and D. Bender, eds, *Textbook of Personality Disorders*. Washington: APA, 431–48.

Silva, J.A. 2009. "Forensic Psychiatry, Neuroscience, and the Law," *Journal of the American Academy of Psychiatry and the Law* 37, 4: 489–502.

Skodol, A., D. Bender, L. Morey, L. Clark, J. Oldham, R. Alarcon, et al. 2011. "Personality Disorder Types Proposed for DSM-5," *Journal of Personality Disorders* 25, 2: 136–69.

Slutske, W. 2001. "The Genetics of Anti-social Personality Disorder," *Current Psychiatry Reports* 3: 158–62.

Soloff, P. 2005. "Somatic Treatments," in J. Oldham, A. Skodol, and D. Bender, eds, *Textbook of Personality Disorders*. Washington: APA, 387–405.

Stern, A. 1938. "Psychoanalytic Investigation of and Therapy in the Borderline Group of Neuroses," *Psychoanalytic Quarterly* 7: 467–89.

Wolff, S., R. Townhend, R. McGuire, and D. Weeks. 1991. "Schizoid Personality in Childhood and Adult Life," *British Journal of Psychiatry* 159: 620–9.

Zanarini, M., and F. Frankenburg. 2001. "Olanzapine Treatment of Female Borderline Patients: A First-Line Placebo-Controlled Pilot Study," *Journal of Clinical Psychiatry* 62: 849–54.

Index

Note: Page numbers in italics indicate illustrations.

12-Step Model of Recovery, 258, 259

Abdullah, T. and T., 2011, 81
Aboriginal Healing Foundation, 119
Aboriginal peoples, 79; anomie and, 102; diagnoses and, 81; federal responsibility for health care, 23–4; indigenous worldview and, *77*; life expectancy, 79; residential schools and, 13, 79; social work assessment and, 76; suicide and, 101–2, 106, 118–19; women, 79
abstinence programs, 258
abuse: elder, 232–4; personality disturbance and, 277
Accreditation Canada, 111
acetylcholine theory, 237–8
Achilles, 132
action plan, 115
"Act respecting Asylums for the Insane, The," 43
acute stress, 126, 136; in DSM, 140, 133–4; interventions for, 139; symptoms of, 207
Addiction Research Foundation (ARF), 257
adjustment disorders, 132
adjustment disorder with depressed mood, 183
admission, involuntary, 43–4, 44–55
adrenergic, 196
adrenocorticotropin-releasing hormone (ACTH), 206
adult day treatment programs, 236
advanced directives, 46–49, 60–61, 288
affidavit, 66, 288
after-care programs, 34
Age and Gender Considerations in Psychiatric Diagnosis, 94
aggression: dementia and, 238; personality disturbance and, 274; substance abuse and, 244; suicide and, 103, 104
agnosis, 226, 228
agonists, 154
agoraphobia, 207, 210
agranulocytosis, 170
Ahmed v. Stefaniu, 51–2
akathisia, 169, 288
Alarcón, R., et al., 95
Alberta: community treatment orders and, 64; consent to treatment in, 55, 60; defining mental disorders, 45; health insurance plans in, 26; involuntary admission and, 45; mental health legislation in, 46; protection of financial security in, 66; spending on health care, 28
Alberta Health, 28
Alberta Mental Health Act, 55
alcohol abuse, 245; biological factors, 246–7; controlled drinking, 257–8; costs of, 244; deaths attributed to, 244; diseases related to, 244; longer-term psychopharmacology for, 263; metabolization and, 247; psychosocial factors, 246; suicide and, 109; withdrawal from, 248, 262; *see also* substance use disorders
Alcohol and Drug Use Monitoring Survey, 251
Alcoholics Anonymous (AA), 257, 258
alpha-adrenergic receptor agonists, 262
Alprzaloam (Xanax), 216
alternative strategies, 115
Alzheimer, Alois, 222, 225
Alzheimer's disease, 220, 222, 225; assessing, 229; course of, 226; family caregivers and, 231; memory loss and, 226; paranoid symptoms, 275
American Psychiatric Association, 94
amnesia: anterograde/retrograde, 195, 293
amphetamines, 152, 154, 251, 253, 262, 288
amygdala, 129, 205
amyloid plaque, 238
analgesia, 252, 288
Anatomy of Melancholy, The (Burton), 133, 175
Anderson, Jordan River, 23–4
Andreae, D., 25
angst, 204
anomie, 102, 103, 288
Antabuse, 263, 264, 288
antagonists, 154
anticonvulsants, 262, 288; cocaine withdrawal and, 264; mood stabilizers and, 238–9
antidepressants, 10, 191; cocaine withdrawal and, 264; for personality disturbance, 285; for trauma and grief, 144
anti-inflammatory drugs, 238
antipsychotics, 10, 154; conventional, 167, 168, 170, 171, 239; for delirium, 234; for mania and bipolar disorder, 197; for personality disturbance, 285; for progressive neurocognitive disorders, 239; for schizophrenia, 167; second-generation, 167, 169, 170, 171, 239; side effects of, 168–70
anti-social personality, 248, 270, 273
anxiety, 217; behavioural symptoms, 208; behavioural theories of, 204; biological factors, 205–7; case example and possible interventions, 201–2, 216–17; causes of, 204–7; cognitive symptoms, 208; cognitive theories of, 204–5; costs of, 203; existential, 204, 290; family cognitive-behavioural therapy and, 214–15; gender and, 203; heritability of, 207; incidence and prevalence of, 203; intrapsychic factors, 204; mindfulness-based stress reduction, 213; nature of, 202–3; pharmacological interventions, 215–16; physical symptoms, 208; psychosocial interventions, 213–15; recovery model and, 212; relapse and, 215; separation, 204, 293; social-environmental factors, 204–5; substance use disorders and, 248; symptoms and types of, 207–12; systematic desensitization and exposure therapy, 213–14; university students and, 203
anxiolytics, 10, 170, 288
aphasia, 226
Appelbaum, P., 67
applied behaviour analysis (ABA), 23
apraxia, 226
arousal symptoms, 134, 288
Asian cultures, somatization and, 80
Asperger's syndrome, 276
assertive community treatment (ACT), 17; for schizophrenia, 163–4
assessments. *See* social work assessments
asylums, 31, 43
atrophy, 225, 229, 288
attachment patterns, 271–2; ambivalent, dependent, and

preoccupied, 272; avoidant and dismissive, 271–2; disorganized, controlling, and unresolved, 272; secure, 271
attachment theory, 190
attention, 91
attention deficit hyperactivity disorder (ADHD), substance use disorders and, 248
autism spectrum, 276
Auton (Guardian ad litem of) v. British Columbia (Attorney General), 23
autosomal dominant, 179–80, 288
avoidance symptoms, 134, 288
avoidant personality disorder , 270, 278–9

"baby blues," 181
baby boom, aging, 28
Bagby, M., 52
Bandura, A., 205
bargaining, stage of grief, 137
bath salts, 253
battery, 56
Beck, A., 188
Beck Anxiety Inventory, 110
Beck Depression Inventory, 110
Beck Hopelessness Scale, 110
Beck Scale for Suicidal Ideation (BSS), 110
behavioural couples therapy (BCT), 257
behavioural self-control training (BSCT), 257
behavioural therapies, traumatic brain injury and, 235
Bentley, K., J. Walsh, and R. Farmer, 10–11
benzodiazepines, 145, 216, 234, 246, 262; opiates and, 263–4; personality disturbance and, 286
benztropine, 169, 288
beta-adrenergic blockers, 145, 262
Bill C-562, An Act to amend the Criminal Code, 112–13
biology: anxiety and, 205–7; schizophrenia and, 152–5; substance use disorders and, 246–7; trauma response and, 129, 130
bipolar affective disorder, 181
bipolar disorder: gender and, 177; genetics and, 179, 180; incidence and prevalence of, 177; interpersonal therapy and, 190; MBCT and, 189; psychoeducational approaches, 187; psychopharmacological treatment of, 197; racial differences and, 177; regional differences, 177; seasonality and, 178; substance abuse and, 179; substance use disorders and, 248; treatment approaches for, 186; typologies I and II, 176, 183, 184
bipolar spectrum disturbances, 183–5
Bisson, J.I. et al., 142
Blackstock, C., 75–6
Blanchard, E.B. et al., 127
Blier, P., 191
blocking, 90
boarding homes, 34
Borden-Wilkins, Walter, 125
borderline personality disorder, 270–1, 277, 280
brain: anxiety and, 205–6; frontal lobes, 273; lesions, 227, 273; parts of, *206*
Brian's Law, 62
brief cognitive screening, 229
brief psychotic disorder, 160
British Columbia: community treatment orders and, 62; consent to treatment in, 55; Health Care and Care Facility Review Board, 60; health insurance plans in, 26; involuntary admission and, 45; mental health legislation in, 46; mental health policy and treatment in, 31–2; protection of financial security in, 66
British North America Act (BNA Act), 21
Brown and Harris, 1978, 178
Building on Values: The Future of Health Care in Canada (Romanow Report), 28
buprenorphine, 256–7
buproprion, 194
Burton, Robert, *The Anatomy of Melancholy*, 133, 175

CAGE screening tool, 254
Campbell, Gordon, 24
Canada: parliamentary system, 21–2; branches of government, 22, *22*; calls for national mental health strategy, 36; health policy in, 31–9; mental health legislation in, 46–9, 51–2; privacy legislation, 68–9
Canada Act, 22
Canada Health Act, 23, 26, 27
Canada's Drug Strategy (CDS), 254
Canadian Alcohol and Drug Use Monitoring Survey (2011), 245
Canadian Alliance on Mental Illness and Mental Health, 37
Canadian Association of Social Workers (CASW), 1, 2, 4, 37; capacity to consent and, 58–9; *Code of Ethics*, 7, 19, 68, 112; *Guidelines for Ethical Practice*, 112
Canadian Blue Cross, 26
Canadian Centre on Substance Abuse, 247
Canadian Charter of Rights and Freedoms, 21, 22–3; involuntary admission and, 51
Canadian Community Mental Health Survey, 6
Canadian Constitution, 21, 22
Canadian Institutes of Health Research (CIHR), Institute for Gender Health, 82
Canadian Journal of Psychiatry, 64
"Canadian Network for Mood and Anxiety Treatments Guidelines for Management of Patients with Bipolar Disorder," 187
Canadian Welfare, 3
cannabis use, 152, 245; psychosocial factors, 246
capacity to consent, 55, 57–9, 60; minors and, 58–9; restriction to hospital and, 57–8; specificity and fluidity of, 58
Caplan, G., 114, 131
caregivers: burden, 231, 236, 237; support and relief, 236
catastrophic thinking, 189
CATIE-AD, 239
Centre for Addiction and Mental Health (CAMH), 3, 31, 110, 162
cerebrospinal fluid, 144, 288
cerebrovascular accidents (CVAS), 227
cerebrovascular disorders, 273, 288
Chadwick, P. and P. Trower, 166
Changeling, The, 194
children: depression and, 178; specific phobias and, 210; treatment of anxiety in, 214–15
cholinesterase inhibitors, 237
Chrétien, Jean, 28
chronicity, 8, 288
Churchill, Winston, 183
circadian rhythms, 238, 288
circumstantial thinking, 89
citizen participation, 25
civil liberties, 42, 44, 288
civil litigation, access to mental health records and, 70–1
clang associations, 90
Clarke, D.S., 31
Clarke Institute, 31

classification, of disorders, 93–5, 94
clock-drawing test, 229, 230
clonidine, 262
clozapine, 169, 170, 171
club drugs, 252–3
Coca-Cola, 251
cocaine, 152, 245, 248, 251, 262; pharmacology for abuse of, 264
Cochrane Review, 191, 192, 237, 238, 257, 260, 263, 264, 283
Coconut Grove nightclub fire, 131
Code of Ethics (CASW), 7, 19, 68, 112
coercion, 54, 59, 288
cognition, 91, 220
cognitive-behavioural therapy (CBT), 141–3; anxiety and, 213; exposure therapy, 141–2; family, 214–15; forms of, 141–2; group treatment methods, 142; mood disturbances and, 186, 187–9; for schizophrenia, 163, 165–6; stress inoculation and training, 141–2; symptom management and, 142–3; traumatic brain injury and, 235; traumatic grief and, 144
cognitive disturbances, 189
Colony Farm, 32
Colquitz Mental Home (BC), 32
Columbia Suicide Severity Rating Scale (C-SSRS), 110
"common-sense perspective," 52
communicable diseases, health legislation and, 25–6
community-based treatment, 33, 34, 39, 62; bipolar disorder and, 187; neurocognitive disorders and, 232
community capacity-building, 5
community treatment orders (CTOs), 62–5
co-morbid, 152, 288
competence, 7
competent practice, 14
complex post-traumatic stress, 126, 134–5, 136; interventions for, 139
comprehensive-holistic rehabilitation programs, 235
compulsions, 212
computerized axial tomography (CAT), 155, 288
concordance, 104, 288
concurrent disorders, 247–9, 288
confabulation, 91, 289
confidentiality, 7, 68, 72; *Code of Ethics* and, 112; legislation, 68–9; duty to warn and protect and, 67–8
Consent and Capacity Board, 51, 60, 289
consent to treatment;
consent to treatment, 55–6; appeals and, 60; capacity to consent, 57–9, 60; elder abuse and, 233–4; elements to, 56–60; emergencies and, 56–7; express, 56; implied, 56; informed consent, 59, 60; provincial and territorial legislation, 46–9; validity of, 56; voluntary consent, 59–60; withdrawal of, 56
Consent to Treatment and Health Care Directives Act (PEI), 55–6
conspiracy of hope, 8, 163
consultation, 5
consumer partnerships, 34–5
contraindicated, 286, 289
controlled drinking, 257–8
Controlled Drugs and Substances Act, 256
coping strategies, 115
correctional institutions, 31; Aboriginal peoples in, 79; prevalence of mental illness in, 35
corticotrophin-releasing factor (CRF), 206
cortisol, 129, 180, 195, 289
cortisol releasing factor (CRH), 180, 195
counselling, 5
Country Asylums Act (UK), 43
crack, 243, 245, 246, 251
Creutzfeldt-Jakob disease, 226
criminal cases, mental health records and, 70–1
Criminal Code, 70, 289
crisis, x, 131, 136, 289; characteristics of, 132; developmental, 131; personality disturbance and, 282; psychological interventions for, 139; situational, 131
crisis intervention, 114–19
crisis/adjustment disorder, 126
crystal meth, 253
Cultural Formation Interview, 81, 95; four domains of, 95
Cultural Influences on Mental Health (CIMH) model, 78–81
culture: help-seeking and, 81; schizophrenia and families and, 159–60; social work assessments and, 77–81, 85; suicide and, 103
cyclothymia, 176, 183, 184, 289

data: analysis, 83; collection, 83; fragmentation of, 38
Daubert v. Merrell Dow Pharmaceuticals, 15
decision-making: citizen, 25; evidence-based practice and, 15–16; substitute, 18, 46–9, 61–2, 66, 293
Deegan, P., 8, 163
deficit-based approach, to mental health social work, xi, 8
deinstitutionalization, 33–4, 35, 39, 43; caregiver burden and, 231–2
Delaney, R., 24–5
deleterious, 251, 289
delirium, 220, 221, 240, 289; approaches to treatment of, 234–5; causes of, 224; due to medical condition, 224; factors contributing to, 223–4; incidence and prevalence of, 222; investigation of underlying cause, 234; management of acute situation, 234; stabilization and recovery, 234–5; statistics and, 2; symptoms of, 222
delirium tremens, 221, 289
Deller, Matthew, 125
delusional disorder, 160
delusions: cognitive-behavioural therapies and, 166; of delirium and, 221; grandeur, 90; progressive neurocognitive disorder and, 228; schizophrenia and, 157, 165, 166; persecutory, 90; somatic, 90
dementia, 93, 222, 289; financial burden of, 222; memory loss, 227; subcorticol, 225; treatable causes of, 229; *see also* progressive neurocognitive disorders
dependence, 252, 289
dependent personality disorder, 272, 279
depersonalization, 90, 91, 289
depression, 175–6, 199; case example and possible interventions, 174–5; cognitive-behavioural therapy and, 188; course and symptoms of, 182–3; diet and, 196–7; electroconvulsive therapy and, 194–6; gender and, 82, 177; genetics and, 179–80; hormones and, 180–1; incidence and prevalence, 176–7; interpersonal therapy and, 190; light therapy, 196; MBCT and, 189; medication and, 191–4; overview of medications, 193–4; pharmacological and medical interventions, 190–7; pharmacological intervention and, 117; post-partum, 181–2; racial differences and, 177; regional differences, 177; seasonality and, 178, 196; social

stressors, 178; stage of grief, 137; substance abuse and, 179; substance-related, 224, 248; suicide and, 108, 183, 186; transcranial magnetic stimulation, 196; treatment approaches for, 186
depressive cognitions, Beck's triad of, 188
depressive spectrum disturbances, 182–3
derailment, 90, 158
derealization, 91, 289
detainment, 43, 289
determinants of health, 29; *see also* social determinants of health
diabetes: schizophrenia and, 171; as cause of dementia, 229
diagnosis, cultural influences on, 80–1
Diagnostic and Statistical Manual of Mental Disorders (DSM), 18, 75, 92–5; advantages and disadvantages of, 92–3; Cultural Formation Interview, 81, 95; editions of, 94–5; history of classification, 93–5; mood disturbances in, 176, 179, 183; neurocognitive disorders in, 220; personality disorders in, 268–9, 274; post-traumatic stress disorder in, 133; post-traumatic stress in, 134; substance-related disorders in, 244; suicide in, 100
dialectical behaviour therapy (DBT), 283–4
dialectic behaviour therapy (DBT), 117, 141
diazepam, 216, 224
Dickens, B., 59
diet, depression and, 196–7
dignity of persons, respect for, 7
dipsomania, 93, 289
discharge planning, 5
disclosure, 14, 59
discrimination : labelling and, 92; of racialized individuals, 79, 164
disinhibition, 247, 289
disorganization, 137
dissociation, 90, 289
dissociative symptoms, 134, 289
disulfiram (Antabuse), 263, 264, 288
dizygotic twins, 104, 179, 289
dopamine, 154, 247
Dopamine Hypothesis, 154
dopaminergic, 196
double bind, 151–2, 289
drugs, of abuse, 249–53; club drugs, 252–3; hallucinogens, 251–2; opiates, 249–51; psychostimulants, 251; *see also* substance use disorders
drug-seeking behaviour, 247
DSM. *See Diagnostic and Statistical Manual of Mental Disorders* (DSM)
Durkheim, Émile, 103; *Suicide*, 103
dysmetabolic syndrome, 170–1, 289
dysphoria, 134, 289
dysregulation, 274, 290
dysthymia, 176
dystonia, 168–9, 290

echolalia, 90
ecological model, 75; *see also* multiple influences model
ecstasy, 253
education: gender gap and, 82; suicide and, 108
education and literacy, 29
efficiency, 25
elder abuse, 232–4; assessment of, 233
electroconvulsive shock therapy (ECT), 33, 186, 194–6
electro encephalogram (EEG), 154, 273, 290
emancipation, 58
employment, 30; suicide and, 106
endocrine, 224, 290
endogenous, 249, 290
endorphins, 247
epigenetics, 104, 290
epistemology, 76, 290
equilibrium, 131, 290
equity, 25
erotomania, 90
Essondale, 32
ethics, 7–8: evidence-based practice and, 12–17; guidelines, 58–9; principles, 19
ethnicity, health status and, 78
etiology, 2, 290
euphoria, 184, 290
euthanasia, 98, 290
evidence-based practice (EBP), 12–17, 19, 290; criticisms of, 12–13; decision-making and, 15–16; definitions of, 15; model of, 16–17, *16*; recovery model and, 17
expertise, legal definition for, 14–15
exposure therapy, 141–2
express consent, 56; *see also* consent to treatment
expression of distress, cultural influences on, 79–80
externalizing cluster, or personality disturbance, 274
extrapyramidal side effects (EPS), 168

families, 18; as caregivers, 231–2; psychoeducational interventions with, 164–5; schizophrenia and, 151–2, 158–60; suicide and, 113
Faris, R.B.L. and H.W. Dunham, 151
Farkas, M. et a.l, 17
Farrant, Gradby, 32
federal government, 21–2; confidentiality legislation and, 68; health insurance and, 26
federal transfer payments, 21
fetal alcohol syndrome (FAS), 102, 290
filtering, 189
financial security, protection of, 65–6
First Nations, social determinants of health and, 30; *see also* Aboriginal peoples
First Nations Child and Family Caring Society of Canada, 24
5-H1AA (receptor), 104, 144
5-HT_{1b} (receptor), 104
5HT/DA ratio, 170
flight of ideas, 90
"flight or fight" response, 206
Floersch, J., 11–12
fluoxetine (Prozac), 192
folic acid, dementia treatment and, 238
follow-up plans, 116
Food and Drug Administration (FDA), 191
formulation, assessment and, 85, 86–7
Foy, D. et al., 142
freedoms, in Charter, 23
Freud, Sigmund, 103
functional impairment: trauma response and, 131, 137; dementia and, 228; schizophrenia and, 164
fungi, with hallucinogenic properties, 252

G8, 36, 290
gabapentin, 262
gamma hydroxybutyrite (GHB), 253
gender: alcohol use and, 245; anxiety and, 203; assessment and, 82; dementia and, 223; depression and bipolar disorder, 177; education and, 82; schizophrenia and, 150; seasonal mood disturbances and, 179; suicide and, 101, 106

general acceptance concept, 15
general adaptation syndrome, 205
generalized anxiety disorder, 203, 207, 211
General Social Survey on Victimization, 232
genetics: mood disturbances and, 179–80; personality disturbance and, 273–4; schizophrenia and, 153; substance use disorders, 247; suicide and, 104; trauma response and, 129
Gilbert, J., 4–5
ginkgo biloba, dementia treatment and, 238
gliosis, 155, 290
global assessment of functioning (GAF), 94, 290
Global Status Report on Alcohol and Health (WHO), 244
Golan, N., 114
Gold, N., 83
gold rush, in BC, 31
Gong-Guy, E., et al., 81
government, 3; branches of, 22; branches of Canadian, *22*; division of powers, 21–2; executive branch of, 22; legislative branch, 22; judiciary branch, 22; jurisdiction over mental health care, 21–5; *see also* federal government; provincial and territorial governments
Graham Report, 35
Great Depression, 26
grief: acute, 137; case example and possible interventions, 125, 146; five stages of, 135–7; intersections with trauma, 135–40, *138*; pharmacological treatment for, 144–5
group treatment methods, 142
growth potential, 17
guided self-change (GSC), 257
Guidelines for Ethical Practice (CASW), 112
Gutheil, T.G., 45, 57

Hacking, Ian, 80
Hall, Emmett, 26
hallucinations, 90, 290; auditory, 91, 157; command, 109; depression and, 183; olfactory, 91; schizophrenia and, 157; somatic, 91; tactile, 91; visual, 91
hallucinogens, 152, 251–2
Harcourt, B., 35
Hardin, Hershel, 42
Harkness, D., 92
harm, term used in involuntary admission legislation, 45
harm reduction, 254, 255; controlled drinking, 257–8; methadone maintenance treatment, 256–7; needle exchange, 255–6
Hawkes, Erin, 42–3
health care: access to, 30; in early Canada, 25–6; as provincial jurisdiction, 26; spending on, 28–9
health insurance, 25–6
Health of Canadians–The Federal Role (Kirby Report), 26–8
health policy, 21, 25–30
help-seeking, 81
hepatitis, 249–51; needle exchange programs and, 256
Herman, Judith Lewis, 277; *Trauma and Recovery*, 134
heroin, 245, 249
High-Risk Construct Scale, 110
Hildebrand, Tanner, 125
Hippocrates, 175
histrionic personality disorder, 278
HIV, 226, 249–51; needle exchange programs and, 255, 256
Hoffman, Albert, 252
Hoffman, A. et al., 2008, 203
holistic, 9, 290
Hollingshead, A.B. and F.C. Redlich, 151
Holubowich, Brendan, 125
Hong Fook Mental Health Association, 164
Hopmeyer, E. and A. Werk, 118
hormones, mood disturbances and, 180–1
Hospital for the Mind, 32
Hospital Insurance and Diagnostic Services Act, 26
Huntington's disease, 225, 226
Hurricane Katrina, 127
Hwang, W. et al., 78, 80
hydrocephalus, 229, 290
hypertensive, 216, 290
hyperthyroidism, 181
hypnotics, 10
hypoglycemia, 224, 290
hypomania, 176, 183, 290
hypothalamic-pituitary-adrenal (HPA), 205–6
hypothyroidism, 181, 225, 290
hysterical anesthesia, 91

iatrogenic treatment, 74, 290
ideas of reference, 90
idiosyncratic, 276, 290
Iliad (Homer), 132
immigrants: health status and, 77–8; mental health status and, 79
impairment, involuntary admission and, 45
income, 29, 78
Incompetent Person's Act (Nova Scotia), 65
inefficacious, 205, 290
influence, multiple levels of, 17–19
informal patients, 51
informed choice, 25
informed consent, 14, 59, 60, 290
Injuries of the Spine and Spinal Cord, without Apparent Mechanical Lesion and Nervous Shock (Page), 133
inmates, prevalence of mental illness among, 35
insidious, 157, 291
insight, mental status examinations and, 91–2
insomnia, 251, 291
insulin shock therapy, 32–3, 291
intake, 3
integrity, 7
internalizing cluster, of personality disturbances, 274
International Classification of Diseases (ICD), 93
International Covenant of Civil and Political Rights, 68
interpersonal therapy (IPT), 117, 141; group intervention, 284; mood disturbances and, 189–90; personality disturbance and, 284–5
interprofessional teams, 4–6, 291
interview, assessment, 83–5
intrapsychic, 103–4, 291
intrusion symptoms, 134, 291
involuntary admission, 43–4, 44–55; in Charter, 51; criteria for, 44–5; means of, 50; perception of clients and, 54–5; provincial legislation and, 46–9
Involuntary Psychiatric Treatment Act, 62–3
Iproniazid, 191–2
irritable heart, 133, 291

Jacka, F. et al., 196–7
Janet, Pierre, 132–3
Johannes, William, 51–2
Johnson, J. and D. Stewart, 82
Jordan's Principle, 24
Judd, Zachary, 125

judges, involuntary admission and, 50
jurisdiction, 45, 291

Kasper, S. et al., 178
ketamine, 252–3
Ketchum v. Hislop, 51
Khat, 253
Kinderman, P. and R. Bentall, 166
Kingston Asylum, 31
Kirby, Michael, 26, 36
Kirby Report, 26–8; conceptual model for mental health care, *37*
Knipe, Roslyn, 51–2
Korsakoff's syndrome, 226
Kraepelin, E., 154, 175
Kress, K., 57
Kübler-Ross, Elizabeth, *On Death and Dying*, 135–7

labelling, 92
labile, 89, 291
language, dementia and, 228
Lara-Cinisomo, S. and B. Griffin, 178
law: expertise and competent practice and, 14–15; mental health, 18, 42–55
learned helplessness, 205
"leash laws," 62
leave certificates, 62
legal considerations, suicidal patients and, 111–13
lesions, 273, 291
"Let's Abolish the Social Service Exchange" (Teicher), 3–4
Lewy body disease, 227
Leyton, M. and S. Cox, 249
light therapy, 196
Lindemann, E., 131
Linehan, Marsha et al., 283
listening, active, 115
lithium, 33; carbonate, 117, 197, 285
Longhofer, J. et al., 11
loosening of associations, 90
lorazepam (Ativan), 216
"Low-Risk Alcohol Drinking Guidelines," 245
LSD (lysergic acid diethylamide), 252
lunatics, 31, 43, 291
Luoma, J. et al., 105
Lurie, S., 35
Lyons, M. et al., 274

McDonald, Joyce, 38
McLachlin, Beverley, 23, 57
MacMaster, S., 255
"mad traveller," 80
magnetic resonance imaging (MRI), 155, 273, 291; depression and, 180
major depressive disorder, 176, 182, 183, 192–4
malapropisms, 228, 291
Mancini, A., P. Griffin, and G. Bonanno, 143
mania, 33, 93, 176, 183–5, 199, 291; case example and possible interventions, 175, 198–9; origins of term, 185; psychopharmacological treatment of, 197; treatment approaches for, 186–7; *see also* mood disturbances
manic-depressive illness
Manitoba: Aboriginal peoples in, 79; advanced directives in, 61; community treatment orders and, 62; defining mental disorders, 45; health insurance plans in, 25–6; involuntary admission and, 44, 45; mental health legislation in, 46; protection of financial security in, 65; substitute decision-makers and, 62
Manitoba Vulnerable Persons Living with a Mental Disability Act, 62
Marshall v. Curry, 56–7
Mask of Sanity, The (Cleckley), 276
May, Rollo, *The Meaning of Anxiety*, 204
Mayou, R., A. Ehlers, and M. Hobbs, 142
MBCT. *See* mindfulness-based cognitive therapy (MBCT)
Meaning of Anxiety, The (May), 204
medical associations, insurance plans, 25
Medical Care Act, 26
medications: meanings ascribed by client, 11–12; placebo effects, 11, 238; psychiatric, 10–12; psychotropic, 10, 292
Mela, M., 58
melancholia, 88, 93, 175, 183, 194, 291; *see also* depression
melatonin, dementia treatment and, 238
memory, 91; long-term, 91; loss, 227
mental disorders, varying definitions of, 45
mental health: calls for national and provincial action plans, 30; case example and possible interventions, 41–2, 71–2; conflict in jurisdiction over, 23; definitions of, 1, 2; dominant model of, xi, 8; funding for, 29; jurisdiction for, 21–5; public spending on, 2; recovery model, 8–10; national strategy for, 36; reform and, 34–9, 43, 52; spending on, 28, 34–5
Mental Health Act, 43, 51
Mental Health Commission of Canada, 8–9, 36, 38
mental health legislation, 72; involuntary admission and, 43; legal decisions, 51–2; in Ontario, 43; provinces and territories and, 46–9
mental health records, 68–71
Mental Hospitals Act, 43–4
mental illness: better understanding of, 2–3; economic burden of, 2; impact in Canada, 1–2; pervasiveness of, xi; public attitudes towards, 37–8
mental status examinations, 87–92; appearance, attitude, and behaviour, 87–8; cognition and, 91; insight and judgement, 91–2; mood and affect, 88–9; overview of aspects of, 88; perception and, 90–1; speech and thought content, 90; speech and thought form, 89–90
mesolimbic dopamine pathway, 247, 291
meta-analyses, 128, 150, 291
methadone, 256, 263
methadone maintenance treatment (MMT), 256–7
methylamphetamine, 251
migration, diagnoses and, 80
Miller, W.R. and S. Rollnick, 259
mindfulness, 283
mindfulness-based cognitive therapy (MBCT), 189, 213
mindfulness-based relapse prevention (MBRP), 257
mindfulness-based stress reduction, 213
mini-mental status examination (MSE), 229–30, 230
minors, consent to treatment and, 58–9
Mishna, F., B. Antle, and C. Regehr, 111, 112
moderate cognitive impairment (MCI), 227
Moderation Management (MM), 258
moderation-oriented cue exposure (MOCE), 257
Mollica, R.F. et al., 127
monoamine neurotransmitters, 180
monoamine oxidase inhibitors (MAOIs), 191–2, 193; anxiety and, 215–16
monoamine oxidase activity, personality disturbance and, 273

monomania, 93, 291
monozygotic twins, 104, 153, 179, 291
mood disturbances, 175–6, 199; biological factors and, 179–81; cognitive-behavioural therapy and, 187–9; combining social/environmental and biological factors, 181–2; factors contributing to, 177–82; genetics and, 179–80; hormones and, 180–1; interpersonal therapy and, 189–90; neurobiology and, 180; psychoeducational approaches, 187; psychosocial interventions promoting recovery, 187–90; recovery model and, 185–7; seasonality and, 178–9; social and environmental factors, 178–9; substance abuse and, 179; substance use disorders and, 248; *see also* bipolar disorder; depression; mania
MoodGym, 186
mood stabilizers, 10, 285
moral management, 32
mother-blaming, 14, 152
motivational interviewing, 258–61
Mott, F.W., 133
Mount Sinai Hospital, 164
Muhlbauer, S., 158–9
multiple influences model, 76, 181
music therapy, 237
Mutual Recognition Agreement on Labour Mobility for Social Workers in Canada, 28
Myers, Laura and Bruce Thyer, 12

Naltrexone, 262, 263
narcissistic personality disorder, 278
National Anti-Drug Strategy (NADS), 254–5
National Association of Social Workers (NASW), 5–6
National Mental Health Strategy, 2
needle exchange, 255–6
negative psychotic symptoms, of schizophrenia, 149, 157, 158, 159
neologisms, 89, 158
neurasthenia, 133, 291
neurobiology: mood disturbances and, 180; personality disturbance and, 273; schizophrenia and, 153–5
neurochemistry, suicide and, 104
neurocognitive disorders, 240; abuse of older people with, 232–4; case example and possible interventions, 220, 239; nature of, 220–2; *see also* dementia; progressive cognitive disorders
neurodevelopment, 155, 291
neuroendocrine, 130
neuroleptic malignant syndrome (NMS), 170, 291
neuroleptic medications, 167, 168, 291; extrapyramidal side effects, 168–9
neurons, 153, 154, 291
neuropsychiatry, 32, 291
neurotransmitters, 153–4, 180, 292
New Brunswick: consent to treatment legislation in, 55; defining mental disorders, 45; involuntary admission and, 45; involuntary admission in, 50; mental health legislation in, 47
Newfoundland and Labrador: consent to treatment legislation in, 55; defining mental disorders, 45; mental health legislation in, 48
nigrostriatal pathway, 168, 292
non-suicidal self-injury, 100
noradrenaline, 104, 144, 180
norepinephrine, 144–5, 249; substance use disorders and, 247
Northwest Territories: involuntary admission and, 45, 50; mental health legislation in, 49
no-suicide contracts, 116
Nova Scotia: community treatment orders and, 62–3; defining mental disorders, 45; health insurance plans in, 25; Incompetent Person's Act, 65; mental health legislation in, 47; mental health reform in, 38–9
Nunavut: involuntary admission and, 45; mental health legislation in, 49
nystagmus, 252, 292

O'Brien, A. and K. Calderwood, 10
obsessive compulsive disorder (OCD),203, 211–12
obstetrical complications: schizophrenia and, 153; depression and bipolar disorder and, 180
O'Donoghue, B. et al., 54–5
Office of Controlled Substances, Health Canada, 256
Office of the Correctional Investigator, 35
Offord, D. et al., 34
omega-3 fatty acid supplements, 238
On Death and Dying (Kübler-Ross), 135–7
One Flew Over the Cuckoo's Nest, 194
Ontario: community treatment orders and, 62, 63–4; Consent and Capacity Board, 60; defining mental disorders, 45; health insurance plans in, 25; involuntary admission and, 45; mental health legislation in, 43, 47, 51; mental health reform in, 35, 35–6, 43; Ministry of Health and Long-Term Care, 33, 35–6; pathways to treatment, *53*; spending on health care, 28; substitute decision-makers and, 62
Ontario Association of Social Workers, 4
Ontario College of Social Workers and Social Service Workers Privacy Toolkit, 69
Ontario Court of Appeal, 65
Ontario Health Care Consent Act, 233
Ontario Mental Health Act, 52, 64, 65, 69
Ontario Mental Health Act and Health Care Consent Act, 62
Ontario's Hospitals for the Insane Act, 65
opiates, 249–51; pharmacology for abuse of, 263–4; withdrawal and, 262
opium, 249
orbitofrontal, 180, 292
O'Reilly, R. et al., 64
orientation, 91
Out of the Shadows at Last, 36–8
overgeneralization, 189
Oxycocet, 249
OxyContin, 249

Page, S., 52
Page, Herbert William, *Injuries of the Spine and Spinal Cord, without Apparent Mechanical Lesion and Nervous Shock*, 133
panic attacks, 202, 205, 292; characteristics of, 209
panic disorder, 203, 208–9; family and twin studies, 206–7; medications and, 216
Paracelsus, 194
paraesthesia, 209, 292
paranoid personality disorder, 270, 274–5
paranoid thinking, 166, 275
parasuicide, 106, 292
paresis, 93, 292
Paris, J., 270
Parkinson's disease, 226, 227
pathognomonic, 228, 292
patient advocacy, 3, 51
PCP (phencyclidine), 252

pejorative, 92, 292
perceived life threat, 128
peritraumatic distress responses, 128–9
perpetuating factors, 85
perseveration, 90
persistent depressive disorder, 176, 182, 183
Personal Information Protection and Electronic Documents Act, 68
personality, 268; change, 227–8; traits, 268, 274
personality disorders, 108, 268, 269, 274, 287; *see also* personality disturbance
personality disturbance, 126, 136; anti-social, 270, 276–7; avoidant, 270, 278–9; borderline, 270, 277, 280; case examples and possible interventions, 267–8, 286; characteristics of, 269; dependent, 279; dialectical behaviour therapy and, 283–4; disordered attachments and, 271–2; externalizing cluster, 274; factors contributing to, 270–4; general issues and approaches, 280–2; genetics and, 273–4; histrionic, 278; incidence and prevalence of, 269–70; internalizing cluster, 274; interpersonal therapy and, 284–5; intrapsychic factors, 271–2; narcissistic, 278; nature of, 268–9; neurobiological factors, 273; obsessive-compulsive, 270, 280; paranoid, 270, 274–5; pharmacological interventions, 285–6; psychological interventions for, 139; psychosocial approaches to intervention, 280–5; schizoid cluster, 274, 275; schizotypal, 270, 275–6; social environment factors, 270–1; types of, 274–80
person involvement, 17
person orientation, 17
Peteet, J.R. and T.G. Gutheil, 286
phenothiazines, 33, 292
phobic disorders, 207
physical environments, 30
Pick's disease, 225, 226, 227
Pikangikum, 102
plants, with hallucinogenic properties, 252
pluralistic society, 25, 292
polarization, 189
Ponniah, K. et al., 92
positive psychotic symptoms, 157–8
positron emission tomography (PET), 154, 180, 292
post-partum: depression, 181–2, 190; psychosis, 181
post-traumatic stress, 126, 133–4, 136, 140; interventions for, 139
post-traumatic stress disorder (PTSD), 126–7, 146, 207, 292; dose-effect model, 127; environmental supports and attitudes, 127–8; event-related factors, 127; genetics and biology, 129; individual experiences and coping, 128; peritraumatic distress responses, 128–9; remission of symptoms, 140–1; sexual assault victims and, 127, 128
power of attorney, 61, 65, 292; financial, 66
POWER project, 82
precipitating factors, 85
predisposing factors, 85
prefrontal lobotomies, 33, 292
preoccupations, 90
President's New Freedom Commission on Mental Health, 8
prevalence, definition of, 150
Prigerson, H.G. et al., 137–8
Prince Edward Island: capacity to consent and, 57; community treatment orders and, 62; consent to treatment legislation in, 55–6; defining mental disorders, 45; involuntary admission and, 45; mental health legislation in, 48
Privacy Act, 68
Prochaska, J. and C. DiClemente, 259
prodromal, 187, 292
prognosis, 149, 292
program: development, 5; management/administration, 5
progressive neurocognitive disorders, 220, 222, 240; agnosis and, 228; caregiver support and relief, 236; case example and possible interventions, 219–20, 239–40; course of, 226–30; elder abuse and, 232–4; factors contributing to, 225–6; functional impairment, 228; incidence and prevalence of, 223; interventions focused on increased cognitive activity, 237–8; language, 228; medications targeting neuropsychiatric symptoms, 238–9; memory loss, 227; personality change, 227–8; pharmacology and, 237–9; psychosis and, 228; reality orientation and, 237; recovery-oriented interventions, 236–9; reminiscence therapy, 236–7; special issues for family members caring for, 231–2; symptoms of, 227–8
propranolol, 145, 262
protective factors, 85
provincial and territorial governments, 21, 22; confidentiality legislation and, 68–9; health insurance and, 25–6; jurisdiction over health care, 26; mental health legislation in, 21, 46–9; qualification for health-care funding, 26; spending on health care, 28–9
Provincial Hospital for the Insane (BC), 32
Provincial Lunatic Asylum (BC), 32
pseudo-Parkinisonism, 169
psilocybin mushrooms, 252
psychoanalysis, 32, 292
psychoeducation, 186, 292; family interventions for schizophrenia, 163, 164–5; individual and family, 5
psychologization, 80, 292
psychopathic personality, 276; *see also* antisocial personality disturbance
psychosis, progressive neurocognitive disorder and, 228
psychosocial programs, 8
psychostimulants, 251
psychotherapy, 5, 141; personality disturbance and, 280
psychotic disorders, related to schizophrenia, 160–1
psychotropic medications, 10, 292
public guardian, 66
public trustee, 65, 66, 292

Quebec: involuntary admission and, 45; involuntary admission in, 50; mental health legislation in, 47

race: depression and, 80, 177; discrimination, 79
Raging Spoon program, 162
randomized controlled trials (RCTs), 192, 283, 284
rape trauma syndrome, 133
Rapp, R., H. Siegal, and N. DeLiberty, 258
rapport, 114
readmission, 3, 8, 292
reality orientation (RO), 237
reasonable patient standard, 14
reasonable physician standard, 14
receptors, 153
recidivism, 3, 292
recourse, 51, 292
recovery, 8–9, 36
recovery model, 8–10, 292; anxiety and, 212; evidence-based practice and, 17; mood disturbances and, 185–7; personality disturbance and, 282; principles

of, 9–10; schizophrenia and, 149–50, 161–2, 163; substance use disorders and, 255; traumatic brain injury and, 235
refugees, 78–9
Regehr, C., S. Stern, and A. Shlonsky, 16
Regehr, C. and T. Sussman, 137, 140
rehabilitation, 4
Reibl v. Hughes, 59
relapse, 3, 8, 64, 293; anxiety and, 215; *see also* recidivism
relationship, traumatic grief and, 140
relaxation techniques, anxiety and, 213
reminiscence therapy, 236–7
renal failure, 224, 293
reorganization, 137
repetitive transcranial magnetic stimulation (rTMS), 196
research, 2–3, 5
Research Agenda for DSM-5, A, 94
residential schools, 13, 79
resilience, 128, 293
resolution phase, 131
resource development, 5
rights, in Charter, 22–3
Riverview Hospital, 32
Roberts, A.R., 114
Rock, Allan, 28
Rodriguez, Sue, 98, 111, 112, 120–1
"Role of a Psychiatric Social Worker, The" (Teicher), 3
Romanow, Roy, 28
Rosenthal, N. et al., 178
Rothbaum, B. et al., 140
Rotman School of Management, University of Toronto, 162
Royal Commission on Health Services, 26
Royal Commission Report on the Asylum for the Insane, 32
Ryder, A. et al., 80

SAD PERSONS Scale, 110
safety, term used in involuntary admission legislation, 44
Salyers, M. and S. Tsemberis, 164
Saskatchewan: community treatment orders and, 62, 64; consent to treatment legislation in, 55; defining mental disorders, 45; health insurance plans in, 26; involuntary admission and, 45; mental health legislation in, 46; protection of financial security in, 65, 66; substitute decision-makers and, 62
schemas, 272
schizoaffective disorder, 160, 161
schizophrenia, 172; alienation and, 158; assertive community treatment and, 163–4; auditory hallucinations, 157; biological factors, 152–5; case example and possible interventions, 148–9, 171–2; cognitive-behavioural therapy and, 163, 165–6; course of illness, 155–6; cultural context for families, 159–60; delusions, 157–8; early symptoms, 156–7; factors contributing to development of, 151–5; factors contributing to successful outcomes, 156; family interventions and, 13–14; fear of being dependent, 158; fear of losing everything, 158; first-year university students and, 156; five phases of family response to, 158–9; gender and, 82, 150; genetics and, 153; incidence and prevalence of, 150–1; indirect costs of, 150; issues for families, 158–60; medications in acute phase, 167–71; minority patients and, 164; nature of, 149–50; negative symptoms, 149, 157, 158, 159; neurobiology and, 153–5; neurodevelopmental model of, 155; obstetrical complications, 153; other related psychotic disorders, 160–1; pharmacological interventions, 166–71; positive psychotic symptoms, 149, 157–8; psychoeducational family interventions, 164–5; psychosocial interventions, 162–6; recovery model and, 149–50, 161–2, 163; regional differences in, 150–1; rural and urban incidence of, 151; social and family influences, 151–2; social implications, 158, 159; social workers role in recovery, 161–2; stages of recovery from, *161*; stigma and, 158, 159, 160; substance abuse and, 152; substance use disorders and, 248; suicide and, 108; symptoms and challenges, 149, 156–60; thought form and content, 158
schizophreniform disorder, 160
schizophrenigenic mother, 13–14, 151, 152, 293
seasonal affective disorder, 178, 196
seasonality: depression and, 196; mood disturbances and, 178–9
secondary loss, 127, 293
selective serotonin reuptake inhibitors (SSRIs), 117, 191, 192, 193, 238, 264; anxiety and, 215
self-determination, 12, 14, 16, 17; schizophrenia and, 161; suicide and, 112
self-efficacy, 205
self-harm, 100, 103, 105, 106; case example and possible interventions, 97, 119; counselling interventions for, 116–17; major, 105; moderate, 105; stereotypic, 105
self-injury, 100
self-schemas, 165–6, 272
self-stigma, 38, 81
Selye, H., 205
serotonin, 104, 105, 144, 192
serotonin norepinephrine reuptake inhibitors (SNRIs), 117, 191, 192, 193
Sevels v. Cameron, 61
sexual assault, trauma and, 127, 128
Shaffer, A. et al., 179
Shamattawa First Nation, 99, 121
Shay, J., 132
Sheehan, K. and T. Burns, 54
shell shock, 133, 293
Skelton, Mora, 3, 4, 33
Smith, Brian, 62
Smith v. Jones, 67
smooth pursuit tracking, 154
Sobell, M. and L. Sobell, 257
social action, 5
social determinants of health, 3, 29–30, 39, 178, 293
social drift, 151
social environments, 30
social justice, 3, 7
social phobia (social anxiety disorder), 203, 207, 210–11, 279
social service exchange, 3–4
social support networks, 29
social work: areas of, 3, 4; aspects in mental health, 5; definition of, 75; interprofessional teams, 4–6; role in mental health, 3–4, 6
social work assessment, 18–19, 74–6, 83–7, 95–6; assessment interview, 83–5; community context and, 75; components of, 84–5; within cultural context, 77–81, 95–6; at family level, 75; gender and, 82; at individual level, 75; multiple levels of influence, 75, *76*, 17–19; multi-perspective formulation, 86–7; perpetuating factors and, 86;

perspective of, 75; precipitating factors and, 86; protective factors and, 86; societal level, 75; written format of, 83–4
social workers, xi; duties of, 4; knowledge of medications, 12; labour mobility and, 28; medications and, 10–12; perspective of, 19; practice of mental health and, xi, 1; role of, 3; role of early, 3; role with clients on medications, 12
Social Work Journal, 4
sociopathic personality, 276; *see also* antisocial personality disturbance
somatization, 79–80, 293
specific medical neurocognitive disorders, 226
specific phobia, 203, 209–10
speech content and form, 89–90
spirituality, 9
spousal caregivers, 231, 236
Stages of Change Model, 259, 260
Standing Senate Committee on Social Affairs, Science and Technology, 26
Starson v. Swayze, 45, 57
statistics, of mental health in Canada, 1–2
stigma, 30, 81, 293; campaign against, 36–8; help-seeking and, 81; labelling and, 92; schizophrenia and, 158, 159, 160
stimulants, 10
Stover, Vincent, 125
stress inoculation and training, 141–2
structured breathing exercises, 143
subdural hematoma, 229, 293
subpoena, 70, 71, 293
substance-induced disorders, 244, 245
substance-induced neurocognitive disorder, 226
substance-related disorders, 244; impact of, 244; incidence and prevalence of, 245; nature of, 243–5
substance use disorders, 244–5, 265; abstinence programs, 258; biological factors, 246–7; case examples and possible interventions, 242–3, 264–5; factors contributing to, 245–7; gender and, 82; harm-reduction interventions, 255–8; HIV and hepatitis, 249–51; management of withdrawal, 262–3; mood disturbances and, 179; motivational interviewing, 258–61; other mental health problems and, 247–9; other psychosocial interventions, 258–61; pharmacological and medical approaches, 261–4; psychosocial factors, 246; screening for, 254; schizophrenia and, 152; self-medication and, 246; suicide and, 109
suicidal behaviour disorder, 100
suicidal patients: ethical and legal duties, 111–13; physicians' obligations, 111; social workers' obligations, 111
suicide, 99–100, 114; Aboriginal peoples and, 101–2, 118–19; Aboriginal youth and, 102; acute risk, 99–100; assessment of risk, 85, 105–10; assisted, 98, 112; case example and possible interventions, 98–99, 120–1; chronic risk, 100; crisis intervention with acute risk, 114–19; culture and, 103; definition of, 99; depression and, 183, 186; factors contributing to, 103–4; family histories and, 108; gender and, 82, 101, 106; genetic and neurochemistry factors, 104; hospitalization for acute risk, 116; impact on family and friends, 113; impulsive behaviour and, 106–8; incidence and prevalence, 100–2; intent, 107, 109–10; interventions for fluctuating risk, 116–17; intrapsychic factors, 103–4; mental disorders and, 101; mental illness and, 108; modifiable risk factors, 107, 108–9; overview of assessment of risk, 107; pharmacological intervention, 117; previous attempts, 106; rates in selected countries, *101*; rates of, 99; as rational decision, 111; scales for assessment, 110; in Shamattawa First Nation, 99; social-environmental factors, 103; social work interventions with families and communities after, 117–18; static risk factors, 106, 107; support groups for survivors, 118; victims' contact with health professionals, 105–6
Suicide (Durkheim), 103
suicide ideation, 99
supervision, 5
supported self-management, 185–6
support groups: for families of schizophrenic patients, 165; for survivors of suicide, 118
Supreme Court of British Columbia, 23; assisted suicide and, 113
Supreme Court of Canada, 23; assisted suicide and, 112; capacity to consent and, 57; client access to records and, 69; consent to treatment and, 55, 56; duty to warn and protect and, 67; informed consent and, 59
Swanson, S. and I. Coleman, 108
Swartz, M.S. and J.W. Swanson, 64
SWOT analysis, 74, 293
systematic desensitization, 213–14

tangential thinking, 89, 158
Tarasoff v. Regents of University of California, 67
tardive dyskinesia, 170, 293
taxation, 22
Taylor, Gloria, 113
teaching, 5
Teicher, Mort, 3–4; "Let's Abolish the Social Service Exchange," 3–4; "The Role of a Psychiatric Social Worker," 3
tension-reduction hypothesis, 248
thought broadcasting, 157
thought content and form, 89–90
thought insertion, 90, 157
thought withdrawal, 90, 157
thyroid hormones, 180–1
Time is Now, The: Themes and Recommendations for Mental Health Reform in Ontario, 35–6
Titus Andronicus (Shakespeare), 132
Toronto Declaration on the Global Prevention of Elder Abuse (WHO), 232
Toronto Lunatic Asylum, 31. *see also* Toronto Psychiatric Hospital (TPH)
Toronto Psychiatric Hospital (TPH), 3, 33, 43. *see also* Centre for Addiction and Mental Health (CAMH)
Toseland, R. et al., 6
Tourette's syndrome, 105, 293
Toward a Healthy Future: Second Report on the Health of Canadians, 29
Towns, A. and K. Schwartz, 6
transient, 269, 293
transinstitutionalization, 35, 293
trauma: case examples and possible interventions, 124–5, 145–6; crisis intervention, 141; dosage or level of, 127; exposure, 127; as intentional, 127; intersections with grief, 135–40, *138*; interventions, 140–5, 146; nature and prevalence of reactions, 126–30; personality disturbance and, 271; as personalized, 127; pharmacological treatment for, 144–5; psychological interventions for, 139; remission of symptoms, 140–1

Trauma and Recovery (Herman), 134
trauma response, 146; acute stress and post-traumatic stress, 132–4; biological correlates of, 130; crisis response and adjustment disorder, 131–2; factors contributing to, *130*; types of, 131–5, 136
traumatic brain injury (TBI), 220, 221, 240; caregiver stress and, 231; case example and possible interventions, 219, 240; comprehensive-holistic rehabilitation programs, 235; factors contributing to, 225; financial burden of, 223; incidence and prevalence of, 223; psychosocial interventions, 235
traumatic events, 126–7
traumatic grief: approaches to, 143–4; model of, 137–40; psychological interventions for, 139
trazodone (Desyrel), 194
treatment, 4; early, 32–3; consent to, 55–60
tricyclic antidepressants (TCAs), 191, 192, 193; anxiety and, 215
Turner, E. et al., 191
tyramine reaction, 192

Ulysses Contract, 61, 293
UN Convention on the rights of the Child, 58
understanding, capacity to consent and, 57
Ungar, Michael, 38
United Kingdom, mental health institutions, 43
United Nations, *World Drug Report*, 245
United States: classification of disorders, 93; community treatment orders and, 62; duty to warn in, 67; public attitudes towards mental illness, 37–8
Universal Declaration of Human Rights, 68
universal health care, 26
Upper Canada Sanitary Commission and Board of Health, 25
US Centers for Disease Control, 256
US Department of Labor, 6
US Supreme Court, general acceptance and, 15

Valium, 145, 216, 224, 246, 286; *see also* benzodiazepines
values, related to health care, 25
Vancouver Island, 31
van Laar et al., M., 248
vascular neurocognitive disorder, 226, 227
Vear Model of Addiction, 250
Vietnam veterans, effects of war on, 132, 133
vitamin B12 deficiency, 225, 229
voluntary admission, 51
voluntary consent, 59–60

waiting lists, for service, 29–30
Walker, E.F. et al., 154–5
warn and protect, duty to, 66–8
Weerasekera, P., 86
Williams C., and A. Collins, 158
withdrawal: from alcohol, 248, 262; management of, 262–3
women: Aboriginal, 79, 101; alcohol and, 245; burden of disease and, 82; post-partum depression and, 181–2; substance use disorders, 246; *see also* gender
word salad, 89
working conditions, 30
World Drug Report (UN), 245, 249–51
World Health Organization (WHO), 1, 2, 3, 149, 150, 293; *Global Status Report on Alcohol and Health*, 244; *Toronto Declaration on the Global Prevention of Elder Abuse*, 232
world views: indigenous, *77*; social work assessment and, 76
worried well, 34

Yehuda, R. et al., 129
youth: anxiety and, 203; depression and, 176–7; *see also* children
Yukon, mental health legislation in, 49